LEISURE
LEADERSHIP

LEISURE
LEADERSHIP
Working with People
in Recreation and Park
Settings

E. William Niepoth
California State University, Chico

PRENTICE-HALL, INC., Englewood Cliffs, New Jersey 07632

Library of Congress Cataloging in Publication Data

NIEPOTH, E. WILLIAM, (date)
   Leisure leadership.

   Includes bibliographical references and index.
   1. Recreation leadership. I. Title.
GV181.4.N53 1983   790′.023   82-18118
ISBN 0-13-530071-1

Editorial/production supervision and interior design by Natalie Krivanek
Cover design by Zimmerman/Foyster Design
Manufacturing buyer: Harry P. Baisley

Printed in the United States of America

10 9 8 7 6 5 4 3 2 1

ISBN: 0-13-530071-1

Prentice-Hall International, Inc., *London*
Prentice-Hall of Australia Pty. Limited, *Sydney*
Editora Prentice-Hall do Brasil, Ltda., *Rio de Janeiro*
Prentice-Hall Canada Inc., *Toronto*
Prentice-Hall of India Private Limited, *New Delhi*
Prentice-Hall of Japan, Inc., *Tokyo*
Prentice-Hall of Southeast Asia Pte. Ltd., *Singapore*
Whitehall Books Limited, *Wellington, New Zealand*

To Marilyn

Contents

3

RECREATION BEHAVIOR   55

4

HELPING AND RELATED INTERPERSONAL RELATIONSHIPS   96

5

LEADERSHIP PROCESSES 126

6

WORKING WITH GROUPS 152

7

TEACHING AND LEARNING 186

8

REFERRAL AND ADVOCACY   223

9

USING RESOURCES: FINANCIAL AND SAFETY
CONSIDERATIONS   250

10

WORKING WITH HUMAN RESOURCES 288

11

SUPPORT PROCESSES 317

Preface

Most people engage in recreation behaviors. The specific nature of these behaviors varies greatly from person to person, in terms of the kinds of activities involved, the intensities with which they are pursued, and the goals that motivate them. Typically they are made possible by the efforts of people other than, and in addition to, the participants: the father who teaches his son to fish, the center director who shows members of an older adult club how to do macrame, the sports supervisor who sets up a tennis tournament, the recreation therapist who assists paraplegic individuals in the hospital pool, and the ranger who takes park visitors on nature walks. In the broadest sense, these people are all leaders.

Leaders use many different processes when they work with others in recreation and park settings. Often, they engage in what we specifically call leadership. At other times, the teaching process is utilized. Leaders might rely on group processes, or they might employ such processes as counseling or manipulation of resources. To the extent that all of these activities are intended to facilitate the change of others' behavior they can be thought of generally as leadership processes.

This book is about these processes. It can be useful to anyone who wants to help others enjoy leisure. It is written especially for personnel in the field of recreation and parks. It is intended for students in leadership courses offered by universities, colleges, and community colleges. In addition, it can be used as a supplementary text in other courses in the leisure services that include content related to working with participants, staff, or the general public; the areas of programming and administration are particular possibilities. Also, it should be a useful reference for people already in the field, or in any human service organization where the emphasis is on working with people.

This book has several essential features:

1. It takes a broad view of leadership as encompassing all those processes used by leisure service workers that are intended to facilitate the change of others' behavior (both participants and staff).

2. It is based on the premise that there are "core processes" that are common to all, or most, of the positions held by people working in the field. The use of any one of these processes is influenced by the worker's personality and by the demands of the situation.

3. Most of the core processes involve interpersonal relationships. In large measure, the nature of these relationships determines the success of the processes and, therefore, the effectiveness of the leisure service delivery system. This dimension is emphasized in this book.

4. A human service perspective is presented. Responsibility for working with people is seen as being based on a holistic and humanistic approach. The text recognizes the interrelationship between the recipients of leisure services and their social and physical environments. People come to our parks and programs as total beings . . . not just with leisure needs, but with all of the problems and potentials that are part of their lives and that influence their leisure behavior. This suggests that personnel must function at times as enablers, facilitators, catalysts, or advocates, as well as leaders, teachers, supervisors, managers, and administrators.

5. The book integrates information about behavior with the uses of the various core processes. Since these processes are intended to facilitate changes in the behavior of others, it follows that their use should be based on understandings of behavior.

6. An eclectic approach is taken that brings together information from such areas as leadership theory, small group theory, and teaching and learning theory.

7. Emphasis is given in the book to the need for the leader to know himself or herself. Personal biases, expectations, values, and anxieties can have negative effects on interpersonal relationships. However, if the worker is aware of these, their influence can be minimized. Self-awareness of strengths permits these to be used more fully.

The skill of working with people, or of exercising leadership in the broad sense, is central to the leisure services field. One does not learn to work with people by reading books. Leadership skills are developed through actual interactions. However, books and other communicative devices can provide information that permits an individual to understand actual experience; to organize it, to learn from it, and to use it in future applications and changing situations. This book is written on the premise that the leadership competencies of recreation and park workers can be improved in at least three ways:

1. By analyzing the core processes, and knowing the expected outcomes and the basic factors involved in their utilization.

2. By developing a concept of participant (and staff) behavior that guides use of the core processes.

3. By becoming more familiar with the use of "self" as a resource in helping relationships.

The purpose of this book is to contribute to these three areas of knowledge.

The book would not have been written without the contributions of many other people. While it is impossible to list all of them individually, I am deeply indebted to former students and to colleagues in the field of recreation and parks. They helped me see the need for the book and to define the content. Many of them exemplified the ideals of effective leadership that are suggested in the various chapters. In that sense they served as role-models. I value the associations I have had with students and colleagues, and the friendships that emerged.

I specifically want to express appreciation to Joe Bannon and Jim Murphy, editors for this series. Joe provided very helpful guidance during the early development of the manuscript and during the review process. Jim encouraged me to submit the initial proposal, and gave continuing support during the writing of the book. His contributions to my work extend beyond this. Over the years, he has been a source of intellectual stimulation and professional excitement about our field.

The persons with whom I worked most closely during the editing and production phases were Alice Dworkin and Natalie Krivanek. Their efforts made it possible for the manuscript to be printed. I appreciate their help and the assistance of many other Prentice-Hall staff members who were involved.

Finally, I want to thank Marilyn, members of our family, and close friends. . . for love and understanding and all those similar things that are so important when you undertake projects such as writing a book. I am grateful for these and many other blessings.

                                                                    EWN

LEISURE
LEADERSHIP

chapter 1

The Leisure Services

"I want to work with people." The young man who sat across the desk from the academic advisor, in the university's Recreation and Park Department, was explaining why he wanted to enroll as a major in the department. The advisor's thoughts were directed momentarily to the stack of new students' folders on her desk; she reflected briefly about how often that phrase was repeated in the letters of application from prospective students.

Hundreds of miles from the university, a recreation and park superintendent was reviewing the program for the upcoming annual conference of the professional society. He noted with interest the listing of several sessions on the topic of human services. He reflected briefly on the association of that term with the overall field of leisure services.

Most people who work in the field of recreation and parks, either on a paid basis or in a volunteer capacity, do work with people. They work with participants in programs, with other staff, and with the general public in a variety of ways. They share this vocational characteristic with all of the myriad of workers whose agencies comprise the field of human services.

WHAT ARE THE HUMAN SERVICES?

The term *human services* is used in publications, at conferences of various organizations, and in the discussions of college and university faculties and administrations. Some speak of the human services as a new profession, developed to serve more effectively the great variety of health, educational, and welfare needs of people in the complex society of today.

> Human Services is a new profession, emerging full force in 1970's America . . . There are already many encouraging indications that America is be-

ginning to settle down and sort things out and develop a new and durable set of people centered values. One of the outstanding examples of our society's intention to chart a new course which gives prominence to personal, not technological, values is the recent creation and blossoming of the human services profession.[1]

Others see the concept as a new linking of existing organizations to form a more effective service potential.

The increasing tendency to designate a community's variety of health and social welfare services as human service organizations reflects not only the desire to provide services more efficiently but also a growing societal, as well as professional, recognition of the common denominator inherent in the varied problems presented to us by clients. It also indicates an appreciation for the generic quality integral to the helping actions of professional and non-professional care givers despite multiple technologies utilized by them . . . it is clear that genuinely effective, comprehensive services can be rendered only through the forging of systematic linkages that bring together the various care-giving agencies needed to provide a complex array of resources, technologies, skills.[2]

Human services may be conceived of very broadly as all those efforts that are made by people who help other people.

A workable definition may be *human services refers to the attention and assistance offered to people by other helping people* . . . human services embraces the work accomplished by physicians, psychologists, social workers, mental health technologists, community service workers, and others.[3]

A somewhat narrower view is taken by those who associate the term with existing fields that possess certain identifying characteristics.

Although human service organizations differ in functions and client populations served, they all have characteristics that distinguish them from other classes of formal organizations.[4]

These organizations are differentiated from other bureaucracies by two fundamental characteristics: (a) their input of raw materials are human beings with specific attributes, and their production output are persons processed or changed in a pre-determined manner, and (b) their general mandate is that of "service," that is, to maintain and improve the general well-being and functioning of people.[5]

Hasenfeld and English noted that, from the standpoint of the individual, human service organizations provide resources and assistance not readily available elsewhere. From the standpoint of society, they provide for socialization, social control, and social integration.

These authors also suggested that human service agencies share some common problems: Specific goals are difficult to define unambiguously because the agencies work with widely differing individuals in diverse socio-cultural settings; technologies used are indeterminant because of the complexities of the human conditions of their clients and because of limited ability to confidently assign cause-and-effect relationships; and they lack reliable and valid measures of their effectiveness.[6]

Human service workers tend to be concerned with the "whole person."

The majority of workers in human services are not specialists in the sense that they can focus on one particular aspect of need. By the very nature of the demands of their jobs, they are required to deal with the totality of individuals, either in helping them cope with the overall demands of living or in enabling them to make use of more specialized service such as education, medical care, legal advice, psychotherapy, and so on.[7]

Brill observed that the types of concerns that the human services have for people permit a grouping of these services into two categories:

. . . (1) Those designed to provide opportunities for maximization of human potential and prevention of individual and social breakdown, and (2) those designed to provide remediation of such breakdown and restoration of capacity for functioning.[8]

Common Elements. While each of the views presented earlier suggests differences, a review of human service literature permits the identification of several common elements. The following are included:

1. *The human services are a collection of agencies, with some characteristics held in common, whose primary functions are to maintain or enhance the well-being of individuals within the framework of societal norms.* The most apparent common characteristic is that they work with and on behalf of people. They seek to change people, or to process people so as to facilitate the work of other agencies, or to enhance the abilities of people to enrich their own lives. In the process of carrying out these basic functions, they marshall and utilize both human and physical resources; and they create or manipulate environments.

2. *Human service agencies adhere largely to a philosophy that focuses on the whole person, on the totality and interrelatedness of an individual's needs and desires.* This is in contrast to the approach of narrow specialization in which agencies deal with isolated aspects of problems or with highly specific attempts at life enrichment. This is not to say that any given human service agency will try to be all things to all people; obviously matters of technological or methodological competence preclude this. But it does assume the basic position that the needs of the person being served are not confined to neat categories that can be worked on separately. Recognition of this fact by agencies leads, in part, to a third basic element.

3. *The type of delivery system used by human service organizations is based on linkages between agencies to provide a broader base of services than any one agency could supply.* The approach is multidisciplinary. In human service organizations, agency personnel familiarize themselves with the purposes and resources of agencies other than their own that have potential for serving the needs of people. They develop lines of communication with other agency personnel and traditions of working together. These linkages, and the resulting interdependence, create a sense of identity among agencies. Though loosely defined, this identity might be thought of as a new profession or as a concept encompassing several existing professions into a larger collectivism.

4. *The effectiveness of human service agencies to a large degree depends upon the relationships between staff and the users of agency services.* Human service agencies usually seek to bring about beneficial or enriching changes in people's lives. Techniques intended to promote or facilitate these changes rely heavily on interpersonal relationships; frequently these are helping relationships.

5. *The users of agency services often are involved in the planning and delivery of services.* A humanistic approach places considerable emphasis on helping people grow in their ability to meet their own needs and on self-determination.

Types of Services.   Hasenfeld and English[9] provided two very useful typologies of human services. One is based on a categorization according to types of clients served (normally functioning or malfunctioning) and the predominant function of the organization (people processing or people changing). *People-changing agencies* utilize various methods that are designed to change clients (or users of agency services) in defined ways. An elementary school is an example. By using instructional techniques, teachers strive to change their students' behaviors. *People-processing agencies*, rather than trying to bring about change directly, attempt to facilitate the work of other agencies that are change oriented. They do this by identifying client needs and characteristics or by evaluating clients' potential for benefiting from change methodologies used by other agencies. A senior information and referral agency that identifies the various needs of older adults in a community would be an example. Another example would be a juvenile court.

The second typology is based on the extent of the agency's interest in the client's biography (limited or extensive) and the means used to obtain clients' compliance with procedures. Three compliance systems are defined: *normative,* which relies on the staff's ability to develop rapport with clients; *utilitarian,* which operates by the agency controlling the resources desired by the client; and *coercive,* where control mechanisms are brought to bear directly on clients.

These typologies can be represented schematically, as shown in Figure 1-1.

Human Service Functions.   Hasenfeld and English's scheme identified two major functions: people processing and people changing. The people-changing function, as suggested earlier by Brill, includes preventive services and opportunities for growth as well as rehabilitative services. A third function suggested directly by Brill and implied by Hasenfeld and

TYPOLOGY BASED ON AGENCY FUNCTION AND TYPE OF CLIENT

Predominant Functioning

People Served by Agency	People Processing	People Changing
Normally Functioning	Employment Placement Service	Public School
Malfunctioning	Juvenile Court	Hospital

(a)

TYPOLOGY BASED ON AGENCY-CLIENT RELATIONSHIP

Interested in Background Information on Client

Compliance System Used by Agency	Limited	Extensive
Normative (Based on rapport between staff and clients)	University	Mental Hospital
Utilitarian (Control of resources desired by clients)	Medical Clinic	Nursing Home
Coercive (Direct control mechanisms)	Police	Correctional Institution

(b)

Figure 1-1 Human service agency typologies.[10]

From Yeheskel Hasenfeld and Richard English, eds. *Human Service Organizations,* (Ann Arbor, Michigan: The University of Michigan Press, 1974), pp. 5, 7.

English is *facilitating.* It might be said that most change agencies are facilitating if they change people in ways the people wish to be changed. However, facilitating in a more direct sense carries the notion of helping people to achieve what they want to achieve. The focus is somewhat more on the self-activation of people and on the role of agency personnel as enablers.

This facilitating function assumes that the individual cooperates in the accomplishment of agency objectives (which must also be, or support, the individual's objectives). It further assumes that the individual comes to, and takes part in, the service voluntarily; and that he or she is functioning well enough to assume this role.

In facilitating, the primary processes used rely on interpersonal relationships and/or on the manipulation of environments on behalf of the individual.

DEFINING THE LEISURE SERVICES

Leisure services are provided by those agencies comprising the field of recreation and parks. These services involve all three functions: processing, changing, and facilitating. Frequently they all are in evidence in one agency. Two of the illustrations provided in Figure 1-2 relate to participants—the psychiatric hospital and the municipal recreation and park department. A third example, a state department of recreation and parks, is related to agency staff.

As suggested in Figure 1-2, processing and changing functions contribute to facilitating. They enable people to engage in leisure behaviors that enrich their lives. In the case of staff, these functions permit a fuller development and utilization of individual talents in the work setting.

Recreation and park agencies use various resources to provide opportunities for people to engage in leisure behaviors. These resources include legal authorizations, money in the form of budgets, the personnel who provide services, and the physical facilities and land and water areas managed by the agencies. Agencies plan for the use of these resources, and they organize and administer them to accomplish the purposes that have been defined for the different specific programs, sites, or user groups which are involved. The purposes or objectives generally are defined in terms of human welfare and the enrichment of the quality of life. Typically, the public being served participates in the development of objectives.

Providing these opportunities, and the planning, management and deployment of resources that are involved, constitutes the leisure service delivery system.

The system, in its entirety, is made up of a great variety of recreation and park agencies. Some of these are tax-supported entities that serve the public at the local, regional, state, or federal levels. Municipal recreation and parks departments, special recreation and park districts, state park systems, and the National Park Service are examples. Other organizations operate in the private sector, either as agencies supported by voluntary giving and membership fees (YMCA, Girl Scouts of America, and so on), or entirely by membership fees (swim and tennis clubs, special interest groups). Still others function in the private enterprise arena, and operate to make a profit (resorts, marinas, ski areas, theaters).

Some leisure service agencies are concerned primarily with parks and natural resources—more specifically, with the public's use of parks and natural resources. Others are more involved with the provision of programs (classes, clubs, tournaments, tours). Some focus their efforts on par-

FUNCTION

Agency	People Processing	People Changing	Facilitating
Psychiatric Hospital	Leisure counseling which identifies an individual's needs, and makes referrals.	Recreation therapist helping an individual who has an emotional problem, learn skills of relating to others in a social sense.	The Hospital Recreation Section providing a party, which encourages social interaction.
Municipal Recreation and Park Department	Registering children for swim lessons; initial screening of students, and assignment to class levels.	Swim lessons, at various levels (beginners, intermediate, etc.)	Recreation, or open swim periods during which time new skills can be used.
State Department of Recreation and Parks	Recruitment of applicants for open positions; testing and interviewing to identify most qualified candidates. Employment and assignment.	Staff training; development of knowledges, attitudes, and skills related to specific assignments.	Ongoing supervision, which supports staff functioning; provision of resources, evaluations and opportunities for advancement.

Figure 1-2   Illustrative human service functions in recreation and park agencies.

ticular subgroups within the general population (the aged, adolescents, the physically handicapped, and so on).

Two Approaches. Two approaches to providing services can be identified. Each of these is a continuum involving two extremes. In one, the continuum is from the provision of *direct service* at one end to an *enabling approach* at the other end. In the direct service approach, the agency provides leisure services in which participants take part, without being involved themselves in the provision of the opportunity. In the enabling approach, the participants are involved in the provision of the service; agency personnel assist the process. Murphy and others described the approaches this way:

> The direct service approach determines or makes some assumptions about peoples' recreation desires and interests; the resources are then provided, ready to be used. The enabling approach serves as a catalyst, and helps people to implement their desires and interests. It assists people in planning and obtaining needed resources. The continuum, then, is from providing opportunities which permit direct and immediate participation to providing services which enable people to develop their own opportunities.[11]

Leisure opportunities, representing different points along the continuum, might be evident in any one agency. Figure 1-3 provides an illustration.

The second continuum is from a *cafeteria* approach to a *prescription* approach.[12] In the cafeteria approach, the agency establishes a general framework of objectives (such as to provide wholesome activities or to foster the learning of new skills). Within this framework, the agency assumes that the users of these services will select, from the range of opportunities, those that most appeal to them individually. In the prescription

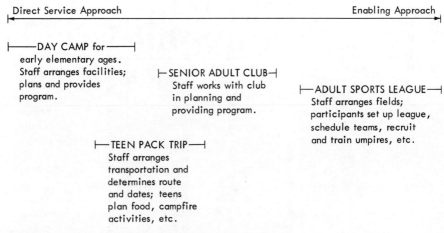

Figure 1-3 Direct service vs. enabling approach continuum.

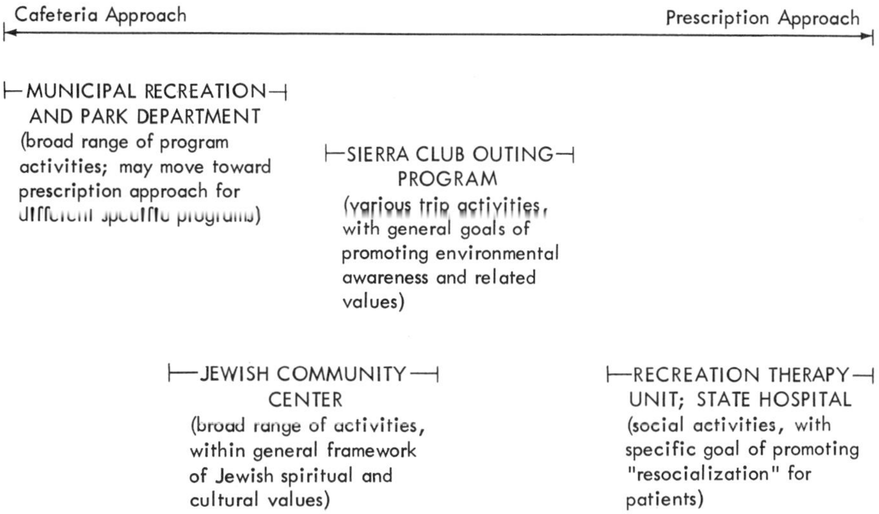

⊢─MUNICIPAL RECREATION─⊣
AND PARK DEPARTMENT
(broad range of program
activities; may move toward
prescription approach for
different specific programs)

⊢─SIERRA CLUB OUTING─⊣
PROGRAM
(various trip activities,
with general goals of
promoting environmental
awareness and related
values)

⊢──JEWISH COMMUNITY──⊣
CENTER
(broad range of activities,
within general framework
of Jewish spiritual and
cultural values)

⊢─RECREATION THERAPY─⊣
UNIT; STATE HOSPITAL
(social activities, with
specific goal of promoting
"resocialization" for
patients)

Figure 1-4 Cafeteria vs. prescription approach continuum.

approach, the agency works to achieve more specific objectives, in terms of the outcomes of participation. Different agencies, or different specific programs in any one agency, will fall at various points along the continuum. Some examples are shown in Figure 1-4.

Agency Cooperation. Leisure service agencies in some communities have developed mechanisms for working cooperatively, together and with other health and welfare agencies, on common problems. These are the "linkages" mentioned earlier in the chapter that are characteristics of human service agencies. These linkages in the leisure services often take the form of federations of agencies or community councils. Such cooperative arrangements usually involve private agencies and, less frequently, both private and governmental agencies. Commercial enterprises are involved infrequently.

Several illustrations can be provided. All those agencies in a community that work with older adults might meet periodically to assess overall services for senior citizens and conduct coordinated planning. A recreation and park district might work closely with a county drug counseling center to develop programs for adolescents with drug problems. Volunteer training sessions might be conducted jointly by two different youth-serving agencies. A commercial bowling establishment and an employee recreation association might cooperatively offer lessons and a novice tournament for beginning bowlers.

All personnel in the field of recreation and parks work with the public they serve. Some are in direct contact with participants (for example, craft instructors, playground leaders, and interpreters in natural resource settings). Others work indirectly with the public (administrators, supervisors, and maintenance personnel).

Agency Organization and Responsibility. Leisure service agencies tend to be organized somewhat similarly. Figure 1-5 shows an illustrative organization chart for a hypothetical municipal recreation and park department.

In this illustration, as in most agencies, there are three basic levels of responsibility: the administrative level, the supervisory level, and the level that either works directly with participants or with some physical function (such as park maintenance). This third level is often called the *functional*[13] or *operational* level. Individuals working at these three levels usually are in a direct line of responsibility (line personnel) for service to the public. Another category of personnel includes those who work in staff positions. These positions support and assist the work of line personnel.

In Figure 1-5, positions one, two, and four are administrative. Positions five through ten are supervisory. Positions in categories eleven through sixteen are functional. All of these are *line* positions; that is, they are in the direct line of accountability for serving the public. Position three is the only staff position shown. Staff positions are those which support or facilitate the work of persons in line positions.

There is an additional method of categorizing responsibility in leisure service agencies. This is to differentiate policy determination, policy recommendation, and policy implementation. All of the numbered positions in Figure 1-5 (one through sixteen) are concerned with implementing (carrying out) policies. The determination of policies usually is the responsibility of a body elected by the public served by the agency. For the agency shown in Figure 1-5, this group is the city council elected by the voters residing within the boundaries of the city. Similarly, in a private organization such as the YMCA, it is the board of directors, elected by the general membership of the organization. In a district it also is the board of directors. The policy recommendation function is somewhat diffused. An agency administrator often recommends policies to the board or council. However, policy-determining bodies frequently appoint citizens (nonstaff) to commissions or committees whose primary purpose it is to recommend policies to the group that appointed them. Figure 1-6 provides a hypothetical illustration for a municipality.

In this illustration, the council (Block one) determines policy; the commission (Block two) makes recommendations to be considered by the council; and the city manager and the recreation and park director (Blocks three and four) are employed to implement policies determined by the council.

The levels of responsibility shown in Figure 1-5 (administrative, supervisory, and functional) and the categorization with respect to policy illustrated in Figure 1-6 (determination, recommendation, and implementation) can be observed in most leisure service agencies.

In addition to paid personnel, many agencies utilize volunteer workers. Volunteers work directly with participants in teaching or leadership capacities; or they provide supportive services, such as transporting the

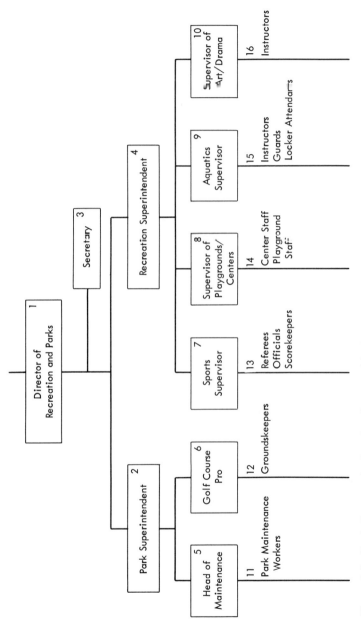

Figure 1-5 Illustrative organization chart for a municipal recreation and park department.

| 1 Director of Recreation and Parks |
| 3 Secretary |
| 2 Park Superintendent |
| 4 Recreation Superintendent |
| 5 Head of Maintenance |
| 6 Golf Course Pro |
| 7 Sports Supervisor |
| 8 Supervisor of Playgrounds/ Centers |
| 9 Aquatics Supervisor |
| 10 Supervisor of Art/Drama |
| 11 Park Maintenance Workers |
| 12 Groundskeepers |
| 13 Referees Officials Scorekeepers |
| 14 Center Staff Playground Staff |
| 15 Instructors Guards Locker Attendants |
| 16 Instructors |

11

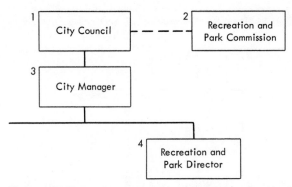

Figure 1-6 Policy recommendation, determination, and implementation levels.

handicapped, registering children for swim lessons, and so on. Sometimes they provide specialized services, such as a doctor giving Little League physical exams without charge, or a lawyer providing free legal advice in the formation of an older adults club; and, of course, those people who serve on recreation and park commissions, boards of directors, or special committees are volunteers.

Regardless of the level at which an individual works, certain activities can be identified that are common to most positions. These might be spoken of as *core processes*—processes in the sense that they are behaviors in which personnel engage as they carry out their responsibilities, and core in the sense that they are associated with most personnel positions. These core processes include such things as communicating, exercising leadership, working with groups, solving problems, planning, and teaching.

Leisure services, then, are those activities carried out by personnel using available resources that provide opportunities for the expression of a wide variety of recreation behaviors.

Influences on Leisure Service Agencies. Personnel who work in the field attempt to serve society. Various conditions influence this attempt, including environmental, economic, demographic, social, and political factors. For example: Fuel shortages directly affect recreational travel; inflation influences the amounts of money that people have available for discretionary spending. A higher percentage of older adults in the society suggests various program modifications.

People's attitudes and expectations are significant influences. Widespread interest in personal growth, self-realization, and holistic health create potential demands for leisure services that vary from traditional patterns. Increasing societal acceptance of varied lifestyles and changes in role expectations associated with such factors as sex identity and aging have important effects upon service delivery. Brill noted the influence of these factors and others on the human services generally. She suggested that several conditions have emerged in society that seem to be fundamental considerations. One of these is the

> . . . developing emphasis on a pluralistic society and on what has been called the communal individual. Two basic values that have been a part of culture in

America since its beginning are being challenged in light of the demands of living together in an increasingly larger, more complex technological society. These are the values related to the concept of the melting pot, wherein all people blend their differences into one great whole, and the concept of the independent person, who "rides alone into the sunset," who is dependent on no one but self.[14]

Another fundamental consideration is the

> . . . emphasis on rights of all people to what has been called social justice and the expansion of the concept of rights to different groups of people such as children and women.[15]

Agency Accountability.   Brill also identified an expectation, held by increasingly larger numbers of people, that has direct influences on the human services, including recreation and parks. She spoke of this as an

> . . . almost impatient demand for what has been called "accountability," for the development of better tools and knowledges about evaluation of outcomes of programs and services and evidence, insofar as is possible, on the basis of empirical research, of the effectiveness of what is being done.[16]

Yet the efforts of human service workers do not permit easy accountability. Human needs and human problems are complex. In today's society, people are subject to a great variety of pressures: economic, social, environmental. Their inability to cope with these pressures may lead to apathetic resignation or, more frequently, to feelings of frustration, anger, and anxiety. Detrimental as they are, these emotions may be better than apathy; they tend to cause people to seek help—to seek out human service workers. Brill contended that the human services have obligations to ". . . teach new ways of dealing with the demands of living . . . ," including the knowledge of ". . . how to use the opportunities that exist in the society we have created."[17] The challenges of helping people use free time seem to be applicable here.

Desires for accountability may be part of a larger, general suspicion of bureaucracies, especially government agencies. A widespread resistance to tax increases probably is attributable to this, as well as to erosion of purchasing power by inflation. Bannon commented on these kinds of political and economic influences on the field of leisure services.

> Most economic predictors indicate a slowed rate of economic growth for the 1980's while most political activity indicates an unsettling taxpayer refusal to fund social and human services to the degree they were funded over the past 20 years. The combination of reduced economic growth and the passage in nearly 20 states of tax- or budget-limiting legislation has put parks and recreation in an unprecedented financial and political bind. And this situation is likely to worsen.[18]

Bannon spoke, however, of the importance of not using these diverse economic and political conditions as reasons for diluting our services to the public.

A clearly defined "bottom line" of behavior must be established beneath which parks and recreation professionals never operate. The easiest asset to lose is a good reputation and the most difficult to remedy is a bad one. Although, as a profession we have a good image and reputation among lawmakers and citizens, this reputation may suffer as pressures mount in the 1980's (most notably economic and fiscal in nature) and we are tempted to cut corners or make deals to insure our livelihood.[19]

Gray observed the influences of economic, political, and other social conditions, and suggested that the field must respond positively.

These social, political, economic, and energy-related changes pose serious challenges for the recreation and park field, but perhaps the most profound challenge facing the field lies in resisting the temptation to meet adversity and change with simple retrenchment. In short, the future's outlook is less a question of coping and more a question of dynamism, initiative and innovation, a question of permitting the recreation and park movement to evolve rather than forcing it to play catch up.[20]

The conditions that pose challenges to the field were reiterated in a paper David Gray and Seymour Greben presented at the 1981 Congress of the National Recreation and Park Association. The authors expressed the strong belief that the problems for our field, created by social and economic conditions and political events, were of "crisis" dimensions.[21] They felt that the central question related to these conditions and events is the role of government.

In the earlier statement, Gray spoke of permitting the ". . . recreation and park movement to evolve. . . ." One aspect of the evolution of the field is related to the human services. Bannon noted the connections between recreation and parks and the human services. He suggested that these connections must be nurtured even though the field faces various challenges.

We are aligned and integrated with other social and human services, and we must never deny these connections in an effort to win favor for ourselves. Our ethical position must remain: the mix of social and human services presently available is essential in any advanced, civilized society.[22]

THE EVOLUTION OF A HUMANISTIC EMPHASIS

A variety of the concerns and conditions mentioned in the previous section are reflected in two interrelated influences that have been felt in the field of recreation and parks. One is greater acceptance of a humanistic approach and a belief that leisure services are justified primarily in terms of their contributions to the enhancement of human potential. Gray and Greben presented a paper in 1973 that was a predecessor to the statement given at the 1981 NRPA Congress. The 1973 paper, also given at a NRPA Congress, was titled "Future Perspectives of the Park and Recreation Movement." This paper had a significant influence on the field's awareness of its close ties with the humanistic movement. The authors contended that

The central concept of the Recreation and Park Movement are ideas whose time has come. The concern for people that has been and is the primary theme in the philosophical foundation of the Recreation Movement has become the major thrust of contemporary life in this country. It is apparent in the humanistic movement that is sweeping the nation and the world. We see it in humanistic psychology, attacks on the abuses of technology, the peace movement, empathy for the poor, the drive for improved medical care, the move to reject possessions as the symbol of identity, the effort to improve education, women's lib, race relations, and in a thousand other ways. These ideas are being acted out in programs and demonstrations and individual efforts all around us.[23]

In their 1981 paper titled "Future Perspectives II: Earning a Place in National Priorities," Gray and Greben noted changes in social conditions that had become more dominant since the 1973 statement. These changes included increased violence and crime, an erosion of purchasing power for many due to inflation, a reduction in social services funded by public agencies, and a diminishing government commitment to regulating environmental quality and consumer and occupational protection.[24] As mentioned earlier, they felt that these conditions, and especially the changing roles of government, create severe challenges for the field of recreation and parks as well as for the general welfare of people. "We believe that what is at stake may well be the continuing vitality of our total movement and, in a larger sense, the meaning and vitality of social progress in our country."[25]

They did not imply that the challenges we face detract from the responsibilities of the field to serve people. They reaffirmed that our central concern is the enrichment of human life. "Recreation exists as a discipline and a philosophy in direct relation to human beings and to human fulfillment. We exist, we have validity, primarily in that kind of world in which human values—and service to human beings—are paramount."[26]

They also noted that our concern includes issues beyond those specifically related to leisure services. "Our concern is for the total human experience, and thus issues such as environmental protection and preservation, financial aid for poor people, conservation of natural resources, etc., are vital to us also."[27]

Murphy's writings also have influenced the field toward a humanistic emphasis. He noted the following approaches and potential contributions:

Recreation and leisure agencies which incorporate a humanistic approach to service seek to promote the capacity and ability of groups and individuals to make self-determined and responsible choices—in light of their needs to grow, to explore new possibilities, and to realize their full potential as well as concern for eliminating barriers which hinder self-development. Recreation and leisure service which does not address itself to the positivistic nature of human behavior will miss the essence of humanism. Humanism is concerned with facilitating man to become what he is capable of being. It asks, "What are the possibilities of man? And, from these possibilities, what is *optimum man*, and what conditions will most probably lead to his attainment and maintenance of such a state?"[28]

The writings of Gray and Greben, and Murphy, served to make the field more conscious of its relationships to the broader field of human services. In a sense, they also reminded us of the fact that our central concern is people, and what happens to people in the opportunities we provide for them. This concern has been expressed by various spokespersons at different times in the history of the recreation movement. In 1931, V. K. Brown, Superintendent of Playgrounds and Sports for Chicago's South Park System, stated

> Long ago, we passed the point where we were interested exclusively in what people do in recreation; the trend is now to consider, as more vital, rather what the thing done itself does, in turn, to the doer of it.[29]

However, the expressed concern for human growth and welfare, evident in the history of the field, did not lead immediately to the development of a humanistic approach. Gray and Greben suggested that until recent times the emphasis was placed on programs and facilities. In their 1973 paper mentioned earlier they wrote

> We should have discovered long ago the nature of the business we are in, but we have not. Only now are we beginning to rethink what recreation is. In the emerging view it is not activities, or facilities, or programs that are central, it is what happens to people.[30]

Neulinger also affirmed that our central concerns should be the experiences people have. He noted the humanistic thrust of the field, and observed that this has brought us into closer alignment with the field of psychology.

> We find a strong turning toward a humanistic orientation in this field, concomitant with an increasing acceptance of at least some subjective aspects in the definition of leisure. To this must be added the recent emergence of leisure education and counseling as areas of intense involvement for recreation professionals. All these trends push recreation in the direction of psychology. . . . Investigations from that perspective no longer imply an interest in time periods and activities as such, but merely as these events constitute conditions for bringing about a certain state of mind—namely leisure.[31]

He suggested that the important questions in the field relate to such matters as how people view their leisure experiences, what meanings these have for them, and what needs are satisfied.

> The quality of the person's experience, and in a larger sense, the quality of life in general, becomes the ultimate concern. It is this aspect, of course, to which the humanistic orientation refers.[32]

A study by D'Amours supported the contention that the field is moving increasingly toward a humanistic orientation. D'Amours used a consensus-seeking method to assess the perceptions of leading recreation and park practitioners and educators relative to future developments in the field. The study pointed to the following conclusion:

> As a general conclusion, the study demonstrates that there will be a shift from a segmentalist activity-oriented approach to an integrative, multi-disciplinary and human-oriented approach in the domain of recreation professional preparation. The new professional will have to perform in different manners. It seems that the fundamental role of a recreation professional will be that of helping relation vis-a-vis the client, as counselor, guide, advisor. Leisure behavior will be considered less and less as a special kind of human behavior performed during free time. A more holistic approach will take place and those particular behaviors, which provide man with a sentiment of self-realization and achievement, will be privileged among others. The justification of professional intervention will refer to social welfare benefits and to the acceleration of human development rather than to the ever-increasing amount of free-time and its activity use.[33]

The Impact of a Changing Society.   In addition to a humanistic approach, a second influence on the field has been the developing recognition that people's leisure needs do not exist independently of the other conditions and forces that affect their lives; and that social changes affect the field of recreation and parks just as they affect other human services. A position statement presented at the 1977 Annual California and Pacific Southwest Conference represents the thinking in this direction.

> The economical, political, social and aesthetic conditions inherent in today's environment create a population replete with alienation, emotional deprivation, unemployment, poverty, crime and disintegrated sense of community. Citizens in urban communities are becoming increasingly mobile, involved in changing family relationships and life-styles, experiencing new or altered patterns of housing, work and leisure are entwined in changing value systems. Human service needs emerge in such areas as adequate shelter, nourishment, mental and physical health knowledge, income, personal development and leisure pursuits.
>
> The recreation and park movement is not immune to the forces of social change which has altered the consciousness of women, minority groups, to the poor, the elderly, the handicapped and the young. The use of leisure time has important implications for human development, community integration, mental health, conservation of resources and the quality of human existence. However, it is necessary to move beyond recreation activities, buildings, and parks and accept the consequences of what we do in terms of making people stronger and improving the quality of community life. Our traditional role of taking care of the parks and offering a program of recreation activities is no longer effective in society's changing social environment.[34]

The implication is not that recreation and park personnel should attempt to be health educators, employment counselors, nutritionists, correctional officers, legal advisors, or housing experts. Rather, the statement suggests that they recognize the holistic nature of the human condition and that they take advantage of the opportunities they have to support efforts by experts in other human services, to refer those individuals who have needs and with whom they have contact to appropriate resources, to advocate for better conditions, and to act as catalysts and enablers. The direct implication is that people working in recreation and park agencies see themselves as human service workers and that they conceive of the agencies in which they are employed as integral parts of the larger human services delivery system.

This implication emerged also at the 1977 Congress of the National Recreation and Park Association. At the congress, two major position papers were presented: One dealt with the human service responsibilities of the field; the other related to energy conservation and environmental quality. The human services position paper stated:

> The disparity between need and resource has forced new social alliances, the need to coordinate and mobilize resources in public and private sectors, the integration of social delivery systems, and . . . new responsiveness to citizen involvement.
>
> The cornerstone of the human service policy statements is understanding the enormous potential of recreation activity to enhance self-concept and the development of a holistic approach to broader program orientation and the adoption of cooperative multi-service delivery systems.[35]

The paper called upon the National Recreation and Park Association
to

> . . . foster the idea that recreation and park services are a fundamental component of the human services movement and promote a vital role for recreation and parks in the human services movement, which may include becoming the lead agency in the delivery and coordination of human services.[36]

How Far to Go?   Delegates to the congress were not unanimous in their support of the position paper. Similarly, there have been differences of opinion among recreation and park personnel. Mostly the differences have revolved around the question, How far should the field of recreation and parks move in the human services direction? The range of possible positions is suggested by a review of eight different human service roles for municipalities identified by Gardner.[37] These include such functions as direct delivery of services, contracting with other agencies for services, serving in referral capacities, or simply encouraging other agencies to provide needed services.

It does appear that recreation and park agencies are providing direct services which go beyond the traditional ones. Kraus reported on two surveys of public recreation and park departments completed in 1971 and 1979.[38] The departments were in cities of over 150,000 population. Thirty-nine percent in 1971 and 32 percent in 1979 reported that they provided antidelinquency programs; 19 percent in both years reported programs for working with drug abuse; and 64 percent (1971) and 75 percent (1979) offered youth employment programs. A variety of services for special populations also were reported.[39]

These programs suggest movement toward a greater human service stance in the field. However, they are not evidence of total acceptance of the validity of such a trend. There is divided opinion, and several basic questions have been raised. Should the field offer direct services other than traditional ones, as the agencies surveyed by Kraus were doing? Should leisure service agencies lead in the coordination and integration of programs offered by other human service agencies? Should leisure service agencies be the "umbrella" under which other agencies function? Should recreation and park personnel operate on the basis of a human service philosophy, and should they use human service methods?

A HUMAN SERVICES PHILOSOPHY AND METHODOLOGY

Earlier in the chapter, the basic characteristics of human service agencies were discussed. These characteristics included a philosophy which focuses on the whole person. Eriksen provided the following additional dimensions of a human service philosophy:

1. A commitment to the premise that human service should be a right of American citizens, not a privilege, and that people should have equal access to service.
2. A belief that the human services are intended to enrich people's lives by helping them correct deficiencies, cope with realities, and experience satisfactions. This assumes the inclusion of both preventive and rehabilitative services.
3. A resolve to actively involve the recipients of services in both the planning and evaluation of programs.
4. A persuasion that those agencies that comprise the field of human services will be most effective if they cooperate.[40]

The following statements suggest several general methods that are appropriate for use by leisure service personnel.

1. They should seek to provide services to all citizens, equally, and on the basis of needs and desires.
2. They should help people become more independent and self-determining, with due respect for the rights, needs, and desires of others.
3. They should be sensitive and responsive to citizens' perceptions (a) of their own needs, and (b) of the effectiveness of the services they receive.
4. They should develop and maintain liaisons with other community human service organizations—organizations that can provide services to meet a wide range of citizen needs and wishes, but that are not within the expertise or authority of their own agencies.
5. They should seek to deploy the resources available to them, and to manipulate the environments within which the recipients of their services live, so as to remove barriers to personal growth and well-being and to create opportunities for the enrichment of life.[41]

We do aspire to create opportunities for all people to engage in recreation behavior. This has been a stated intention of recreation and park personnel, historically, though we have often fallen short of this ideal. Through these opportunities we hope to encourage the growth of those who use our services; generally, we aspire to help these people become self-determining and independent. We use a variety of processes to determine the leisure wishes of people. Elected boards of directors, advisory commissions, and other citizens groups have responsibilities for representing the interest of the public. In addition, we frequently use various survey methods to assess what services people want. These boards, commissions, and surveys help us to evaluate the effectiveness of our services. The general expectations of the public for more accountability on the part of governmental and other human service agencies give added importance to these evaluations. Part of our effectiveness in providing service is influenced by the degrees to which we avoid gaps and overlaps. To do this requires at least minimal liaison with other agencies that provide leisure opportunities. The development also of liaison with other human service agencies, such as health departments and school districts, makes it easier to explore ways of sharing resources and facilitates possibilities for referring people to the most appropriate sources of help. Recreation and park personnel do all of these things, in the final analysis, to create opportunities through which people can enrich their lives. As we engage in these activities, we are using methods consistent with a human services philosophy—and, of course, we are working with people.

WORKING WITH PEOPLE

The responsibilities, tasks, and functions of recreation and park personnel do, indeed, involve working with people. This is not unique. Almost everybody works with people in one way or another. However, recreation and park personnel, operating within a humanistic and human service perspective, have specific responsibilities to work with people in ways that enrich individuals' lives through leisure. This process may be schematically illustrated, in broad dimensions, as shown in Figure 1-7. This figure suggests the following activities and relationships:

　　1. The basic purpose of the leisure service worker (1)* is to encourage and facilitate recreation behavior on the part of the *user* (2) so that the user's life is enriched. The worker does this directly by relating to the user, or indirectly by creating or manipulating the *physical and social environment* (3). For example, the swimming pool manager relates directly to users when he teaches a class for beginning swimmers; he relates indirectly when he develops the work schedule and assigns guards, sets and checks pool filtration, chlorination, and heating equipment to assure proper water quality and temperature, and posts basic safety rules on the dressing room wall where swimmers enter the pool.

　　The superintendent of recreation also works indirectly with these users when she administers the overall department budget (which includes the pool budget for staff, supplies and equipment), when she provides staff

*Numbers refer to the related position, entity, or process shown in Figure 1-7.

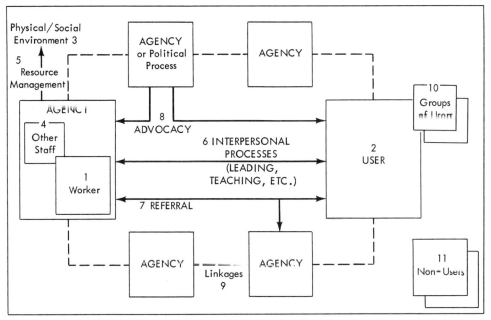

Figure 1-7 Working with people in recreation and park settings. (a schematic representation.)

training in interpersonal relationships for all department staff including pool staff, and when she meets with the high school principal to renegotiate the agreement that permits the department to use the school pool. All of these activities ultimately are intended to facilitate the users' recreation behavior.

2. Much of what the worker does, individually and cooperatively with other *staff* (4), is designed to get people to engage in desired behaviors—such as participate in program activities, support environmental causes, and adopt new leisure skills. This usually involves the *management of resources* (5), such as making facilities available and assigning staff. It often involves leadership of users and staff, if other staff are involved; and it may involve teaching and the use of group processes. In all of these tasks, the worker relies heavily on his or her *interpersonal relationship* (6) with the users (or staff). In many circumstances, this is a helping relationship, such as might be found in therapeutic settings or leisure counseling. If the needs of the user require expertise beyond that possessed by the worker, the activities of *referral* (7) might be brought into play; suggesting and facilitating contacts with health departments, social welfare agencies, legal aid and other human services. In some cases, the worker may assume an *advocacy* (8) role, working for changes in the community that benefit the users with whom he or she works. As an illustration, the recreation superintendent might appear before the board of directors of the transit agency to encourage them to offer Sunday bus service, which would permit more older adults to use the city recreation centers.

3. These basic processes (leading, teaching, and so on) are enabled by the support processes of communicating, planning, problem solving, organization, and evaluation. Obviously, they also require the gathering of relevant information about the community and about users, and they require the development of working arrangements, or *linkages* (9) with other agencies.

4. The basic processes and the support processes require knowledge about behavior in at least four categories:

> **a.** User behavior, *individually* and in *groups* (10),
>
> **b.** Staff behavior, in those cases where workers relate to other staff as either coworkers or as supervisors,
>
> **c.** The behavior of nonusers of leisure services (11), to the extent that workers might encourage or facilitate participation,
>
> **d.** Knowledge about self (the individual worker) or, more specifically, about personal values, attitudes, and biases that influence the worker's use of the basic and support processes.

This basic scheme symbolizes leisure leadership, in the broad sense of working with people in recreation and park settings.

SUMMARY

The human services include those agencies that enable people to cope with the problems they encounter and to live fuller, richer lives. They tend to operate on holistic and humanistic philosophies. They often develop linkages with each other that enable them to serve people more effectively.

Recreation and park agencies exist, in large part, to provide opportunities for people to engage in recreation behavior. Directly or indirectly they are concerned with the enrichment of life. To carry out this basic purpose they utilize the resources of law, money, areas and facilities, and personnel. These leisure service agencies frequently develop cooperative relationships with each other or with other community organizations. Their staff members aspire to meet the needs of all those for whom the services are intended, to recognize the wholeness of people, and to involve people in determining the nature of the services provided. In these ways, recreation and park agencies do show human service characteristics.

Leisure service personnel inevitably work with people—the users of agency services and other staff members. In doing so, they operate within physical and social environments. In these environments, they use various processes, often interpersonal.

The remainder of this book examines the processes used by those who provide leisure leadership. Chapter 2 is devoted to a general consideration of competency as a function of the interrelatedness of the worker, the recipient of services, the processes used, and the situation within which services occur. Chapter 3 presents an overview of behavior applicable to both users of recreation and park services and staff. Chapter 4 discusses elements in the relationship between the worker and the individual or individuals served, including such processes as helping and counseling. Chapters 5 through 10 deal with the basic processes of leadership, working with groups, teaching, referral and advocacy, and utilization of resources. Chapter 11 briefly examines the support processes of communicating, planning, problem solving, organizing, working with other agencies, and evaluating.

A summary is provided at the end of each of the following chapters in the book. You might want to look ahead and review each of the summaries before reading the rest of the book. This would give you a more detailed overview of the concept of working with people that is presented and it would help you to understand how the various parts of the concept fit together.

REVIEW QUESTIONS

1-1 What are the characteristics of the human services?

1-2 What basic purposes do the human services accomplish?

1-3 What are the major purposes of the leisure services, or the field of recreation and parks?

1-4 What are some of the conditions (social, economic or political) that influence the field of leisure services?

1-5 In what ways can the field of recreation and parks be considered a human service?

1-6 What basic methods are appropriate for our field, if it is to function as a human service?

TO DO

Recreation and park personnel usually keep lists of things to do. This "to-do" list might be kept by the day, or week, or perhaps month. In Chapter 11, you will read about the ways such lists help you use your time more effectively. By the number of each "to-do" item is a small box. Check off the item after you have completed it.

Save the materials (descriptions, charts, and so on) that you develop as you complete these lists. You will be asked to refer back to them in future chapters.

1-A Write a brief description of the first (or next) full-time job you probably will have in the field of recreation and parks. What will be the probable title of the job? In what kind of an agency or organization will you work? What will be your major responsibilities? Where will the organization in which you are working be located (in what type of city or geographic area)?

1-B For the agency in which you probably will be working (described in item 1-A), draw an organization chart. Include all of the probable positions at the administrative, supervisory, and functional levels. Show the policy-determining and recommending groups, if they are likely to be involved.

1-C If you are taking a class with other recreation and park students, share your career objectives with two or three other people. Find out about their future professional plans.

END NOTES

1. Karin Eriksen, *Human Services Today* (Reston, Va.: Reston Publishing Company, Inc , 1977), pp. 1, 6.

2. Herbert C. Schulberg, Frank Baker, and Sheldon R. Roen, eds., *Development in Human Services*, vol. I (New York: Behavioral Publications, 1973), pp. 7–8.

3. Evaline D. Schulman, *Intervention in Human Services* (St. Louis: C. V. Mosby Co., 1974), p. 4.

4. Yeheskel Hasenfeld and Richard A. English, eds., *Human Service Organizations*, (Ann Arbor: University of Michigan Press, 1974), p. 9.

5. Hasenfeld and English, *Human Service Organizations*, p. 1.

6. Ibid., pp. 9–14, 21.

7. Naomi I. Brill, *Working with People*, 2nd ed., (Philadelphia: J. B. Lippincott Co., © 1978), p. 108. Reprinted by permission of Harper & Row, Pub.

8. Brill, *Working with People*, p. xii.

9. Ibid., pp. 4–7.

10. The format of the typologies and the agency examples are taken from Hasenfeld and English, *Human Service Organizations*, pp. 5, 7.

11. James F. Murphy and others, *Leisure Services Delivery System: A Modern Perspective* (Philadelphia: Lea and Febiger, 1973), p. 70.

12. Murphy and others, *Leisure Services Delivery System*, p. 71.

13. Jay S. Shivers, *Recreational Leadership: Group Dynamics and Interpersonal Behavior* (Princeton, N.J.: Princeton Book Company, Publishers, 1980), pp. 177–85.

14. Brill, *Working with People*, pp. xii–xiii.

15. Ibid., p. xiii.

16. Ibid., p. xiii.

17. Ibid., p. xiii.

18. Joseph Bannon, "Management," *Parks & Recreation* 15, no. 7 (July 1980): 32.

19. Bannon, "Management," 33.

20. David E. Gray, "State of the Art . . . Future Challenge," *Parks & Recreation* 15, no. 7 (July 1980): 26.

21. David Gray and Seymour Greben, "Future Perspectives II: Earning a Place in National Priorities" (San Diego, Calif.: Institute for Leisure Behavior, Department of Recreation, San Diego State University; 1981), p. 19.

22. Bannon, "Management," 33.

23. Seymour Greben and David Gray, "Future Perspectives of the Park and Recreation Movement," Paper presented at the National Congress for Recreation and Parks; Washington, D.C. (October, 1973) p. 13.

24. Gray and Greben, *Future Perspectives II*, pp. 4, 6–7.

25. Ibid., p. 15.

26. Ibid., p. 20.

27. Ibid., p. 17.

28. James F. Murphy, *Recreation and Leisure Service* (Dubuque, Iowa: Wm.C. Brown Co., 1975), p. 2.

29. V. K. Brown, "Trends in Recreation Service," *Recreation* 25, no. 1 (April 1931): 63.

30. Greben and Gray, "Future Perspectives of the Park and Recreation Movement," p. 14.

31. John Neulinger, "Introduction," in *Social Psychological Perspectives on Leisure and Recreation*, ed. Seppo E. Iso Ahola (Springfield, Ill · Charles C Thomas, Publisher, 1980), pp. 12–13.

32. Neulinger, "Introduction," p. 13.

33. Max D'Amours, "The Views of Recreation Educators and Practitioners on the Future of the Leisure Service Professions as a New Source of Guidelines for Recreation in Higher Education," (Report to study panelists, Department of Human Sciences, Université du Québec à Trois-Rivières, P.Q., Canada, 1975), p. 23.

34. "Human Service Statements," *Leisure Lines: A Monthly Action Report* (Sacramento: California Park and Recreation Society, Inc., 3, no. 1, February 1977).

35. Jack Foley, "Human Service National Policy Statement, Draft #2, National Recreation and Park Association." Paper presented at the National Congress for Recreation and Parks, Las Vegas, Nev., October, 1977.

36. Jack Foley, "Human Service National Policy Statement, Draft #2," National Recreation and Park Association, October 1977.

37. Sidney L. Gardner, "The Changing Role of Local Governments," in *Managing Human Services*, ed. Wayne F. Anderson, Bernard J. Frieden, and Michael J. Murphy (Washington, D.C.: The International City Management Association, 1977), pp. 62–63.

38. Richard Kraus, "Urban Recreation, A Greatly Exaggerated Demise," *Parks & Recreation* 16, no. 7 (July 1981): 26–30, 54.

39. Kraus, "Urban Recreation, A Greatly Exaggerated Demise," p. 29.

40. Eriksen, *Human Services Today*, pp. 10–12.

41. E. William Niepoth, "Human Service Methods in the Field of Recreation and Parks," *Special Report on Human Services* (Sacramento: State of California, The Resources Agency, Department of Parks and Recreation, July, 1981), p. 21.

chapter 2

Competency in the Leisure Services

PREVIEW

Chapter 1 suggested that leisure services are part of the overall human service field. While there are differences of opinion about the precise role which recreation and parks should play in the human services, there is considerable agreement that human service methods of working with people are appropriate in recreation and park agencies.

The basic reason that we work with people is to provide opportunities for them to engage in recreation behavior. A model, depicting the activities of recreation and park personnel as they work with people, was presented in Chapter 1. In this chapter, we will take a closer look at these activities. We will examine competency.

The chapter begins with a discussion of the general concept of competency, and suggests that to be competent is to be able to do something in an effective or adequate way. This is followed by a brief description of several different efforts to define competency in our field: a text related to different aspects of program leadership, two investigations of competencies in commercial recreation, a group of projects focused on therapeutic recreation competencies, and a study of general competencies that are found commonly in most leisure service settings. This general definition is a major part of Chapter 2. It suggests that competency is a function of the interrelationships of certain core processes, worker characteristics, and situational demands. Each of these elements will be discussed.

Special attention will be given to the influences of self-awareness on competency. The chapter also describes some professional responsibilities that enhance our abilities to provide effective services.

The campus union director had just finished meeting with a student delegation. The group was complaining about the seeming ineffectiveness of a member of the director's staff. The director had listened to them and promised to talk with the staff member. As he sat at his desk, he was somewhat confused. The staff member had, in the past, worked with several campus organizations and the feedback from these groups was favorable. In a couple of cases, it was excellent. True, different groups were involved. The group whose members complained was smaller than any of the others with whom the staff member had worked. And it was made up almost entirely of graduate students, whereas the others were comprised mostly of undergraduates. Still, it seemed strange that the staff member's performance varied from group to group, if the complaining group's perceptions were correct.

In a suburban area several miles from the university, the executive director of a Camp Fire Council was preparing an announcement of an open position on her staff. The announcement would be sent for publication to the professional organization and to universities in the state. The position was a new one, just authorized by the Council's board of directors. While she knew generally what she wanted the new staff member to do, she found it difficult to write the announcement. After crumpling up the third attempt and throwing it in the wastebasket, she put down her pen and pushed back her chair. "Just what do I want the new person to be able to do? What kind of individual am I really looking for?" She found herself saying the thoughts audibly even though she was alone.

Questions about what recreation and park personnel do, or should do, raise the issue of competency. What makes for competency in the field? What is it that personnel do as they meet their professional responsibilities? What factors influence their effectiveness?

CONCEPTS OF COMPETENCY

To be competent is to be able to do something well. The something usually is fairly specific, rather than general. A person is competent in public speaking, in archery, or in medical practice. That is, we usually say or infer that someone is competent in some particular field or topic. Synonyms for the word *competent* include such terms as *qualified, capable,* and *able.* They imply a level of ability or capacity. A competent person is able to perform at an adequate or acceptable level. Competency related to work situations is the ability to perform adequately in one's field. In recreation and parks, it is the ability to carry out effectively those responsibilities that will allow leisure service agencies, and the publics they serve, to achieve their goals.

Much has been written about competency. The field of teacher education has devoted considerable effort to the identification of teaching competencies, and probably more work on competency development has been undertaken in this field than in any other. This work started as early as 1957.[1] In the leisure services there is considerable information about the responsibilities of workers and about qualities that seem to relate to effectiveness. Although relatively little of this information is stated in terms of specific competencies, some work has been completed.

Leadership in the Leisure Services Program. Ball and Cipriano developed an extensive list of competencies related to different aspects of program leadership. The competencies are grouped together in several modules, which represent relatively independent units of study.[2] Included are such areas as interpersonal communications and group processes, first aid and safety, leisure counseling, leadership and supervision, and program activities. The specific competencies in each of these modules are defined in terms of objectives—skills and knowledges to be learned and demonstrated as evidence of each particular competency. In the program activities module, objectives are presented for social recreation, informal activities, games of low organization, sports, music, arts and crafts, dance, and dramatics. The following objectives for low-organized games are illustrative:

1. To define low-organized games.
2. To describe advantages of leading games of low organization.
3. To determine the significance of low-organized games.
4. To describe types of low-organized activities.
5. To indicate characteristics of low-organized activities.
6. To conduct games of low organization.
7. To adapt games of low organization.
8. To identify types of low-organized games.
9. To develop a portfolio of games of low organization.
10. To depict considerations in leading games of low organization.
11. To develop a format to lead low-organized games.[3]

A similar pattern is presented for each of the other modules. Overall, 195 sets of objectives and statements that evidence the achievement of competency are presented. These objectives and statements provide a useful definition of what it is that recreation personnel do as they work with people in program settings and in some special settings, such as leisure counseling.

Commercial Recreation.   In the area of commercial recreation, preliminary definitions of competencies have been completed. Klar made an "exploratory field study" of those competencies that were seen by commercial recreation workers as being most important in their field.[4] Communicating orally, engaging in public relations, and communicating in written forms were the most highly rated competencies, in that order. Sales, management, safety, and scheduling were competency areas that also received high ratings. The author cautioned that the findings were based on limited response to the questionnaire that was used to gather data, and that the respondents were not representative of all aspects of commercial recreation. However, the study does provide some insights. Klar noted that the results suggested the importance of competencies in both the recreation area and the business area.

A key message seemed to repeatedly emerge: to prepare properly for the commercial recreation sector, graduates should be prepared in both recreation and business related concepts. Respondents did not overemphasize the business aspects at the expense of recreation, nor was the reverse the case. The need for both was a clearly expressed theme.[5]

In an earlier report, Langman and Rockwood defined the attributes of entry-level personnel, according to the perceptions of commercial recreation administrators.[6] They identified fifty-one specific attributes, which were grouped in the three categories of "technical," "human/behavioral," and "conceptual." Included among the fifty-one were such things as communicative, supervisory, and planning skills; knowledge about commercial recreation values and processes; and understanding of participation trends, motivations, and other aspects of behavior particularly focused on users of commercial services. The authors indicated that attributes in the human/behavioral category were the most significant ones.

Therapeutic Recreation.   Competencies related to therapeutic recreation were defined in a project conducted at Temple University. The project was funded by a grant from the Federal Bureau of Education for the Handicapped. The approach used in the study was to identify functional roles of therapeutic recreation professionals, to define the tasks related to these roles, and to identify the competencies (including knowledge and skills) needed to perform the tasks. Sixty-four tasks were defined, which were related to six functional roles: administrator, consultant, supervisor, educator/trainer, leader/therapist/counselor, and researcher.[7] These sixty-four tasks then were categorized into the following thirty competencies, grouped under five "Segments of Therapeutic Recreation Service" as shown.

I. MANAGEMENT
1. Ability to formulate a department philosophy of therapeutic recreation that is consistent with the philosophies of agencies providing a therapeutic recreation program.
2. Ability to develop departmental policies and procedures that incorporate the department's philosophy, and which detail how the department will function in providing its recreation services within the structure of an agency.
3. Ability to hire staff through proper utilization of personnel practices and procedures.
4. Ability to prepare, present, and defend an adequate budget for a therapeutic recreation program.
5. Ability to organize and prepare routine reports required by agencies.
6. Ability to participate appropriately and effectively in administrative meetings.
7. Ability to identify funding sources and to develop, write, and submit proposals for grants.
8. Ability to utilize public relations to enhance therapeutic recreation programs.

      9.   Ability to facilitate and promote interagency coordination.
   10.   Ability to provide consultation services.

II. SUPERVISION
   11.   Ability to effectively supervise staff.
   12.   Ability to effectively supervise practicum field-work students.
   13.   Ability to effectively utilize and supervise volunteers.

III. STAFF TRAINING
   14.   Ability to identify individual and group training needs of staff and volunteers.
   15.   Ability to develop learning objectives from identified training needs.
   16.   Ability to identify and develop training activities to meet specified learning objectives.
   17.   Ability to evaluate the cost and effectiveness of training programs.

IV. PROGRAMMING
   18.   Ability to develop and implement a basic recreation program that incorporates currently accepted recreation principles and goals.
   19.   Ability to retrieve, interpret, and apply current research to recreation program development.
   20.   Ability to plan and conduct program evaluation.
   21.   Ability to organize, service, and maintain equipment and supplies.
   22.   Ability to function effectively as a member of a treatment team.
   23.   Ability to assess a client's functional level as a basis for his or her involvement in therapeutic recreation services.
   24.   Ability to develop treatment plans for clients.
   25.   Ability to analyze activities to determine their functional elements and potential therapeutic value for clients.
   26.   Ability to plan and conduct therapeutic recreation activities to meet individual client needs and treatment objectives.
   27.   Ability to write clinical reports and records concerning clients and their involvement in therapeutic recreation services.
   28.   Ability to provide leisure counseling services for clients.
   29.   Ability to implement and maximize integration of clients into the community.

V. RESEARCH
   30.   Ability to plan, conduct and report research.[8]

    The project staff developed a list of knowledges and skills for each competency. For example, knowing what information is included in a job description, and potential sources for recruiting new employees were part of the listing for the competency of using proper personnel procedures to hire staff members (number I-3). Skills for this competency included the ability to write a job description, and to use different sources to recruit staff.

The Temple study was part of the development of a graduate program in therapeutic recreation. Another study, conducted for the National Therapeutic Recreation Society (NTRS), defined competencies for entry-level personnel. The study identified ninety competencies, grouped under these twelve categories:

1. Concepts and Philosophy of Therapeutic Recreation
2. Human Growth and Development
3. Characteristics of Special Populations
4. Facilitation and Communication Skills
5. Activity Selection and Utilization
6. Program Planning
7. Program Implementation
8. Program Evaluation
9. Administration, Supervision, and Consultation
10. Resources and Services
11. Professionalism
12. Research[9]

Most of the competencies were stated in terms of understandings. For example, the concept and philosophy category included basic understandings about leisure and recreation, goals of therapeutic recreation, and concepts of rehabilitation and therapy. The facilitation and communication category included understandings about group processes, leadership techniques, and teaching. The category for resources and services included knowledges of community resources, inter-agency relationships, referral processes, and legislation.

The Temple and NTRS studies provided information about the work of recreation therapists. A third project identified competencies needed by entry-level professionals who work with special populations in community settings. Educators and practitioners who responded to the study felt these skills and knowledges were important:

1. The ability to use proper first aid and safety procedures (such as in lifting and transporting disabled persons and responding to diabetic reactions).
2. An understanding of ways to develop positive attitudes toward special populations.
3. The ability to recognize individual needs, interests and attitudes.
4. An understanding of the concepts of mainstreaming and normalization; of ways to help disabled persons participate in regular programs and services.[10]

Other important competencies were understanding the responsibilities of community-based professionals for serving special populations, knowing how to define objectives for services, knowing ways to design facilities that are accessible to the disabled, knowing useful community resources, being able to plan activities that are appropriate to the functioning level of the individual, and teaching.

General Competencies.   Attention to general competencies in recreation was given in a study funded through the California State University Fund for Innovation and Improvement in Education.[11] The study team included recreation and park faculty from three CSU campuses, educational psychology faculty from one of the campuses, and recreation and park faculty from three California community colleges. This project focused on the field of recreation generally. One of its primary purposes was to identify competencies to be achieved by graduates of recreation curricula. The team worked within the following conceptual framework:

The field of recreation and parks is comprised of a diversity of agencies, including agencies in therapeutic recreation, as well as agencies in such areas as municipal recreation, park and outdoor recreation resource management, voluntary organizations, and private enterprise recreation. This condition suggests that there are many different competencies to be found, and that these will differ from agency to agency and from one level of responsibility to the next. That seems to be true. However, we can identify several processes that are used by most workers in most agencies. These are *core processes*—core in that they are commonly found and that other job-specific processes are built upon them or are related to them. One example is the process of working with groups. All three of the basic levels of responsibility in recreation and park agencies (administrative, supervisory, and functional) are related in some way to groups. Administrators work with boards and commissions and with a variety of citizen groups. A supervisor works primarily with staff members. Functional level workers frequently work with groups of participants (such as members of a teen club, the cast of a play, or park visitors in an interpretive program). This illustration could be applied more specifically to a variety of different agency settings.

However, the administrator of a state park, working with an advisory group of environmentalists, might work somewhat differently from another park superintendent working with the same group of people. And either administrator might rely on quite different processes in working with a different group, such as the maintenance staff of the park. Specific use of the core processes is influenced by both the character of the worker and the character of the situation. In that sense, competency may be defined as the ability to effectively perform required core processes, compatible with the personal characteristics of the worker in those situations typically encountered.

This general idea of competency can be represented as shown in Figure 2-1, using communication as the illustrative process.[12] Three major

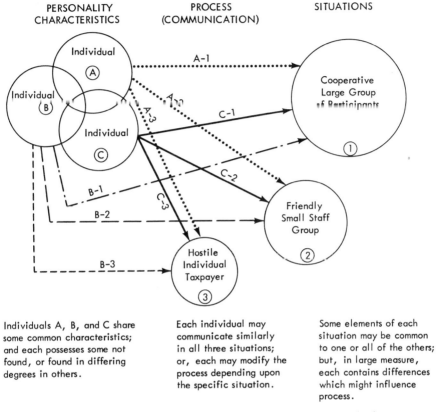

PERSONALITY CHARACTERISTICS   PROCESS (COMMUNICATION)   SITUATIONS

Individual (A)

Individual (B)

Individual (C)

A-1

Cooperative Large Group of Participants

C-1

C-2

C-3

A-3

A-2

B-1

B-2

B-3

Hostile Individual Taxpayer ③

Friendly Small Staff Group ②

①

Individuals A, B, and C share some common characteristics; and each possesses some not found, or found in differing degrees in others.

Each individual may communicate similarly in all three situations; or, each may modify the process depending upon the specific situation.

Some elements of each situation may be common to one or all of the others; but, in large measure, each contains differences which might influence process.

Figure 2-1   A representation of competency using the process of communication.

elements are represented in Figure 2-1: basic or core processes, situations, and personal characteristics.

Basic or core processes are those activities in which most recreation and park workers engage, regardless of their specific positions. The activities represent knowledge manifested in performance. That is, the ability to do something improves as one possesses knowledge about what is to be done. For example, the ability to communicate is enhanced by knowing the elements of effective listening and speaking. However, the primary characteristic of the basic processes is that they are activities—things that people do or perform. Other examples, in addition to communicating, include leading, teaching, planning, and evaluating.

Situations are the differing environments within which recreation and park personnel carry out the basic processes. Different situations influence the specific ways in which the basic processes are used. In the example in Figure 2-1, there are obvious differences among the three communication targets. It may be necessary to use a different style of communication when speaking to an angry taxpayer, for example, than one would use with a group of friendly staff members. Further, large groups might require a different approach from smaller groups.

While each situation probably is unique in some respect, categories of situations can be identified. Most important in these categories are the characteristics that may influence the ways in which the basic processes are used.

Personal characteristics include the vast array of differences which make each person unique. Included are such things as self-concept, interests, attitudes, and past experience. While each of us is unique, we nearly all are alike in some ways. In Figure 2-1, individuals A, B, and C probably share some common characteristics. They may have had similar past experiences. Perhaps they all work for the same leisure service agency; or they may all have graduated from a university. It is likely that they are motivated by similar general goals: to be recognized as capable individuals, to be liked by others, and to enjoy good health, for example.

However, each person is an individual, with certain characteristics not found, or found in differing degrees, in others. One person might be intensely motivated by a need for recognition. Another might conceive of himself as an aggressive, outgoing individual. Another might have had unsuccessful prior experiences working with large groups. Each of these differences can affect how the individual will communicate.

As suggested in Figure 2-1, individual A might communicate differently in working with a large group of participants (A-1), a small staff group (A-2), and an individual, angry taxpayer (A-3). Differences also might be observed for individual B (B-1, B-2, B-3) and individual C (C-1, C-2, C-3). Examples also could be developed for such processes as leading, teaching, and supervising.

These interacting influences of personal characteristics and situational demands could be operating in the campus union situation described at the beginning of the chapter. The staff member had been successful with other groups, but the present group—the one complaining about the staff person's performance—is different. Therefore, the situational demands are different. It is possible that his characteristics, and the particular ways in which he used various processes, made the staff member ineffective when the situation changed.

CORE PROCESSES

The California State University project identified sixteen core processes. The study focused on entry-level positions. However, the list of sixteen seems applicable to most positions, regardless of level. The sixteen processes were developed through a series of interviews with recreation and park personnel, and a questionnaire study of recreation and park educators. The processes that were identified were not mutually exclusive. For example, the process of communication is a part of almost every one of the other processes. The sixteen do, however, have enough identity to be considered distinct activities. They are described later. The study attempted to assess the degree to which each process was related to a worker's effectiveness. The sixteen are listed in the approximate order in which they were seen as contributing to effectiveness (process 1, most related to effectiveness; process 2, next most, etc.). The processes are written as behaviors.[13]

1. *The entry-level worker should be able to communicate in both written and oral forms.* Communication processes enable and influence almost every activity of the entry-level worker. All relationships with participants, staff, and the general public are based on communication. The processes of leadership, supervision, and teaching rely directly on both written and oral communication efforts.

Oral forms include communications related to teaching, supervising and other functional processes, as well as those found in relationships with the general public (day-by-day contacts and more formal presentations appropriate for meetings and larger assemblages of people). A special type of oral communication is involved in interviews, which are used in staff recruitment and in systematic information-seeking situations. The worker should be able to communicate both orally and in writing, using commonly accepted standards and observing appropriate channels and timing, so that the meaning is clear.

2. *The entry-level worker should be able to utilize leadership processes.* Most of the work of the entry-level worker is getting other people to do things: participate in programs, observe regulations, support fund drives, carry out duties as volunteers or part-time staff, and so on. In general, these activities are encouraged and accomplished by the exercise of leadership.

Leadership relies heavily on motivating people—structuring situations so that people desire to engage in the expected behavior. The creation of motivating circumstances is based on such factors as goal augmentation, persuasion, influence, and so on.

In some cases, workers must control or regulate disruptive or potentially hazardous behavior by participants. In some special settings (for instance, resource-area management) law enforcement activities might be involved. While this control is not synonymous with leadership, leadership processes are involved in varying degrees, depending upon the specific situation. The worker should be able to use leadership processes appropriate to the situation so that desired behaviors are brought about with the optimum degree of satisfaction to the affected individual(s) and the greatest contribution to the specific objectives being sought.

3. *The entry-level worker should be able to carry out both program planning and organizational planning.* The primary purpose of any recreation agency is to provide opportunities for individuals and groups of people to engage in leisure behavior. At the most basic level, all of the resources of the agency are devoted to this objective. The complex of opportunities which the agency provides is its *program*.

Program planning is basic and fundamental to all recreation personnel and agencies. Program planning can range from establishing the year-round program of an agency to planning a campfire program at a national park, a dedication ceremony for a new community center, or a birthday celebration at a convalescent home.

Program planning involves consideration of participant and agency goals, and available resources. The planner must deal with questions of timing (schedules, dates, durations), promotion (letting people know about opportunities) and evaluation.

Organizational planning is concerned with overall agency operations that support the program offerings: budgeting, staffing, training, facility development, and more. The entry-level worker should be able to develop program plans that meet participant and agency goals as fully as possible, and that make optimal use of available resources. The worker should be able to develop plans, related to the general operations of the agency for which he or she has responsibility, that appropriately support and enable the implementation of program plans.

4. *The entry-level worker should be able to teach.* The entry-level worker carries considerable responsibility for teaching.

In relationship to participants, the worker may teach a variety of skills depending upon the specific situation (crafts, dance, sports, camping, aquatics). In some settings, the worker is responsible for contributing to the development of attitudes and values. This situation is most often found in youth agencies and institutional settings, but it might be a responsibility in all agencies to some degree. To the degree that attitudes and values are learned, the worker has the opportunity to teach them.

In relationship to staff, the worker who has any responsibility for supervising other staff (paid or volunteer) probably will be teaching. Educational experiences for staff must be provided that orient them to their respective positions and develop and maintain their effectiveness.

The worker should be able to define the objectives to be achieved by teaching, to plan and provide the educational experiences which will bring about these objectives, and to assess the degree to which the objectives have been achieved.

5. *The entry-level worker should be able to organize available resources and his or her own time and energies.* Organization is related to planning as well as to other processes such as problem-solving and managing. In terms of resources, the basic process of organization is one of breaking a total task into appropriate units, assigning resources to these subtasks, and then relating the units (resources) to each other so that they can function efficiently. The units might be defined around a specific function (such as maintenance, accounting, special facility operation, provision of program specialties), around clientele service (such as teens, senior citizens), and/or around geographic locations (districts within a city or wards in a hospital, for instance). The entry-level worker is likely to be involved with such functions as publicizing a special event, arranging facilities for specific programs, recruiting volunteer staff, and so on.

The assignment of resources to subunits of the total task typically involves the scheduling of staff and the allocating of other supporting resources such as budgets and physical facilities. Entry-level workers most frequently deal with part-time and volunteer staff. The relating of the subunits to each other essentially involves the establishment of channels of communication and lines of responsibility and authority of staff. The intent is to provide for a coordinated and efficient effort in achieving an overall task.

If other staff are not involved, the basic task of organizing is one in which the worker assigns his or her own time and energies to the subunits. This requires the ability to set realistic expectations and to establish priorities, if time is limited.

The worker should be able to organize available resources so that they are used efficiently and optimally in the pursuit of agency goals. He or she should be able to organize personal energies so that required tasks are accomplished, according to plan, without undue pressure, and with appropriate regard for quality.

6. *The entry-level worker should be able to evaluate both programs (or operations) and staff.* The process of evaluation is basic to planning, which is a necessary prerequisite to management of resources and implementation of programs. Evaluative information is needed in order to determine whether or not objectives have been met.

The two primary aspects are the evaluation of programs or operations and the evaluation of staff. In both cases the process involves the definition of objectives or performance standards, and then the measurement of the degree to which the objectives have been achieved or the standards met. A variety of measurement devices might be used. The worker should be able to judge when evaluation is needed, to select and employ appropriate techniques, and to interpret the results so that operations and/or staff performances are improved.

7. *The entry-level worker should be able to manage resources, including both budgetary resources and others such as personnel, facilities, and supplies.* Agency and community* resources enable a worker to accomplish objectives and provide services for the clientele he or she serves. If service is to be adequate, the resources must be managed effectively.

This process involves the identification of existing and potential resources. It requires that the worker know what monies are available, what physical facilities can be utilized, and what sources of personnel can be tapped. It also requires that the worker possesses some awareness of potential resources that lie outside of the regular agency jurisdiction.

Management, then, involves the effective utilization of available resources, in the planning, organization, and implementation of programs and ser-

---

Community is used here, and afterward in this section, to mean the potential service population or area with which the worker's agency is identified. For a therapist, it might be the hospital; for a youth agency worker it could be several communities.

vices. Scheduling contributes to appropriate deployment of facilities and staff; budgeting and accounting procedures assume optimum use of financial resources. Supervisory activities, including training, are employed to help staff make best use of resources. If the worker is responsible for other staff, paid or volunteer, the definition of job descriptions and performance standards and the communication of these to staff are essential aspects of resources management.

The worker should be able to identify and utilize resources so that agency objectives are accomplished without either an overextension of monies, personnel, and facilities or the accumulation of surpluses.

8. *The entry-level worker should be able to work with groups.* The worker typically relates to numerous groups, which fall into one or more of the following categories: participant groups, groups composed of staff members, and various citizen groups (service clubs, advisory groups, and so on). Some groups may be primarily task-oriented (staff groups, advisory commissions, etc.); others will give greater emphasis and attention to processes and interactions among group members (social clubs, certain types of classes).

In these different groups, the worker may play many roles: leader, member, resource person, observer. Thus, a variety of other processes may be involved, including communicating, teaching, and leading. To be effective, the worker should be aware of the goals of the group, the resources available, and the time required to accomplish these goals. The worker should be aware of basic aspects of group process and of the potential influence of the group on the behavior of individuals. In most situations, the worker should be able to help the group to achieve its goals and enhance the enjoyment of the members in being a part of the group.

9. *The entry-level worker should be able to implement programs or services.* Programs and services are the basic reasons for the existence of recreation and park agencies. From the agency standpoint, the justifications for personnel are in terms of their abilities to implement programs and services. Program implementation follows planning; it, in turn, is followed by evaluation. It requires both organization and the management of resources. It may involve teaching or leading.

At a more specific level, program implementation requires that appropriate facilities and supplies be available, that personnel (if needed) be assigned, and that time constraints be observed (the program starts at a predetermined time, runs for a given period). The worker should be able to implement programs (or services) so that participants have the opportunity to engage in activities they enjoy and that are compatible with agency objectives.

10. *The entry-level worker should be able to solve problems.* In some ways, all that goes on in an agency could be called problem solving. In a more restricted sense, problem solving is a technique that is employed when the routine operations of an agency cannot be carried out normally or when some desired state cannot be achieved by regular procedures. (Of course, problem solving itself can be conceived of as a regular or routine procedure.)

Problem solving involves the subprocesses of identifying the desired state, the factors that prevent it from being achieved, and the alternative courses of action. The probable consequences of the various alternatives then are defined and a decision is made with respect to the most feasible or realistic course of action.

The worker should be able to utilize the problem solving process to take appropriate action when regular procedures are ineffective.

11. *The entry-level worker should be able to perceive relevant information about the population and community he or she serves that has potential for influencing service.* The worker must be familiar with the characteristics of the people for whom he or she provides recreation and park opportunities. This requires the ability to discover and use demographic information available through such sources as planning departments and census reports. In addition, it may necessitate the development, administration, and interpretation of surveys designed to obtain data about service populations.

The worker also must understand those governmental, community, and institutional decision making processes and influence sources which are potentially related to his or her own responsibilities. A basic knowledge of bureaucratic functioning and a sensitivity to pressure groups contribute to the worker's effectiveness.

The worker should be able to obtain and interpret information about the community or service population which will enable effective planning, implementation, and evaluation of recreation and park services; and he or she should be able to work within existing decision-making structures and with an awareness of sources of influence in the community.

12. *The entry-level worker should be able to develop appropriate relationships with other professional and community groups.* In most situations, the agency in which the worker is employed is one of several in the community that provide recreation and park services. A knowledge of these other agencies, and rapport with the personnel employed in them, enhances the chance that the overall resources of the community will be used most effectively. Such knowledge and rapport permit the worker to refer potential participants to other appropriate agencies when his or her agency does not offer the desired services. It also permits personnel from the various agencies to share resources, when feasible, and to engage in such mutually beneficial activities as problem-solving sessions, joint training efforts, and so on. Further, these contacts minimize interagency conflicts over such matters as jurisdictional questions and resource allocation (as in United Funding). And they contribute to easier communication and conflict resolution when problems do arise.

Recreation and park personnel also have opportunities to relate to staff members from other social service agencies (health, welfare, education, law enforcement, probation). Again, knowledge of these agencies and open relationships with their staffs facilitate the recreation and park worker's efforts to serve his or her population most effectively. The worker may have opportunities to refer participants to other helping agencies; the recreation and park agency may be able to cooperate with various other efforts to solve community problems or enhance the quality of community life.

The worker should possess sufficient knowledge of other community agencies to be able to cooperate with them in the solution of common problems and, as appropriate, in the implementation of joint projects designed to enhance community life.

13. *The entry-level worker should be able to perceive and work within the framework of legal considerations.* The services offered by any recreation and park agency are based on some type of legal authority. This authority typically spells out what the agency may do, what kinds of services it may provide, what financial procedures it must follow, and other procedural matters.

In addition, the operating practices of most agencies are subject to the regulatory control of various specific pieces of either state or local legislation. For example, state codes usually describe the conditions under which residential treatment centers and camps must operate; state laws and local laws regulate swimming pool operations, and so on.

Further, every agency employee bears a legal responsibility to conduct himself or herself so as to provide service in a reasonable, prudent fashion with due regard for avoiding negligent acts.

The worker should be able to conduct his or her professional activities so that they are consistent with the overall purposes of the agency as defined in its basic legal authority, so that they conform both to state and local regulations, and so that they are immune from successful charges of negligent practice.

14. *The entry-level worker should be able to verbalize a philosophy on which his or her professional practices can be based.* Workers in the field of recreation and parks make some assumptions about (1) the nature of the society (public) they are attempting to serve, and (2) the responsibilities of the generic institution within which they operate (government, voluntary agencies, or the commercial sector). Frequently, these assumptions are not clearly articulated; quite possibly they include unintegrated or inconsistent elements. Nonetheless, the assumptions in their totality are the elements of a professional philosophy. Unless the workers operate in a completely random, opportunistic fashion, the assumptions condition and influence practices.

An internally consistent statement of assumptions and beliefs, which can be verbalized, enables the worker to be more rational in his or her approach to providing service. If it can be verbalized, it can be applied more consistently and with more awareness; and it can be tested against experience and modified or reinforced.

A specific dimension of a professional philosophy is the set of beliefs related to the professional organization—its role, its contribution to effective service and to professional growth, and so on.

The worker should be able to verbalize a set of professional assumptions and beliefs that are internally consistent and logically defensible; he or she should be able to perceive the relationship between this philosophy and professional practices.

15. *The entry-level worker should be able to understand and use the "special language," if any, that is associated with his or her professional responsibilities.* The worker has a responsibility to be able to communicate with people, both within and outside of his or her special area of interest. Contacts with individuals outside of the specialty are based on sound communicative practices, where jargon normally should be avoided. However, effective communication within a specialty often requires the use of more esoteric terminology. The recreation therapist communicates within an institutional environment and with members of other medically or therapeutically oriented fields. The worker with responsibilities in the area of park maintenance deals routinely with operations, chemicals, and equipment that can be understood most fully in technical terms.

Technical or esoteric terminology should not be used for the sake of exclusiveness or the aggrandizement of either the field or personnel working in it. But, in those cases where full meaning can be obtained by its use, it is justified. In such cases, the worker should be able to understand and use the special language so that he or she communicates in the most effective manner.

16. *The entry-level worker should be able to perform a variety of general technical skills related to office practices, paperwork management, and media utilization.* Whatever the worker's specific position, he or she probably will engage in the routines of making and receiving phone calls, keeping office appointments, answering correspondence and maintaining files (or seeing that they are maintained). In many situations, the worker will operate duplicating equipment such as Xerox machines, mimeograph and ditto machines. In some positions, the operations of movie and slide projectors and tape recorders will be required. The amount of involvement the worker has with these activities will vary greatly, depending upon the size of the agency and the particular position held by the individual. In any case, the worker should be able to manage paperwork so that files and records are systematically stored and readily available. He or she should be able to handle telephone contacts and office receptions so that the purposes of the contacts are carried out to the optimum satisfaction of the parties involved. When audio-visual and reproductive equipment are used, the worker should have the skills and knowledges necessary to achieve the desired results with due regard for appropriate operations of the specific piece of equipment.

Two additional activities were identified by the study team and were felt to be commonly used by recreation and park personnel. However, they were not included in the basic list of sixteen because each of them involved so many of the other processes. The two were (1) *supervision* and (2) *developing desirable public relations*. The process of supervision, as used in the study, was concerned with the relationships between supervisor and staff members rather than among a staff member and participants. Supervision was viewed as an enabling process that helped staff members do their jobs more effectively both in terms of agency goals and personal satisfaction.[14] Supervision was a combination of almost every one of the other processes, especially communicating, leading, teaching, planning, managing resources, organizing, working with groups, and evaluating. The second process, developing desirable public relations, also was seen as drawing upon many of the other processes, particularly communicating and those skills related to planning and providing services for the public (such as organizing, conducting programs, managing resources and working with groups).

A process that was not addressed directly in the project is *helping*. Helping is based on the interpersonal relationships that develop between helpers and the persons being helped. The general purpose of helping is to enable people to grow in their abilities to solve, or cope with, the problems they confront. In a sense, leading, teaching, and supervising are helping processes. To that extent, the process of helping is an element in these other activities of recreation and park personnel. However, there are times when a staff member "helps" a user of agency services or another staff member in ways not directly associated with leading, teaching, and supervision. In these cases, the staff member should be able to interact with the other person in ways that encourage personal growth.

All of the processes described in this section are related to working with people. Some are more directly related, especially leading, working with groups, and teaching. Later chapters will focus on these topics, and on the development of effective interpersonal relationships.

SITUATIONAL FACTORS

The situations in which recreation and park personnel work vary greatly. The California project identified several categories of situational differences.[15]

One type of difference is the nature of the *physical environment* within which personnel carry out their responsibilities. Some workers are employed in large urban areas; others work in small towns; still others operate largely in wilderness settings. One ranger might be assigned to a seashore and another to a desert park. One therapist might function on a ward in a large military hospital; another might cover several small convalescent homes. For any one worker, the physical environment might be familiar or unfamiliar. The available resources might be extensive or they might be limited.

Another category of differences between situations is the nature of the *psychological environment*. Included in this category are such things as the demands made upon workers, the presence of either clearly defined expectations or ones that are vague and ambiguous, and the restrictions or freedom that are perceived by workers. The degree of stability in work conditions and the rapidity of change also are factors.

Situations differ also in the *relationships personnel have with other people*. In some instances, workers relate to others in authority roles—as administrators or supervisors. Some people function consistently as subordinates carrying out directions given by others. Many recreation and park workers operate in both roles. Also, workers often relate to others as peers, taking neither a superior nor subordinate role. Work situations sometimes are structured so that individuals function nearly independently; in others, people may depend upon one another for the successful completion of responsibilities. Workers also may relate to others either cooperatively or competitively. In some situations there is conflict. The situation depends on the relationships among the individuals, which influence the psychological environment.

Another difference in situations has to do with the *numerical composition of relationships*. A recreation therapist might work with one patient, or with ten patients. The park naturalist sometimes takes small groups on nature hikes; sometimes he or she speaks to large audiences at campfire programs. The ceramics instructor might have five students in one class and twenty-five in another.

Relationships also differ in terms of *function*. For example, a recreation supervisor might relate to each of the following groups in the course of carrying out responsibilities: other staff, participants in programs, general community groups (such as service clubs and Parent-Teacher Associations), and other allied community or professional groups (such as public school personnel, health department staff, and committees of the state professional organization).

These groups, and the individuals who comprise them, differ in terms of *socio-psychological composition*. Recreation and park personnel typically work with people of different ages, different income levels, different racial or ethnic identities, and different educational backgrounds. Some groups are fairly homogeneous with respect to these various factors; others are relatively heterogeneous.

The *nature of work arrangements and expectations* is another category of differences. In some situations, workers function as individuals; in others they operate as a team. Here one is a leader; elsewhere he is a follower.

These categories of differences are not mutually exclusive. For example, the work arrangements and expectations often directly influence the nature of relationships and the psychological environment. However, the categories do suggest some of the major differences among work situations. Various types of differences usually will be involved. For example: A state park ranger is employed at a coastal park, near a large, urban area (the physical environment). The park has the supplies and equipment needed to operate the facility. The ranger has been assigned to the park for four years, so he is very familiar with the setting. The park superintendent supervises all personnel. The superintendent's style is democratic; rangers are involved in making decisions, and they have some considerable autonomy in carrying out their responsibilities (the psychological environment).

The park is used heavily, and, as a result, the ranger's work load is heavy, especially on weekends. Demands change frequently, according to the composition of the user groups. The ranger interacts with users of the facility as well as with other staff (the nature of relationships with other people). Relationships with users tend to be pleasant and informal. However, there are times when disruptive user behavior results in conflict situations; at times control measures must be used. Contact with users ranges from the one-to-one or small-group interactions at the entrance station up to groups of over 100 at evening campfire programs (the numerical composition of relationships). The ranger also participates in periodic staff meetings, and cooperates with a local citizens' committee to develop a tidepool nature trail (functional composition of relationships). Most users of the park are from the nearby urban area; they are all ages and overall the user population is fairly heterogeneous (socio-psychological composition).

As indicated earlier, the ranger works under the supervision of the superintendent. The work usually involves direct responsibility for various functions, but at times the ranger serves in a support capacity (the nature of work arrangements and expectations).

While it is difficult to make any general statements about the ways in which these situational differences influence a worker's specific use of basic or core processes, it is important to recognize that different situations call for different responses. The selection of specific methods is a matter of knowing something about the process to be used, (ideally having had some experience with it), knowing something about yourself, and being as sensitive as possible to the demands of the situation.

PERSONAL CHARACTERISTICS

The third element in an overall concept of competency is the factor of personal characteristics. This factor includes such considerations as the personal traits of individuals who choose careers in the leisure services, and the influence of these characteristics on effectiveness in the field.

General Qualities.   Much has been written about the relationships of personal characteristics to effectiveness in the field of recreation and parks. A considerable amount of this literature has consisted of descriptions of the qualities of effective leaders.[16] Frequently mentioned qualities include enthusiasm, sensitivity to the needs of others, good judgement, integrity, flexibility, and a sense of humor.

Shivers, using the term *leader* in the generic sense or as a synonym for personnel, contended that there are two essential characteristics.

> Of the many characteristics associated with leaders, only two are inherent and absolutely essential for a potential leader. First, the individual must have the desire to become a leader. . . . The second inherent quality the potential leader must possess is intelligence.[17]

Shivers suggested that the abilities to verbalize and to empathize are both aspects of intelligence. The latter aspect he identified as "social intelligence." He also discussed "moral intelligence," or the ability to know what is morally right, and "communicative intelligence."[18]

In addition to these two basic characteristics, Shivers identified several character traits, including such qualities as loyalty, integrity, discretion, reliability, responsibility, tolerance, sociability, perseverance, and initiative.

Ross and Hendry, and Stogdill completed extensive reviews of research on leadership and presented summaries of related personal qualities. These are discussed in Chapter 5. Most of the research that has been done has not focused directly on effectiveness in recreation and parks. However, some studies are available. In his research on leadership personnel standards in public recreation, Anderson included a section on essential qualities. He presented ten qualities: consideration, courage (willingness to defend personal beliefs), mental and physical health, intelligence, leadership (initiative, enthusiasm, ability to influence others), professional knowledge, efficiency, sociability, judgment, and dependability.[19]

Kammeyer's research dealt specifically with personal characteristics associated with successful leadership in recreation. She identified several successful behavior patterns.

> On the basis of frequency of expression, the following aptitudinal patterns are important for successful recreation leadership: displaying security and lack of fear in the position of leadership; maintaining a tolerant, flexible atmosphere toward the participants; demonstrating a lack of fear of discipline problems; accepting the respect of participants; and exhibiting sensitivity and empathy for the problems of participants.[20]

Characteristics as Measured by Personality Inventories. Kammeyer's investigation involved a rating scale. Other research has been based on some type of personality inventory. Kirkish studied personality traits associated with the selection of recreation as a college major, using the California Personality Inventory (CPI) and a rating scale.[21] She found that recreation majors scored higher, on the self-acceptance scale, than typical college students. In addition, male students in the sample scored higher than females on the scales for sociability and dominance, but lower on responsibility and achievement via independence. Scores on some CPI scales varied according to student probability for success in the field, as perceived by faculty members. Recreation majors who were rated high scored higher on the following scales: achievement via independence, intellectual efficiency, psychological mindedness (such traits as spontaneity, resourcefulness, and social ascendancy), flexibility, capacity for status (ambitious, forceful, self-seeking), and sense of well-being.[22]

McCormick studied the differences in responses to the CPI of part-time recreation leaders who were rated as "superior" as compared to those rated "mediocre."[23] The leaders were rated by trained evaluators. The CPI scores for females and males were analyzed separately. McCormick observed that superior male leaders scored higher than their mediocre colleagues on the CPI scales for dominance, achievement via conformance, intellectual efficiency, psychological-mindedness, and sense of well-being.

Superior female leaders scored higher than those who were rated mediocre on the scales for capacity for status and tolerance, but lower on the scale for communality (higher scores indicate dependability, tact, patience, honesty, conscientiousness).[24] However, McCormick cautioned that the ability of the CPI to yield data by which high-potential leaders can be selected is not clearly proven. He noted that psychologists differ in their opinions about the usefulness of the CPI for making personality assessments.[25]

Two different personality inventories were used in the California competency assessment project discussed earlier in the chapter. The Omnibus Personality Inventory (OPI) and the Personal Orientation Inventory (POI) were administered to groups of recreation majors, faculty members, and field personnel in an attempt to identify characteristic traits.

The OPI is intended to measure personal characteristics that are related to intellectual orientation and personal adjustment. Intellectual interests, theoretical concerns (liberal versus conservative attitudes), and socio-emotional characteristics are the three major areas of the OPI.[26] The results of the testing, using the OPI, indicated that, while there were some differences between groups (recreation majors, faculty, and field personnel), all groups generally scored within the average range when compared with the norm groups.[27] Scores for the field personnel group were somewhat higher than average. Individuals in this group were included in the overall study because they were perceived as effective practitioners. The study team concluded that their scores, as a group, suggested a general personality type who, as a person

> . . . is socially and emotionally adjusted, who has a concern for the welfare of others and the problems of society, who is independent in thinking, who has a tolerance for new experience, who likes to explore ideas, and who values creativity.[28]

The POI is intended to assess personal variables that are related to Maslow's concept of self-actualization. The inventory measures two major personality aspects: *time competence,* the degree to which a person lives in the present, reflectively uses the past, and relates future expectations to present goals; and *inner support,* the degree to which a person is autonomous and self-directing, as opposed to being influenced primarily by others.[29] There were no statistically significant differences between group scores on the POI. Overall, scores for all groups tended to be fairly close to the norm; that is, in general, the groups tended to be no different in responses to this instrument than the typical adult population.[30] As in the OPI, field personnel scored above the average on all but one of the twelve scales, suggesting that this group tended to be relatively higher than the norm group in self-actualization as defined by the POI.[31]

The different tests, used in the studies that have been described, tend to measure different traits. Different study populations were used. And, of course, the limitations of the various studies, in terms of sample size and representativeness, make it inappropriate to generalize broadly. However, the data suggest that recreation groups tend not to be much different from the general population, in terms of the inventories used. There are some differences between subgroups. Again, the studies suggest that those individuals who are perceived to be more effective in field practice (or if students, to have more potential for effectiveness) tend to score higher on certain scales, on the different inventories.

Qualities as Perceived by Practioners and Educators.   The California competency assessment project also included interviews of selected field personnel. In the interviews, recreation and park professionals were asked to talk about those personal characteristics of entry-level workers that made them most effective. Responses to the same question—Which personal characteristics are related to effective performance?—were solicited from recreation and park educators using a written survey form. The study team analyzed the perceptions of both groups and found considerable agreement between them. The study team identified eight "clusters" of personal characteristics. These are shown in the approximate order in which field personnel felt the various specific traits, which comprise each cluster, contributed to effectiveness (first listed contributing most).

1. A work enthusiasm cluster (illustrations of terminology used by interviewees: willing, energetic, aggressive).
2. Work efficiency cluster (confident, emotionally stable, independent, mature, shows common-sense).
3. Sensitivity cluster (empathetic, accepting, understanding, perceptive, unselfish, patient).
4. Flexibility cluster (flexible, cooperative. Flexibility as a single notation was mentioned by more respondents than any other personal characteristic).
5. Likeableness cluster (friendly, optimistic, possesses sense of humor, likeable).
6. Health-appearance cluster (appearance, health, and endurance).
7. Intelligence cluster (knowledge of field, alertness, intelligence).
8. Creativeness cluster (imaginative, creative, innovative).[32]

Beliefs and Perceptions as Personal Characteristics.   Combs and several associates have identified the personal characteristics of helpers who are perceived by those with whom they work as being effective.[33] While Combs's work involved counselors, teachers, pastors, and nurses, the information he generated seems to apply to a discussion of competency in recreation and parks. He observed that the "perceptual organization," or *belief system,* of a worker is a key factor in his or her effectiveness.[34] Combs noted that effective helpers tend to be oriented to people rather than to things, that they hold a generally positive view of people, and that they believe that people have the capacities to grow and help themselves. Effective helpers seem to be empathetic; they tend to have a belief in the importance of the internal states, feelings, and perceptions of the people with whom they work. They see themselves as "one with mankind, as sharing a common fate."[35] They appear to see their own responsibilities as ones designed to free people rather than to control them.

The above beliefs of effective helpers concern views they have about those with whom they work. A second set of major personal characteristics are the beliefs helpers have about themselves. Effectiveness seems related to a clear concept of self and positive self-regard.

> The tasks of professional workers can be accomplished only by entering into some kind of relationship with others. Since one cannot have a relationship with a nonentity, effective helpers must have a clear sense of self.[36]

Helpers must feel reasonably adequate and feel that their own needs are fairly well met before they can respond to the needs of others.

> With a firm base of operations to work from (a positive self-concept) such persons can be much more daring and creative in respect to their approach to the world and more able to give of themselves to others as well.[37]

Self-Awareness. It seems clear that self-awareness is an important personal characteristic. Brammer stated it this way, in discussing effective helpers:

> There is universal agreement among practitioners and writers that helpers need a broad awareness of their own value positions.[38]

Self-awareness seems equally valuable for recreation and park personnel. The more we know about ourselves, the more effective we should be in working with or relating to others. If we know what our own goals are, we can work directly with others to achieve them. If we know our own biases and prejudices, we can attempt to overcome them or neutralize them in our relations with others. If we know our strengths, we can capitalize on them; if we know our weaknesses, we can try to improve and grow.

We learn about ourselves, in part, by reflecting on our experiences—by introspection. We also learn about ourselves through interacting with others.

Luft presented a useful symbolization of self-awareness, based on interaction, called the "Johari Window."[39] This concept is shown in Figure 2-2. Luft described the Johari Window this way:

> The four quadrants represent the total person in relation to other persons. The basis for division into quadrants is awareness of behavior, feelings, and motivation. Sometimes awareness is shared, sometimes not. An act, a feeling, or a motive is assigned to a particular quadrant based on who knows about it. As awareness changes, the quadrant to which the psychological state is assigned changes.[40]

The model is based on the assumption that we often have limited awareness of the sources of our behavior, and of how our behavior affects others. Further, it assumes that we do not reveal to others all of those things we know about ourselves.

It is in Cell 1, the open cell, that we interact most freely with others. We can expand the size of this cell through the processes of "self-disclosing" and being "receptive to feedback."[41] *Self-disclosure* is letting other people know how you are reacting to, or feeling about, what is going on in the

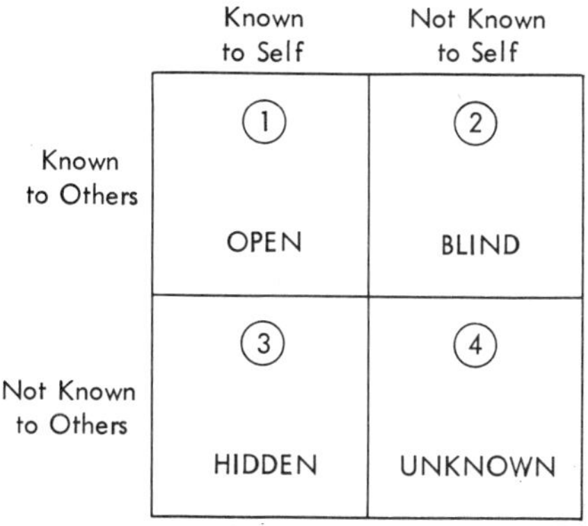

Known to Self Not Known to Self

Known to Others

① OPEN ② BLIND

Not Known to Others

③ HIDDEN ④ UNKNOWN

Figure 2-2 The Johari Window. From *Of Human Interaction* by Joseph Luft by permission of Mayfield Pub. Co. Copyright © 1969 by National Press, p. 13.

present, and giving them any information about the past that helps them to understand your present feelings and reactions.[42] *Feedback* is giving other people information about how you are reacting to their behavior.[43] It is a form of self-disclosure. *Receptivity to feedback* is the extent to which you are willing to hear and accept (or consider) the reactions of others to your behavior. As a person self-discloses appropriately, the open cell of the Johari Window expands, and the hidden cell contracts. As feedback is received, and accepted or considered, the hidden cell contracts and the open cell expands.

These processes of feedback and self-disclosure will be discussed further in Chapter 4; for now, just remember that self-awareness is a personal characteristic which seems to be related to professional effectiveness. Self-awareness allows us to adapt more appropriately to the varying situations we encounter. It permits us to modify our uses of the various processes to take advantage of our own strengths and minimize our biases. These are the key factors in terms of personal characteristics.

A Composite Picture. It is difficult to draw a precise description of those personal characteristics that are associated with effectiveness. However, the image that emerges is that recreation personnel tend to be not greatly different, in the aggregate, from the general population. Effective workers tend to be aware of their own values and attitudes, and they are somewhat more self-actualizing and self-accepting. They are motivated to work with people; they tend to hold positive beliefs about those with whom they interact; and they tend to be empathetic and accepting of others. In general, they are enthusiastic about their work.

Remember, though, that personal characteristics do not exist in isolation. They function as interacting influences with the demands of each particular situation.

PROFESSIONAL RESPONSIBILITIES

Competence also means professionalism. Professionalism can have three different meanings. First, a professional worker can be thought of as any person who is employed (in contrast to a volunteer who receives no pay for services). A second view is that a professional worker is one with a sense of commitment and who performs at a high level. A third perspective is that a professional worker carries out certain responsibilities to provide quality service. This last view has implications for a concept of competency in the field of recreation and parks.

Professional fields have several characteristics in common.[44] Typically, they serve relatively complex social needs. There is public recognition of the value of the field. Professionals do not use routine methods; rather they adjust their methods to the changing needs they encounter. Professions validate these methods through research, and they require candidates for the field to undergo periods of educational preparation. They control entry into the field through systems of licensing or registration. They establish codes of ethics that provide guidelines for the relationships between workers and the people they serve. Several of these characteristics result from the field carrying out certain responsibilities that require collective action. Therefore, professions usually develop organizations or associations of workers. The basic premise is that the meeting of professional responsibilities leads to more effective service.

Kinney and Thomas and Smith developed a concept of professional maturity as the degree to which a field carries out professional responsibilities.[45] In this sense, a field may be relatively mature in one area—for example, educational preparation—but relatively immature in another area. The responsibilities that are met by the field suggest certain behaviors on the part of personnel who make up the field.

Niepoth developed a list of eighty-two behaviors or activities based upon the professional responsibilities defined by Smith.[46] The list was intended to identify the professional role of recreation administrators. The assumption was that the activities, which constituted the professional role, would show an administrator's acceptance of professional responsibilities.

The professional responsibilities as defined in Niepoth's study were as follows:

1. Working with the public in the definition of the aims and objectives of recreation.
2. Defining and enforcing standards of ethical conduct.
3. Conducting and/or encouraging and supporting research related to recreation theory and method, including testing the effectiveness of operational procedures and techniques and disseminating the resulting body of knowledge.
4. Working with colleges and universities in the development of programs of professional preparation, including the establishment of standards for selecting candidates, and the development and administration of accreditation procedures.
5. Developing and administering or encouraging in-service training efforts designed to increase and maintain the competency of those individuals who are working in recreation agencies.
6. Recruiting new members into the field of recreation and fostering the development of pride in the profession and dedication among those already in the field.

7. Developing standards for identifying the competent and qualified professional worker, and administering, or cooperating with an agency charged with the responsibility for administering, a program of certification or licensure based on such standards.

8. Encouraging the establishment and maintenance of adequate salaries and working conditions for recreation personnel, including protection from unwarranted attack upon character or ability.

9. Maintaining a strong, financially sound, well supported professional organization to facilitate the fulfillment of the preceding responsibilities.[47]

The list of eighty-two behaviors comprising the administrator's professional role was developed from the above nine responsibilities. The behaviors related to research (Responsibility 3) are illustrative:

1. Taking time to read and attempting to utilize the findings of research that have implications for recreation.

2. Keeping staff members informed of research findings related to their functions and encouraging them to attempt to utilize these findings.

3. Engaging in and/or supporting and cooperating with formally organized research projects that relate to recreation.

4. Discussing, with recreators in other departments, findings of pertinent research and/or studies that I have done or that have come to my attention.

5. Evaluating operating procedures used in my department in an effort to determine whether or not they effectively contribute to the objectives of the department.

6. Analyzing (or delegating authority for analyzing) successful and unsuccessful procedures in an effort to isolate and document factors that contribute to success or failure.

7. Consulting with recreators in other departments when seeking solutions to problems in my own department.

8. Requiring staff members to evaluate their activities and to attempt to isolate and document factors that contribute to the effectiveness or lack of effectiveness of the operational procedures they use.

9. Studying the characteristics, needs, and desires of people and basing operational procedures on the accumulated knowledge.[48]

The approaches to professionalism described in this section suggest that the concept of competency should include professional behaviors. It seems clear that we will be able to serve people better if we engage in these behaviors. For example, using relevant research findings, when available, as bases for our methods should allow us to be more confident that what we are doing is effective. Taking advantage of appropriate educational opportunities (such as enrolling for coursework in colleges and universities, attending workshops and conferences, and reading related journals) should help us improve and maintain our effectiveness. Becoming active members of professional organizations (such as the National Recreation and Park Association or a state professional society) should lead to many opportunities to improve our abilities to work with people, as well as to contribute to the continued development of the field.

SUMMARY

The field of recreation and parks is complex, with many different types of agencies. Personnel in these agencies carry out diverse responsibilities. However, it is possible to identify professional activities that are common to most situations. The activities can be thought of as *core* processes. How these processes are used is influenced by the demands of the particular situations within which recreation and park personnel work, and by the personal variables of each worker. Competency can be thought of as the ability to perform required processes effectively, compatible with personal characteristics and in work situations.

Working in a professional manner is also an aspect of competency. Assuming the responsibilities of professionalism will allow us to provide more effective leisure services for the people we serve in recreation and park agencies.

REVIEW QUESTIONS

2-1 What does the term *competency* mean?

2-2 What are *core processes*?

2-3 How is the use of core processes influenced by differences in the situations where they are used, and differences in the personal characteristics of the person using them?

2-4 Overall, do leisure service workers seem to have personal characteristics that are different from the general population?

2-5 How does self-awareness help you to work more effectively with people?

2-6 What are some of the things leisure service personnel do that evidence professional maturity? In what ways do these help workers provide better service for people?

TO DO

2-A Look back over the list of core processes discussed in this chapter. Using a key word or two for each (such as written communication, leadership, problem solving) list the sixteen processes on the left-hand side of a piece of paper. Now, work with the list in the following way:

1. Mark an "X" behind the five processes that you feel are your strongest areas at the present time. Consider any past experience you have had working with people (in any setting, paid or volunteer). Consider also things you have learned in classes, by reading, or in any other way. Which five of the processes can you do best? In the space to the right of each of these, briefly indicate why you feel the process is one of your strongest ones.
2. Mark an "O" behind the five processes in which you are least strong.
3. Underline the five processes that seem like they would be the most important ones in the job you described in item 1-A (Chapter 1).

These might or might not be ones you have marked with an "X" or "O." "Important" means the processes that would contribute most directly and most frequently to your effectiveness as a worker in that job.

4. For each underlined process that has an "O" marked behind it, write a brief description (in the space to the right) of what you could do in the next six months to improve your ability. Be as specific as possible.

END NOTES

1. For discussions of competency development in the field of teacher education, see W. Robert Houston and Robert B. Howsam, eds., *Competency-Based Teacher Education: Progress, Problems, and Prospects* (Chicago: Science Research Associates, Inc., 1972) and Dan Anderson and others, *Competency Based Teacher Education* (Berkeley, Calif.: McCutchan Publishing Corp., 1973).

2. Edith Ball and Robert E. Cipriano, *Leisure Services Preparation: A Competency Based Approach* (Englewood Cliffs, N.J.: Prentice-Hall, Inc., 1978).

3. Ball and Cipriano, *Leisure Services Preparation*, pp. 51–52.

4. Lawrence R. Klar, Jr., "Competencies Needed in Commercial Recreation: An Exploratory Field Study" (Paper presented at the National Congress for Recreation and Parks, Phoenix, Arizona, October 1980).

5. Klar, "Competencies Needed in Commercial Recreation," p. 10.

6. Robert R. Langman and Linn R. Rockwood, "Be Prepared . . . For a Career in Commercial Recreation," *Parks & Recreation* 10, no. 7 (July 1975): 30–31.

7. Jerry Jordan, Project Director, "Process Analysis Approach to the Development of a Competency-Based Curriculum in Therapeutic Recreation at the Masters Degree Level," (Philadelphia: Temple University, Department of Recreation and Leisure Studies, 1978), p. 9.

8. "A Process Analysis Approach to the Development of a Competency-Based Curriculum in Therapeutic Recreation at the Masters Degree Level," pp. 13–15.

9. Carol Ann Peterson, Ellyn Newmyer and Peg Connolly, "Final Report: Identification and Validation of Entry Level Therapeutic Recreation Competencies." Submitted to the National Therapeutic Recreation Society Board of Directors (September 30, 1978), pp. 2–14.

10. David R. Austin and Lou G. Powell, "What You Need to Know to Serve Special Populations." *Parks & Recreation,* 16, no. 7 (July, 1981) 40–42.

11. E. Niepoth, Project Director, "Competency Assessment Processes in Recreation Curricula," 1973–74. (Report filed at the Office of the Chancellor, The California State University, Long Beach, California.)

12. "Competency Assessment Processes in Recreation Curricula," p. 17.

13. These processes are adapted from "Competency Assessment Processes," pp. 31–50.

14. This concept of supervision is similar to the one presented by Margaret Williamson in *Supervision: New Patterns and Processes* (New York: Association Press, 1961), pp. 19–20.

15. "Competency Assessment Processes in Recreation Curricula," pp. 61–63.

16. For example, see George D. Butler, *Introduction to Community Recreation*, 4th ed., (New York: McGraw-Hill Book Company, 1967), p. 119; Reynold Edgar Carslon and others, *Recreation and Leisure: The Changing Scene*, 3rd ed., (Belmont, Calif.: Wadsworth Publishing Company, Inc., 1979), pp. 301–4; Richard G. Kraus and

Barbara J. Bates, *Recreation Leadership and Supervision: Guidelines for Professional Development* (Philadelphia: W. B. Saunders Company, 1975), pp. 14–16; Maryhelen Vannier, *Methods and Materials in Recreation Leadership*, rev. ed. (Belmont, Calif.: Wadsworth Publishing Company, Inc., 1966), pp. 18–19.

17. Jay S. Shivers, *Recreational Leadership: Group Dynamics and Interpersonal Behavior* (Princeton, N.J.: Princeton Book Company, Publishers, 1980), p. 166.

18. Shivers, *Recreational Leadership*, pp. 168–71.

19. Jackson M. Anderson, "The Development of Personnel Standards for Leadership Duties in Public Recreation" (Ph.D. diss., New York University, 1948), p. 61.

20. Shirley J. Kammeyer, "The Development of an Aptitude Inventory and Rating Scale for Community Recreation Leaders" (Ph.D. diss., The State University of Iowa, 1959), pp. 82–83.

21. Merton Kirkish, "Some Personality Traits Associated with Choice of Recreation as a Major" (Masters thesis, San José State College, 1964).

22. Kirkish, "Some Personality Traits Associated with Choice of Recreation as a Major," p. 48.

23. Stuart McCormick, "A Comparative Study of Personality Characteristics Associated with Superior and Mediocre Part-Time Recreation Leaders" (Masters thesis, San José State College, 1964).

24. McCormick, "A Comparative Study of Personality Characteristics Associated with Superior and Mediocre Part-Time Recreation Leaders," p. 66–67.

25. Ibid., pp. 26–27.

26. "Competency Assessment Processes in Recreation Curricula," p. 54.

27. Ibid., p. 104.

28. Ibid., p. 61.

29. Ibid., p. 158.

30. Ibid., p. 170.

31. Ibid., p. 54.

32. Ibid., pp. 51–52.

33. Arthur W. Combs and others, *Florida Studies in the Helping Professions* (Gainesville: University of Florida Press, 1969), pp. 21–75; and Arthur W. Combs, Donald L. Avila, and William W. Purkey, *Helping Relationships: Basic Concepts for the Helping Professions*, 2nd ed. (Boston: Allyn and Bacon, Inc., 1978), pp. 5–12.

34. Combs and others, *Florida Studies in the Helping Professions*, p. 71; Combs, Avila, and Purkey, *Helping Relationships*, pp. 9–12.

35. Combs and others, *Florida Studies in the Helping Professions*, p. 71.

36. Combs, Avila, and Purkey, *Helping Relationships*, p. 11.

37. Combs and others, *Florida Studies in the Helping Professions*, p. 74.

38. Lawrence M. Brammer, *The Helping Relationship-Process and Skills* (Englewood Cliffs, N.J.: Prentice-Hall, Inc., 1973), p. 21.

39. Joseph Luft, *Of Human Interaction*, by permission of Mayfield Pub. Co. © 1969 by National Press, p. 13.

40. Luft, *Of Human Interaction*, p. 13.

41. David W. Johnson, *Reaching Out: Interpersonal Effectiveness and Self-Actualization*, 2nd ed. (Englewood Cliffs, N.J.: Prentice-Hall, Inc., 1981), pp. 20–21.

42. Johnson, *Reaching Out*, p. 16.

43. Ibid., p. 22.

44. For discussions of professionalism and the field of recreation and parks, see Richard Kraus, *Recreation and Leisure in Modern Society*, 2nd ed. (Santa Monica, Calif.: Goodyear Publishing Co., Inc., 1978), pp. 280–301; and H. Douglas Sessoms, Harold D. Meyer, and Charles K. Brightbill, *Leisure Service: The Organized Recreation and Park System*, 5th ed. (Englewood Cliffs, N.J.: Prentice-Hall, Inc., 1975), pp. 311–29. Professional characteristics are defined in Earl Kauffman, Jr., "A Critical Evaluation of Components Basic to Certain Selected Professions with a View to Establishing Recreation as a Profession" (Ed.D diss., New York University, 1949); and E. W. Niepoth, "The Professional Maturity of Recreation Administrators" (Ed.D. diss., Stanford University, 1962).

45. Lucien B. Kinney and Lawrence G. Thomas, *Toward Professional Maturity in Education* (San Francisco: California Teachers Association, 1955); Richard A. Smith, "Maturity of Education as a Profession," (Ed.D. diss., Stanford University, 1956).

46. Niepoth, "The Professional Maturity of Recreation Administrators," pp. 107–21.

47. Ibid., pp. 107–21.

48. Ibid., pp. 110–11.

chapter 3

Recreation Behavior

PREVIEW

Chapter 2 dealt, in part, with the behaviors of recreation and park personnel. In this chapter, we will examine some ideas about participant and staff behavior. The logic for doing this is that when personnel work with other people, either participants or staff, they are involved with others' behaviors. They provide opportunities directly or indirectly for people to engage in recreation activity. As they work with other personnel in the provision of these opportunities, they encounter the behaviors of these staff members. It follows, then, that recreation and park workers should know something about human behavior. Chapter 3 examines some dimensions of behavior that have particular relevance for our field.

First, two major views of behavior are presented. Then, some of the general characteristics of recreation behavior are discussed. Following this is an overview of some theoretical explanations of recreation and play and a brief discussion of different approaches to the study of these phenomena.

A description of a general model of recreation behavior is a major part of the chapter. The model serves as a framework for understanding different aspects of recreation behavior, and it provides a useful background for discussions of such processes as leading and teaching, which are the subjects of later chapters.

Several major generalizations about recreation behavior are discussed after the presentation of the model. These give attention to such things as motivation, perception, individual variations (related to age, occupation, personality and other factors), and environmental influences.

Since recreation and park personnel try to serve as many people as possible, consistent with agency purposes and available resources, some information is pro-

vided on why people use (or do not use) leisure services. A general concept of use and nonuse factors is presented.

The last section of the chapter provides a brief explanation of how the general model of behavior applies to staff behavior.

Somewhere in the Sierra Nevada, two men move slowly upward toward the notch in the ridge through which the trail passes. At 11,000 feet, their progress is slow and their breathing labored. The packs are heavy, even though each item of food, clothing and equipment was considered and weighed carefully. At the crest, they slip out of their loads and lean back against the rock wall which rises above the trail. The wind cools and dries their sweat-drenched shirts as they gaze out over the vastness to the south.

Two hundred miles away, a woman bends over a ceramic wheel and digs her thumbs into the mound of clay which spins on the wheel. Carefully, she brings up the cylindrical wall, the clay responding to her search for evenness. Several revolutions of the piece against the sponges, and she straightens to exchange a few words with her neighbor on an adjacent wheel.

At home, the neighbor's ten-year-old shakes the dice and counts out five spaces on the board. As directed by the square he landed on, he draws a *Chance* card. Dismay replaces anticipation as he reads, "Go directly to jail. Do not pass GO. Do not collect $200."[1]

All three of the above are descriptions of recreation behavior.

The basic responsibility of recreation and park personnel is to provide, directly or indirectly, opportunities for people to engage in recreation behavior. The goals, in terms of individual growth and enrichment, that the field attempts to accomplish are sought through the medium of recreation behavior. It follows then, that to be effective recreation and park workers must understand the behavior of those who use their services. Personnel will also be more effective if they know something about those who do *not* use recreation and park services. Such knowledge may enable the agency to provide opportunities for these people.

HUMAN BEHAVIOR: TWO MAJOR VIEWS

Behavior is an extremely complex subject. The field of psychology is devoted to the study of human activity. Many theories have been developed to explain why people do what they do and the influences of different factors. Much research is available, which deals with the great range of specific aspects related to behavior. It would be presumptious to try to explain behavior in a single chapter. Yet, some basic information can be provided that is useful to recreation and park personnel as they work with both participants and staff.

While there are many different theories of behavior, there are two major points of view.[2] One point of view is the *behaviorist tradition,* which focuses on the observable aspects of behavior. That is, the focus is on elements in the environment that stimulate the individual, and on the observable responses of the individual to these stimuli. The second point of view, the *humanist tradition*, emphasizes the internal states of the individual. Theories in this category are concerned about such matters as the ways different people perceive things and the influences of their own self-concepts and attitudes.

As an illustration of these points of view, assume that we are watching a swim instructor working with a group of children in a beginners' class. The children are lined up at the shallow end of the pool; they are standing about ten feet out, facing the end of the pool. The instructor is on the deck giving directions and suggestions as the children practice pushing off from the bottom and gliding in a prone position. We observe that the instructor jumps down into the water each time one of the learners fails to reach the end of the pool in a prone-glide position. The instructor, while in the water, has the child try again and gives verbal encouragement. If we were to examine the instructor's behavior from the behaviorist perspective, we would give greater attention to the instructor's responses, which we can see, and to the external conditions that seem to have brought them about (the student's behavior). We would be concerned about what the instructor did and about the details of the environment within which the behavior occurred. Does the instructor get into the pool every time a child is unsuccessful? Does he encourage each child in the same way? How does he respond when a previously unsuccessful child completes the prone-glide as intended? Does he get into the water or offer encouragement under other conditions? If we examined the instructor's behavior from the humanist point of view, we would be more interested in what was going on in the instructor's mind. What purpose does he think is being accomplished by getting into the water? How does that act relate to effective teaching, as he sees it? How does he see himself as a teacher, and how does his behavior relate to that concept?

Mannell, in a discussion of strategies in studying leisure experiences, commented on the limitations of a behaviorist approach. He stated that the leisure experience is a "mental experience; therefore it is a private experience."

> Obviously the adoption of a strictly behavioral approach would rule out the study of leisure experiences. . . . So-called behavioral data, which might consist of the frequency of attendance at cultural events, the number of rapids negotiated during a canoe trip, or the time spent on the golf course, are limited in their ability to provide explanations of leisure and the contributions of various recreation, entertainment, and art engagements to the quality of life.[3]

He noted, however, that observable and measurable events can be used to make inferences about the internal, psychological states of the individual.[4]

Clearly the two positions are not mutually exclusive. In any behavior there will be the elements of the external stimuli, the individual's observable response, *and* the internal conditions of the individual that are related to the response (including such things as attitudes, the recollections of past experience, and concepts of self). The difference between the two major views may be more a matter of emphasis. The behaviorist perspective focuses more on observable stimuli and responses, while the humanist perspective gives greater attention to internal influences on behavior. The position taken in this text is that attitudes, values, self-concepts, and other internal states are all important influences and must be recognized in any attempt to explain behavior.

RECREATION BEHAVIOR: SOME GENERAL CHARACTERISTICS

In a general sense, theories of behavior also explain that particular kind of behavior called *recreation* or *play* (for purposes of this chapter, these terms will be considered interchangeable). In addition, there is a body of literature related specifically to recreation behavior. Some of this literature focuses on the general characteristics of recreation; some is concerned with theoretical explanations; and some takes the form of research on specific aspects of leisure behavior.

Driver and Tocher developed a "behavioral interpretation of recreational engagements" that provides a useful framework for understanding some general characteristics of recreation behavior.[5] These authors offered their interpretation as a contrast to what they saw as a prevailing tendency to view recreation simply as participation in activities. Their conceptualization includes five postulates.

1. Recreation is an experience that results from recreation engagements.
2. Recreational engagements require a commitment by the recreationist.
3. Recreational engagements are self-rewarding; the engagement finds pleasure in itself and of itself, and recreation is the experience.
4. Recreational engagements require personal and free choice on the part of the recreationist.
5. Recreational engagements occur during nonobligated time.[6]

The authors noted that these postulates can be combined to produce a definition of recreation as a human experience.

Driver and Tocher used the term *recreationist* to mean the person who engages in recreation behavior—who takes part in recreational engagements. The term *engagements* is used, rather than *activity,* to denote the broader psychological dimensions. They stated that Postulates 2, 3, 4, and 5, collectively, are descriptors of the differences between recreation and other forms of human behavior. *Commitment,* referred to in Postulate 2, is the allocation by the recreationist of personal resources (such as energy, time, and money). Driver and Tocher raised some interesting questions about differing degrees of commitment that might be associated with different recreation experiences.[7] For example, do different time periods (such as weekends and longer vacations) involve different levels of commitment?

Postulate 3 focuses on the nature of gratifications in recreation engagements. Driver and Tocher suggested that recreationists receive value from the attainment of "goal-objects" in the recreational experience. These goal-objects are rewarding in and of themselves. That is, they are pursued primarily for their own sake, not for some secondary value.

Postulates 4 and 5 suggest the voluntary nature of recreation behavior. The authors noted that the freedom to make choices falls along a continuum from total restraint to complete freedom. While situations will vary from individual to individual, and from time to time, recreation behavior falls at the end of the continuum where restraints are least in evidence. Freedom to choose is a function of both environmental factors (the relative presence or absence of opportunities) and personal variables (availability or lack of such resources as time, money, health, and skill). Obligation also falls along a continuum. We sometimes feel rather heavily obligated to do something; there is a sense of being bound to the activity, and often a sense of urgency about doing it. At other times, we feel relatively free from obligation. Recreational engagements fall at this end of the continuum.

Levy identified the "salient characteristics of recreation behavior as (1) intrinsic motivation, (2) suspension of reality, and (3) internal locus of control.[8] *Intrinsic motivation* means that the behavior itself is rewarding. It is not pursued primarily for some other benefit. This is the same idea as Postulate 3 in the concept developed by Driver and Tocher. *Suspension of reality* means that, in recreation, the "real" world is forgotten temporarily or de-emphasized. Everyday responsibilities and roles are put aside. *Internal locus of control* means that the participant feels that he or she is in control of the behavior and the outcomes.

Iso-Ahola also observed that recreation behavior is characterized by intrinsic motivation.[9] He suggested that intrinsic motivation is a function of perceived freedom and perceived competence. The participant chooses the recreation activity and the circumstances of participation (when, where, and with whom). The choice is made with the expectation that the activity will be successful. This promotes a feeling of competence, an intrinsic reward.

Iso-Ahola discussed an additional characteristic of recreation behavior—*optimal arousal*.[10] Optimal arousal is that point on a continuum, from boredom to stress (or distress), that is most desired by a participant at a particular time. This state is also an intrinsic motivation.

Greben and Gray contended that recreation is characterized by certain emotional states. They developed this conceptualization:

> Recreation is an emotional condition within the individual human being that flows from a feeling of well-being and self-satisfaction. It is characterized by feelings of mastery, achievement, exhilaration, acceptance, success, personal worth, and pleasure. It reinforces a positive self-image. Recreation is a response to aesthetic experience, achievement of personal goals, or positive feedback from others. It is independent of activity, leisure or social acceptance.[11]

Other writers have contended that leisure behavior is characterized by concentration and lessened awareness of time.[12] The participant tends to be deeply absorbed with the activity or experience and often loses track of time and surrounding events.

Several authors have suggested that recreation behavior includes more than the "on-site" experience. Jensen identified four phases: anticipation of the experience, planning and preparation, participation itself, and recollection of it afterward.[13] Chubb and Chubb developed an expanded scheme with eleven phases, including four related to awareness and decision making.[14]

The general model of recreation behavior presented later in this chapter is compatible with the general characteristics discussed in this section.

TYPES OF RECREATION BEHAVIOR

The activities described at the beginning of the chapter—backpacking, ceramics, and playing Monopoly—are different behaviors. The goals of the participants may be similar: to sense achievement or to enjoy interactions with other persons. But the basic nature of the activities differs. For example, backpacking requires a different kind of physical energy than do ceramics or Monopoly. Ceramics involves a type of hand-eye coordination that is not as prevalent in the other two. Monopoly requires an opponent; ceramics and backpacking do not. Various other differences could be described.

The range of recreation behaviors is extremely broad. Almost any experience could be thought of as recreational in nature if the elements suggested earlier are present. A categorization presented by Murphy and others provides an illustration of the variety of behaviors that can be observed.[15] *Socializing behaviors* include such things as parties, dating, and visiting friends. *Associative behaviors* are those in which participants meet to pursue a common interest: for example, antique car restoration, model railroading, or gourmet cooking. *Acquisitive behaviors* involve collecting things such as stamps, dolls, and coins. *Competitive behaviors* and *testing behaviors* are similar in that participants use skills to achieve some objective. In competition, there is an opponent. In testing, the participant might match skills against the environment as in mountain climbing. Testing behaviors often are *risk-taking behaviors*. Risk activities vary from physically hazardous forms like hang-gliding to such activities as playing slot machines and betting on horses. *Explorative behaviors* may be illustrated by travel, sightseeing, nature study and other activities where the participant encounters new environments. When we encounter events or environments through the eyes of someone else, as in reading or attending movies, the activities can be thought of as *vicarious experiences*.

Some activities are pursued because they provide *sensory stimulation;* consumption of alcohol and listening to music fall into this category. *Physical expression* is the use of the body—running, jumping, dancing and other activities where enjoyment results primarily from movement. *Creative behaviors* and *appreciative behaviors* often are related to the arts—music, painting, sculpture, dance and so on. In *variety-seeking behavior* participants seek a change from routine. Finally, recreation experiences frequently involve *anticipatory* and *recollective behaviors*. Often, looking forward to a trip or a game and remembering it afterwards can be considered as leisure experiences themselves. Nor are these different categories mutually exclusive: For example, a SCUBA diving trip could be exploratory and involve risk. If divers were members of a club, the activity could also be associative. Even so, the categories do suggest the very wide range of participant behaviors that are evident in recreation and park settings.

THEORETICAL EXPLANATIONS OF RECREATION AND PLAY BEHAVIOR

While recreation is behavior, and while general theories of behavior help to explain recreation behavior, various theories directed specifically toward recreation and play have been developed.

"Classical" Theories. Interest in explaining play behavior began in the late 1800s and early 1900s. Several theories were developed during this time that are frequently referred to as "classical" or "early" theories. While exact terminology varies, the following theories generally are included: surplus energy, instinct-practice, recreation, relaxation, and recapitulation. In brief, the *surplus energy* theory suggested that people (and animals— much of the early interest in play stemmed from observation of animal activity) play because they have energy not needed for survival. The *instinct-practice* theory postulated that children play to practice behavior that they will need in later years. That is, play provides a preparation for later life. The *recreation* and *relaxation* theories were closely related. They suggested that we play as a means of enjoying a change from the other routines of life (that is, to relax). This change enables us to return to the routines, such as work, more able to function. We recreate our capacity to work or study or engage in other life functions. The *recapitulation theory* assumed that children relived, in play, the major cultural epochs through which the species passed in its evolution.

The classical theories presented some ideas that continue to seem valid. Energy does lead to activity. Children do play at adult activities. We do seek changes from routine. Yet each of the theories falls short of a comprehensive explanation of recreation behavior. Many of the classical explanations focused largely on children's play, and often these theories made no attempt to explain the form play takes.

Recent Theories. Other theories have been developed in more recent times. Ellis described several that appeared after 1900.[16] One group of theories explains play in terms of antecedent experiences. Play is seen as ". . . a strategy for erasing or working out the effects of those experiences."[17] Included are explanations based on generalization, compensation, catharsis, and psychoanalytic theory. In *generalization,* people are thought to seek out in play those situations which are similar to ones in which they experience success in nonplay activity. That is, they seek to generalize the satisfactions of nonplay situations to play. In *compensation,* people try to find satisfactions that they do not achieve in other areas of life; they attempt to compensate for these through play. The *catharsis* explanation takes the position that the direct expression of negative emotions, especially aggression and hostility, is suppressed in society, but that in play these emotions can be expressed in acceptable nonharmful ways. In so doing, the person is purged or released from these emotions. Play explanations derived from *psychoanalytic theory* emphasize the function of play in helping relieve the unpleasantness of negative experience. This is accomplished by reliving or repeating the experience in play, where the individual can control conditions or where the individual can reverse roles and become master of the event rather than the victim.

Ellis's discussion of recent theories also includes explanations based on human development and learning. The *developmental* explanation suggests that play is conditioned by the developmental levels through which children pass. The ways in which a child thinks influence how he or she perceives the world and how the child reacts to it. The cognitive structures of children influence the form of play. As cognitive structures become more complex with increasing age in children, more complex reactions, including more complex play behaviors, are evident. Also, children's play behaviors can be seen as resulting from *learning*. Children learn to seek out pleasurable experiences and avoid unpleasant ones. Play usually is pleasant, and they "learn" to play. The society within which children live influences this learning by providing certain opportunities but not others. Learning also is influenced by the ways in which society (including such elements as the family and peers) rewards or reinforces some behaviors but not others.

"Modern" Theories. Ellis discusses two additional explanations, more recent than those just described, in a category labelled "modern" theories.[18] One of these is the *competence-effectance theory,* in which play is thought to result from individuals' needs to feel competent in the situations in which they find themselves, and to feel that they can cause things to happen (that is, to feel "effectance"). The assumption is that play provides opportunities for these feelings to occur. The second theory is *play as arousal-seeking.* In this theory, Ellis contends that we seek conditions of optimal stimulation—not so much arousal as to be stress producing, nor so little as to be boring. There will be different optimal levels for different individuals. We attempt to achieve and maintain these optimal levels of arousal. Play usually occurs when we desire greater stimulation. Ellis suggests that play can be defined in this manner:

> . . . *play is that behavior that is motivated by the need to elevate the level of arousal towards the optimal.*[19]

Ellis observed that, given the variety of theories that exist, one is faced with two alternatives: to take the position that one is most correct and all of the others are less adequate, or to assume that an integration of several of the theories leads to the best explanation. His persuasion is that an integration of the arousal-seeking theory with developmental and learning points of view produces the most adequate explanation of play.[20]

APPROACHES TO THE STUDY OF RECREATION
AND PLAY BEHAVIOR

It is possible to identify some general approaches to the study of play behavior and play theories. Herron and Sutton-Smith presented a review in which six different approaches were identified: normative, ecological, psychoanalytic, comparative, cognitive, and developmental.[21] Each of the theories discussed in the previous section could be placed in one of these categories.

Normative studies attempt to identify the play forms in which children typically engage. *Ecological* approaches attempt to find relationships between play environments and play behavior. As indicated earlier, *psychoanalytic* studies relate play to the reduction of anxiety and hostility and to the development of a sense of being in control of events. *Comparative* studies tend to focus on play as observed in animals. *Cognitive* approaches emphasize the relationships of exploration, competence-seeking, and intellectual development to play. Finally, *developmental* approaches emphasize characteristics of play that are apparent at sequentially different levels of human development.

Levy also identified several categories of play theories. These included some of those presented by Herron and Sutton-Smith, and an additional category that he termed "socialization theories of play behavior."[22] Explanations in this category are based on the influences of such processes as learning and socialization. Levy included generalization and compensation theories in this category, as well as conflict-enculturation and attribution theories.

Generalization and compensation were discussed earlier. In *conflict-enculturation* theory, play is seen as a means used by individuals to reduce anxieties and stresses that result from socialization processes. *Attribution* theory is concerned with people's perceptions of the causes of their behavior, particularly the degrees to which individuals feel that their behavior is attributable to internal (personal) factors or to external (environmental) factors.

Levy suggested that there is no overall "grand theory" of play.

> Although each of them [the various theories] . . . has a strong contribution to make, what is needed is an all-encompassing theory that would subsume the most salient features of these microtheories in order to account for more of the behavior referred to as play.[23]

He presented a conceptual paradigm as a step in the direction of an all-encompassing theory.[24] The paradigm is comprised of these dimensions: antecedents or determinants of play behavior, the structure of play behavior, and consequences of play behavior.

The *antecedents of play behavior* include such things as cultural values and dominant beliefs of the society within which play occurs, child-rearing practices, and other socio-cultural factors which are part of the socialization process. Anatomical and physiological factors (height, coordination, visual acuity, muscular strength), and psychological makeups (personality, motivation, emotional states) are also antecedents or determinants. In addition, environmental factors are antecedent influences. Levy suggested that leisure behavior results from the interactions between individuals (each with different characteristics and circumstances) and environments.

The *structure of play behavior* includes elements, settings or conditions, and processes. Elements of play behavior are those skills and capabilities that the individual must possess to participate in a particular activity. Settings or conditions are factors surrounding the activity that are necessary for participation. For example, snow is required for cross-country skiing; an opponent is needed in competitive badminton. Processes ". . . deal with the way the individual player decides to consciously manipulate the *elements* and *conditions* for specific effects and outcomes."[25]

Consequences of play behavior include outcomes that may be beneficial or dysfunctional, or both.[26] Disruptive spectator behaviors at athletic events, and emotional pressures sometimes associated with children's sports are examples of dysfunctional outcomes.

Kaplan developed a detailed model for studying and understanding leisure in society.[27] It is comprised of a system of components, at several different levels. The system is dynamic in that the various components interact with each other. Each has potential for influencing the others. The first level is the "institution of leisure." Other levels describe aspects of society or culture that influence leisure.

In presenting his first level, Kaplan provided insights into leisure behavior. At this level, he suggested four different components: condition, selection, function, and meaning.[28] *Conditions* are those factors that have potential for determining behavior, including such things as age, place of residence and income level. *Selection* is "the process of choice that may lead one to a game of cards instead of to a book, a walk, a television show, a conversation or other possibilities."[29] *Function* has to do with the purposes served by leisure, the purposes desired by the person, and the results that occur. *Meaning* is simply the meaning that leisure has for the individual (and for society). These four components interact with each other. For example, the amount of time any person has available for leisure is influenced by other conditions (including age and occupation). Available time influences the selection process. We select different leisure experiences to meet different functions; these have different meanings for us. Certain experiences may come to have important enough functions and meanings that we will devote greater amounts of time to them, even if we must save time somewhere else.

Kaplan provided detailed descriptions, with useful illustrations, of how these four components interact with each other. He also described, with illustrations, the interactions of all of the components of the model.[30]

While conditions (such as age and occupation) determine leisure behavior, no one factor alone explains why a certain leisure choice is made. They function in combination. An individual may go surfing because she is young and has the physical energy and ability to do so, because she lives near the ocean, because her job permits enough time off to go, because she has a sufficient income level to afford to do so, and because she enjoys the climate and scenery at the coast. Kaplan noted this interaction of conditions. He also indicated that personality and other internal factors, such as need and desire, serve as influences. Further, he observed that a great variety of "mediating factors" may contribute to the actual selection of a specific activity: a deliberate thought about the activity, a feeling, an advertisement on television, a change in the weather, the suggestion of a friend, the force of habit, or any one or a combination of many other influences.[31]

A GENERAL MODEL OF RECREATION BEHAVIOR

The various characteristics and theoretical approaches described so far in this chapter illustrate the complexity of recreation behavior. This complexity is illustrated further by a growing body of research on various specific aspects of the leisure experience.[32] Overall, the amount of theoretical and research information available is considerable and diverse. For those reasons, a general model of recreation behavior, which provides a framework within which other relevant information can be considered, is presented in this section. The model is based on a conceptualization of human behavior and learning developed by Cronbach.[33] It is useful in that it identifies major dimensions of behavior with which recreation and park personnel are involved. It is compatible with many of the theoretical explanations described previously. It recognizes the influences of the external environments, within which behavior occurs, as well as the influences of such factors as the attitudes, perceptions, and self-concept of the individual. It presents behavior dimensions in a clear, straightforward manner; this is an advantage, but a note of caution is required. Remember that behavior is exceedingly complex. To simplify it is to miss the full reality of it. However, the model provides sufficient information to serve as a background for discussion of such processes as leadership and teaching in later chapters.

Dimensions of Recreation Behavior.   At the beginning of this chapter, three illustrations were given. The individuals involved were two backpackers, one ceramicist, and a Monopoly player. These three illustrations depict recreation behavior. All three contain dimensions that can be defined in most examples of recreation behavior. While these dimensions interact in a fluid, dynamic fashion in actual behavior, it is possible to isolate them artificially for the purpose of defining a concept of participation as behavior.

1. *The participant's goal or goals.* It seems safe to assume that all three of the individuals involved are engaged in activity for a reason (probably for multiple reasons). The goals may be grand or mundane; they may be sought after intensely or casually, immediately or with an eye to ultimate achievement.

2. *The influences of some of the individual's personal characteristics.* In addition to goals, each individual possesses many characteristics, some of which influence leisure behavior. The health and fitness of the packers influence the scope of their hike. The work of the ceramicist is influenced by her skills; and her son's play depends upon his knowledge of the rules. Other influencing factors include financial resources, attitudes, feelings about self, coordination, and strength. In some respects, these personal characteristics are similar to those possessed by all other members of any given society; for example, we all experience fear to some degree when placed in situations that we perceive as hazardous. In other ways personal characteristics tend to be highly individual; each person's past experiences, and the specific influences of those experiences on such factors as attitudes and feelings about oneself probably are completely unique.

Between the two extremes (near-universal traits and complete individuality) exists a useful concept of "modal" or "typical" characteristics for various subgroups within the society. For example, we can describe some typical characteristics of teenagers, with reasonable confidence. They tend to be interested in members of the opposite sex; they tend to be seeking independence from adult authority; and so on. Certainly, not all teens exhibit these traits at the same time. Some do not exhibit them at all. However, they are typical behaviors for relatively large percentages of adolescents. Most backpackers are conservationists; most mothers feel a responsibility for their children's welfare; and most fifth-grade boys are more interested in playing with boys than with girls. Understanding typical characteristics helps us understand recreation behavior, when we have a deep and continuing appreciation for the wide range of possible individual differences, and when we guard against the tendency to see what is expected rather than what is actually present.

3. *The sociophysical setting within which the behavior takes place.* The two men could hike in almost any outdoor environment, but the Sierra Nevada offers particular values in terms of scenery, challenge, and relative isolation. The influencing elements in the pottery studio include not only the wheels, the clay, light, heat, and other physical factors; the presence of other people also becomes a consideration. The nature of participation may be changed by the individual's interaction with the instructor and with other participants. The emotional climate (relaxed, friendly, formal) is also a potential influencer. The setting within which the Monopoly game is being played includes not only the board, the deeds, and the money, but also the complex web of psychological and emotional relationships that exists among the players.

The actual setting for most recreation behavior is greater than that portion which the participant experiences. There are infinitely more potentially influencing factors within and beyond the ceramic studio than any one of the participants perceives. Perhaps an amateur pottery show is being held in an adjoining community. A knowledge of this might prompt a different kind of effort from the ceramicist in this illustration. Perhaps an unexpected visitor is waiting for her at home; a knowledge of this condition might terminate her participation for the day. Both the pottery show and the visitor are part of the total setting within which the ceramicist behaves;

both are potential influencers of her behavior. However, if they are not part of her awareness at the time, she will not feel their influence. She might also be influenced by factors that she does not perceive accurately. For example, it is possible that the wheel on which she is working is faulty. She may interpret her failure to throw a pot well as lack of skill, rather than as a fault of the wheel. In this sense, an element in the environment (the faulty wheel) contributes to a modification in her behavior. However, until she is aware of the actual source of her failure to perform, she will behave on the basis of her perceptions. That is, she probably will continue to try to improve her techniques.

The influences of the characteristics of the individual and those of the sociophysical setting interact. Assume that one of the backpackers once suffered frostbite when he was caught for several days at a high elevation by a late summer storm. This past experience is part of his unique individual characteristics. This man may perceive a cloud buildup quite differently from his companion, who has not had a similar experience. In this instance, the influence of the physical setting probably will be different for each of the two men.

4. *The participant's plan for achieving the goal(s).* If one of the goals of the hikers is to enjoy an environment of relative isolation, they probably formulated a plan by which to achieve this objective. They may have looked over various maps of the Sierra Nevada and selected their route based on what appeared to be the least-used trails. They also may have decided to go in mid-September, rather than over the Labor Day weekend. This planning process may be long and involved or it may be immediate and relatively concentrated. It also is continuous, as ongoing behavior is adjusted to problems and opportunities that arise. The ceramicist may plan the shape and size of a particular pot for several days. Then, during the throwing, as she attempts to make the pot according to plan, she may make several modifications. These also are plans, even though they happen in the ongoing behavior. She may find the consistency of the clay inappropriate for what she intends to do; or she may happen upon a new shape accidentally that she wishes to incorporate into the overall design. Planning usually is a continuous process that is woven into the total behavior sequence. At the early stages, as with the backpackers going over maps, it can be observed rather directly. As they make adjustments on the trail, planning becomes part of the total experience and therefore is more difficult to differentiate.

The selection of a particular plan by any individual may be influenced by all of the previously mentioned elements (goals, personal characteristics, and perceptions of the setting). An attractive setting (for example, a well-equipped ceramics studio) may generate new goals, or it may intensify existing ones. The setting also may suggest a plan for achieving goals. The example of other people throwing pots, or techniques described and illustrated on a bulletin board, may lead to a plan of intended behavior. The setting may be experienced directly, or indirectly through television or printed materials. Similarly, the recollection of past experiences may contribute to goal development or to plans for achieving goals. Plans may be based on adaptions of earlier successful behaviors and experiences. Or we may imitate the behaviors of others in defining our own plans. Much of our recreation behavior is probably based on examples provided by family and friends. In a sense, we follow their plans.

Some of our recreation behaviors may become almost habitual and relatively unplanned. Given certain recurring goals, we may engage in an activity with relatively little planning, or without any reappraisal of an earlier plan on which the response is based. For example, we may frequently seek relaxation after dinner. Watching television has satisfied this goal in the past. Given the circumstances—an early evening in the home with the goal of relaxation—we may turn on the TV set without really evaluating whether that behavior has the greatest potential for satisfying our goal, consistent with available opportunities and our own resources, such as energy level and time.

5. *The behavior or participation.* It is this element that recreation personnel most frequently encounter directly, and it is this aspect that is most easily observed. For the participant, it is the recreation experience. It is the act of hiking, of throwing a pot, of playing Monopoly. It does not exist in isolation from all of the other elements. The participant's goal(s), his or her characteristics and perceptions of the setting, and the plan which has been conceived all are part of the total experience. However, we typically think of the behavior as it is manifested when we think of participation.

The behavior or activity may involve quite different expenditures of energy. In this sense, listening to music is an activity, as are square dancing and playing the guitar.

As indicated earlier, several authors have suggested a useful expansion of the concept of participation. They contend that the total recreation experience includes such phases as anticipation, planning, and reminiscence, as well as the actual participation. While these phases may be part of the same recreation experience, they also may be viewed as three different recreational experiences. That is, the planning of the pack trip, and the recollections of it (slide viewings, discussions with friends) probably contain the elements of goal(s), individual characteristics, settings, plans, responses, and consequences, as does the actual trip itself. The distinction is not important however, as long as the observer of recreation behavior is sensitive to the fact that anticipation and recollection of recreation experiences may in themselves be recreational.

6. *The participant's perceptions of the consequences of his or her behavior.* The backpackers, the ceramicist, and Monopoly player all experience the consequences of their behaviors. Usually, they perceive these consequences in terms of varying degrees of satisfaction. The packers may enjoy the solitude or the view, or they may meet a large group on the trail and the weather may be unfavorable and they are disappointed.

Perceptions of satisfaction or dissatisfaction probably occur as a continuing part of the ongoing flow of behavior and as an overall feeling about the recreation experience at its conclusion. The feeling of satisfaction may be rather intense, or it may be diffused and generalized.

Satisfaction and enjoyment, or the lack of these elements, are largely a function of the degree to which goals are achieved. We can predict with some confidence which kinds of experiences will be satisfying. However, the perceptions of the individual are the determining factors in any specific experience. Suppose the ceramicist throws a pot that is admired greatly by her family and other members of the class. Will this condition produce satisfaction and enjoyment? Probably, but we cannot be sure. If she aspired to an invitation to show the pot at the County Fair and the invitation was not forthcoming, she might be quite dissatisfied despite the admiration of family and friends. On the other hand, she may aspire to no more than completing a pot, regardless of its beauty. In this case, she might find real satisfaction even in the absence of recognition from others.

One backpacker may aspire to hike five miles a day; another may wish to hike a 100-mile section of trail in five days. These varying levels of aspiration influence whether or not satisfaction is experienced. The phenomenon seems to be present in most recreation behavior.

If a participant experiences satisfaction from an activity or a particular behavior, the behavior tends to be repeated when conditions occur that are similar to the earlier behavior. When the hikers have free time during the summer months, there is greater likelihood that they will engage in backpacking rather than in a less-satisfying activity. If satisfaction is not achieved, there is a tendency to do one of two things: (1) try a new or modified plan for reaching the same goal, or (2) give up the goal in favor of other goals. If the ceramicist does not receive the admiration she seeks with her first pot, she may try again, using some modification in her technique. Given rather consistent failure to receive admiration (assuming this to be the goal), she may turn her free-time energies from ceramics to other activities with other potential rewards. These become new goals.

Schematically the elements discussed above may be represented by the relationships shown in Figure 3-1.

The *individual participant* (A) exists within a total environment, which includes an infinite number of potentially influencing factors. These factors constitute the *actual setting* (B). However, the individual will be mainly influenced only by those factors that are part of his or her awareness—the *perceived setting* (C). Within this setting, the individual defines *a goal or goals* (D). The goal may be a result of one or more *stimulus factors* (E): needs the individual feels, satisfactions from past experiences, an attractive and stimulating environment, or group or peer pressures. The individual mentally formulates *a plan* (F) for achieving the goal. *Other possible courses of action* may have been planned, but not selected (G). The plan leads to *a response* (H). The response may include emotions and appreciations, as well as more readily observable activity. The participant does something. He or she hikes, or goes to the ceramics studio, or moves to Park Place. As a result of the activity, the participant perceives *a result*. The result may be *satisfying* (I) or *dissatisfying* (J). If the results are satisfying, the tendency to *repeat the response* will be strengthened (K). If not, the individual may try *a modified*

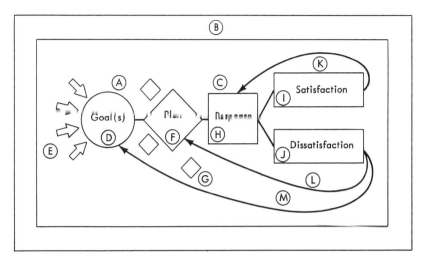

Figure 3-1 A representation of recreation behavior.

plan (*L*), in an attempt to achieve the same goal. Or, *a new goal* may be selected (*M*).

SOME MAJOR GENERALIZATIONS ABOUT RECREATION BEHAVIOR

The model described above, and the material presented earlier in the chapter, suggest the following major generalizations about recreation behavior:

Recreation Behavior Is Purposeful and Goal Directed. Recreation behavior is motivated by the rewards inherent in the experience itself. It is engaged in primarily for its own sake, rather than for some secondary reason such as economic gain. If asked, most people would say they engage in recreation for enjoyment or fun. Satisfaction and enjoyment tend to be emotional states brought about by certain conditions; and they tend to be individualistic. For some people, the emotional state—enjoyment—comes from experiencing a condition of relaxation; for others, enjoyment results from sensing achievement.

Tinsley reported on several investigations of why people engage in leisure behavior.[34] His report identified the psychological needs met through participation. He noted that different activities satisfy different needs. Some needs are satisfied more fully by certain activities, while others appear to be satisfied more or less equally by participation in *any* leisure activity.

Tinsley, Barrett, and Kass termed these two types of needs "leisure activity specific" and "leisure activity general." Drawing on the work of several other researchers, they developed a list of forty-five needs that might be met through recreation. They then investigated the degrees to which these needs were satisfied by participation in five different leisure activities. Forty-two of the needs appeared to be activity specific.[35]

The prevalence of leisure needs that are specific to certain activities was confirmed in a replication and extension of the original study. However, in the second investigation there was increased evidence that some needs are more general.[36]

Hawes conducted a nationwide survey of 1000 households to determine leisure satisfactions.[37] He used a list of fifty activities and a set of thirty-two satisfactions statements. He suggested that the benefits represented by the statements were components of "an overall global feeling of 'satisfaction'." The statements rated most important by women were "peace of mind," "chance to learn about new things," "chance to get the most out of life while I can still enjoy it," and "a chance to escape home or family pressures." Important satisfiers for men were "peace of mind," "chance to get the most out of life while I can still enjoy it," and "adventure and excitement." Enjoying an "old familiar activity" and "happy memories" also were important.

Ragheb and Beard developed a "Leisure Satisfaction Scale (LSS)," in which they identified six dimensions of satisfaction. These different dimensions, defined as subscales, were psychological, social, educational, relaxational, physiological, and aesthetic.[38] In the psychological subscale, satisfactions are related to such benefits as a sense of freedom and involvement. The nature of the benefits, and satisfactions, in the educational, social and relaxational subscales, is suggested by the title of each subscale. The physiological part of the LSS is concerned with such benefits as health and physical fitness. The aesthetic part relates to the enjoyment of beauty.

The satisfactions associated with a recreation experience may be the result of secondary activities, as well as the primary activity. Buchanan and Burdge, in a study of fishing, found that other activities which participants engaged in during a fishing trip (such as visiting with friends, sitting around a campfire, and going for a walk) contributed to satisfactions received along with the main activity of fishing.[39]

Whatever the particular reasons why people engage in recreation behavior, it seems clear that they do so purposefully and to achieve certain goals. That is, they are motivated to engage in the behavior. There are differing points of view among psychologists regarding the nature of motivations. Yet it is possible to identify several considerations that are useful to recreation and park personnel as they seek to understand recreation behavior.

1. *Multiple goals and satisfactions.* Any segment of recreation behavior may be motivated by more than one goal. Assume surfing as a recreation behavior, and an imaginary person, June Whitman, who is a beginning surfer. Whitman may engage in surfing both because of the sense of excitement it produces and because she enjoys the companionship of friends who surf. Both of these rewards might be operative in the same behavior. The effects of secondary activities might also be operative, as suggested earlier.

Crandall's studies lend support to the notion of multiple goals and satisfactions. He investigated relationships of leisure and social behavior, and noted that some activities, such as partying and visiting friends, essentially are based on social interaction; other leisure activities may be pursued primarily to avoid social contact and to experience a sense of relative isolation. He suggested that activities between those two extremes might be motivated, to varying degrees, both by satisfactions intrinsic to the activity and by social interaction.

> In addition to its role as a leisure activity, social interaction is also important as a motivation for participation in other leisure activities, and as a source of satisfaction or need fulfillment derived from them. Many activities such as team sports, games, organizational memberships and crafts may include an important social component.[40]

Crandall's work focused on social interactions in leisure. Other multiple goals and satisfactions might involve such elements as achievement and new experience; both of these might be motivating factors in learning a new skill, such as tennis. Or aesthetic appreciation and relaxation might be factors in attending an art show. And, as Crandall's studies suggest, social interactions might be involved in addition to these other multiple goals and satisfactions.

2. *Immediate, Process, and Long-range Goals.* People are motivated by goals that have different time dimensions. For example, the surfer may wish to experience the thrills of surfing in the particularly good wave conditions that exist today. This is an immediate goal. Or she may enroll in surfing lessons as a means of improving her skills (a process goal) so that she can reach her long-range goal to enter a surfing competition in Hawaii.

3. *Social Motives.* Many theorists support the idea that there are motives, or *wants*, that are widespread in our society. Kretch, Crutchfield, and Ballachey provided an illustrative list. They used the term *social wants* to differentiate from physiological needs, such as food and shelter. Five major social wants were presented: to be affiliated, to acquire things, to experience prestige, to express altruism, and to satisfy curiosity.[41] The authors contended that most people in present western society are motivated, at different times and to different degrees, by one or more of these social wants. To continue our example, June Whitman may surf to experience companionship (affiliation) or to sense achievement and the recognition of others (prestige). She may be satisfying a curiosity about the sport, or she may wish to learn to surf so she can help others learn (altruism). Her long-range goal of competing in surfing may include a desire to earn trophies, to take photographs during competition, or to collect souvenirs from trips taken to different surfing areas (acquisition). All of these wants seem appropriate to recreation behavior, and many other illustrations could be given. The six subscales of Beard and Ragheb's Leisure Satisfactions Scale also probably describe categories of fairly common motivations.

4. *Maslow's Scheme.* Abraham Maslow generated a theory of motivation based on differing human needs. Maslow contended that some needs are more dominant or potent than others; that a hierarchy of needs exists. At the bottom are physiological needs, for such things as food and water. Next are security or safety needs: protection from harm. Following these, in ascending order, are social or belonging needs, needs for self-esteem and recognition, and the need for self-actualization.[42] Until the lower-order needs (physiological and security) are satisfied more or less consistently, the higher-order needs do not become operative. Suppose that the basic motivation for Whitman's surfing is her desire for affiliation (belonging). Maslow's scheme suggests that she would not be motivated to engage in this recreation behavior unless, or until, her more basic needs have been met. Further, she might stop surfing if she feels a strong enough threat to her safety (fear of drowning, being hurt by the board in a fall, or shark attack).

On this point, it is useful to point out that her perception of the degree of risk is what is important. Surfing (and many other recreational behaviors) involves hazards. For many people, the presence of risk is one of the elements that attracts them to such activities. However, as long as Whitman sees the risk as acceptably low, the safety needs will not become dominant.

The levels of needs that most frequently are apparent in recreation behavior are social or belonging needs and esteem needs. The self-actualization needs, or the needs to reach one's own fullest level of functioning in any given situation, probably are found less frequently. Yet the potential for expressing oneself fully in recreational engagements can be a strong motivation.

5. *Conflict.* It is possible for the multiple motives that operate in recreation behavior to conflict. Four such conflict situations have been defined in psychological literature: approach-approach conflicts, approach-avoidance conflicts, double approach-avoidance conflicts, and avoidance-avoidance conflicts. In *approach-approach* conflicts, we are faced with two equally attractive opportunities at the same time. If Whitman were planning to go to the coast for a surfing trip on Saturday and she learned that a friend whom she wanted to see very much was to be in town on the same day, an approach-approach conflict might exist. An *approach-avoidance* conflict exists when one activity has both positive and negative attractions that are equally strong. Whitman might be attracted by the possibility of entering the beginners competition on Saturday, but fearful of embarrassing herself in front of friends if she did not perform skillfully. *Double approach-avoidance* involves two activities, equally attractive and with equally strong negative factors. *Avoidance-avoidance* conflicts rarely are considerations in recreation behavior; since free choice is a characteristic of such behavior, situations with only negative elements usually can be avoided.

6. *Substitutability.* The notion of substitutability has to do with recreation values, specifically, the degree to which one recreational engagement can substitute for another in terms of the values derived. If, for example, Whitman moved to the Midwest and could not surf, could participation in some other activity produce satisfactions and benefits that she previously enjoyed from surfing? Considerable attention has been given to the idea of substitutability.[43] While the full implications have not been defined, the concept seems useful. The idea presented earlier that leisure needs may be activity specific or nonspecific (general) is a relevant consideration.

7. *Level of Aspiration.* Another understanding related to motivation is that people may seek the same goal, but have different expectations in terms of satisfying it. As suggested earlier, in the illustration of the ceramicist, what is seen as a satisfying performance by one individual may be disappointing to another. Both Whitman and a surfing friend may wish to "have a good day at the meet." For Whitman this may mean that she hopes to be able to complete all of her runs without falling, and in sufficiently good form to not be identified as an obvious beginner. For her friend, a good day may mean taking first place in the competition. Whitman and her friend have different levels of aspiration. People will tend to be satisfied to the degree that they meet or exceed their levels of aspiration.

8. *Antecedent and In-Progress Influences on Goals.* Driver and Tocher provided some useful insights into factors that have potential for increasing the values received from recreation behavior. It follows that if value is increased, the motivation for engaging in the behavior probably is increased. The authors noted the influence of the attractiveness of the goal of the behavior, itself. They also identified two other sets of factors— conditions that are *antecedent* to the behavior, and variables that are encountered by the participant *during* the behavior or *enroute* to the site of participation.[44] In a general sense, any motive to participate arises from antecedent conditions, from conditions that existed prior to the behavior. More specifically, some conditions have greater influences upon the magnitude of the values received from the behavior, and the strength of the motivation to engage in it. An incidence of heavy air pollution in their home communities might increase the motivation of the two backpackers mentioned earlier to get into the high country. Being given a new surfboard as a birthday present might intensify June Whitman's desire to go surfing.

Witt and Bishop suggested that the situations in which an individual has been, immediately prior to engaging in recreation, influence such things as moods and needs, and that these in turn influence the nature of the recreation behavior.[45] For example, the student who has just spent an afternoon in the library satisfactorily completing a reading assignment might seek different subsequent leisure activities than an individual who spent a frustrating day running all over campus trying unsuccessfully to locate a set of lost notes from a history class.

Variables encountered enroute to or during the recreational engagement also influence motivational intensity. If the backpackers encounter bad weather, their desire to hike might be lessened, possibly eliminated. On the other hand, a chance meeting in a small town near the trailhead with two other friends who intend to pack into the same area may intensify the motivation for all four individuals.

   An Individual's Perceptions and Attitudes Are Key Determiners of Recreation Behavior.   Reality is what we perceive it to be. It is possible that two different people might perceive the same situation in quite different ways. The two backpackers might view differently the same afternoon cloud buildup in the mountains. For one with little prior experience in the mountains, the gathering clouds might seem so threatening that he suggests cancelling the trip. For the other, whose prior experience is that such cloud buildups usually produce only two or three hours of rain and then clear, the situation calls for keeping rain gear handy but not cancelling the trip. The different perceptions, until modified by interaction between the two individuals, will lead to different behaviors.

   We behave in accordance with the situations we encounter *as we perceive them.* In this sense, our perceptions govern our behavior. These perceptions are influenced by such things as our past experience, our attitudes and values, and our concepts of ourselves. The surfer who sees herself as a cautious person will view a moderately heavy surf differently than another individual who sees herself as a daring person.

   Combs, Richards and Richards observed that

> the perceptual field of any person is both much less and much more than the field which is potentially available in the immediate physical environment.[46]

That is, there are elements in any situation of which we will be unaware. Some of these might have potential for influencing our behavior, but they will not do so if we are not aware of them. Also, we bring to the situations our own unique past experiences and our interests and attitudes; these create the meanings the situations have for us, and, in this sense, make the situations "larger" than they would be otherwise.

   Attitudes are closely related to perceptions. Our perceptions influence the attitudes we form, and the attitudes we hold may modify our perceptions. Iso-Ahola noted both the nature of leisure attitudes and the potential they have for motivating behavior.

> Perhaps the most frequently offered label (reason) for leisure participation is "because I like it." It is this concept of *liking* or feeling or affect that constitutes the heart of the construct called attitude. Thus a positive leisure attitude toward an object may be viewed as a special case of intrinsic leisure motivation.[47]

Mobley, Light and Neulinger, in a study of the attitudes of university students and recreation participation, concluded that positive leisure attitudes were related to participation in free-time activities.[48] They cautioned, however, that causal relationships had not been established and that participation is influenced by multiple factors.

   Neulinger devised a questionnaire intended to measure leisure attitudes. Items in the questionnaire are grouped under five factors that suggest the various dimensions of leisure attitudes. The five factors are: "Affinity for Leisure" (Factor I), "Society's Role in Leisure Planning" (Factor II), "Self-definition through Leisure or Work" (Factor III), "Amount of Leisure Perceived" (Factor IV), and "Amount of Work or Vacation Desired" (Factor V).[49] Factor I is concerned with the degree to which a person likes, and perceives a personal capacity for, leisure. Factor II relates to a person's feelings about the kinds of activities that should be encouraged and the general responsibilities of agencies in society. The relative importance of work and leisure and the contributions of these elements to personal identity are elements in Factor III. Factors IV and V deal with an individual's perception of amounts of leisure available, general satisfactions with these amounts, and amounts desired. Similar to Iso-Ahola, Neulinger contended that leisure attitudes are potent influencers of recreation behavior. He suggested that consideration of leisure attitudes is a necessary condition for the provision of effective leisure services.

> If we wish to provide adequate leisure services, if we wish to improve such services and anticipate what people really want, it is an absolute necessity that we know what their attitudes on leisure are.[50]

Crandall and Slivken suggested that leisure attitudes are, in fact, more important than leisure behaviors.

> If we define leisure in terms of mental states, such as perceived freedom, attitudes become more important than behaviors! Leisure activities and facilities should be designed not because we care about specific leisure behaviors, but because we want to create a positive leisure experience, or state of mind, in the participant![51]

Regardless of the relative importance with which attitudes are viewed, it is clear that they influence recreation behavior. It also is clear that they are related to perception, and that an individual's perceptions are key determinants of behavior.

Other Personal and Environmental Factors Influence Recreation Behavior. As suggested earlier, the individual conditions or circumstances that characterize any one person serve as influences on recreation or leisure behavior. Neulinger described the breadth of these influences.

> Leisure, no matter how defined, is part of the person's total life experience. It is subject to all the forces, personal or environmental, impinging on the individual and, in turn, it leaves its mark on the individual's life style.[52]

Broadly, these influences can be described as biological, psychosociological, or environmental. The *biological* category includes such conditions as health, physical fitness, coordination, strength, height, and visual acuity. *Psychosociological* factors include personality differences and influences associated with such things as education, occupation, and income level. *En-*

vironmental influences result from differing places of residence or location, with the attending differences in climate, land and water areas, population densities, and environmental quality.

Individual Development.   Some of the influences noted above largely are a function of an individual's stage of development. For example, a typical six-year-old does not have the strength or coordination of a typical sixteen-year-old. Also, the six-year-old usually is not granted as much independence from parental authority as is the teen-ager. We would expect the teen to be more interested in the opposite sex than the younger child would be.

Societal Demands.   Other influences result more from the expectations or demands of society. One of the implications of being sixteen years old is that, in most places, you can become licensed to operate a motor vehicle. This is a societal expectation in the form of a law, and it has considerable influence on recreation behavior. Another implication is that you legally cannot consume alcoholic beverages as a sixteen-year-old. This is another law. Other expectations are not expressed in legal forms, but nonetheless can be potent influences. Peer pressure is an example. The sixteen-year old's interest in the opposite sex may be the result of social pressure as well as chronological maturation.

The individual influences on recreation behavior that have been studied most frequently are age, income level, educational level, occupation, sexual identity, and ethnic or racial identity.[53]

Age.   While age may not be the factor that most influences recreation behavior,[54] it probably is the one that is used most in recreation planning. Kraus contended that "the single most significant basis of recreation program planning is the age of the participants."[55] The age of potential participants can be determined rather easily, and therefore it is an operationally effective factor for use. As suggested earlier, the influences of age are both developmental and cultural. Kraus defined four characteristics of play behavior related to chronological development: increasing social content in play as children grow older, a narrowing of recreational interests, greater independence from home and parents, and more involvement with the opposite sex.[56] The combined influence of maturation and societal expectations can be seen in these trends. They also can be seen in characteristic recreational patterns of the aged. As an illustration, older adults often experience declining levels of energy and physical activity. In addition, there may be social pressures on the aged to "slow down" and to "act their age."

Sexual Identity.   Cultural expectations are evident in the ways in which sexual identity influences recreation behavior. These are changing rapidly, however, and it is difficult today to identify leisure pursuits as primarily masculine or feminine.

Income Level.   The influence of income level on recreation behavior seems to be both direct and indirect. In a direct sense, it costs money to engage in many leisure pursuits—money for equipment, lessons, entrance fees, and transportation to and from the site. Indirectly, income influences where an individual lives, how mobile he or she is, and frequently how healthy he or she is. All of these factors have potential for directly influencing recreation behavior. There are some suggestions that rates of participation increase with increases in income levels—up to a point.[57] Cheek and Burch observed that different specific studies suggest differing relationships between income and leisure behavior. Overall, however, they concluded that

> Persons in higher class (income) and status (prestige) groupings have higher participation rates in nearly all nonwork activities.[58]

Knudson also noted the varying nature of research on income and participation and contended that the influence of income might be felt more in terms of the types of activity pursued rather than the overall amount of participation.

> At least in terms of overall participation, people are not limited by finances. Changes in income would be more likely to affect the activity mix rather than total participation.[59]

To the extent that income is a factor in social status, it influences the kinds of opportunities a person has.

> It would seem that position within the larger social structure has a continuing pervasive influence upon the life chances and opportunities of those in a particular stratum.[60]

The life chances of a person with a very restricted income will be different than those of a more affluent individual. The poor person may have fewer leisure opportunities of any kind, and may be preoccupied with other concerns (such as seeking work, improved living conditions, or adequate medical care).

What is important in terms of understanding recreation behavior is the amount of discretionary income—the amount available for leisure expenditures. A young, single adult might have a relatively small income compared to an older individual with a large family. But the young adult might have more money available for recreation because he has relatively fewer financial responsibilities and fixed costs.

Education.   Income, education, and occupation are interrelated, to an extent. Frequently, higher levels of education lead to higher paying jobs. However, both education and occupation seem to have additional influences. Education seems to have the effect of exposing people to new experiences, many of which have the potential of leading to new recreation behaviors. These exposures happen through formal coursework, general out-of-class activities, and contacts with other people.

The social contacts people have are influenced in part by levels of education. The factors of exposure and social contact, and the relationship of education to occupation (and therefore income) contribute to the strength of educational level as an influence on recreation behavior. Murphy noted that this influence might be more dominant than other socioeconomic factors.

> It is increasingly recognized among researchers of leisure behavior that educational attainment seems the best predictor of nonwork behavior.[61]

Occupation.   Work appears to have several effects. The type of work we do influences the amounts of free time we have. The location of the work is also a factor, involving such things as commute time and the availability of leisure opportunities near work sites. The nature of the work itself could be an influence. Physically demanding work might predispose a person to seek more passive recreation experiences (as suggested by the relaxation theory). Or, one might seek to express in free time those skills and abilities that are similar to ones used on the job (as suggested by the generalization theory). An additional factor might be the influence of certain social or community expectations associated with different occupations.[62] It is possible, in some communities, that doctors, for example, are expected to belong to certain organizations or to attend certain community activities. Friendship circles, based on work contacts, also might be influences. Cheek and Burch made this observation:

> It would seem that the organizational milieu of some occupations predispose one to participate with a particular social circle and to share its particular life style variation.[63]

Racial or Ethnic Identity.   One of the influences of racial and ethnic identity is that of a desire to preserve certain elements of a group's heritage. This desire is manifested in such events as celebrations of special days, teaching of folk arts and ethnic dance, and the holding of various festivals. It also might take the form of reading history and other literary works related to an individual's or group's heritage.

Patterns of segregation and discrimination influence recreation behavior.[64] These factors have contributed to overrepresentation of minority groups at lower income levels. Income influences behavior, place of residence, and health; these affect the opportunities people have to engage in recreation.

In the history of the recreation movement, in both the public and private sectors, many illustrations of segregated facilities and discriminatory practices can be found. Parks and other leisure services often were limited in number or were of lesser quality in areas where minority populations lived. Situations such as these may influence the development of attitudes and skills. People who are prohibited from, or discouraged from, using certain recreation facilities probably will develop neither the skills or concepts of themselves as participants that are appropriate to the specific activity. To illustrate, the person who in earlier years was denied access to public and private golf courses probably did not develop further interests or skills related to golf; and he probably did not incorporate golfing into his self-image. The lack of concept of self as a participant also may result if other factors, such as low income status, are involved. For example, in the past most of our national parks were located at considerable distances from urban areas. For minority persons living in urban areas who also were poor, travel to a national park was relatively impossible. Under such circumstances, it would have been unusual for such persons to see themselves as park visitors. The influences of segregation and discrimination have declined in proportion to improvements in the civil rights areas and in the efforts of the field to provide services for all peoples. Therefore, it is probable that the effects they have had on attitudes and self-images are more evident among older members of minority populations.

Interactions Among Factors. In considerations of racial and ethnic identity, as with other factors such as age and education, it is difficult to identify one condition and examine it in isolation from other variables. In any recreation behavior, a variety of individual characteristics, in combination and in interaction, have potential for influencing behavior. Murphy and others provided this illustration.

> A middle-income, American Indian female who is employed as a reading consultant on a rural county school superintendent's staff is a totality. Her financial status does not operate as an influencer independently of her sex identity, her racial heritage or her occupational role. The overall influence of these conditions is a result of the fact that they occur and operate together. One may be a more potent influencer; but even so, it does not exist in isolation of the other factors.[65]

Moreover, individual characteristics do not operate independently of the situational influences on recreation behavior. Bishop and Witt's study of the sources of variance in leisure behavior[66] supports this idea. The researchers compared two major sources of influence: the person and situational events or experiences. The *person* category assumed that individuals make relatively free choices of activities and that these choices are not influenced appreciably by external conditions or events. Rather, they are influenced by the individual's personality. The *situations* category assumed that events or experiences occurring prior to an individual's leisure behavior have direct influence on the choice of activity. That is, the selection is not free from the influences of situations. Bishop and Witt concluded that

> . . . neither persons nor situations, in terms of their simple effects have a great deal of influence on reported leisure behavior. The various interactions accounted for substantially more of the variance than did main effects of persons, situations, or modes of response.[67]

The combined influence of individual variables such as age and sexual identity may be relatively little when compared to other factors such as personality. Mueller and Gurin reported on a nationwide survey of the relationships of socioeconomic factors to outdoor recreation participation. The factors studied included income, education, occupation, place of residence, sex, age, life cycle and race. While the analysis did reveal relationships between these factors and participation, the influence was not great.

Taken together these factors account for approximately 30 percent of the variance in the measure of outdoor activity. It follows that characteristics additional to the socioeconomic characteristics included in the analysis are major determinants of levels of outdoor recreation activity. A number of factors come to mind readily—such as time available, access to facilities, the goals and interests which the individual seeks in his leisure time, recreation preferences of other family members and friends, psychological factors, recreation experiences in childhood, etc.[68]

Burch noted the "consistently poor fit between standard social variables and leisure behavior."[69] He suggested that these variables focus on the past and are inadequate for predicting future behaviors. Knudsen felt that the failure of socioeconomic variables to adequately explain recreation behavior was due to techniques of measurement.

Thus, socioeconomic variables, as measured, do not adequately explain the outdoor recreation participation patterns of people. Much of this is probably attributable to the manner of measurement of such variables and not to any lack of connection. Further work or more refined measurements and inferential analysis may help in making more reliable statements about socioeconomic variables as predictors of recreation behavior. Intuitively, one feels that the relationships seem to exist.[70]

Personality. Some researchers have taken the position that an individual's personality is a very potent influencer of leisure choices. Havighurst suggested that leisure behavior is an aspect of an individual's personality, that it occurs in response to personality needs, and that the significance of it is more determined by personality than by variables such as age, sex, and social class.[71] However, Neulinger questioned the usefulness of personality traits as predictors of behavior. He observed that correlations between different personality traits and different recreation behaviors have been found to be relatively low for practical use in predicting the leisure choices a person will make.[72] He suggested that

The main problem in trying to predict leisure behavior from personality traits may be that any given activity may fulfill different needs for different people, or even the same person at different times.[73]

In spite of the problems associated with attempts to use personality measures as predictors of behavior, it is apparent that personality traits do influence leisure choices.

Individuality. While general personality traits have been described by various theorists and test makers, each person is a unique individual. Brill observed that in some ways we are like all other people, in some ways like some others, and in some ways like no other person. Each person's individuality results from ". . . a unique genetic heritage in continuous and dynamic interaction with a unique life experience."[74]

As suggested earlier, it is possible to describe typical characteristics or behaviors that are associated with different age groups, for example, or different income groups. However, these descriptions cannot be thought of as applying to all members of the group in question. As an illustration, older adults typically experience a decline in physical energy. Even so, there is wide individual variation; some senior citizens have immense energy, and some middle-aged persons have relatively little. Our reactions to aging are only partly physical; mental outlook, emotional health, earlier life habits, and a host of other factors combine to create for each older person the "unique life experience" of which Brill spoke.

Environment.   The environments in which we live and play also influence our recreation behaviors. One obvious factor is the availability of leisure opportunities. Coastal areas permit surfing behavior; deserts ordinarily do not. The nature of the environment, including the various elements of land and water areas and the presence or absence of other people, influences the goals we seek as well as the activities in which we engage. For example, there is some evidence that people seek out, in free time, those environments which are comprised of different elements from the ones they occupy during nonfree-time periods. In a study of the environmental determinants of recreation behavior, Knopp suggested that

> Recreation may be thought of in terms of the environments as well as the activities man selects in his leisure. The environment may be more closely related to the functions or satisfactions derived from recreation than are activities or form.[75]

Knopp compared the values placed on outdoor recreation experiences by rural and urban populations. He concluded that

> . . . these groups placed relatively more value on several elements of the outdoor recreation experience which were less evident in their home and work environments.[76]

In a broad sense, the environments in which we live seem to have widespread and pervasive influences on behavior, generally. Different authors have described the effects of various types of living spaces, and differences in perceptions of personal space, or our zones of privacy.[77] Some of these factors have potential influence on recreation behavior. Writing specifically about leisure behavior, Cheek and Burch discussed the influences of "leisure locales" and presented a tentative classification. They suggested that there are relationships between the particular design or characteristic of each different type of environment and the types of behavior which occurs.[78] The particular characteristics of each locale include not only the physical design of spaces but also the sizes and the interrelationships of the groups that use them, and the symbolic meanings the locales have for people.

In Recreation Behavior, the Individual Interacts with Elements of an Environment.   Recreation behavior involves an individual doing something in an environment; the environment is the setting within which the behavior occurs. The setting includes all of the physical elements, as well as other people who might be present. For example, the setting within which downhill skiing occurs includes such elements as the mountainside, the lift, the trail or run markers, and the varying snow conditions and current weather. It also may include other people: friends with whom one is skiing, other people on the hill, lift operators, ski patrol members, and possibly spectators on the lodge deck. As suggested earlier, these factors have potential for influencing the behavior of any one skier. Different skiers may be influenced differently. Unbroken snow may be sought eagerly by the expert and avoided by the intermediate skier. The difficulty, or steepness of the slope, will attract skiers of different skill levels as well, perhaps, as those with different personalities. Some skiers may ski differently in the presence of friends than they would if skiing alone. As pointed out earlier, however, only those elements of the setting which the person is aware of will affect behavior.

The relationship between an environment and people engaging in recreation behavior is not unilateral. Behavior influences the environment. The presence of one skier on the slope creates a different environment than if the person were not there. If that individual skis recklessly, without regard for others on the hill, the environment is changed even further. A person who rides a trail bike illegally into a wilderness area changes the environment. A person who litters in a city park changes the environment. In a sense, the relationships between the participant and the environment might be thought of as a temporary ecological unit. The behavior is in response to the environment; if the behavior changes the environment, the modified setting may produce changes in subsequent behavior.

Some Things About Recreation Behavior Cannot Be Observed Directly.   Assume that we are watching someone ski a steep section of a hill at a major resort. We can observe, directly, the actual behavior—skiing the hill. We can see how the person handles the hill; we can observe the form, the speed of the run, the aggressiveness of the skier. But we cannot observe the skier's motives. We cannot see why the person is skiing that section. We do not know if the person is confident or frightened. We cannot see what the run means to the skier. All of these things must be inferred. We can make guesses about them, or we can ask the person.

If we make inferences, it is well to remember that behavior is best understood from the point of view of the person involved. Combs and Richards provided this insight into understanding others' behaviors.

> However capricious, irrelevant and irrational our behavior may appear to an outsider, from our point of view at the instant of the behavior it is purposeful, relevant, and pertinent to the situation as we understand it.[79]

USE AND NONUSE FACTORS

The general model of recreation behavior presented earlier and the major generalizations discussed in the previous section all focus primarily on the user of recreation and park services. Some factors are suggested, however, that help to explain why people do not use our services. For example, individuals may not see the recreation opportunities we offer as being related to their goals. They may not have the personal qualifications needed to participate; or they may not perceive that the opportunity to participate is available. All of these possible factors seem to fit within a second general model or scheme.[80]

The Basic Elements.   Assume the following situation. Edward Sebastian, a 27-year-old accountant, just moved to Sacramento from San Diego, California. He is in excellent health, and he has a good income. He engages in several low-energy leisure pursuits (for example, reading, attending movies, and other spectator events), but his physical recreation activity has been limited to surfing. In Sacramento, he has relatively little opportunity to surf.

Shortly after joining the firm, in December, he meets another accountant who skis. They eat lunch together two or three times and talk about skiing in the Sierra Nevada. Sebastian also sees a couple of ski reports on television. One day, on his way to work, he walks by a sports shop. He drops in and picks up some brochures on ski areas in the nearby Sierra Nevada, and gets information on equipment rental.

On Friday, he stops at the shop and rents skis, boots, and poles. Saturday morning, early, he departs for the mountains.

At the ski area, he purchases a lift ticket. Three hours later, he is wet, tired, bruised, and discouraged. He has spent more time on his back than on the skis, and he is convinced that he is lucky to have escaped with all limbs intact. After lunch at the lodge, he goes home.

Two weeks later, Sebastian bumps into an old friend who has just moved to Sacramento. The friend works for the Pacific Gas and Electric Company and has a week-end job teaching skiing at one of the areas at Lake Tahoe. He encourages Sebastian to come up and take lessons.

Over the remainder of the season, Sebastian develops his skill in week-end classes. His interest and his enjoyment continue to increase.

Sebastian's involvement in skiing might be represented by the model illustrated in Figures 3-2, 3-3, and 3-4.

Awareness.   Sebastian was a potential user (that is, a potential skier). However, there was no likelihood that he would become a participant until he became aware of the activity. This condition simply says that one factor contributing to use or nonuse is awareness.

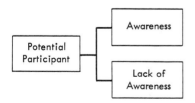

Figure 3-2 Use/nonuse factors (awareness).

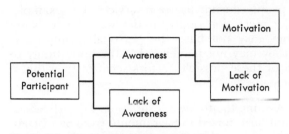

Figure 3-3 Use/nonuse factors (motivation).

The participant must have at least some awareness of the activity for it to be a possible behavior for him or her.

Motivation. Awareness alone does not lead to participation. The individual must want, to some degree, to engage in the activity. Somewhere along the line, Sebastian developed a desire to try skiing. His interest may have been sparked when he talked to the fellow accountant, when he saw the television reports, or when he dropped into the sport shop. It may have been strengthened by a deeper desire for physical activity, perhaps as a replacement for surfing. Whatever the particular combination of events and conditions, he was motivated to try skiing. Without such motivation, he would have been a nonuser.

Opportunity. However, motivation alone will not assure use. There must be opportunity. Opportunity and motivation are linked. The presence of perceived opportunity might create motivation. Conversely, if a person is strongly motivated, opportunity might be created.

Sebastian had the opportunity. Skiing was geographically accessible to him; he had adequate health and fitness for the activity and sufficient time and financial resources to participate. Initially, he lacked skill, but he overcame this restriction.

These elements—geographic and environmental resources, health and fitness, financial resources, time and knowledge and skill—seem to define the immediate limits of an individual's opportunities to participate. They are subject to change, but they influence the immediate capacity to

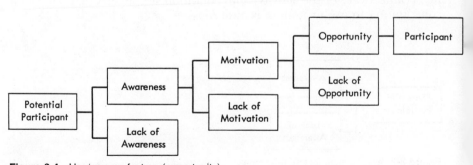

Figure 3-4 Use/nonuse factors (opportunity).

use or not to use facilities and programs. Endless examples could be offered. It is difficult to climb mountains in Iowa. The older adult, with cardiac problems, may not be able to hike into wilderness areas. The poverty mother may not be able to afford the ceramics class. The physician may not have time to participate in the community orchestra, while the young pianist may not have sufficient skill to do so.

Another factor might be added. The climate for participation must be at least somewhat encouraging or accepting if we are to become users. As suggested earlier, some environments are prohibited by law; minors cannot legally frequent bars and the unlicensed driver cannot legally operate a motor vehicle, even if he has the skill. Restrictions are also imposed, more subtly, in terms of social sanctions and expectations. The beginning tennis player who would like to join the club may not because he does not have appropriate apparel or because he does not know the modes of behavior which are expected on and off the courts. The woman who enjoys billiards may find in some communities, even today, social expectations strongly against her participation. Restrictions based on expectations and sanctions seem to be lessening. However, such restrictions continue to exert some influence on the opportunities any given individual possesses.

Whatever the specifics, each person's unique complex characteristics interact with the environment to produce what might be called an *opportunity framework*. For some, this framework is fairly large. For others, the framework of opportunities is consistently limited. The aged, the poor, the ill, and the disabled are typically in this category. These are the people who seem most often to be nonusers—not by choice, but because of environmental and personal restrictions.

A Community Illustration.   The skiing illustration embodied the basic notions of use and nonuse. The following hypothetical situation illustrates these factors in a public recreation and park department:

The Broderick Street Recreation Center recently initiated a new morning program for preschool youngsters. The program was well planned by the center staff, and there was a high participation potential because many young families live in the area. However, there were very few sign-ups for the program and only two or three mothers have been bringing their children. Analysis by the area supervisor revealed the following contributing factors:

Awareness.   The program was publicized in the community newspaper by two announcements and one article. The center director also asked the Broderick Elementary School principal if he would ask the three primary-grade teachers to send notes home with the children in their classes. Some nonuse potential was introduced at this point. Many residents of the neighborhood do not subscribe to the paper, and two of the teachers forgot to send home notes with the children.

Motivation.   Broderick Recreation Center has an excellent program staff. They have a good reputation in the community for providing effective programs. However, earlier cutbacks in the departmental budget required that the city's maintenance staff be reduced. As a partial result, all of the centers have been less well maintained. The grass has not been cut as often as it was previously; trash has been collected less frequently; and the general condition of the building has deteriorated somewhat. In addition, older, out-of-school youth have recently been hanging around the center grounds during the morning. These conditions led to some conflict situations on the part of those parents who were aware of the program. The reputation of the center staff contributed to a desire to enroll their children. However, the presence of the older youth created some parental fear that younger children might be bothered, and the deteriorating appearance of the center tipped the balance in favor of avoiding the situation and not participating.

Opportunity.   The center staff decided to set up the preschool program on a partially self-supporting basis. A nominal fee was planned to cover the costs of supplies. The program also was organized using mothers as aides. Each mother was to volunteer one morning, every other week. These two conditions ruled participation out for most of the parents who knew about the program and who wished to participate. The registration fee, even though nominal, was excessive for young families on very limited budgets. In addition, several mothers also had infants who required care during the times when they would be expected to assist with the program.

The Decision Making Process.   At various points in the earlier illustrations, individuals decided to either participate or not participate. Chubb and Chubb presented a comprehensive description of the participation process, that includes four decision making stages.[81] These stages contribute to an understanding of use and nonuse.

1. Based on initial awareness of an activity (for example, backpacking), the potential participant *assesses the relative value* of the activity in comparison with other activities. "Will I get more satisfaction from backpacking than from tennis?"

2. If the answer is "yes," the individual then *assesses the probability that participation actually will result in the possible benefits.* "If I hike in Grand Teton National Park will I really enjoy it? Would it be better if I went to the Summit Lake Wilderness area, that is familiar and closer to home?"

3. If the original idea seems likely to produce the expected satisfaction, the individual then *assesses personal suitability.* "Is this activity really for me? Do I want to drive that far? Will I be comfortable in a new and unfamiliar area?"

4. If answers to questions in the third stage are "yes," then the individual *assesses the feasibility* of going. "Do I have enough vacation time? Am I in good enough physical condition to hike in that kind of country?"

The above examples suggest that if we want to expand the numbers of people who directly use our services, we first need to be certain that they are aware of the opportunities that are available to them.

We need to use our resources so as to provide for services that appeal to a broad range of possible motivations or goals. And we need to do what we can to help people see how our services can contribute to goals they may have.

If we wish to reduce the numbers of nonusers in our communities, we need to make some inferences about the opportunity frameworks within which people live. We need to define restrictions and to identify those over which we may have influence. In some agencies, these kinds of analyses probably will have to be made on a group basis or in terms of "modal" characteristics—at least initially. However, the more our efforts can be individualized the more effective we will be.

Perhaps most basically, we need to become more sensitive to the sociopsychological and environmental factors that influence the behavior of the people we serve and those we do not serve.

STAFF BEHAVIOR

The material presented in this chapter is intended to provide some insights about recreation behavior. However, much of the information is applicable to an understanding of the behavior of staff members. The model of behavior discussed earlier also can be used to understand the actions of staff members. As an illustration, assume that you are the chief ranger at a state park, and that you have an interpreter on your staff who is in charge of the park's visitor center. The interpreter will have certain goals that she hopes to achieve. Assume that one of these is to help visitors understand more fully the importance of not feeding wildlife encountered on the park's several nature trails. She might think of several ways to accomplish this— that is, several plans, one of which she will select for trial. This leads to a response—say a new slide show in the visitor center designed to show the undesirable effects of wildlife eating and becoming dependent upon nonnatural foods. She then evaluates the results of her response. If people seem to feed the animals and birds less, we can assume that she feels some satisfaction and that she would continue using the slide show. If the behaviors of users do not change, she might try a different plan.

Assume that another ranger wishes to get a pay raise (a goal). He believes the way to do so is to write a letter (a plan) to your supervisor, complaining about how he is underpaid. He does so (the response). Your supervisor returns the letter to him (result), asking if he has discussed the matter with you, and if not, to do so. Countless other examples could be described.

Staff behavior also is influenced by all of the various generalizations discussed in this chapter. Staff behavior usually is purposeful and goal directed. It is influenced by a great variety of personal and environmental factors. As staff interact with the environments within which they work, both their behaviors and the environments might be changed. There are aspects of staff behavior that often cannot be observed directly, such as their goals, feelings, and self-concepts. And, finally, the key to understanding staff behavior is to try to see it from their perspectives. The perceptions they have, individually, are the bases upon which they understand reality, and therefore are the bases for their behaviors.

Since most recreation and park personnel consistently work with other staff members, understandings of staff behavior are important.

SUMMARY

Recreation and park personnel who possess some basic understandings of behavior have advantages in working with people.

In attempting to develop these understandings, we can view behavior from two major perspectives: the behaviorist tradition, which focuses on observable phenomena, and the humanist tradition, which gives greater emphasis to internal influences such as attitudes and perceptions. The views are not mutually exclusive, and an awareness of both perspectives contributes to an overall understanding.

Recreation behavior itself is characterized by the participant's perception of relative freedom and by the fact that the behavior is motivated primarily by direct enjoyment of the activity in which the person is engaging. The behavior results in an experience; this experience and the attending emotional state produced in the individual might be thought of as the essence of recreation.

Various theories have been developed that attempt to explain recreation behavior and play. While these theories are not completely compatible, and while some have apparent shortcomings, they do contribute to our understandings of such questions as why people engage in recreation and what factors influence such behavior. The theories that have been generated can be cast into several categories, based on such factors as the importance given to the idea of instinct, the relative emphasis on development and learning, the degrees which recreation serves needs different from or similar to other aspects of life, and the general types of benefits thought to result from leisure activity. Several approaches to studying play also have been developed that identify the influences of such factors as cultural values, personal characteristics, and social and environmental variations.

It is possible to define a general model of recreation behavior. The model suggests that there are several different elements in any unit of such behavior: the participant, the participant's goal (or goals), a plan for achieving this goal (or goals), the observable response, the participant's perceptions of the consequences of behaving or of the response, and the setting within which the behavior occurs. These elements interact in a fluid, on-going way; however, to facilitate understanding an artificial separation of them can be made.

The model also suggests several generalizations about recreation behavior. It is purposeful and goal oriented. People engage in recreation to achieve certain goals. The nature of the behavior, directed toward achieving these goals, is influenced significantly by people's perceptions of themselves and of the environments in which they are behaving. Recreation behavior also is influenced by a variety of other personal and environmental factors, such as age, education level, personality, and place of residence. Since many of these factors, including perception, are not directly observable, some aspects of recreation behavior are understandable only by inference. Environmental influences are not unilateral; the individual is influenced by the characteristics of the environment, and he or she in turn changes that environment.

There are some general factors that lead to recreation behavior. For such behavior to occur, an individual must be aware of the activity, must be motivated to engage in it, and must have the opportunity to do so.

The model of recreation behavior, and the associated generalizations, also apply largely to staff behaviors. Recreation and park personnel usually function as part of agency staffs. This means they interact with other staff members in their own agencies as well as in other related agencies. Understandings of behavior can be drawn upon in these situations, to help personnel function more effectively.

REVIEW QUESTIONS

3-1 What are the characteristics of recreation behavior? How is this kind of behavior similar to any other behavior? How is it different?

3-2 What different theoretical explanations of recreation behavior have been developed? Which of these seem most logical to you? Why?

3-3 In the general model of behavior several different dimensions or aspects were described. What are these?

3-4 What variables influence the form recreation behavior takes for different individuals? For example, why does one person tool leather, another watch TV, and yet another race automobiles?

3-5 How does perception influence recreation behavior?

3-6 What factors lead to nonuse of leisure services? What are barriers to participation?

TO DO

3-A Think about your own recreation behavior. Identify several favorite activities—things you like to do. Write these down on the left-hand side of a piece of paper. Now, work with this list in the following ways:

1. Behind each activity (in the space to the right) briefly describe why you engage in the activity. What are your motives? What do you expect to get out of it?

2. Mark activities on your list according to these symbols (as they apply). Use the space immediately to the left of each activity.

> 6–   I engage in this more than six times a year.
> $10   This costs more than $10 each time I engage in it.
> 12H   This requires fairly large blocks of time
>   (at least one full day).
> I   This is something I can do by myself.
> N   This is something I started doing in the last year,
>   something new I learned.

3. Look back over the list, your comments and the symbols, and write a short statement that characterizes your overall leisure behavior.

3-B Write down several recreation behaviors that you would like to engage in but do not. For each one, list why you do not engage in it. What factors keep you from participating?

3-C In the job you described in item 1-A (Chapter 1) what kinds of people will you probably be trying to serve? Write a brief description of them—their probable ages, income levels, occupations, and so on. What do you think will be the primary reasons that these people will use your services? What factors might limit their participation?

END NOTES

1. This illustration, and the general model of recreation behavior and the discussion of use and nonuse factors presented later in the chapter, are taken from E. William Niepoth, "Users and Non-Users of Recreation and Park Services" in *Reflections on the Recreation and Park Movement,* ed. David Gray and Donald A. Pelegrino, (Dubuque, Iowa: Wm.C. Brown Company, Publishers, 1973), p. 132. Used with permission of the publisher.

2. Arthur W. Combs, Donald L. Avila and William W. Purkey, *Helping Relationships: Basic Concepts for the Helping Professions* 2nd. ed. (Boston: Allyn and Bacon, Inc., 1978), pp. 106–11; Nelson F. DuBois, George F. Alverson and Richard K. Staley, *Educational Psychology and Instructional Decisions* (Homewood, Ill.: The Dorsey Press, 1979), pp. 39–41.

3. Roger C. Mannell, "Social Psychological Techniques and Strategies for Studying Leisure Experiences," in *Social Psychological Perspectives on Leisure and Recreation,* ed. Seppo E. Iso-Ahola (Springfield, Ill.: Charles C Thomas, Publisher, 1980), p. 69.

4. Mannel, "Social Psychological Techniques and Strategies for Studying Leisure Experiences," in *Social Psychological Perspectives on Leisure and Recreation,* pp. 70–71.

5. B. L. Driver and S. Ross Tocher, "Toward a Behavioral Interpretation of Recreational Engagements, with Implications for Planning," in *Elements of Outdoor Recreational Planning,* ed. B. L. Driver (Ann Arbor: University of Michigan, University Microfilms, 1970), pp. 9–31.

6. Driver and Tocher, "Toward a Behavioral Interpretation of Recreational Engagements, with Implications for Planning," in *Elements of Outdoor Recreation Planning,* p. 10.

7. Ibid., p. 21.

8. Joseph Levy, *Play Behavior* (New York: John Wiley & Sons, Inc., 1978) pp. 6–19.

9. Seppo E. Iso-Ahola, "Intrinsic Motivation: An Overlooked Basis for Evaluation," *Parks & Recreation* 17, no. 2 (February, 1982): 32–33.

10. Iso-Ahola, "Intrinsic Motivation," p. 33.

11. Seymour Greben and David Gray, "Future Perspectives of the Park and Recreation Movement" (Paper presented at the National Congress for Recreation and Parks, Washington, D.C., October 1973), pp. 14–15.)

12. For a discussion of these characteristics, see Mannel, "Social Psychological Techniques and Strategies for Studying Leisure Experiences," in *Social Psychological Perspectives on Leisure and Recreation,* pp. 75–77, 81–84.

13. Clayne R. Jensen, *Outdoor Recreation in America: Trends, Problems and Opportunities,* 3rd ed. (Minneapolis, Minn.: Burgess Publishing Company, 1977), pp. 10–11.

14. Michael Chubb and Holly R. Chubb, *One Third of Our Time? An Introduction to Recreation Behavior and Resources* (New York: John Wiley & Sons, Inc., 1981), pp. 230–35.

15. James F. Murphy and others, *Leisure Services Delivery Systems: A Modern Perspective* (Philadelphia: Lea and Febiger, 1973), pp. 73–76.

16. M. J. Ellis, *Why People Play* (Englewood Cliffs, N.J.: Prentice-Hall, Inc., 1973), pp. 49–79.

17. Ellis, *Why People Play*, p. 49.

18. Ibid., pp. 80–111.

19. Ibid., p. 110.

20. Ibid., pp. 112–18.

21. R. E. Herron and Brian Sutton-Smith, *Child's Play* (New York. John Wiley & Sons, Inc., 1971).

22. Joseph Levy, *Play Behavior* pp. 156–81.

23. Levy, *Play Behavior*, p. 72.

24. Joseph Levy, "A Paradigm for Conceptualizing Leisure Behavior: Towards A Person-Environment Interaction Analysis," *Journal of Leisure Research* 11, no. 1 (1979):48–59. Also, Levy, *Play Behavior*, pp. 52–72.

25. Levy, *Play Behavior*, p. 64.

26. Levy, "A Paradigm for Conceptualizing Leisure Behavior," pp. 57–58.

27. Max Kaplan, *Leisure: Theory and Policy* (New York: John Wiley & Sons, Inc., 1975), pp. 30–44.

28. Kaplan, *Leisure: Theory and Policy*, pp. 35–36.

29. Ibid., p. 35.

30. Ibid., pp. 52–85.

31. Ibid., pp. 113–14.

32. Studies on various aspects of recreation behavior are reported in such publications as the *Journal of Leisure Research* and *Leisure Sciences*. In addition, the National Recreation and Park Association publishes abstracts of research reported at NRPA Congresses. For example, see the "Psychology of Leisure," "Play Behavior," and "Sociology of Leisure" sections in *Abstracts From the 1980 Symposium on Leisure Research* (Arlington, Va.: National Recreation and Park Association, 1980). Also, related research may be found in journals such as the *Journal of Personality and Social Psychology*.

33. Lee Joseph Cronbach, *Educational Psychology* (New York: Harcourt Brace Jovanovich, Inc., 1954), pp. 45–47, 49–51. The model of recreation behavior is taken from Niepoth, "Users and Non-Users of Recreation and Park Services," in *Reflections on the Recreation and Park Movement*, ed. Gray and Pellegrino (W. C. Brown Co., Publishers), pp. 132–36.

34. Howard E. A. Tinsley, "The Ubiquitous Question of Why," *New Thoughts on Leisure: Selected Papers from the Allen V. Sapora Symposium on Leisure and Recreation*, ed. D. James Brademas (University of Illinois at Urbana-Champaign: May, 1977), pp. 86–98.

35. Howard E. A. Tinsley, Thomas C. Barrett and Richard A. Kass," Leisure Activities and Need Satisfaction," *Journal of Leisure Research* 9, no. 2 (1977):110–19.

36. Howard E. A. Tinsley and Richard A. Kass, "Leisure Activities and Need Satisfaction: A Replication and Extension," *Journal of Leisure Research* 10, no. 3 (1978): 191–202.

37. Douglass K. Hawes, "Satisfaction Derived From Leisure-Time Pursuits: An Exploratory Nationwide Survey," *Journal of Leisure Research* 10, no. 4 (1978): 247–64.

38. Mounir G. Ragheb and Jacob G. Beard, "Leisure Satisfaction: Concept, Theory, and Measurement," in *Social Psychological Perspectives on Leisure and Recreation*, pp. 336–38.

39. Thomas Buchanan and Rabel J. Burdge, "Satisfactions and Secondary Activities: A Canonical Analysis," in *Abstracts From the 1980 Symposium on Leisure Research*, p. 11.

40. Rick Crandall, "Social Interaction, Affect and Leisure," *Journal of Leisure Research* 11, no. 3 (Third Quarter 1979):166.

41. David Krech, Richard S. Crutchfield, and Edgerton L. Ballachey, *Individual in Society* (New York: McGraw Hill Book Co., 1962), pp. 89–99.

42. Abraham H. Maslow, "A Theory of Human Motivation," *Psychological Review* 50, no. 4 (July 1943): 370–96. Maslow's theory is accepted widely. However, some questions about it have been raised. See Seppo E. Iso-Ahola, *The Social Psychology of Leisure and Recreation* (Dubuque, Iowa: William C. Brown Company Publishers, 1980) pp. 233–36.

43. For discussions of the substitutability concept, see: Robert Baumgartner and Thomas A. Heberlein, "Process, Goal, and Social Interaction: What Makes an Activity Substitutable," *Leisure Sciences* 4, no. 4 (1981):443–58. James E. Christiansen and Dean R. Yosting, "The Substitutability Concept: A Need for Further Development," *Journal of Leisure Research* 9, no. 3 (Third Quarter 1977): 188–207; John C. Hendee and Rabel J. Burdge, "The Substitutability Concept: Implications for Recreation Research and Management," *Journal of Leisure Research* 6, no. 2 (Spring 1974): 157–62; and William Moss and Stephen C. Lamphear, "Substitutability of Recreational Activities in Meeting Stated Needs and Drives of the Visitor," *Environmental Education* 1, no. 4 (Summer, 1970): 129–31.

44. Driver and Tocher, "Toward a Behavioral Interpretation of Recreational Engagements, with Implications for Planning," in *Elements of Outdoor Recreation Planning*, pp. 16–18.

45. Peter A. Witt and Doyle W. Bishop, "Situational Antecedents to Leisure Behavior," *Journal of Leisure Research* 2, no. 1 (Winter 1970): 64–77.

46. Arthur W. Combs, Anne Cohen Richards, and Fred Richards, *Perceptual Psychology: A Humanistic Approach to the Study of Persons* (New York: Harper & Row, Publishers, 1959), p. 22.

47. Seppo E. Iso-Ahola, "Toward a Dialectical Social Psychology of Leisure and Recreation," in *Social Psychological Perspectives on Leisure and Recreation*, p. 31.

48. Tony A. Mobley, Stephen S. Light, and John Neulinger, "Leisure Attitudes and Program Participation," *Parks and Recreation* 11, no. 12 (December 1976): 20–22.

49. John Neulinger, *The Psychology of Leisure: Research Approaches to the Study of Leisure* (Springfield, Ill.: Charles C. Thomas, Publisher, 1974), pp. 57–60.

50. Neulinger, *The Psychology of Leisure*, p. 130.

51. Rick Crandall and Karla Slivken, "Leisure Attitudes and Their Measurement," in *Social Psychological Perspectives on Leisure and Recreation*, p. 262.

52. Neulinger, *The Psychology of Leisure*, p. 92.

53. For example, see James F. Murphy, *Concepts of Leisure* 2nd ed. (Englewood Cliffs, N.J.: Prentice-Hall, Inc., 1981), pp. 134–52; and Neulinger, *The Psychology of Leisure*, pp. 92–114.

54. R. Schmitz-Scherzer and I. Strodel, "Age Dependency of Leisure-Time Activities," *Human Development* 14, no. 1 (1971): 47–50.

55. Richard G. Kraus, *Recreation Today: Program Planning and Leadership* 2nd ed. (Santa Monica, Calif.: Goodyear Publishing Company, Inc., 1977), p. 103.

56. Kraus, *Recreation Today*, pp. 106–7.

57. Clayne R. Jensen, *Outdoor Recreation in America*, p. 182.

58. Neil H. Cheek, Jr. and William R. Burch, Jr., *The Social Organization of Leisure in Human Society* (New York: Harper & Row, Publishers, 1976), p. 71.

59. Douglas M. Knudson, *Outdoor Recreation* (New York: MacMillan Publishing Co., Inc., 1980), p. 72.

60. Cheek and Burch, *The Social Organization of Leisure in Human Society*, p. 49.

61. Murphy, *Concepts of Leisure*, p. 139.

62. Kaplan, *Leisure*, p. 94.

63. Cheek and Burch, *The Social Organization of Leisure in Human Society*, p. 70.

64. Murphy, *Concepts of Leisure* 2nd ed., pp. 145–51; Neulinger, *Psychology of Leisure*, p. 104.

65. Murphy and others, *Leisure Services Delivery System*, p. 86.

66. Doyle W. Bishop and Peter A. Witt, "Sources of Behavioral Variance During Leisure Time," *Journal of Personality and Social Psychology* 16, no. 2 (October 1970): 352–60.

67. Bishop and Witt, "Sources of Behavioral Variance During Leisure Time," *Journal of Personality and Social Psychology*, p. 358.

68. Eva Mueuer and Gerald Gurin, *Participation in Outdoor Recreation: Factors Affecting Demand Among American Adults* (Washington, D.C.: Outdoor Recreation Resources Review Commission, Study Report 20, 1962), pp. 69–70.

69. William R. Burch, Jr., "The Social Circles of Leisure: Competing Explanations," *Journal of Leisure Research* 1, no. 2. (Spring 1969): 125.

70. Knudson, *Outdoor Recreation*, p. 43.

71. Robert J. Havighurst, "The Leisure Activities of the Middle-Aged," *American Journal of Sociology* 63, no. 2 (September 1957): 152–62.

72. Neulinger, *The Psychology of Leisure*, p. 110.

73. Ibid., p. 111.

74. Naomi J. Brill, *Working with People*, 2nd ed. (Philadelphia: J. B. Lippincott Co., © 1978), p. 28. Reprinted by permission of Harper & Row, Pub.

75. Timothy B. Knopp, "Environmental Determinants of Recreation Behavior," *Journal of Leisure Research* 4, no. 2, (Spring, 1972): 129.

76. Knopp, "Environmental Determinants of Recreation Behavior," *Journal of Leisure Research*, p. 129.

77. For example, see: J. Douglas Porteous, *Environment & Behavior: Planning and Everyday Urban Life* (Reading, Mass.: Addison-Wesley Publishing Company, 1977), pp. 19–58; Marvin E. Shaw, *Group Dynamics: The Psychology of Small Group Behavior* (New York: McGraw-Hill Book Company, 1971), pp. 117–52; and Robert Sommer, *Personal Space: The Behavioral Basis of Design* (Englewood Cliffs, N.J.: Prentice-Hall, Inc., 1969), pp. 12–73.

78. Cheek and Burch, *The Social Organization of Leisure in Human Society*, pp. 154–57.

79. Combs, Richards and Richards, *Perceptual Psychology*, p. 20.

80. This section on use and nonuse factors is taken from Niepoth, "Users and Non-Users of Recreation and Park Services," in *Reflections on the Recreation and Park Movement*, pp. 137–52.

81. Chubb and Chubb, *One Third of Our Time?* pp. 237–40.

chapter 4

Helping and Related Interpersonal Relationships

PREVIEW

Understandings of behavior help recreation and park personnel carry out their responsibilities more effectively. This is especially true for activities that involve working with people. The common element evident in these activities is an interpersonal relationship between the leisure service worker and the individual or individuals who use agency services.

Leading, teaching, and working with groups all involve the development of appropriate interpersonal relationships. These processes will be considered in later chapters. Chapter 4 will focus on some general aspects of interpersonal relationships.

A large part of the chapter will be devoted to a look at the helping process. This is a particular way of working with people that enables them to grow in their abilities to solve their own problems. Recreation and park personnel often have opportunities to help others deal with a variety of personal problems. In addition, the elements of the helping process are applicable to interpersonal relationships generally. For these reasons, helping is given considerable attention in this chapter. Types of requests for help, some basic assumptions about helping, and helper characteristics will be discussed; and the various steps involved in helping will be examined.

Helping, and other interpersonal relationships, rely on the worker's use of "self"—that is, on the use of personal skills and knowledges in combination with the worker's own unique personality. In this sense, the "self" becomes a resource or an instrument to be used in working with others. The use of self requires self-awareness. Factors that contribute to such awareness will be considered.

Contacts between people often result in conflict. Some ideas about conflict will be presented.

The chapter will conclude with a brief look at counseling as a type of interpersonal relationship.

An older patient was in the secluded corner of the convalescent home's lounge. With her sat the patient activities director. Except for the two of them, the lounge was empty, but the cluttered remains of a birthday party were apparent—decorations, the last of the cake, and wrappings from presents. It was obvious that she had been crying, and that she was still upset. The director was holding her hand and listening as she talked.

In a state park, east of the community in which the convalescent home was located, a new ranger was facing his first day of boat patrol on the park's lake. His new assignment required checking safety equipment on board boats using the lake, enforcing speed limits in restricted areas, and giving citations for violations. He had just completed six weeks of police school, and he was armed. But he was not comfortable with the authority role he was assuming, and he was apprehensive about his ability to do the job. He sat in the park superintendent's office, somewhat reluctantly telling the superintendent how he felt. The superintendent listened, encouraged the ranger to talk about his feelings, and shared his confidence in the ranger's ability.

Personnel in recreation and parks inevitably assume responsibilities for working with people.

A ranger requests a group of park users to comply with regulations in the campground; an interpreter leads a sixth-grade class along a nature trail; a recreation therapist conducts an on-ward party for neuropsychiatric patients; a Girl Scout district executive provides a Saturday training session for adult volunteers; a recreation supervisor convenes a weekly staff meeting; a park superintendent works with a conference planning committee of the professional organization; the general manager of a recreation and park district meets with a citizens committee to promote an upcoming bond election; and a youth center director meets with a school counselor and a juvenile officer from a probation department to discuss several adolescent problem cases. All of these individuals are working with people. The list of illustrations could be expanded almost endlessly. All of these activities involve interpersonal relationships.

THE NATURE OF INTERPERSONAL RELATIONSHIPS

Interpersonal relationships are interactions between people. Usually, two people are involved in any relationship, even if it occurs in a group setting. For example, the interpreter will interact with various students in the sixth-grade class. While the interactions will tend to be similar, each may result in a different relationship between the interpreter and the specific child. The Girl Scout district executive will work with all of the volunteers in the training session, but probably will interact with each individual as she does so. Different relationships may develop. These and other relationships will exist over time. Some are fairly brief: others last for many years. They involve feelings, and they are behaviors. The various generalizations about behavior, discussed in the last chapter, are applicable. Our interactions are influenced by our perceptions, needs and motives, self-concepts, and past experiences in relating to other people. Interpersonal relationships include both direct contacts and the remembrances or anticipations that result from direct contacts. The relationship between the youth center director and the juvenile officer probably was initiated by direct contact—a conversation, meeting, phone call, or perhaps a letter. The relationship probably developed as the two individuals had further contacts. However, the relationship continues between these times of actually working together. Each individual remembers the other, and each probably has expectations about working together in the future. That is, the relationship continues, based on past experiences and the anticipation of future interactions. The direct contacts, upon which relationships are built, occur through various forms of communication.

Griffin and Patton presented a useful concept of how a relationship develops, based on the perceptions and needs of the two individuals involved.

> As you meet another person for the first time you carry along with you your own needs for interaction; perceiving these needs of your own is the first step in the process of forming a satisfying relationship. Second, you perceive the potential of the other person for satisfying these needs. Some people tend to slight the next two steps in the process, thus antagonizing persons with whom they interact; for a full and satisfying relationship to develop, steps three and four are critical. The third step is to perceive the interpersonal needs of the other person. Step four is to perceive one's own ability to satisfy the other person's needs.[1]

The authors observed that three types of needs are involved; needs related to social interaction, needs to reach agreements about control, and needs related to the giving and receiving of affection or to reducing hostility.[2] Control is concerned with how decisions in a relationship will be made and by whom. It involves such things as dominance, influence, and the use of power.[3]

Griffin and Patton indicated that these three needs form the basic dimensions found in most human relationships; the amounts of involvement and control, and the emotional tone. Assume the weekly staff meeting called by the recreation supervisor. Interpersonal relationships will exist between the supervisor and the various staff members. These relationships will differ with the differing amounts of involvement: how much interaction occurs between the supervisor and an individual staff member, and the importance it has for each of them. Control also will be present: the degree of authority exercised by the supervisor, and the extent to which the staff member accepts it or rejects it. Finally, there will be an emotional tone that exists between the two; the tone may be friendly and accepting or it may be more hostile or cold.

If the staff has worked together for a period of time, the degree of interaction between the supervisor and each member will probably be stable; at least relatively so, even though there are routine and expected variations from day to day. This is true in most relationships. Therefore, the dimensions of control and emotional tone are the most important considerations.[4] Griffin and Patton observed that each of these dimensions exists along a continuum; from dominance to submission for power, and from affection to hostility for emotional tone.[5] They suggested that any interpersonal relationship can be described by identifying the points along each of the continuums that best characterizes the interactions between the two individuals involved. The recreation supervisor's relationship with a particular staff member might be described as friendly, in which decisions that influence each of them are shared. The park ranger's relationship with a campground user, who is violating a minor regulation might be described as neutral in emotional tone, with the ranger in a dominant role.

HELPING AS AN INTERPERSONAL RELATIONSHIP

Often the act of working with people takes the form of a helping relationship—an interpersonal exchange where one person helps another person (or persons) accomplish a goal. This could involve the recreation and park worker with participants, as in the case of a senior adult center director helping an individual cope with an unfavorable housing situation. Or it might be in a staff relationship, where the center director is helping a new leader be more sensitive to the needs and feelings of older adults. The park superintendent helping the new ranger deal with anxiety is another illustration.

In the broad sense, teaching and leading and most of the other things recreation and park personnel do, as they work with people, can be thought of as helping relationships. This is a true and useful generalization. The characteristics of helping relationships are also applicable to other interpersonal processes.

In a more limited sense, however, helping is the act of relating to another person in such a way that the person grows in the ability to cope with problems. We all encounter a great variety of problems in our everyday lives. Some are small, insignificant, and easily solved. Others are more difficult or more significant. Usually we are able to handle the problems we face, often with the help of others. Sometimes the help comes from someone we go to on a professional basis—a physician or a lawyer, for example. Frequently, a friend or family member helps us. Recreation and park personnel often help either participants or staff members to solve problems which they confront.

The question might be asked, Should we do this? Isn't doing so going beyond our area of responsibility? The answers to these questions grow out of a reexamination of our purposes. The field exists to help people enjoy leisure opportunities. That means that as recreation and park professionals we are concerned with the enrichment of life; with enjoyment. If there are problems which people face that detract from their capacities for enjoying free time, and if we can help in the solutions of these problems, then our attempts to help will be consistent with our overall responsibilities. True, we cannot get into attempts to help that are beyond our abilities; we are not marriage counselors, pastors, psychoanalysts, or probation officers. Also, we must weigh the costs of any particular helping attempt, in terms of time and energy, against the probable values, in terms of our overall responsibilities. But to fail to be sensitive to opportunities for providing appropriate help in appropriate situations is to miss an important part of the delivery of leisure services. The following anecdote will illustrate:

> The Senior Adult Club advisor's door opens and one of the members greets her cheerfully. He enters and sits down across from her. The conversation moves easily from the weather and club happenings to the main reason for the visit. The advisor begins by recalling that, during their last visit, the member had expressed the worry that he was not getting along well with other members of the club. He had felt that he was losing friends and that he found it more difficult to be comfortable with other members. The director had encouraged him to talk and express his feelings; then she and he together had explored possible reasons why he felt as he did. They had agreed to meet again today, and she had reassured him that their discussions would be kept confidential.
>
> After the brief review of the previous meeting, the advisor helps the member explore possible courses of action that might help him feel better. Together, they discuss alternatives and plans. With her support, he decides upon some initial behaviors to try and an overall, longer-range plan. They agree to meet again next week.

The advisor may have no direct responsibility for working with the club member in the improvement of his interpersonal relationships. However, the capacity of the member to enjoy the activities of the club probably is dependent directly upon his relationships with the other members.

Similarly, the park superintendent mentioned at the beginning of the chapter may have no professional concern for the feelings and anxieties of his staff members. However, he does have the responsibility to help them work as effectively and as efficiently as possible. This responsibility, if none other, would cause him to be concerned about their problems, since it is clear that personal problems influence a worker's ability to perform on the job.

There are additional reasons for developing competence in helping. Helping depends upon certain kinds of behaviors on the part of the helper and on certain beliefs about people. These behaviors and beliefs seem most applicable to the everyday activities of recreation and park personnel as they work with people. Personnel who develop effective helping skills will become more effective, generally, in interpersonal relationships.

THE NATURE OF REQUESTS FOR HELP

Gazda, Asbury, Balzer, Childers and Walters have identified four categories of requests for help: (1) requests for something to be done, (2) requests for information of some kind, (3) requests for "inappropriate interaction," and (4) requests for understanding and involvement.[6]

Requests for action and information are common. A member of the Senior Adult Club might ask the advisor to start a great books discussion group, or to post a current city bus schedule. He might ask for information about next month's program or about medical care facilities in the community.

Requests for inappropriate interaction are statements that have potential for damaging relationships. Gazda and his colleagues included the following types of requests:

> . . . (1) gossip, (2) inordinate griping, (3) rumor, (4) solicitation of a dependency relationship, and (5) encouragement of activities that are counter to the benefit of other persons or the organization. . . .[7]

Such requests usually cannot be honored, but in refusing them the helper needs to be careful not to destroy a relationship. Sometimes such requests are symptomatic of legitimate problems with which the person needs help.

Requests for understanding and involvement seem to have at least two characteristics: first, the feelings of the person making the request are involved and are an important dimension in the request, and second, the request usually is for a relationship rather than for a direct answer. Sometimes a request for understanding and involvement is stated as a request for information or action because the person making the request cannot express the need directly. For example, a child in a beginning swimming class might say something like, "What happens if I won't put my face in the water?" What she may mean is, "I am afraid of putting my face in the water, and I hope you can understand how I feel." Or, as suggested earlier, an inappropriate request might be a disguised request for understanding and involvement.

This chapter is concerned primarily with helping relationships based on understanding and involvement. The premise is that recreation and park personnel have frequent opportunities to help with problems that do not require the expertise of other specialized professionals such as social workers, therapeutic counselors, and rehabilitation specialists. It assumes that personnel will be working with people who are functioning more or less normally and that if their behavior becomes seriously abnormal, staff members will make referrals.

While it may sound contradictory, people find it difficult to ask for help. To do so, one must admit to himself and to another person (the helper) that something is wrong and that he is not able to solve the problem on his own. A request for help implies a willingness to let someone else get involved in our lives, to trust someone. Further, it implies a willingness to change some of our present behaviors.

TWO BASIC ASSUMPTIONS ABOUT HELPING

There are several general assumptions upon which helping relations are based.

1. *The growth principle.* Helping assumes that people generally want to solve their problems and want to learn to cope with the demands they face. Moreover, it assumes that people seek not just to solve their problems but to meet their needs and achieve their aspirations as fully as possible. Combs referred to this as the "growth principle."

> Growth is characteristic of the very essence of life and finds expression in all of life's ramifications. . . . The entire organism strives toward growth. People do not just seek to be physically adequate; more important, they strive for personal fulfillment.[8]

Helping also assumes that people have the capacity to grow in their abilities to solve problems.

2. *The helper as a facilitator.* The assumptions that people wish to grow in their capacities to lead more satisfying lives, and that they have the capacities to do so, condition the methods used in helping relationships.

> Helping another human being is basically a process of enabling that person to grow in the directions he chooses. . . . The aim of all help is self-help and eventual self-sufficiency.[9]

Combs writes about "open" and "closed" systems of working with people.[10] In *closed* systems, the assumption is that the helper knows the answers to the problems faced by those being helped. An example of a closed system is the traditional medical model, where the doctor diagnoses the problem and prescribes a solution. The doctor has the responsibility to define what the patient should do, while the patient takes a passive role. We frequently use this approach, in the field of recreation and parks, as administrators, supervisors, or teachers; and it is often most appropriate to do so. However, in helping, we are interested in maximizing a person's ability to reach his or her potential more fully, to be more self-determining and less dependent. For this purpose, an *open* system approach seems to be more effective. In an open system there is greater emphasis on the perceptions of the person who is having the problem, and on related feelings and choices. In these circumstances, the helper relies much less on predetermined objectives and avoids giving expert advice or direction.

> The emphasis in open systems is on participation by all with shared power and decision making. The role of the helper is not director but facilitator.[11]

The role of the helper becomes one of interacting with others in such ways that the solutions to problems are discovered and that people grow in the process.

HELPER CHARACTERISTICS

Several characteristics seem to be related to effective helping.[12] These were discussed in Chapter 2, as they related to competency. In terms of the more specific functions of helpers as facilitators of growth, the following characteristics seem apparent.

Effective helpers are seen by the people with whom they work as being empathetic, caring, and genuine, and as having respect for others they are attempting to help.[13] Katz provided a useful description of empathy.

> When we experience empathy, we feel as if we were experiencing someone else's feelings as our own. We see, we feel, we respond, and we understand as if we were, in fact, the other person. We stand in his shoes. We get under his skin.[14]

Katz also provided a useful differentiation between empathy and sympathy. He noted that in empathy the focus is on the feelings of the other person. In sympathy, there is a preoccupation with the close similarity of our feelings to the feelings of others.

> When we sympathize, we are aware of our own state of mind and much of our attention is devoted to our own needs. When we empathize, we cannot fully escape our own needs but we discipline ourselves to use our own feelings as instruments of cognition.[15]

With empathy the helper becomes aware of how the other person is feeling. Also, as empathy is expressed, the other person has the feeling that he is being understood, that the helper knows how he feels. This seems to be an important element in the development of rapport.

Rapport also is facilitated by the expression of caring and positive regard for others. Caring is a showing of concern and interest in the other person. Positive regard has to do with the helper's acceptance of the other person as an individual, and a positive sense of the person's worth.[16] Clearly, it will be difficult to establish a helping relationship if we are seen by others as not being concerned about them or as not accepting them as individuals worthy of our attention.

The helper's expressions of concern must be seen by the person with whom she is working as being genuine if rapport is to develop. Genuineness means that the helper's statements of concern are consistent with her behavior—that is, the nonverbal messages of the helper must support what she says. The effective helper is authentic. She is seen by others as being a believable person.

THE HELPING PROCESS

Helping others often is a spontaneous, unplanned act that involves very little time. In other circumstances, a considerable amount of interaction will occur, and much time and thought will be given to it. Brammer suggested that the formality of any specific helping relationship falls along a continuum from relatively unstructured (as in family and friendship interactions) to highly structured (as in interactions with professionals such as psychiatrists and ministers).[17] Regardless of how formal or how spontaneous the helping effort is, certain elements of the process can be identified.

There is a beginning and an end to any helping encounter. Someone asks you for help, or is referred to you, or you perceive that help is needed and initiate the interaction. (In this later situation, some extra sensitivity is needed. One can offer help but in such a way that the other person is not threatened or offended.) The success of the relationship depends upon the willingness of both persons involved to participate; the relationship cannot be forced. Further, the helper must be careful not to confuse his or her professional role and personal relationships. Recreation personnel do have frequent opportunities to help colleagues and friends. But it is especially important here that the help is requested.

> The helper who seeks to be teacher or counselor to [his] wife, friends or colleagues may only succeed in frustrating and antagonizing them. . . . Treating a person who has not asked for it, or teaching a person who does not want such a relationship, can be a blatant lack of acceptance. It imposes a relationship, and so robs others of their right to choose for themselves.[18]

At some point the helping interaction terminates. Usually, it cannot be useful if it continues indefinitely. The helper does not have unlimited time to devote to any one interaction. Also, the goal of helping is to promote growth; a relationship that continues too long may produce dependence.

Building Rapport and Exploring Feelings.   The initial phase of the helping process is the development of rapport, or the reinforcement of it if it is already established. Helping will occur, most readily, or perhaps only if the other person trusts the helper and believes that the helper understands the problem and the associated feelings. It is at this stage that empathy is most important. People with problems have feelings about them. They are hurt, or disappointed, or fearful. The helper who responds to the expression of these feelings in an accepting, nonjudgmental way is being empathetic. This builds rapport.

> Empathy, the listener's understanding response to the feelings of the speakers, is important because it allows the speaker to feel safe and accepted, not judged or condemned because of his feelings.[19]

Often, the person with a problem does not realize all of the feelings which are present. Sometimes these feelings are hidden; we suppress them because we feel that it is not right to have strong feelings. Society tells us, in many general ways, that we should control our emotions. However, it seems that the helping process can proceed only if the person involved explores the feelings related to the problem, and accepts them.

> The helper's job is to enable that person to discover and understand these feelings. To rectify a problem, a person must first understand his own feelings about it. Then and only then does it make sense to decide on a course of action designed to solve the problem.[20]

As suggested, the key to showing empathy, and to facilitating the exploration of feelings, seems to be the response the helper makes to the other person's initial statements. There are several different kinds of responses you might make. Gillispie and Dendy described five different categories of responses.[21]

1. A situational response. This response focuses on the situation related to the problem (the other people involved, the physical setting, and the details of what happened), but ignores the feelings of the other person.
2. A judgmental response. A response that suggests that the feelings or actions of the other person are right or wrong.
3. A solution response. In this response, you either suggest a solution to the problem or you ask the other person what he thinks he should do.
4. A sympathetic response. This response says that you feel sorry for the other person, but implies that you cannot do anything about the situation.
5. An empathetic response. This response tells the other person that you understand the feelings involved, that you accept them, and that you can relate to them.

Gillispie and Dendy spoke of this as "responding to feelings. . . ." It is

> . . . the process whereby the listener hears the speaker's feelings and gives them back in a positive reflective statement that lets the speaker know that the listener has heard his feelings. He "mirrors" what he has heard.[22]

Johnson also identified five different types of responses, based on the underlying intentions of the person speaking. These are similar to those described by Gillispie and Dendy.[23] They include advising and evaluative responses, analytical or interpretive responses, responses that reassure and support, those that probe for more information, and those that show understanding.

As an illustration of these various types of responses, assume the following situation. You are the supervisor of maintenance in a suburban park and recreation district. One day while you are turning in the time sheets for your crew, the district secretary makes this comment to you: "I really like my job here and I like the people with whom I work, but I am concerned. I can't seem to please the park superintendent. The harder I work, the more it seems he expects me to do." Suppose also that you make one of the following remarks in response:

1. "These people are nice to work with, aren't they? But the superintendent does expect a lot of work from the staff."
2. "I don't think you should complain. Sure, he expects a lot from all of us, but, like you say, it is a good place to work."
3. "The thing to do is stand up to him. If you let him push you around now, things will never get any better."
4. "That's too bad. I'm really sorry to hear that the boss keeps piling the work on you."

5. "It sounds like you are worried about your job, and confused about what you have to do to satisfy the boss."
6. "I know how you feel. I've been living with that same situation for six years."
7. "How long have you felt this way?"

How do these seven responses correspond to the various response types? Response 1 is a situational response. In it, you are commenting on the elements of the problem, but ignoring the secretary's feelings. Response 2 illustrates a judgmental or evaluative response. Here, you are implying that the secretary is wrong. In Response 3, you are advising and suggesting a solution. Again, feelings are ignored. They also are ignored in Response 4, which is a sympathetic response. Response 5 does focus on what seem to be the secretary's feelings. In this comment, you are reflecting what you hear, in a nonjudgmental way, and one in which advice is not given. In a sense, you are saying that you understand the feelings that are involved. This response is most likely to show empathy. Response 6, a supportive response, sounds like it focuses on feelings and evidences understanding. However, the feelings are unspecified, and the comment shifts the focus from the other person's feelings to your own. Moreover, you are implying that the secretary is worrying needlessly; you have been "living with the same situation for six years" and you are still on the job and life is still going on. In a *probing* response, illustrated by Response 7, there is the possibility that the secretary may feel that she has to defend or explain her feelings. Probing can be appropriate at different times, but in an initial relationship it seems to work against the showing of empathy.

In the initial phases of a helping relationship, empathetic responses are much more likely to produce rapport between the helper and the person who is seeking help. Also, they facilitate the exploration of feelings, the first phase of the helping relationship.

It is during this initial phase also that mutual understanding about roles and procedures are established. Brammer spoke of this as establishing a structure;[24] Brill talked of establishing a contract.[25] What is involved is an agreement about what will be done, and about the expectations of each person for the relationship. When helping is formal, the structure may be defined very carefully. In more informal encounters, it tends to be defined more informally. In either case, it serves to avoid the disappointments or frustrations that come from expectations that are unrealistic or cannot be fulfilled. Also, in either case, care should be taken in the establishment of structure so that rapport is not damaged.

As the helping encounter proceeds, it is quite possible that the agreements about roles and procedures may change as the problem is understood more fully or as other circumstances change.

Clarification of Problem and Exploration of Attitudes and Values. The nature of the problem will begin to emerge during the exploration of feelings. And the problem needs to be understood well enough for initial agreements about methods. However, there is a need to go beyond these initial definitions. This usually involves helping the person integrate his feelings about the problem and his thinking about it, and an exploration of his values and attitudes which influence the problem. The following example illustrates how feeling, thinking and the holding of certain values might be involved.

Assume that you are the chief recreation therapist at a large urban hospital. A colleague, who is the patient activities director at another large medical center across town, has just dropped in to see you. The two of you are having coffee in the hospital lounge. He has a worried look. After some casual, initial conversation he says

> I just received a memorandum from the hospital manager indicating that we have to make a cut in personnel next month because of budget problems. That means laying off some full-time personnel, and I don't know how to begin doing that—who to lay off. Most people have been on the staff for a fairly long time, and—well—I just don't know what to do.

Your friend might be experiencing feelings of worry or fear or helplessness. He might be thinking, "How can I pick who is to be released? What will the manager think of me if I can't make a decision? What will the staff think of me when I tell them that someone has to go? What will happen if I make the wrong decision?" These thoughts might grow out of some values which your friend holds. For example, he might believe strongly in being a good employee who is dedicated to the agency for which he works. He might value personal effectiveness on the job. He might also value the respect and good will of the staff members who work under his supervision. In this situation, this value may conflict with the value he places on being an effective worker in the agency. This conflict might be the source of his feelings of worry or helplessness.

If you could help your friend understand the ways in which his feelings, thoughts and values are related, you would be helping him to clarify the problem. You could do this by listening to him and responding in nonjudgmental ways. This would help him explore possible conflicts in values and attitudes.

The purpose of this phase is to help the other person understand how his "feelings, thinking, and behavior fit together."[26] This information helps to clarify the actual problem, and it provides the basis for making decisions about solving the problem.

Problem Solving. The final aspect of the helping process, as discussed here, is problem solving: the definition of goals to be achieved, the exploration of alternative courses of action, and the selection and implementation of the most appropriate action. The helper's role, again, is to facilitate these things happening—*not to do them for the other person.* By responding to the other person's statements, by asking questions, by making suggestions, and by reinforcing actions with encouragement and praise, the helper facilitates another's problem solving.

You might ask, "If someone comes to me for help, and I don't solve the problem directly, won't the person be disappointed or angry?" Remember that the kinds of requests for help that are emphasized here are those for involvement and understanding or action. Remember also that the focus in helping is on the growth of the other person. These conditions suggest that you help the other person most appropriately when you do not take responsibility for the problem, but rather help him solve the problem himself. Helping is facilitated by acceptance, rapport, and the other individual's perception of you as an empathetic person. By taking direct responsibility for the problem, you often miss the opportunity to show your understanding of the feelings involved. The following example provides an illustration.

Assume that you are a supervisor of maintenance in a city park department, and that one of your staff members arrives late to work. He says

> I'm sorry I'm late coming in this morning. When I got up, I found a note on the kitchen table from my daughter—she's sixteen—saying that she is unhappy with things at home right now and that she is going to spend a few days at a friend's house until she can think things out. I don't know where she has gone, or what she is doing.

In response, you might say something similar to one of the following:

1. "Don't worry about being late—and don't worry about your daughter. I have a friend who works for the Juvenile Division of the Police Department. I'll call her and see if she can get a lead on where your daughter is."
2. "I can understand why you're late—and don't worry about your daughter. I know how you feel. My oldest girl did the same thing when she was fifteen. She stayed away for a couple of days at a friend's house and then she came home."
3. "I can understand why you're late. It sounds like you really are worried about your daughter—worried about where she is, and who she is with— and afraid that she really will not come home in a few days. Would you like to talk about it?"

In Statement 1, you are taking responsibility for doing something about the situation. It might seem as though the staff member would be relieved that you are doing so. He might appreciate your action. Or he might not; he might feel involving the police is inappropriate. In either case, he probably will not see you as very empathetic. You did not respond to the feelings he might be having, except to advise him not to worry. He might be very angry, or embarrassed, or fearful. You've given him no indication that you understand how he feels. Further, you've done nothing to help him develop the capacity to deal with this problem or similar future problems.

Statement 2 may seem like an empathetic response, but it falls short of showing an understanding of the other person's feelings. It is what was identified earlier as a sympathetic response. It is comforting for someone who is having a problem to realize that someone else has experienced a similar situation. However, the feelings involved might be quite different.

You may not know how the other person feels; to state that you do discourages the other person from telling you. Also, by suggesting that the problem really isn't a problem you are suggesting that the feelings are not important. Again, you haven't helped the person grow in the ability to deal with this and other similar problems.

In Statement 3, an empathetic response, you are focusing on the feelings first. Your assumption that the other person is worried is a fairly safe one; but even if it is not, you leave the conversation open for the staff member to tell you how he really feels. You are reflecting the feelings you hear in a nonjudgmental way. You are not saying how he should feel, and you are not saying that his feelings are right or wrong. This kind of a response seems to contribute most to the other person's perception of you as an understanding individual.

Maybe the staff member does not want to talk more about the situation. Maybe he doesn't care. However, if he does want to talk, your conversation eventually might get into the ways he feels about such things as family unity, parental responsibility, and proper adolescent behavior. Again, your reflective, nonjudgmental responses might help him develop greater understandings about values and attitudes he has that reflect upon this immediate situation. He might come to a better understanding of why he is angry, or fearful. At that point, your suggestions, or reactions to his ideas, and your encouragement can lead to problem-solving behavior on his part.

This whole sequence might take only a few minutes or it might involve two or three meetings and several hours. You might decide you can't devote that much time. Or you might, after some initial interaction, feel that some specialized help is needed. In that case, you might suggest he see someone else. Whatever you do, your initial focusing on his feelings stands a greater chance of evidencing empathy and building an appropriate relationship upon which helping can be based. Also, your not offering solutions helps him to grow in his ability to solve problems. Obviously, if there is a situation where immediate action is necessary, and if you have an appropriate solution, then it should be offered. However, these situations usually are requests for direct action rather than for the kinds of help that are emphasized in this chapter.

It should be emphasized that the different phases of the helping process outlined here are not recipes or formulas. They cannot be followed in "cookbook" fashion. Rather, the helper should be aware of them, and should attempt to incorporate them as naturally as possible into interactions that are intended to help others deal with problems.

THE "SELF-AS-INSTRUMENT" CONCEPT

The idea of competency described in Chapter 2 suggested that the helping process and the other interpersonal processes used by recreation and park personnel are influenced by the unique, personal characteristics of the individual worker. The "self-as-instrument" concept, presented by Combs, suggests that these personal characteristics are resources through which workers, or helpers, accomplish goals.

> Professional helpers must be thinking, problem-solving people; the primary tool with which they work is themselves. This understanding has been called the *self as instrument* concept. In the helping professions, effective operation is a question of the use of the helper's self, the peculiar ways in which helpers are able to combine knowledge and understanding with their own unique ways of putting them into operation.[27]

This concept seems most appropriate to recreation and park situations. In many ways, what we are doing when we lead or teach or supervise is using the special skills that, when used as each different person uses them, are unique. Our uses of our abilities to communicate, to establish rapport, to be sensitive to situations, to make appropriate decisions, and to use resources are, in a sense, uses of ourselves.

APPROPRIATE SELF-DISCLOSURE AND CONSTRUCTIVE FEEDBACK

To use ourselves most effectively, we need to be aware of those aspects of self that have potential for influencing our relationships with others and our work performance generally. This point was noted in Chapter 2 with a presentation of the Johari Window. As suggested there, we learn about ourselves, in part, through our interactions with others, as we reveal things to others about ourselves and as we receive feedback from them.

Self-disclosure helps us to understand more about ourselves by receiving feedback from others and, of course, it helps others to know more about us. This process seems a necessary part of developing healthy interpersonal relationships. Johnson defined self-disclosure as

> revealing how you are reacting to the present situation and giving any information about the past that is relevant to understanding how you are reacting to the present.[28]

He observed that self-disclosure focuses more on feelings than facts.

> Reactions to people and events are not facts as much as they are feelings. To be self-disclosing means to share with another person how you feel about something he or she has said or done, or how you feel about the events which have just occurred. Self-disclosure does not mean revealing intimate details of your past life.[29]

Johnson defined several characteristics of appropriate self-disclosure. Primarily, it must be relevant to the relationship you have with the person to whom you are disclosing and appropriate to the situation within which it is happening. For example, assume that you and I are working together on a grant application to fund a demonstration leisure services program for older adults. Suppose I tell you that I don't like to work under pressure, and that it makes me uncomfortable when you postpone or reschedule our meetings when the deadline for submitting is close at hand. To do so would be disclosing feelings I have that are relevant to our present relationship and situation. Perhaps it would be useful also if I told you that, in the past, I worked frequently with another person whose procrastination caused me to miss several important deadlines. This might help you to understand my present feelings. It probably would not be helpful, or appropriate, if I disclosed facts or feelings about financial problems I might be facing, or details about a conflict I might be having with another staff member. This is not to imply that self-disclosure should be superficial, rather that it should pertain to our present relationship, and that it should be offered because I want to improve our present relationship.

The appropriateness of self-disclosure also is a function of the amount of information revealed and the degree of intimacy involved. Revealing too much of oneself, too quickly, can be threatening to the other person. Similarly, disclosing intimate details about oneself, when the relationship is *not* intimate, also can be threatening. On the other side, superficial or limited self-disclosure usually does very little to improve relationships; it permits little opportunity for the kind of feedback that contributes to self-awareness. Egan made this observation:

> A group in which all disclosures are overly safe soon becomes stilted and boring. On the other hand, if the risks taken in disclosing yourself are too high, others may become frightened and may respond unpredictably, as frightened people do. When this happens, the climate of support disappears and you are left on a limb, exposed.[30]

Egan noted that trust must exist if self-disclosure is to occur, and that trust develops gradually. Therefore, the amount and depth of self-disclosure should increase gradually if they are to be increased.[31]

Relationships are built on trust. Trust develops when two people are willing to take risks by self-disclosing appropriately, and when they are accepting and supportive of each other. Johnson described the importance of acceptance and support.

> In order to build a relationship, you must learn to create a climate of trust that reduces your own and the other person's fears of betrayal and rejection and promotes the hope of acceptance, support, and confirmation.[32]

Risk is involved in self-disclosing. There is a chance that someone will make fun of you or even reject you. Culbert contended that the degree of risk is influenced by the intensity of the self-disclosure and the degree to which the other person hears the disclosure as it is intended, and responds as expected. Risk is intensified when the disclosure is intense, that is, when information is involved that is important to the person doing the disclosing. Risk is reduced when there is a high probability that the receiver of the information will understand the message as it was intended and will react in expected ways.[33]

Luft provided a useful summary of the value of taking reasonable risks, in self-disclosing, as a way of developing greater self-awareness.

> The risks of being more open and more transparent must be borne not only for the satisfaction and enjoyment of people and of self, but for increased realization of self. Lest that last phrase slip by as just another platitude, I'd like to rephrase it something like this. Your talents and your potentials have a better chance of being developed if you as a person have access to your own feelings, your imagination, and your fantasy. If you can be open and free with but one other person there is greater likelihood that you can be in touch with self.[34]

Another way of finding out more about yourself is to be receptive to the reactions of other people to your behavior. This usually is spoken of as being open to "feedback." Luft observed that we receive feedback from many sources, but that human response is the most influential kind.

> That morning look at the mirror is a kind of feedback. The mirror speaks loud and clear, but it doesn't have much of a memory. A camera does, and for this reason it can be a bit more threatening. Videotape playback has become an important means for teaching and learning about behavior, and it has enlarged on the function of the tape recorder for this purpose. But the most powerful form of feedback is the human response. People can be excellent mirrors, cameras, and tape recorders. Optimal learning, however, requires sensitivity and judgment in the feedback process, and for this reason human response remains the most powerful instrument.[35]

Some kinds of feedback are nonverbal—facial expressions, posture changes, or body movements often suggest one person's reaction to another. Much of the feedback we give and receive is verbal. Luft defined five different kinds of feedback: (1) the giving of information, (2) personal reactions, (3) judgmental reaction, (4) forced feedback, and (5) interpretation.[36] Forced feedback is feedback that is unsolicited. Interpretation is an attempt to identify reasons or motives for behavior. Luft suggests that feedback that is judgmental, forced, or interpretive may not contribute positively to an interpersonal relationship. Personal reactions, however, are seen as important sources of information about self, which also have potential for enhancing the relationship between two people.

This potential seems most achievable if the feedback is nonthreatening. Johnson noted some of the characteristics of nonthreatening feedback.[37] In general, feedback seems most effective when you react to the specific behavior of another person at the present. For example, suppose you and I are working together as coleaders at a teen center and that I arrive late for work this afternoon, for the third time this week. Assume also that my tardiness makes you angry. If you say to me, "You were late again today, and that puts extra pressure on me and I get angry when you do that," you are focusing on my present, observable behavior. If instead, you say, "You are a person who is always late, and who doesn't seem to care about his work," you are focusing on me as a person, and you are moving from observation of my behavior to inferences. This kind of feedback is much more threatening.

The comments about different response styles are appropriate here, also. Judgmental feedback or feedback that offers advice or solutions seems to contribute less to creating effective relationships. It is more threatening, and therefore it has less potential for contributing to self-awareness. Timing and the place where feedback is given are also important. To say that my tardiness makes you angry may be very useful information for me. But to tell me that in the presence of other people may embarrass me so much that I become defensive, and I fail to hear all that you would like to say to me. Also, the amount of information given in feedback should be adjusted to what the receiver can readily accept. Overloading can be threatening.

Feedback and self-disclosure are very similar. When you give someone else feedback about how you are reacting to her behavior, you are also self-disclosing. The differences between the two might be illustrated best by relating them to the Johari Window. Self-disclosure is intended to let other people know more about you; that is, it is intended to reduce the size of the *hidden* cell in the Johari Window. Feedback is intended to help another person know more about herself—to reduce the size of the *blind* cell. For this to happen most effectively, the person must be receptive to feedback. However, the distinction between self-disclosure and feedback is less important than the generalizations that (1) both of these processes contribute to self-awareness, and (2) that self-awareness is an important factor in developing effective interpersonal relationships and in the use of self as an instrument for working with others.

CONFLICT IN INTERPERSONAL RELATIONSHIPS

Whenever we establish interpersonal relationships with other people, we create potentials for conflict. It might even be said that conflict is inevitable. Johnson suggested that a relationship in which there is no conflict may not be a relationship at all.[38] Roark noted that not only is conflict inevitable, but that the potential of it occurring in a relationship increases as interaction, interdependency, and intimacy increase.[39]

The kind of conflict discussed in this section is not the same kind of conflict identified in Chapter 3. The *approach-approach* and *approach-avoidance* situations presented in Chapter 3 are intrapersonal, that is, they arise within an individual. Interpersonal conflicts occur *between* individuals.

> An *interpersonal conflict* exists whenever an action by one person prevents, obstructs, or interferes with the actions of another person. There can be conflicts between what people want to accomplish, the ways in which they wish to pursue their goals, their personal needs, and the expectations they hold for each other's behavior.[40]

Assume that you and I are both recreation therapists working at a medical care facility for children with long-term illnesses. An interpersonal conflict might develop between us over such things as differences in our perceptions about what we should be trying to accomplish with any given patient or the methods we should be using. Our own needs and expectations might be involved. I might expect you to seek my advice and to defer to my suggestions regarding program decisions you have responsibility for making. I might desire this to help satisfy my needs for status and recognition; and I might feel it is appropriate since I am older and have more experience. However, you may expect me to not become involved in your areas. You may also have needs for status, recognition, and independence. These differing expectations and competing needs might create conflict.

Recreation and park personnel can deal with conflict in several ways. Conflict can be avoided—that is, you can avoid getting into conflict situations with other people. The problem with this approach is that you pay a price for the apparent peacefulness that results. Gordon suggested that avoiding conflict rather predictably results in one or more of the following conditions:[41] If the issues that lead to the conflict situation are not faced, people may build up resentments. The feelings that people have about the potential conflict may be displaced; they may be expressed in other situations with other people. In addition, unresolved conflict in a staff situation may lead to poor morale.

> The point is that you cannot afford to run away from conflicts, because resentment will build up, feelings will get displaced, or there will be symptoms of the discontent and hostility people experience when conflicts exist among the people with whom they work. Conflicts should be brought out into the open and resolved, not shoved under the rug or suppressed.[42]

There is a difference between avoiding conflicts and preventing them. Avoidance is failing to recognize the existence of conflict, doing nothing about it. Prevention is taking action that minimizes the probability that conflict will occur. The suggestions for showing empathy, discussed earlier, are helpful in preventing conflict. When people feel that you have listened to them, and that you understand their feelings, the potential for conflict is reduced. Appropriate self-disclosure also lessens the potential for conflict. When other people know how you feel, and what your perceptions and reactions are, there is less probability that conflict will develop. The development of trust also helps prevent conflict. As suggested earlier, a trusting relationship is one in which both parties realize that the actions of either one of the persons can benefit or harm the other. When you trust the other person, you have confidence that you will not be hurt. When trust exists, you view the other person's motives and actions more positively and with less suspicion. This contributes to a reduction in conflict potential.

Once conflict develops, there are actions that can be taken to manage it, that is, to resolve it or reduce it to a point where it is not disruptive. Roark suggested two models for dealing with interpersonal conflict—a technique labeled GRIT (Graduated Reciprocation in Tension-reduction) and a consensus model.[43] GRIT is based on a conflict deescalation process.

> GRIT requires that one side initiate tension-reducing steps and openly announce the intention to de-escalate the conflict. Along with the announcement of the action to de-escalate the conflict, a specific invitation is made for reciprocation by the opponent. If the opponent reciprocates in kind, bigger steps toward de-escalation are initiated.[44]

Roark indicated that this method is not a "subtle way of giving in." Instead, it is a method that attempts to build mutual confidence and trust.

The consensus model essentially is a problem-solving model, in which the persons involved in the conflict attempt to reach agreement on the nature of the conflict and to understand one another's feelings about it. These agreements and understandings become the bases for agreeing on an acceptable solution and on the changes each person would be willing to make to achieve the solution. Johnson also suggested a problem-solving model. He noted that, in agreeing about the nature of the conflict, it is useful to define the conflict as narrowly as is realistic.

> Think small! The more limited the definition of the conflict, the easier it is to resolve. The larger and more vague the description of the other person's actions, the harder it is to resolve the conflict.[45]

Remember the situation where you and I are recreation therapists in a children's hospital? In that conflict, you might say something like this.

> I am having a hard time working with you because you give the impression that you know all there is to know about working with our patients. I would appreciate it if you minded your own business.

Or, you could say something like this.

> When you give me suggestions for working with a patient when I have not asked for your advice, it makes me feel that you do not trust me or you think I am not capable. This makes me angry.

The second statement is consistent with Johnson's suggestion to "think small." It specifically describes my behavior and your feelings.

Johnson suggested further that viewing the problem as one to be solved jointly enhances the probability of a constructive solution. A cooperative approach helps to avoid a win-lose situation.

In the problem-solving process, it seems necessary to make sure that our perceptions of the situation are as accurate as possible. Johnson noted that we often have "perceptual distortions" about our own behavior and the behavior of the other person. Frequently, we feel that we are correct and that the other person is attacking us; the other person has this same feeling of being an "innocent victim."

In most conflicts, both people are firmly convinced that they are right and the other person wrong; that they want a "just" solution but the other person does not.[46]

With respect to wins and losses, Gordon presented three possibilities: "I win, you lose," "You win, I lose," and a "no-lose" alternative.[47] He noted that there are significant disadvantages in any win-lose situation. Those who lose in the resolution of a conflict are very apt to be resentful and angry. Those who win often do so by using power. Both of these conditions work against the establishment of effective, ongoing interpersonal relations. Gordon suggested, instead, that the no-lose method provides for the mutual satisfaction of the needs of the people involved. The no-lose method also is a problem-solving method. It involves the steps of defining the problem, developing possible alternative solutions, selecting the most acceptable one, implementing it, and doing a follow-up evaluation.[48]

As suggested initially, the potential for conflict seems inevitable in interpersonal relationships. There are significant disadvantages in not recognizing this potential, and dealing with the conflict if it occurs. On the other hand, the development of the ability to prevent and to manage conflict contributes considerably to the interpersonal effectiveness of recreation and park personnel.

COUNSELING AS AN INTERPERSONAL PROCESS

The helping process that has been discussed in this chapter might be thought of as counseling. In fact, the National Institute for Drug Abuse, whose model for helping was presented earlier, identifies the process as *short-term client counseling.* That is, the helping relationship is seen as a counseling relationship—short-term in that it exists over a relatively short span of time. This kind of interpersonal relationship is similar to what Tyler described as "minimum change therapy."[49] She suggested that the difference between counseling and therapy is in the degree and nature of change expected as an outcome. *Therapy* seeks personality change; *counseling* is directed toward modifying the other person's behavior, but not toward causing basic personality changes.

> The aim of therapy is generally considered to be personality *change* of some sort. Let us use *counseling* to refer to a helping process which is not to change the person but to enable him to utilize the resources he now has for coping with life.[50]

Wicks suggested that the goals of counseling and therapy may overlap; therefore, the differences between the processes are not sharp. However, he emphasized the helping nature of the relationship.

> Counseling is an interpersonal process in which the professional attempts to help the client or patient develop or rediscover his or her problem-solving skills.[51]

Similarly, Dyer and Vriend saw counseling as a helping relationship.

> Counseling is an interpersonal helping procedure which begins with client exploration for the purpose of identifying thinking, feeling, and doing processes which are in any way self-defeating or which require upgrading.[52]

The authors noted the central role of the client in the process.

> The client determines and declares to the counselor what the counter-productive behaviors are and makes decisions about which ones can be worked on. The counselor helps the client to set goals in which more positive thinking and feeling will lead to the acquisition of self-enhancing behaviors which had not previously been part of the client's repertoire.[53]

Dyer and Vriend emphasized the importance of the client moving toward better self-understanding as a part of the counseling process.

These perspectives are congruent with Tyler's concept. She identified three characteristics of counseling, or "minimum change therapy."[54] The first of these is the *exploration of resources.* In the process of counseling, both the counselor and the person being helped develop greater understandings about the nature of the problem and the attendant feelings. In addition, in this phase, the counselor and the other person explore the resources possessed by the person which might be used in a solution. These include certain personality traits, such as a sense of humor or the ability to adjust, which might be strengthened or enlarged.

A second characteristic is the *structuring of the situation.* This involves the identification of the other person's expectations for the relationship, and a clarification of the counselor's role.

The third feature of minimum change therapy is the use of the *relationship between the client and the counselor* to reduce the client's anxiety and provide support.

> Support does not mean inspirational pep talks, shallow reassurances, or the encouragement of dependence. What it does mean is the act of lending one's own strength to the client for the period during which he needs it, so that he can be certain that his world is not going to fall apart if he moves.[55]

Wicks described counseling as a process which is "brief and oriented to deal with a specific problem."[56] He presented eight stages. These involve characteristics similar to those described by Tyler. The first three stages include the establishment of the initial contact between the counselor and client, and the exploration of feelings. The client is encouraged to talk, and the counselor begins to understand the client's situation. Wicks uses the terms "ventilation," "reconnaisance," and "reflection" to identify what happens in these initial stages. These stages are followed by a period of "clarification and elaboration." This leads to "problem-solving" and "support for action." The counselor helps the client explore alternatives, and provides support for implementing those which are seen as appropriate.

> To be effective, the counselor must avoid putting the client in a dependent position; rather he or she must work with the person to discover ways of handling the problem, refraining from giving advice, except when basic information is required.[57]

The final stages involve a review of what has been done, and a termination of the relationship.

These views of counseling are congruent with the concept of helping presented earlier. They suggest that recreation and park personnel frequently have opportunities to help others, staff members and users of agency services, with problems that detract from their abilities to function effectively or to participate fully. The process of helping described in this chapter is within the capabilities of recreation and park workers who are sensitive, who adhere to the basic premises, and who can make appropriate determinations about when helping is appropriate. In this sense, leisure service personnel might engage in counseling.

A crucial sensitivity that they must develop, however, is the ability to recognize their limits of expertise. Some workers will have greater responsibilities to use counseling processes because of the nature of their jobs. Others, at varying times in their careers, will have opportunities to help by using counseling techniques even though they have no direct responsibilities for doing so. In either case, it is important for workers not to exceed their abilities to use these techniques.

LEISURE COUNSELING

Some leisure service workers will engage in leisure counseling. This is a type of counseling that may involve elements of the helping process, but which takes several different forms. Its purpose is to help people enjoy leisure more fully.

> Leisure counseling, then, can help the individual make meaningful and informed choices consistent with his essential nature (beliefs, attitudes, values toward leisure) and his particular circumstances (possible barriers toward potential leisure involvement, such as physical limitations, economics, geography, cultural, etc.).[58]

Kinney and Dowling emphasized the helping aspects.

> Leisure counseling . . . is a helping relationship with the ultimate aim of growth through leisure. This growth may create cognitive or behavioral change, but change is not the essence of the process. Leisure counseling is primarily an educative process with the goal of self-determination.[59]

Allen and Hamilton identified the various forms that leisure counseling may take. They suggested that the particular form or "orientation" that is used will depend upon the "situational factors (needs, functional strengths, environmental influences and problems) of the individual."[60] Their various orientations include the following:

1. Leisure resource guidance
2. Leisure skills development
3. Leisure lifestyle awareness
4. Leisure-related behavioral problems
5. Leisure as a rehabilitative asset[61]

Leisure resource guidance essentially is a matter of exploring an individual's leisure interests and then providing information about opportunities for engaging in activities that match interests. A skills development approach helps the individual develop skills in those areas where existing deficiencies keep the person from enjoying leisure as fully as he would otherwise. The skills involved might relate to the performance of some particular activity, such as square dancing or swimming, or they might be related to interpersonal relationships. The leisure lifestyle awareness orientation is a broader approach, intended to assist a person

in understanding and clarifying his or her lifestyle and the implications of leisure on all of life's components. This orientation is based upon the assumptions that leisure, in and of itself, can be beneficial to an individual and that, through understanding one's attitudes, values, and behaviors related to leisure, a person is more likely to realize leisure's benefits.[62]

The fourth orientation focuses on leisure-related behavioral problems. It assumes that there is some problem, more general than skill deficiency, that is keeping an individual from functioning satisfactorily in a leisure sense. For example, feelings about leisure might be involved.

Due to the individual's inability to utilize free time effectively, he or she may develop feelings of boredom, guilt, anxiety, nervousness, and so forth. These problem areas may result from one's inability to adapt to the rapid changes taking place in our society or from dramatic change in one's life situation.[63]

This fourth orientation overlaps somewhat with the third orientation. Allen and Hamilton suggested that the approach in Orientation 3 is basically developmental, in which the individual is assisted ". . . in moving beyond his or her current state of normal functioning."[64] Orientation 4 is appropriate in cases where problems exist and where normal functioning is not evident. The approach here is remedial as well as developmental. The fifth orientation also is problem oriented. However, the problems that the individual is having may not be related specifically to leisure. Rather, some general condition may be involved. The authors use as an illustration severe depression. The facilitator (counselor) would work with the person in the exploration and clarification of the problem. Following this, various opportunities would be explored in an effort to discover leisure experiences which might help reduce the depression. Allen and Hamilton caution that this orientation and Orientation 4 are "very similar to conventional forms of counseling or psychotherapy." They recommend that these orientations be used only by persons with appropriate training, and that a team approach involving mental health specialists be used.

Allen and Hamilton suggested that these five orientations can be viewed as a continuum, progressing in terms of counselor involvement and degree of client risk in self-exploration, from Orientation 1 to Orientation 4. In Orientations 1 and 2, the interactions between the counselor and the client are considerably less than in Orientations 4 and 5; and the psychological risk or threat experienced by the client as self-exploration occurs is less in the earlier orientations. In fact, the authors suggested that Orientations 1, 2 and 3 might be identified more accurately as leisure education and awareness processes, even though counseling is involved.[65]

While much attention has been given to the concept, leisure counseling is a relatively new development. There is controversy in the field of recreation and parks over issues such as how leisure counselors should be trained and which of the various orientations are most appropriate. Compton, Witt, and Sanchez noted this condition in a "state-of-the-art" article on leisure counseling. They observed that leisure counseling seems to be more prevalent in rehabilitative programs, but that there is little evidence related to its effectiveness. They provided this summary.

> Leisure counseling may have its strongest support in the rehabilitation sector and its weakest in the public sector. Practice is little more advanced than five years ago. Obviously, there are more applications of various techniques to different consumers and clients, but no clear empirical or scientific evidence exists to support the effectiveness of leisure counseling. In order for leisure counseling to develop into an accepted discipline, there will be a need for more substantive and reliable evidence with which to support the practice of leisure counseling.[66]

Sessoms contended that three fundamental questions had to be answered affirmatively before leisure counseling could reach its full potential. These questions are (1) whether or not the field has defined the "ideal leisure state" operationally and conceptually, (2) whether or not we have developed adequate counseling methods and assessment devices, and (3) whether or not our involvement in leisure counseling is expected and has been sanctioned by the public. He observed that, at the time of his writing, none of these questions could be answered in the affirmative without qualification.

> Regardless of the direction we travel in leisure counseling, the basic problems of theory, methodology, and social mandate must still be resolved. Without some resolution of these problems, we are only playing mind games, using cosmetic words to enhance our status, and, in the end, deluding ourselves.[67]

Kinney and Dowling also noted conditions in leisure counseling that they saw as counterproductive.[68] Like Sessoms, they observed that leisure counselors have been overly concerned with status, and that the field has focused more on testing and assessment than on the overall process of counseling. This, they felt, leads to client dependency, rather than freedom and self-determination, which should be the end results.

Edwards took the position that leisure counseling should be left to those persons who are trained in counseling or psychology. She observed that, while the field of recreation and parks gave early leadership to the leisure counseling movement, it should no longer be involved.

> Recreation and park professionals should stop trying to force an unnatural alliance with leisure counseling and content themselves with bringing in trained leisure counselors whenever they need them.[69]

While there is controversy regarding various issues related to leisure counseling and while its effectiveness is yet to be documented fully, it is a process that seems to have potential for helping people. Kinney and Dowling suggested that, if the issues could be resolved, leisure counseling could become "the most dynamic element of all recreation services. . . ."[70]

SUMMARY

Interpersonal relationships are involved in those activities of recreation and park personnel that fall into the general category of working with people. These relationships have potential for meeting the needs of the various different people who are interacting. In an interaction, you perceive your own needs, the needs of the other person, the other person's potential for meeting your needs, and your potential for meeting his or her needs. Three types of needs might be evident: needs related to involvement, control, and affection.

Some relationships in recreation and parks take the form of helping. Helping involves one person engaging in the kinds of behaviors that encourage and enable another person to solve or reduce the effects of personal problems.

In requests for help, as discussed in this chapter, the person with a problem usually is seeking the understanding and involvement of the helper. The basic assumptions upon which responses to such requests are based are (1) that individuals have the capacities to grow in their abilities to solve their own problems and (2) that the helper's role is to facilitate this growth.

Certain personal characteristics are associated with the helper's role as a facilitator. These include empathy, genuineness, and caring and respect for others.

The helping process itself involves several different steps. Three primary ones were described. The first involves the expression and exploration of feelings, associated with the problem, by the person being helped. During this phase, the helper's role is to respond in nonjudgmental, reflective ways that evidence understanding. The second step involves assisting the person in the clarification of the problem, including an examination of possible conflicts in personal values which might be present. This leads to problem-solving, the third step. Many of the assumptions involved in these steps in the helping process are applicable to general interpersonal relationships.

As recreation and park personnel work with people they use various skills and knowledges that are expressed through the uniqueness of their own individual personalities. In a sense, they use themselves. In the helping professions broadly, this has been referred to as the "self-as-instrument" concept. Effective use of yourself as an instrument for helping others requires that you know yourself—your attitudes, biases, needs, and aspirations which have potential for influencing interpersonal relationships. You can learn more about yourself through appropriate self-disclosure and by being receptive to feedback from others.

Often we encounter conflict in our relationships with others. While conflicts should not be ignored, they can be prevented or minimized; and they can be managed once they develop. Problem-solving methods that attempt to produce "no-lose" solutions and techniques that help to "deescalate" or lessen the intensities of conflict are appropriate management approaches.

In many ways, counseling is a helping process. Recreation and park personnel frequently have opportunities to engage in counseling. It is appropriate that they do so when the counseling is not aimed at personality change, and when personnel clearly recognize the limits of their training and expertise.

Some leisure service workers have responsibilities for leisure counseling. The forms of this special type of interpersonal relationships range from the exploration of interests and the provision of information about opportunities, to developmental or remedial efforts aimed at minimizing some problem that prevents the individual from enjoying leisure more fully.

REVIEW QUESTIONS

4-1 It was suggested in this chapter that in every human relationship the dimensions of *involvement, control,* and *emotional tone* can be observed. What do these three terms mean, as they relate to interpersonal relationships?

4-2 What is the helping process? What basic steps are involved? When might this process be used by a leisure services worker?

4-3 Upon what two primary assumptions are helping relationships based?

4-4 How would you describe an effective helper? That is, what are the characteristics of a recreation and park staff member who uses this process effectively?

4-5 What suggestions could you give a friend about appropriate self-disclosure? What things would you keep in mind when giving constructive feedback to someone else? In what ways do these activities contribute to self-awareness?

4-6 What is leisure counseling? What are the various forms of leisure counseling, and what are the different purposes of each?

TO DO

4-A On the left side of a sheet of paper, list the names of five or more people with whom you have interpersonal relationships. The individuals you list should be ones (1) with whom you interact more than casually (that is, where the outcome of the interaction is at least somewhat important to you); (2) where the interaction occurs more than once or twice a week; and (3) who are not members of your immediate family.

Make three columns to the right of the list of names. In column one, rank the names according to the degree of involvement you have with each. Put a number 1 behind the name of the person you are most involved with, number 2 behind the one you are next most involved with, and so on. In column two, indicate (for each name) who you believe is most in *control* of the relationship—you or the other person. Or are you equally in control? In the third column, behind each name, write an adjective or a noun that best describes the *emotions or feelings* involved in the relationship.

Now look over the list and then complete this sentence: My interpersonal relationships seem to be ones in which

4-B Complete each of these sentences also:

1. The thing I enjoy most about interacting with other people is
2. The thing that irritates me the most in an interpersonal relationship is to have the other person
3. My interpersonal relationships would be improved if I

4-C If you are enrolled in a class on working with people, ask one other person in the class to participate with you in the following:

1. Individually review the list of strengths and weaknesses each of you developed in item 2-A (Chapter 2). Share these with each other.
2. Share the responses you each made to item 4-B in this "to-do" list. Discuss the reasons why you completed each statement as you did. Respond to the other person's statements and reasons.

In these activities, you will be engaging in self-disclosure and feedback. Discuss with the other person any feelings you have when you engage in these activities. Talk about how you might feel if the subject were more personal or threatening. Discuss the values of appropriate self-disclosure and constructive feedback.

END NOTES

1. Kim Griffin and Bobby R. Patton, *Personal Communication in Human Relations* (Columbus, Ohio: Charles E. Merrill Publishing Co., 1974), pp. 29–30.

2. Griffin and Patton, *Personal Communication in Human Relations*, p. 31.

3. Ibid., pp. 57–58.

4. Ibid., p. 56.

5. Ibid., pp. 57–58.

6. George M. Gazda and others, *Human Relations Development: A Manual for Educators* 2nd ed. (Boston: Allyn and Bacon, Inc., 1977), p. 39.

7. Gazda and others, *Human Relations Development*, p. 42.

8. Arthur W. Combs, Donald L. Avila, and William W. Purkey, *Helping Relation-*

ships: Basic Concepts for the Helping Professions 2nd ed. (Boston: Allyn and Bacon, Inc., 1978), p. 38.

9. Lawrence W. Brammer, *The Helping Relationship: Process and Skills* (Englewood Cliffs, N.J.: Prentice-Hall, Inc., 1973), pp. 3, 5.

10. Combs, and Purkey, *Helping Relationships*, pp. 101–6.

11. Ibid., p. 105.

12. For discussions of characteristics related to effective helping, see: Brammer, *The Helping Relationship*, pp. 18–36; Combs, Avila, and Purkey, *Helping Relationships*, pp. 5–12; also Gerard Egan, *The Skilled Helper: A Model for Systematic Helping and Interpersonal Relating* (Monterey, Calif.: Brooks/Cole Publishing Company, a Division of Wadsworth Publishing Company, Inc., 1975), pp. 22–24. A general discussion of helper characteristics as well as behaviors is given as a part of a presentation of the overall helping process in Robert R. Carkhuff, *The Art of Helping* (Amherst, Mass.: Human Resource Development Press, 1973).

13. Brammer, *The Helping Relationship*, pp. 29–34.

14. Robert L. Katz, *Empathy: Its Nature and Uses* (New York: The Free Press of Glencoe, a Division of the Macmillan Company, 1963), p. 3.

15. Katz, *Empathy*, p. 9.

16. Brammer, *The Helping Relationship*, pp. 31, 33–34.

17. Ibid., pp. 12–13.

18. Combs, Avila and Purkey, *Helping Relationships*, p. 209.

19. Beth J. Gillispie and Robert F. Dendy, *Counselor Training: Short-Term Client Systems*, (Rockville, Md.: National Drug Abuse Center for Training and Resource Development, 1977), p. (1-3-2).

20. Gillispie and Dendy, *Counselor Training*, p. (1-3-2).

21. Ibid., pp. (11-7-1)–(11-7-4).

22. Ibid., p. (11-7-4).

23. David W. Johnson, *Reaching Out: Interpersonal Effectiveness and Self-Actualization* 2nd ed. (Englewood Cliffs, N.J.: Prentice-Hall, Inc. 1981), pp. 150–55.

24. Brammer, *The Helping Relationship*, pp. 59–62.

25. Naomi I. Brill, *Working with People: The Helping Process* (Philadelphia: J.B. Lippincott Company, 1978), pp. 100–101.

26. Gillispie and Dendy, *Counselor Training*, p. (111-0-1).

27. Combs, Avila, and Purkey, *Helping Relationships*, p. 6.

28. Johnson, *Reaching Out*, p. 16.

29. Ibid., p. 16.

30. Gerard Egan, *Interpersonal Living: A Skills/Contract Approach to Human-Relations Training in Groups* (Monterey, Calif.: Brooks/Cole Publishing Company, a Division of Wadsworth Publishing Company, Inc., 1976), p. 52.

31. Egan, *Interpersonal Skills*, p. 52.

32. Johnson, *Reaching Out*, p. 50.

33. Samuel A. Culbert, *The Interpersonal Process of Self-Disclosure: It Takes Two to See One* (Washington, D.C.: NTL Institute for Applied Behavioral Science, 1967), p. 8.

34. Joseph Luft, *Of Human Interaction*, by permission of Mayfield Pub. Co. © 1969 by National, p. 129.

35. Luft, *Of Human Interaction*, p. 116.

36. Ibid., pp. 117–21.

37. Johnson, *Reaching Out*, pp. 23–25.

38. Ibid., p. 195.

39. Albert E. Roark, "Interpersonal Conflict Management," *Personnel and Guidance Journal* 56, no. 7 (March, 1978): 400.

40. Johnson, *Reaching Out*, p. 195.

41. Thomas Gordon, *Leader Effectiveness Training* (New York: Wyden Books, a division of P.E.I. Books, Inc., 1977), p. 147.

42. Gordon, *Leader Effectiveness Training*, p. 148.

43. Roark, "Interpersonal Conflict Management," pp. 401–2.

44. Ibid., p. 402.

45. Johnson, *Reaching Out*, p. 221.

46. Ibid., p. 208.

47. Gordon, *Leader Effectiveness Training*, pp. 149–54, 175–90.

48. Ibid., pp. 194–98.

49. Leona Tyler, "The Work of the Counselor," in Jack T. Huber and Howard L. Millman, eds., *Goals and Behavior in Psychotherapy and Counseling* (Columbus, Ohio: Charles E. Merrill Publishing Company, 1972), p. 147.

50. Tyler, "The Work of the Counselor," in Huber and Millman, *Goals and Behavior in Psychotherapy and Counseling*, p. 144.

51. Robert J. Wicks, *Counseling Strategies and Intervention Techniques for the Human Services* (New York: J. B. Lippincott Company, 1977) p. 62.

52. Wayne W. Dyer and John Vriend, *Counseling Techniques That Work: Applications to Individual and Group Counseling* (Washington, D.C.: APGA Press, 1975), p. 17.

53. Dyer and Vriend, *Counseling Techniques That Work*, p. 17.

54. Tyler, "The Work of the Counselor," in Huber and Millman, *Goals and Behavior in Psychotherapy and Counseling*, pp. 148–52.

55. Ibid., p. 157.

56. Wicks, *Counseling Strategies and Intervention Techniques for the Human Services*, pp. 64–73.

57. Ibid., pp. 64–73.

58. Chester F. McDowell, Jr., "Toward A Healthy Leisure Mode: Leisure Counseling," *Therapeutic Recreation Journal* 8, no. 3 (Third Quarter 1974): 99.

59. Walter Kinney, Jr. and Dorothy Dowling, "Leisure Counseling or Leisure Quackery?," *Parks & Recreation* 16, no. 1 (January 1981): 71.

60. Lawrence R. Allen and Edward J. Hamilton, "Leisure Counseling: A Continuum of Services," *Therapeutic Recreation Journal* 14, no. 1 (Fall Quarter 1980): 18.

61. Allen and Hamilton, "Leisure Counseling," pp. 18–21.

62. Ibid., p. 19.

63. Ibid., p. 20.

64. Ibid., p. 19.

65. Ibid., p. 21.

66. David Compton, Peter A. Witt and Barbara Sánchez, ". . . Leisure Counseling," *Parks & Recreation* 15, no. 8 (August 1980): 27.

67. Douglas Sessoms, "Leisure Counseling: A Frank Analysis of the Issues," *Parks & Recreation* 16, no. 1 (January 1981): 107.

68. Kinney and Dowling, "Leisure Counseling or Leisure Quackery?," p. 70.

69. Patsy B. Edwards, "Leisure Counseling: Recreators, Keep Out!" *Parks & Recreation* 16, no. 6 (June 1981): 43.

70. Kinney and Dowling, "Leisure Counseling or Leisure Quackery?," p. 70.

chapter 5

Leadership Processes

PREVIEW

Some Interpersonal relationships are initiated and sustained for the purpose of influencing others in the accomplishment of some specified goal. Teaching is an example; through relationships with students, teachers attempt to cause students to engage in behaviors which lead to learning something. Supervision of staff is another example. In the broadest sense, all of the processes used by leisure service personnel as they work with people involve interpersonal relationships and are intended to lead to behavior changes of some kind. We often refer to these activities as leadership. *This use of the term as a collective label for the things we do when working with people is appropriate. However, there are some specific processes that we call leadership, in the more limited sense of the term, which are used by recreation and park personnel. This chapter examines these.*

The chapter begins with a concept of leadership. Then, several ways in which people become leaders are defined.

A major part of the chapter is devoted to presenting several basic things that leaders do in their attempts to influence others. This discussion will include a look at the relative importance of the leader's own personal characteristics.

Considerable attention will be given also to different styles of leadership. The characteristics and consequences of autocratic, democratic and laissez-faire styles will be examined. Task-oriented and relationship-oriented styles will also be presented, as well as the influences on these styles of such factors as leader position power, task structure, and group maturity.

After a short period of friendly conversation, the five people sat down at the table. They were meeting in the conference room of a large electronics manufacturing firm. Those in attendance were members of the state professional society's legislative committee. The company's recreation director, the elected chairperson of the committee, called the meeting to order. He explained that their purpose in meeting was to develop a strategy for the society's efforts to influence a major piece of legislation. If it passed, the bill would have considerable influence on the field of recreation and parks.

Saturday morning, on the day after the meeting, the recreation director was walking quietly down a trail in a 2000-acre regional park. With him were his eight-year-old son, seven other Cub Scouts, and one other father. He encouraged the boys to walk quietly so they might be able to see some of the small animals that inhabit the park.

The recreation director in the paragraphs above might be called a leader. The local scout executive probably would refer to him as an "adult leader." His colleagues in the state professional society no doubt view him as a leader because of his committee work if for no other reason. And it is likely that at least some of the employees of the firm for which he works would see him as a leader. On the other hand, he might be seen as a conscientious volunteer, an effective chairperson, and a helpful organizer of activities, without any direct reference to his status as a leader. However he is identified, most people would agree that he uses leadership processes. To the extent that he does, he is engaging in activities that are commonly used by recreation and park personnel.

A CONCEPT OF LEADERSHIP

There are many different ways of viewing leadership processes. Stogdill conducted a comprehensive review of the literature published between 1902 and the early 1970s, and identified eleven different meanings of the term *leadership:*

1. A focus of group processes
2. Personality and its effects
3. The art of inducing compliance
4. The exercise of influence
5. An act or behavior
6. A form of persuasion
7. A power relation
8. An instrument of goal achievement
9. An effect of interaction
10. A differentiated role
11. The initiation of structure[1]

He concluded that the variety of definitions of leadership "suggests that there is little agreement as to the meaning of the concept and that little exists in the way of unifying theory."[2]

However, it is possible to find relationships among these eleven meanings. In a broad sense, leadership is what a leader does (meaning 5). Whatever this is, it is intended to cause others to act or behave in certain ways.

Inducing compliance (meaning 3) suggests a unilateral process; the leader determines what the desired actions are and sees to it that they are performed by followers or group members. The exercise of influence (4) and persuasion (6) points of view change the approach from one of domination and control by the leader to ones that recognize the reciprocal nature of the leader's wishes and the wishes of the followers or group members. These three perspectives focus on the behavior of the leader. Leadership as a power relation (7) suggests that follower or group member behavior results from the power possessed and used by the leader. Some types of power are a function of the leader's behavior, such as the promise of rewards and the threat of punishment. Other types of power are the result of qualities possessed by the leader (expertise in a relevant skill or subject area) or the leader's position (the job or office held by the leader). The leader's position often is a differentiated role (10); that is, the leader occupies a position or carries out a role in the group that is different from the positions and roles of other members.

Similarly, leadership as a focus of group processes (1) suggests in a general way that the leader holds a central position in the group. The position may be reinforced by structures initiated and developed by the leader (11). The leader might arrive at this central position by appointment (employment) or election; or he or she might emerge as the leader because of the particular talents needed by the group at a certain time. Regardless of the means, and except in highly structured and coercive situations, in the final analysis *the group must confer leadership.* That is, the group must accept the leader's attempt to exercise influence or to obtain compliance. Individuals who help others achieve their goals (8) are more likely to gain group acceptance.

Even though the leader may be the central person in the group, other members frequently contribute to the group's purposes. In this sense, leadership might be seen as a result of interaction among group members (9).

The leader brings to the central position a variety of personal characteristics (2). The relationship of any of these to the leader's effectiveness is influenced by the demands of the specific situation. Stogdill made the following observations:

> Theorists no longer explain leadership solely in terms of the individual or the group. Rather, it is believed that characteristics of the individual and demands of the situation interact in such a manner as to permit one, or perhaps a few, persons to rise to leadership status.[3]

Implied in the above statement is the idea that an understanding of leadership is dependent upon an understanding of the leader, the group, and the situation. Hershey and Blanchard stated it this way.

> Most management writers agree that leadership is *the process of influencing activities of an individual or a group in efforts toward goal achievement in a given situation.* From this definition of leadership, it follows that the leadership process is a function of the *leader,* the *follower,* and other *situational* variables. . . .[4]

The concept of leadership presented in this chapter is consistent with Hershey and Blanchard's definition. The chapter is based on the general position that leadership is a specific process designed to produce changes in others' behaviors through the use of interpersonal influence. This concept of leadership also is consistent with the notion of competency presented in Chapter 2. That is, competency in the field of recreation and parks can be viewed as a function of the interrelationship of professional processes (including leadership), personal characteristics, and situational demands.

HOW PEOPLE BECOME LEADERS

Leaders become leaders by various means. Sometimes they are elected to the central position they occupy, as in the case of the state legislative committee chairperson. Often they are appointed. The volunteer scoutmaster probably is appointed (recruited) by the local scout council; the industrial recreation director is appointed by the firm that employs him. Leaders may "emerge," and temporarily be afforded a central position by the group because of special talents needed in particular situations. An illustration would be a member of the legislative committee who had worked previously as an aide to a state senator and who had considerable experience with lobbyists. She might emerge as a temporary leader in the group during that period when the committee is considering ways of developing effective contacts with members of the legislature.

The emergent leader has the advantage of group acceptance; that she emerges shows that the group recognizes that she can help them. To a lesser degree, the elected leader also has the advantage of group acceptance. However, it is a tentative acceptance; successful election suggests that the group believes the leader has the potential to help the group meet its goals, but he has to prove that potential by his actions after the election. The appointed leader has the advantage of his position and title; people expect him to engage in certain kinds of leadership attempts because of the position he holds. The disadvantage he faces is that he often is appointed (employed) by one group (in this case the company management) and must work with another group (the employees). He has to earn the acceptance of the group in which he expects to exert influence.

It appears that certain conditions must be present in any situation for a person to exercise leadership.[5] Assume again the situation of the person who had been a legislative aide. Under what circumstances would she attempt leadership in the committee? First of all, she must perceive that leadership is needed. She might see this need because the designated leader is not performing expected tasks. The individual also must feel that she has the necessary abilities to make the attempt with a reasonable expectation for success and that is safe to do so. Most leadership attempts involve a degree of risk. To influence others, the legislative committee member has to suggest a plan of action and, at least to a degree, must assume some responsibility for the behaviors of other members who accept her plan. This opens her up to possible criticism or perhaps ridicule if the plan is not accepted. Another factor that contributes to a person's willingness to attempt leadership is the perception that others expect the attempt to be made. If the former aide feels that other members are looking to her for leadership, she will be more inclined to make an attempt. Sometimes, this perception results from being in a central position in an organization.

Whatever the means by which an individual has the opportunity for leadership, the followers or group members must be aware that the leader is attempting to influence their behavior. Awareness of the leader's intent, on the part of the followers, is a prerequisite to their actions in response to it.

A person can influence behavior without the knowledge of those being influenced. This might be called *indirect leadership* or it might be manipulation. It sometimes is associated with the use of resources. A simple illustration would be the arrangement of chairs in a meeting room to bring about a desired seating pattern. The desired behavior (the seating pattern) might be achieved without any knowledge of those attending the meeting that the arrangement was intended. Another illustration would be the placement or removal of certain toys in child's play environment as a means of encouraging certain kinds of play behaviors and eliminating others. These illustrations probably would be appropriate activities on the part of a leader. However, there are ethical considerations involved in the manipulation of resources, information, events, or relationships to obtain behavior changes without the knowledge of the intended followers. Such manipulation reduces or eliminates the individual's ability to choose whether or not to engage in the behavior desired by the leader; and it does not contribute to the person's capacity for self-direction and growth. Also, it fails to reveal the leader's motives, and it might be based on misrepresentations.

LEADERSHIP BEHAVIORS AND CHARACTERISTICS

Several basic things which leaders do can be identified.

1. *Leaders develop congruence between their goals and group or individual goals.* As indicated in Chapter 3, behavior is goal oriented; people engage in those behaviors that help meet their needs or help them to achieve their goals. To do this they develop a "plan"—a mental image of how to behave in order to meet their needs or achieve their goals. The leader's behavior is no different. His or her behavior is goal oriented and is a result of a plan or series of plans. The basic task of the leader is to cause, or facilitate the development of, congruence between the goals and plans of the followers (or individual group members) and his or her plans. This involves showing or convincing others that the behavior desired by the leader will help the followers or group members meet the goals they have. The idea can be illustrated as shown in Figure 5-1. In Situation A, there is greater congruence between the leader's goal and plan and the follower's goal and plan than there is in Situation B. Therefore, there is greater potential in Situation A for leadership to occur. In a sense, this message is directly or indirectly communicated to the follower: "If you behave on the basis of the leader's plan, you will achieve your goal."

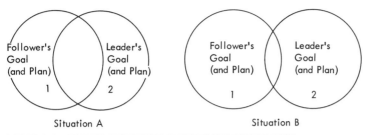

Situation A   Situation B

Figure 5-1 Relative congruence of leader and follower goals.

Ideally, leaders and followers could operate in situations where there is total congruence between goals and plans (that is, where there is total overlap) as in Figure 5-2.

This often is the case, particularly when the leader emerges from the group or when the leader adopts a style which is based on and responsive to follower participation. A democratic style, in which decision making is shared, frequently leads to complete congruence between leader and follower goals. However, the leader often operates in situations where he or she is responsible for achieving agency goals. These goals might be quite different from the personal goals of various group members.

Suppose the scoutmaster's goal is to get the boys to clean up a short section of the trail they are on, which has been littered badly by a previous group of hikers. The primary goals of the boys, on the other hand, are to play and have fun. If the scoutmaster can propose a plan of action that will both achieve the cleanup and be fun to do, he will be in a good position to exercise leadership. In a sense, the one plan (leading to a certain kind of behavior) accomplishes both the leader's and the boys' goals, even though these goals are different. What is important in this illustration, as in any leadership attempt, is that the followers see the leader's plan as one which will meet their goals. The *perceptions* of the followers determine their behavior.

The followers might realize that the leader's goal is different from theirs. They may still follow the plan if they see behavior leading to an "equitable social exchange"; that is, if the efforts they spend engaging in the behavior desired by the leader appear to be worth it in terms of their goals. Gordon stated the idea this way:

> Research has shown that effective leaders are those whose group members feel their needs are getting satisfied and the leaders themselves feel they are getting their own needs met: what some call an "equitable social exchange."[6]

Figure 5-2 Total congruence of leader and follower goals.

Another consideration related to goal congruence is *resistance to change*. Leadership processes are intended to result in changes in behavior. The would-be leader usually is trying to get another person, or members of a group, to do something. Typically, the leader hopes that the would-be followers will change their behavior—that is, do something that they were not doing previously. However, there is ample evidence that we often resist change. The amount of resistance seems to be related to two factors: (1) the degree to which the new behavior is different or departs from the would-be follower's present behavior, and (2) the intensity with which the present behavior or position is held.[7]

Assume the situation with the Cub Scouts described earlier. The scoutmaster wants to get the boys to clean up a section of trail. The new behavior is trail cleaning—picking up litter, essentially. This behavior is not very different from the boys' present behaviors of hiking along the trail. Picking up litter along a trail probably is not greatly different than cleanup activities expected at home (in their rooms or in the yards). The scouts' resistance to the activity probably would be relatively low.

However, if the scoutmaster wanted the boys to attend a joint meeting with a Girl Scout Brownie troop, he might encounter considerable resistance. Boys of this age tend not to interact socially with girls of the same age. Or, if the scoutmaster suggested that the boys invite parents to a special meeting at which each scout would give a short speech, he probably would meet resistance. Again, this behavior (speech making) departs considerably from what boys of this age usually do. Of course, there will be variations from one boy to another, in terms of how willing or unwilling they are to engage in the new behavior. In part, this will be due to the differing strengths of their present positions. A boy who is very shy probably will resist the speaking idea more than will a more outgoing member of the Cub pack; that is, he probably will hold his present position of not speaking before groups more intensely than the other boy.

2. *Leaders make choices between the uses of persuasion and the uses of power.* The leader has two basic means that can be used to obtain congruence between his or her plan and the plans or goals of the followers—logical persuasion, and the use of power.

a. *Logical persuasion* involves convincing others that the behavior desired by the leader is appropriate and that it will lead to the achievement of their goals. It is possible, in some situations, that the group may be convinced of this without any direct persuasive effort on the part of the leader. The leader's actions, related to the demands of the situation, may be so obviously related to their own needs that no further persuasion is needed. If persuasion is used, the logic of it is judged by the followers. If it appears logical to them, then it will be convincing. Shivers presented the essential characteristics of this approach.

> There are many occasions when logical persuasion can be used to gain an objective. In order to evoke properly a satisfactory response, the leader must identify and be thoroughly acquainted with the problem. He must gather suitable evidence of a factual nature and present it with clarity, directness,

and sincerity. He must anticipate the probable objections to his aims and know alternative courses of action to take.[8]

Cartwright and Zander commented on the appropriateness of the approach, particularly in situations where a democratic style is used. They noted two pertinent features of persuasion:

> First, when a person O attempts to influence P [the person upon whom the attempt is made] solely by means of persuasion, he applies no extraneous inducements (rewards and punishments) for accepting his message. P is constrained only by his own evaluation of the merits of the message, even though this evaluation may be colored by his feelings toward O. Second, when O employs persuasion to control P's overt behavior, he still permits P to behave "voluntarily" or "freely." A successful act of persuasion affects P's behavior only indirectly by influencing the beliefs, attitudes, and values that guide his behavior, and P feels that his behavior is under his own control. Persuasion, then, respects the integrity of the individual.[9]

The use of this approach by the professional society's legislature committee chairperson, for example, would involve telling the committee members of the importance of the society's support for the proposed bill, its influence on services they provide for the constituents of their agency, the ways in which it would make their work easier, the undesirable consequences of failure of the bill to be passed, and the relationship of the committee's work to the obtaining of support by the society.

b. The chairperson could attempt a use of *power*. Theorists and researchers have identified several different types of power. French and Raven defined five which are cited widely in literature on leadership: expert power, referent power, coercive power, reward power, and legitimate power.[10]

Expert Power is based on the follower's perception of the competence (skill, knowledge) of the leader. The member of the professional society's legislative committee who had worked for a state senator might move into a position of influence because of her expertise, as related to the committee's needs.

Referent power is based on such factors as liking and respect for the leader. In the situation with the Cub Scouts, one of the older boys who is popular and who is admired by the rest of the pack might exercise influence because of the boys' feelings toward him.

Coercive power and *reward power* are based on the leader's ability to "impose penalties for noncompliance," or "facilitate the attainment of desired outcomes by others."[11] If the scoutmaster promised the boys that he would take them swimming after the hike if they cleaned up the littered portion of the trail, he would be using reward power (assuming that the boys liked to swim). If, instead, he threatened to cancel a planned camping trip if they did not pick up the trash, he would be relying on coercive power.

McGregor's concepts of "needs augmentation" and "needs reduction" are related to reward and coercive powers.[12] The emphasis here is on whether or not the followers see the leader's plan as increasing (augmenting) or reducing their possibilities for need satisfaction. The promised swim augments the chances for fun in the immediate future. The threat to cancel the camping trip reduces the chances for future enjoyment.

McGregor noted the disadvantages of a needs reduction approach.

> There is plenty of evidence (both experimental and common sense) that emphasis upon reduction frequently does not induce the behavior desired [by the leader]. . . . Moreover, reduction tends to be frustrating and frustration typically creates aggression.[13]

Gordon also commented on the disadvantages of coercive power.

> Nobody wants to be coerced into doing something that results in deprivation. No wonder that power provokes such a variety of reactions in people—fighting it, avoiding it, defending against it, or trying to nullify its effects on them. The technical term for such reactions to power is "coping mechanisms."[14]

Legitimate power is based on the expectations of followers that the leader will behave in ways associated with his or her role. Typically, legitimate power relates to the authority of a position or office. The legislative committee chairperson has the opportunity to exercise legitimate power by virtue of his elected or appointed office. That is, the committee members expect that in the role of chairperson he will ask them to do certain things in their roles as members. His authority to do this is legitimized by his election (or appointment).

Hershey and Blanchard added another dimension to an understanding of power. Borrowing from the work of Amitai Etzioni, they discussed the concepts of "position power" and "personal power."[15] *Position power* comes from holding a position in an organization. This is similar to legitimate power. For example, a recreation supervisor is expected to cause certain staff behaviors to occur; this expectation is shared by the staff members and by the agency's administrator. These expectations derive from the position the supervisor holds. Reward and coercive powers also are potentially involved. The supervisor can grant rewards, such as praise and recommendations for pay raises, or punishment, such as reprimands or recommendations for layoffs.

Personal power is similar to referent power. It is based on the willingness of others to respond because of the liking or respect they have for the leader. Respect and liking might be the result of the leader's expertise. A leader may have both position and personal power, as would be the case if the supervisor were well-liked and respected.[16]

Usually, position power is delegated downward in an organization. Personal power comes from follower acceptance and flows upward through the organization.[17] This difference is related to a difference between successful leadership and effective leadership. Hershey and Blanchard, incorporating Bass's distinctions, noted that a leadership attempt might be successful but not effective. They observed that if a person, for example a supervisor, wants to get someone else to do something, the attempt will be seen as successful if the desired behavior occurs. However, if the supervisor depends only upon position power, the attempt might be successful but not effective.

> If A's leader style is not compatible with the expectations of B, and if B is antagonized and does the job only because of A's position power, then we can say that A has been successful but not effective. . . . On the other hand, if A's attempted leadership leads to a successful response, and B does the job because he wants to do it and finds it rewarding, then we consider A as having not only position power but also personal power.[18]

As suggested earlier, some of the uses of power have potential disadvantages. The leader who chooses such approaches needs to weigh the expected effectiveness of the specific leadership attempt against the possible negative reaction on the parts of the followers.

3. *Leaders consider their own personal characteristics and the characteristics of the group and the situation when selecting the approaches they will use.* There appears to be no single best style of leadership. Hershey and Blanchard, after a review of research, noted that

> . . . the evidence is clear that there is no single all-purpose leader behavior style that is effective in all situations.[19]

The activities of the leader and the ways in which he or she relates to the group are, as suggested by Hershey and Blanchard, influenced by the situation, as well as by the personal characteristics of the leader.

There has been considerable speculation about the importance of the leader's personal traits. Early leadership research focused heavily on the identification of such traits. Later studies supported the notion that there are few if any personal characteristics of leaders that are applicable in all situations. Rather, the research suggests that characteristics required of a leader vary from situation to situation. However, this does not discount the idea that leader traits are influencing factors. Considerable evidence exists that the characteristics of the leader and the demands of the situation interact. Stogdill observed that

> Most recent theorists maintain that leader characteristics and situational demands interact to determine the extent to which a given leader will prove successful in a group.[20]

Also, an individual's personality traits may contribute to his or her emergence as a leader. In a review of leadership research up to 1957, Ross and Hendry concluded that individuals who possessed certain identifiable traits would have more chances to move into leadership positions.

> While there is a good deal to the thesis that leadership is situational, this should not distort our view of the importance of the characteristics of the leader, of the type of personality the leader must be. . . . The leadership role will vary, it is true; but the leaders with the qualities detailed in this chapter

> [of their book] will undoubtedly have greater opportunities to lead and will be
> called upon more frequently to lead than persons without these qualities.[21]

The qualities noted by these authors included empathy, consideration,
consistency, and emotional stability. They also observed that leaders tend
to be identified with the norms and values of the groups with which they
are working.[22]

Later research supported the idea that personality is an important
quality for leadership. In his review, published in 1974, Stogdill noted

> Research on the characteristics of leaders indicates that they do indeed exhib-
> it personality, and personality is an important factor in emergence as a leader
> and in maintaining the role.[23]

There appears to be little support, on the one hand, for the contention that
there are generalized leadership traits that are common to all situations.
On the other hand, there is evidence that some leadership behaviors are
applicable in widely differing situations. In Ross and Hendry's 1957 review
of leadership research, the authors identified several things that an effective leader tends to do when working with most groups. These include: (1)
helping the group achieve its goal; (2) initiating new ideas and projects; (3)
analyzing the problem or project being addressed by the group, as well as
analyzing the group itself; (4) facilitating communication within the group;
(5) establishing a structure that enables the group to function effectively;
and (6) implementing a philosophy that promotes the growth and well-
being of the members of the group.[24] Two other behaviors are closely
related to leadership effectiveness. The first of these is contributing to
viscidity in the group, that is, helping the group work together as a unit.

> Viscidity is one of the most important criteria of group effectiveness. At the
> same time, the adequacy of the leader tends to be judged by his contribution
> to this aspect of group life.[25]
>
> The effective leader must perform in such a way that his actions will contrib-
> ute substantially to the ability of the group to pull together as a team.[26]

A second behavior identified by the authors as being related to effectiveness, is contributing to *hedonic tone,* that is, to the pleasantness that
comes from being a member of the group. Ross and Hendry noted the
relationship of these two factors to leadership effectiveness.

> We may suggest the hypothesis, therefore, that viscidity and hedonic tone are
> critical factors in measuring or predicting effectiveness of the group. If this
> be so, the leader who is realistic and alert will consistently seek to evaluate his
> own work in terms of his contribution to viscidity and hedonic tone in his
> group.[27]

The authors observed that all of the behaviors mentioned are closely
related; they are not independent functions. They also noted that group

effectiveness depends upon member behaviors and contributions as well as upon leader behaviors.

The leader behaviors identified by Ross and Hendry make logical sense, especially the ones of contributing to group unity and pleasantness. A recreation center staff that can work together as a unit will be more effective in reaching its goals. Members of a community art guild, setting up an exhibit for local artists, will be more likely to remain involved in guild projects if the experiences are pleasant. If the chairperson of the state professional society's legislative committee mentioned at the beginning of the chapter can help members work cooperatively and in mutually supportive ways, committee goals will be more attainable. As goals are achieved, member satisfaction should increase, both from the sense of achievement and the pleasantness of cooperative and supportive interactions. Members of the committee will thus be more interested in continuing their work or in being reappointed to the group.

Stogdill's review supports these probabilities. He concluded that

> Studies of leader behavior indicate that leaders described high (by followers) in both initiating structure (letting followers know what to expect) and consideration (looking out for the welfare of followers) tend to promote high degrees of follower satisfaction and, in some cases, group performance.[28]

Initiating structure seems closely related to promoting the ability of the group to work together, and consideration probably contributes directly to the pleasantness of the group experience for members.

While it does seem valid that some specific behaviors are related to leadership, this does not contradict the notion that leadership is a function of the group and of the unique demands of the situation.

Most individuals who attempt to exercise leadership processes in recreation and park situations arrive at the opportunity to do so by election or appointment. The above discussions suggest that the person who holds a central position in a group, by virtue of election or appointment, must do several things if he or she wishes to exercise leadership. The would-be leader must analyze the situation to assess such things as group and individual needs, group and individual capabilities, available resources, and other factors. He or she must answer such questions as, What is the nature of the task to be accomplished? What are the people like with whom I will be working? What is my relationship to these people at this time? Do they know me or have any particular feelings about me? What do we have to work with? How much time do we have?

Further, the would-be leader must take stock of personal characteristics, in light of the situational demands, asking, What relevant skills and knowledges do I have? What are my specific shortcomings in terms of this situation? How do I feel about the task, the people involved, and my own chances for success?

The intended leader should recognize that different answers to the above questions will suggest different specific approaches. No single technique or method will fit all specific situations.

The intended leader should also recognize that the demands of the particular situation may be such that someone else will be more capable of exercising leadership at that particular time, even though that person may not be the designated leader.

Finally, he or she must recognize that conditions will change as each situation develops. The meeting of some needs, or the solving of some aspects of a task, often creates other needs or tasks. The abilities and attitudes of group members may change as they interact with each other and with the leader. In this sense, situations are dynamic and changing. Persons wishing to exert leadership must remain alert to these possible changes.

STYLES OF LEADERSHIP

> The park superintendent was meeting with the two ranger-interpreters and four volunteers who staff the park visitor center. The topic of the discussion was a major revamping of the interpretive program offered at the center. The meeting, the most recent in a series of several devoted to planning the changes which were to be made, had been in progress for about two hours. Several agreements had been reached, and the group was deciding on the relocation of some exhibit cases.

> The phone rang. A ranger on the other end reported the outbreak of a small fire in the upper northeast section of the park. The superintendent quickly asked for some details about the fire. He told the ranger to do what she could to contain it and promised to send help. As he hung up, the superintendent made several decisions—which units to dispatch to the fire, whether or not to request immediate backup assistance from an outside agency, and whether or not to evacuate at this time a campground downwind of the fire.

In both these instances, the superintendent was engaging in leadership behavior. In both, he hoped to see the staff perform in such a way as to bring about desired objectives. But his style was somewhat different in the two situations. In the visitor center example, he functioned as one member of a decision-making group. In the fire example, he directly assumed responsibilities for making decisions.

As suggested in Chapter 3, each individual is unique. These uniquenesses of our individual personalities also influence our uses of leadership processes. Thus the methods we use will be somewhat different. However, we can identify several basic leadership styles.

DEMOCRATIC AND AUTHORITARIAN STYLES

One common definition of style is based on the degree to which a leader shares the making of decisions with the group. A leader who operates in an autocratic fashion tends to make decisions for the group; the democratic leader involves the group in decision making. The authoritarian leader might seek the opinions of group members and might take these into consideration. The leader also might provide considerable information for the group about the reasons for the decision which he or she makes. However, if group members do not participate in actually making the decision, the style is autocratic.

White and Lippitt conducted a study of democratic and autocratic leadership styles that defined characteristic behaviors of leaders in both styles and the typical consequences in terms of group member reactions.[29] The study involved the structuring of several clubs for elementary-school-age boys, a rotating assignment of adult leaders who worked with the clubs, and the observation and analysis of the reaction of the boys under different leadership styles. The adult leaders used democratic, autocratic, and laissez-faire approaches at different times with different groups.

In the laissez-faire style, the leader stayed apart and aloof from the group except to give information when asked. For the purposes of this chapter, a laissez-faire style can be considered essentially a nonleadership approach since no direct attempts to cause changes in behavior are involved. The one exception would be where a leader remains uninvolved as a strategy for causing others to take action in the absence of the leader's activity. As an illustration, the scoutmaster referred to earlier might purposefully avoid organizing a cookout for the Cubs as a means of getting the boys to do their own planning.

In the White and Lippitt study, authoritarian leaders gave many more direct orders than did democratic leaders. The investigators noted this behavior as the primary characteristic of the autocratic approach.

> Forty-five percent of the verbal behavior of the autocrats, in contrast to 3 percent in democracy and 4 percent in laissez-faire, consisted of this simplest form of the imposition of one human will upon another.[30]

In contrast, democratic leaders much more often provided guiding suggestions; 24 percent of leader behavior, as opposed to 6 percent in the authoritarian style. Democratic leaders also more frequently gave information, engaged in behavior that the researchers described as "jovial" and "confiding," and stimulated self-direction among group members.[31]

The study pointed to several consequences of the different leadership styles, in terms of member behavior.[32]

Autocracy frequently led to two different reactions: (1) hostility and aggression expressed within the membership group, including aggressive behavior against "scapegoats"; or (2) submissiveness and generally subdued behavior. Also, in the autocratically led groups, there was more dependence upon the leader and less individuality. There was a greater "drop-out" rate in autocracy, suggesting that this style of leadership more often creates dissatisfaction among members.

In the democratic groups, members expressed greater friendliness and group-mindedness. More sharing behavior was evident. The amount of work completed (related to the activities undertaken in the clubs—model building, soap carving, and so on) was somewhat greater in autocracy. However, the quality of the work completed under democratic conditions was better than under autocracy.

Democratic approaches to leadership have some clear advantages over autocratic methods. However, there are times when an authoritarian style would be more appropriate. A democratic approach appears to be most effective if followers are highly motivated, have the necessary abilities to carry out the tasks with which they are involved, and have "relatively high needs for independence."[33] If these characteristics are not present, an autocratic approach might be more effective.

Also, in situations where rapid action is needed to prevent the imminent development of hazardous or other highly undesirable circumstances, shared decision making might be inappropriate. The park superintendent responding to the reported fire is in this kind of a situation. Obviously, hasty action that is poorly thought out is useless and may contribute more to the problem than to the solution. But when quick decisions are required, and when the person making the decisions has competence to do so, an authoritarian approach might be the most appropriate. Further, the members of the group probably would expect the leader to behave autocratically in such a situation. When members expect either democratic or authoritarian behavior, the leader who attempts a contrary approach may encounter group resistance, at least initially.

In some situations, the leader will not have the opportunity to elect a democratic approach. Agency policies, which are established by policy boards or administrators, usually must be implemented by personnel at supervisory and functional levels. It would be inappropriate, if not absurd, for the park superintendent to solicit a vote from staff members on whether or not the park will continue to be open to the public. Unless there are unusual circumstances, the responsibility for that decision rests at a higher level. Some leaders attempt to give the appearance of a democratic approach when, in fact, the decision has already been made. They do so to gain the support of group members for the decision, in the hope that the members will decide upon the course of action that has already been established and think that the decision is their own. This approach is dishonest, at the least, and if the group elects a different course of action, the leader must admit the deceit and announce the predetermined course. Obviously, this works against group trust and respect for the leader.

Overall, it seems that democratic or participatory leadership has significant advantages. However, there will be times when the leader chooses to act autocratically for various reasons. When the leader does so, he or she must consider the probable consequences, in terms of staff morale and long-term effectiveness, and must determine whether the gains are worth the possible costs.

TASK-ORIENTED AND RELATIONSHIP-ORIENTED STYLES

Another approach to leadership behavior relates to the degree of "task-oriented" behaviors or "considerate, relationship-oriented" behaviors engaged in by the leader. Fiedler developed a comprehensive "contingency model" of leadership effectiveness that encompasses these two styles. In the *task-oriented* style, the leader's emphasis is on completing the task and the satisfaction derived from doing so. In the *relationship-oriented* style, the leader gives greater emphasis to establishing and maintaining good interpersonal relationships.[34] Fiedler contended that the appropriateness of either of these styles is contingent upon three conditions related to the group and the task: (1) the position power held by the leader; (2) the personal relationship between the leader and the group members; and (3) the degree to which the task is structured.[35]

Fiedler's model suggests that a task-oriented style is most appropriate when the conditions with which a leader is working are either highly favorable or relatively unfavorable. Favorable conditions would be those (1) where the leader is respected, trusted, or liked by group members; (2) where the task is structured and clearly defined; and (3) where the leader has position power or legitimate power (the authority of an office, with the attendant abilities to reward or withhold rewards). Unfavorable conditions would involve negative feelings toward the leader on the part of the group members, an ambiguous or vague task, and weak position power held by the leader. Fiedler provided these examples:

> In the very favorable conditions in which the leader has power, informal backing, and a relatively well-structured task, the group is ready to be directed, and the group members expect to be told what to do. Consider the captain of an airliner in its final landing approach. We would hardly want him to turn to his crew for a discussion on how to land.

> In the relatively unfavorable situation, we would again expect that the task-oriented leader will be more effective than will the considerate leader who is concerned with inter-personal relations. Consider here the disliked chairman of a volunteer committee which is asked to plan the office picnic on a beautiful Sunday. If the leader asks too many questions about what the group ought to do or how he should proceed, he is likely to be told that "we ought to go home."[36]

The relationship-oriented style is most effective where the situations within which the leader is operating are only moderately favorable or are moderately unfavorable. In these situations, the leader might be well liked by group members but the task may be unstructured. Or the task might be clearly defined, but the leader does not have the trust and respect of the group. If the task is unstructured, the leader who has the support of the group can be effective if he or she can provide the kind of group environment that encourages members to participate and make suggestions. In this way, the potentials of individual members to contribute to the greater structuring of the task can be maximized. The leader who is not on good terms with the group will have a better chance of obtaining members' commitment to a task if it is unambiguous and well defined, and if he or she is sensitive to the feelings of the group and makes an effort to consult with members and minimize their resistance.

Assume that the park superintendent, mentioned earlier, was relatively new to the job, and that the staff had some negative feelings toward him because of rumors about his style of administration in a former position. Assume also that the task of modifying the program of the interpretive center was fairly structured. That is, the objective to be achieved was clear. There were some different approaches which could have been taken in the modification, but the major aspects of the project could be identified readily. And the outcome of the group's work would be easy to evaluate, both by visual examination and by periodic observations of the reactions of visitors. In addition to the factors of staff distrust and task structure, assume also that the superintendent has only a moderate amount of position power. He has the authority to recommend promotions or terminations, but his ability to actually give raises or fire employees is limited by civil service procedures.

These conditions would be neither highly favorable nor highly unfavorable. They would be somewhat favorable, but not clearly so. Under these circumstances, Fiedler's model would suggest that the leader give considerable effort to building better relationships with the staff. According to the research upon which Fiedler's model is based, this approach would produce better results (that is, better planning of the program modification) than would an approach that focused more directly on getting the job done.

Fiedler contended that leader-member relationships have a greater influence on the degree to which a situation is favorable or unfavorable than do position power and task structure. A leader who has good relationships with the group—who is trusted and well-liked—does not have much need for position power.[37]

Task structure appears to be next most influential in determining favorableness. Fiedler noted that the organization for which the leader works can do a great deal to structure the task. It does so by developing standard operating procedures, performance manuals, and methods of quality control. In the illustration of the fire in the park, standard operating policies and procedures related to fire suppression no doubt would have been developed; and they would be followed by fire crews. These procedures probably would be written in manuals and crews would be trained on the basis of the written procedures. These factors all would contribute to task structure.

> The structured task is, in effect, one way of influencing member behavior by means of organizational sanctions which can be imposed, and it reinforces position power. Alternatively, we may say that a group which is engaged in a highly structured task does not need a leader with as much position power because the leader's influence is implied by the instructions inherent in the task.[38]

Since the leader often is attempting to accomplish tasks desired by the organization, the organization has a stake in the leader's success.

Of course, the leader may do a variety of things to create greater or lesser task structure in addition to or in place of what the organization does.

Fiedler used four dimensions, developed by Shaw, as measures of task structure:

1. The degree to which the correctness of the decision can be demonstrated by authority, logic, or feedback.
2. The degree to which members understand what the goal is.
3. The degree to which one path to the goal is evident (the lack of multiple paths to the goal).
4. The degree to which one solution is more correct (the lack of more than one correct solution).[39]

Position power is the third and least influential factor in determining favorableness. However, the relative influence of position power, as compared to leader-member relations and task structure, is not fixed.

> Large differences in rank and position power may outweigh relatively slight differences in task structure. An extremely structured task . . . may outweigh the importance of poor leader-member relations. However, these . . . are likely to be the exception rather than the rule.[40]

The measure of position power (or legitimate power) is related to such things as the leader's authority to hire and fire, and give rewards (promotions, pay raises), and to identifying symbols (job titles, uniforms, size of office).[41]

Edginton and Williams suggested that position power has declined in influence, in relation to personal power.

> In today's organization there is a great shift away from position power and greater increase in personal power. . . . This shift is the result of many circumstances: the effects of unions, civil rights, legislation, and changes in emphasis in government to more power to the citizenry.[42]

The authors noted that threats of being fired or of having other disciplinary actions taken are no longer the strong motivators they once were.

The generalization that emerges from a review of Fiedler's theory is that the leader should base his or her style on the degree to which the situation is favorable or unfavorable. A task-oriented style will be more effective in highly favorable or highly unfavorable situations. A relationship-oriented style will be more appropriate in situations that are neither highly favorable nor highly unfavorable.

The question might be asked, Are these two styles synonymous with autocratic and democratic styles of leadership? They are not. A democratic leader can give greater emphasis either to the task at hand or to personal relationships and still share decision making with the group. Similarly, an authoritarian leader can give greater attention to either dimension without relinquishing his or her prerogatives to make the decisions. However, there are some probable relationships between the styles. On one hand, a democratic style tends to produce better group morale; to this extent, leader-member relations might be enhanced by a democratic approach. A leader working in a situation where a relationship-oriented style is suggested might achieve this style more readily by operating democratically. On the other hand, there might be situations where a task-oriented style would be enhanced by using autocratic methods. In a highly favorable situation, a leader would have greater opportunity to use an authoritarian approach, especially because of position power. Nonetheless, the leader who elects to operate autocratically must weigh the benefits against the possible costs in terms of member morale.

INFLUENCES OF GROUP MATURITY ON STYLE

Hershey and Blanchard developed a concept of leadership style that they called a *Situational Leadership Theory*. Like Fiedler, these authors based their theory on two primary leadership behaviors: task-oriented behaviors and relationship-oriented behaviors. They provided these definitions of the two basic behaviors:

> Task behavior—*The extent to which leaders are likely to organize and define the roles of the members of their group (followers); to explain what activities each is to do and when, where, and how tasks are to be accomplished; characterized by endeavoring to establish well-defined patterns of organization, channels of communication, and ways of getting jobs accomplished.*
>
> Relationship behavior—*The extent to which leaders are likely to maintain personal relationships between themselves and members of their group (followers) by opening up channels of communication providing socio-emotional support, "psychological strokes," and facilitating behaviors.*[43]

The definitions are adopted from concepts developed in the Ohio State Leadership Studies.[44]

Unlike Fiedler, Hershey and Blanchard held that these behaviors were not two ends of the same continuum.

> Most evidence indicates that leader behavior must be plotted on two separate axes rather than on a single continuum. Thus, a leader who is high on task behavior is not necessarily high or low on relationship behavior. Any combination of the two dimensions may occur.[45]

Hall and Williams noted the existence of differing points of view on this question.

> Some leaders feel that the two concerns [for purpose or for people] are mutually exclusive—they can only be concerned about one or the other. . . . Other leaders feel that they can work toward some kind of balance between the two. . . . Still other leaders see the two concerns as functionally related, and feel that both can be given maximum emphasis simultaneously. . . .[46]

Hershey and Blanchard held that concern for the task and a concern for relationships (between the leader and group members) are different factors. However, the behaviors related to both concerns might be in evidence, in varying degrees, in any particular leadership attempt. Their Situational Leadership Theory suggests that the mix of the two behaviors used by the leader at any one time is dependent upon the situation or, more specifically, upon the maturity of the group members. Maturity is defined as the capacity to be self-directing. It is the extent to which group members are able to set realistic goals, and their willingness and ability to engage in behaviors directed toward meeting these goals.[47] A mature group or individual would be motivated to engage in the desired behaviors and would have the necessary skills and knowledge to do so. A relatively immature group or individual would lack these qualities. Hershey and Blanchard emphasized that maturity must be thought of as related to specific tasks, rather than as a generalized condition. Any one individual's maturity probably will vary from task to task. They also noted that maturity involves both ability to carry out the task (*job maturity*) and self-confidence and self-respect (*psychological maturity*).[48]

The basic premise of the theory is that with immature individuals or groups the most effective leadership approach will be a mix of high-task and low-relationship behaviors. As the maturity of the individual or group increases, the effective leader will increase relationship behaviors, and decrease task behaviors. With further increases in maturity, the leader also decreases relationship behaviors. With a highly mature individual or group, the most effective leadership style will be low in both task and relationship behaviors.

Hershey and Blanchard used a diagram similar to the one shown in Figure 5-3[49] to symbolize the relationships between maturity and leadership style. The dotted line represents the mix of task-oriented and relationship-oriented leader behaviors.

The application of this theory to the illustration of the park interpretive program, earlier in the chapter, would suggest the following behaviors on the part of the superintendent. If the ranger-interpreters were immature (were poorly motivated and had little capacity for the task at hand), the superintendent would be most effective if he focused primarily on defining and organizing the rangers' work—explaining the jobs to be done and indicating how and when they should be done. This might be represented as Point A in Figure 5-3. The assumption is that the superintendent must be fairly direct if staff motivation and ability is low. At Point B, the staff has some ability and some motivation; therefore, the superintendent's task would be to nurture these conditions by increasing his attention to relationships, while at the same time continuing to provide sufficient direction. With the higher levels of staff ability and motivation, present at Point C, the superintendent could reduce the amounts of direction given to staff. At the upper levels, for example at Point D, he could let staff members work essentially on their own in the program modification.

In the Situational Leadership Theory, a key word is suggested for each of the four cells shown in Figure 5-3.[50] The key word in Cell 1 (low group maturity; high task and low relationship leader behaviors) is "telling." Here, the leader tells the group members what to do, how to do it,

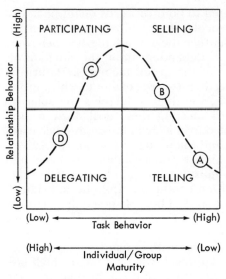

Figure 5-3 Situational leadership theory (adapted from Hershey and Blanchard, 1982).

and when to do it. In Cell 2 (low-to-moderate group maturity; high-to-moderate task and moderate-to-high relationship leader behaviors) the key word is "selling." The leader defines what is to be done, as in Cell 1, but engages also in supporting behavior intended to contribute to the group's willingness to work at the task. "Participating" is the key word in Cell 3 (moderate-to-high group maturity; moderate-to-low task and high-to-moderate relationship leader behaviors). Under these circumstances, the leader and the group provide the structure needed for task accomplishment; the leader facilitates this process. In Cell 4, "delegating" is the key word. As suggested earlier, when a group shows high maturity the leader who engages in both low task behaviors and low relationship behaviors will be most effective. That is, the effective leader in these conditions delegates the task to the group.

The authors also noted the relationship between the Situational Leadership Theory and a participatory (democratic) style of leadership. They suggested that as individuals and groups become more mature, a participatory approach becomes increasingly effective, up to a point, after which it levels off. Conversely, the lower the maturity, the less the likelihood that a democratic approach will be useful.[51]

SOME SUGGESTIONS RELATED TO STYLES

The three approaches to leadership style discussed above are not necessarily incompatible. What is suggested in all of them is that the leader should carefully assess the situation within which he or she will be working. There is ample evidence the nature of the task to be completed and the characteristics of group members influence the specific behaviors of the leader. This means that the ability to analyze and diagnose situations, and the ability to make accurate inferences about the feelings, expectations, and capabilities of group members are both necessary prerequisites to effective leadership. It also means that leaders must be able to adapt their styles to varying circumstances. This is not easy—we tend to find a particular method of leading and use it consistently, usually one with which we had initial success. Also, some styles of leadership tend to be more comfortable and natural for us than others. The challenge is to adapt appropriately to meet the demands of changing situations without violating our basic personality structures—that is, without "trying to be persons that we are not." Part of the challenge is to be more open to ways of growing and changing that will permit us to be more adaptable.

Changes in style should not be made for the sake of change alone. Enough consistency in style is needed so that those with whom the leader works will know what to expect, and not be confused.[52] Modifications in style are called for when the circumstances change within which the leader is working, and when the leader's current approach is ineffective. Also, it is possible that a leader may not be effective in some situations, regardless of the style he or she selects.[53] The objective in adapting to circumstances is to maximize one's effectiveness—to become as effective as possible and to change when appropriate. However, temporary setbacks or failures to achieve objectives may not be causes for change. Sensitivity is required in determining when to continue with an approach and when to modify it.

As suggested in both Fiedler's and Hershey and Blanchard's theories, the leader may, depending upon the circumstances, select a style that gives greater or lesser emphasis to task-oriented and relationship-oriented behaviors. However, this does not mean that, in situations where there is a relatively greater focus on task-oriented behaviors, the leader can ignore completely the matter of interpersonal relationships. A leader's emphasis on the task need not be carried out in ways that alienate or threaten group members. The general notions about developing effective relationships that were discussed in Chapter 4 are also applicable in leadership situations.

SUMMARY

The concept of leadership presented in this chapter is one in which one individual attempts to influence the behavior of another individual (or individuals) toward the attainment of certain goals.

The opportunity an individual has to engage in leadership behavior results from either appointment or election to a position, or from the emergence of the person in direct response to a particular situation.

An individual's decision to attempt to exercise leadership is dependent upon whether or not the person recognizes the need for it, feels capable of doing so, and believes that it is safe to do so.

Leaders attempt to develop congruence between their goals and the goals of groups or individuals with whom they are working. They do this through the use of persuasion or different types of power. Differing circumstances will suggest which general approach is. most appropriate. In some uses of power, the leader may generate undesirable follower behaviors, such as anxiety, frustration, or hostility.

The key elements in the leadership process are the characteristics of the attempted leader, the nature of the followers (or group), and the demands of the particular situation. These factors influence the particular style of leadership that is selected.

One consideration in selecting a style is the degree to which the leader shares decision making with others. In democratic approaches, decisions are shared; in autocratic methods, they are not. Another style consideration is the relative emphasis on task-oriented behaviors or relationship-oriented behaviors by the leader. In Fiedler's theory, task-oriented behaviors are more effective in situations that are either highly favorable or relatively unfavorable for the leader. "Favorableness" is defined in terms of the relationships between the leader and group members, the degree to which the task is structured, and the position power of the leader. In Hershey and Blanchard's theory, high task-oriented and low relationship-oriented leader behaviors are more effective with groups that are less mature. Maturity is the degree to which group members are willing and able to engage in appropriate behaviors related to the task. With mature groups, low task-oriented and low relationship-oriented leader behaviors are most effective. For groups that are neither highly mature nor immature, a combination of task-oriented and relationship-oriented behaviors seems to be the most appropriate leadership style.

REVIEW QUESTIONS

5-1   What is leadership, as discussed in this chapter?

5-2   Individuals can become leaders by being elected or appointed, or by emerging in a specific situation. Leisure service personnel usually are appointed. What advantage does an emergent leader have over one who is appointed?

5-3   What is meant by the idea that leaders develop congruence between their goals and the goals of those with whom they are working?

5-4   What different kinds of power can be used by a leader? What are the disadvantages of using power? What other alternative is available to the leader?

5-5   In what basic way does autocratic leadership differ from democratic? How do each of these styles affect followers? Under what conditions should each style be used?

5-6   In what ways are the theories developed by Fiedler and by Hershey and Blanchard similar? How do they differ?

TO DO

5-A Watch several television programs some evening. Often, at some point in each program, someone is trying to get someone else to do something. If you see a behavior on a program that you think could be called leadership, make some brief written notes about what happened. Later, go back over these notes to remind yourself of the incidents. In each, decide whether the person engaging in leadership used persuasion or power. If power were involved, what kind was used?

5-B Visit a recreation and park facility of some kind (such as a park or center), and observe leisure service personnel working with participants or with staff. Look for situations where staff members are engaged in leadership behavior. What different styles seem to be in evidence? What specific staff behaviors are cues to the style used?

5-C Think of something that you would like to get another person to do—something that you have to do that could be done by the person if he or she would do it, or something you feel the person should do for himself or herself. It should be something that would take more than a simple request. How could you get the desired behavior to take place? What leadership methods might be effective in this situation?

END NOTES

1. Ralph M. Stogdill, *Handbook of Leadership: A Survey of Theory and Research* (New York: The Free Press, A Division of Macmillan Publishing Co., Inc., 1974) pp. 7–15.

2. Stogdill, *Handbook of Leadership*, pp. 15–16.

3. Ibid., p. 23.

4. Paul Hershey and Kenneth H. Blanchard, *Management of Organizational Behavior: Utilizing Human Resources*, 4th ed.,© 1982. Reprinted by permission of Prentice-Hall, Inc., p. 83.

5. Dorwin Cartwright and Alvin Zander, eds., *Group Dynamics: Research and Theory* 3rd ed. (New York: Harper & Row Publishers, Inc., 1968), p. 310.

6. Thomas Gordon, *Leader Effectiveness Training* (New York: Wyden Books, A Division of P.E.I. Books, Inc., 1977), p. 3.

7. Cartwright and Zander, *Group Dynamics*, p. 227.

8. Jay S. Shivers, *Leadership in Recreational Service* (New York: Macmillan Publishing Co., Inc., 1963), p. 35.

9. Cartwright and Zander, *Group Dynamics*, p. 221.

10. John R. P. French, Jr. and Bertram Raven, "The Bases of Social Power," in *Group Dynamics*, pp. 262–68.

11. Stogdill, *Handbook of Leadership*, p. 287.

12. Douglas McGregor, "The Staff Function in Human Relations," *The Journal of Social Issues* 4, no. 3 (Summer 1948): 11.

13. McGregor, "The Staff Function in Human Relations," *The Journal of Social Issues*, p. 12.

14. Gordon, *Leader Effectiveness Training*, p. 159.

15. Hershey and Blanchard, *Management of Organizational Behavior*, pp. 107–8.

16. Ibid., p. 107.

17. Ibid., p. 110.

18. Ibid., p. 109.

19. Ibid., p. 122.

20. Stogdill, *Handbook of Leadership*, p. 411.

21. Murray G. Ross and Charles E. Hendry, *New Understandings of Leadership: A Survey and Application of Research* (New York: Association Press, 1957), p. 59.

22. Ross and Hendry, *New Understandings of Leadership*, p. 59.

23. Stogdill, *Handbook of Leadership*, p. 411.

24. Ross and Hendry, *New Understandings of Leadership*, pp. 70–86.

25. Ibid., p. 65.

26. Ibid., p. 67.

27. Ibid., pp. 68–69.

28. Stogdill, *Handbook of Leadership*, p. 412.

29. Ralph White and Ronald Lippitt, "Leader Behavior and Member Reaction in Three 'Social Climates,'" in *Group Dynamics*, pp. 318–34.

30. White and Lippitt, "Leader Behavior and Member Reaction in Three 'Social Climates,'" in *Group Dynamics*, p. 320.

31. Ibid., pp. 321–24.

32. Ibid., pp. 326–33.

33. James V. Spotts, "The Problem of Leadership: A Look at Some Recent Findings of Behavioral Science Research," in *Behavioral Science and the Manager's Role*, ed. William B. Eddy and Others (Washington, D.C.: NTL Institute for Applied Behavioral Science, 1969), p. 152.

34. Fred E. Fiedler, *A Theory of Leadership Effectiveness* (New York: McGraw-Hill Book Co., 1967), p. 13.

35. Fiedler, *A Theory of Leadership Effectiveness*, pp. 22–34.

36. Ibid., p. 147.

37. Ibid., pp. 29–31.

38. Ibid., pp. 27–28.

39. Ibid., p. 28.

40. Ibid., p. 144.

41. Ibid., p. 23.

42. Christopher R. Edginton and John G. Williams, *Productive Management of Leisure Service Organizations: A Behavioral Approach* (New York: John Wiley & Sons, 1978), pp. 187–88.

43. Paul Hershey and Kenneth H. Blanchard, *Management of Organizational Behavior*, 4th ed. p. 96.

44. Roger M. Stogdill and Alvin E. Coons, eds., *Leader Behavior: Its Description and Measurement*, Research Monograph No. 88 (Columbus, Ohio: Bureau of Business Research, The Ohio State University, 1957), pp. 42–43.

45. Hershey and Blanchard, *Management of Organizational Behavior*, p. 95.

46. Jay Hall and Martha S. Williams, "How to Interpret Your Scores from the Styles of Leadership Survey," A companion booklet to *Styles of Leadership Survey* (Woodlands, Tex.: Teleometrics, International, 1968), p. 1.

47. Hershey and Blanchard, *Management of Organizational Behavior*, pp. 151, 157.
48. Ibid., p. 157.
49. Ibid., p. 152.
50. Ibid., pp. 153–54.
51. Ibid., pp. 168–69.
52. Edginton and Williams, *Productive Management of Leisure Service Organizations*, p. 184.
53. Ibid., p. 186.

chapter 6

Working with Groups

PREVIEW

The process of leadership often occurs in a group setting, and recreation and park personnel work with a wide variety of different groups. Chapter 6 is devoted to an examination of these groups.

What is a group? What are some of the characteristics of groups? Does a group—for example, the members of a local chapter of the Audubon Society who meet to discuss a future outing—differ from a collection of individuals who happen to be assembled in one place at the same time, as in the case of the audience at a lecture on migratory waterfowl? The chapter will begin with some answers to these questions.

Groups typically seem to develop through some rather predictable stages. These will be identified and discussed.

The stages of development through which a group usually passes result largely from the collective behaviors of the individual members. These behaviors are influenced both by the personal characteristics of members and by the group itself. Attention will be given in the chapter to individual behaviors in the group, and to influencing factors.

Some groups are more effective than others. Some seem to function smoothly and without significant problems. Others, for various reasons, encounter difficulties. Often these difficulties interfere with the continued development of the group. Occasionally, they lead to a break-up of the group. Group problems will be examined, and some ways of working with groups and helping them function more effectively will be presented.

The six boys sitting around the table in the downtown YMCA were noisy and energetic; several attempted to talk at the same time and there was much rattling of chairs and movement of bodies. They were planning a canoe trip down a section of a nearby river. The leader took an active part in the discussion, and was encouraging the boys to do some clean-up at different popular stopping places along the river bank as a part of their outing. The boys seemed to be developing enthusiasm for his ideas.

After working with the boys, the leader attended a staff meeting called by the Y program secretary. The secretary indicated that the main purpose of the meeting was to get a staff decision on the date, time, and place of the annual father-son banquet. The secretary suggested that it be held on the same date and at the same location as last year. Two or three of the staff members raised some objections; a general discussion followed during which the secretary explained his reasons for suggesting the same date and location.

Recreation and park personnel inevitably work with groups. One type of group is comprised of users of an agency's services (such as a YMCA club planning a river trip). Another type of group is the agency staff with whom the individual member works. Personnel also relate to various other citizen groups, such as service clubs, advisory committees, and boards and commissions. In different groups, or in one group at different times, the worker may play a variety of roles: leader, member, resource person, or observer.

To work effectively with any group, the individual should be aware of basic aspects of group processes and of the potential influences of the group on individual members. He or she should also be able to identify the goals of the group and the resources available to achieve these goals. The worker should be able to facilitate the ability of the group to accomplish its purposes and maximize the satisfaction members experience from being in the group.

WHAT IS A GROUP?

There are many different definitions for the term *group*.[1] In everyday usage, we often speak of any collection of people as a group, the essential feature being the presence of more than one person. However, this is a general concept that is not very useful for our purposes. The typical kinds of groups with which recreation and park personnel work have additional characteristics, found in most groups. One of these characteristics is that of interaction, which leads to mutual influences among members. Shaw's definition focuses on this aspect.

> A group is defined as two or more persons who are interacting with one another in such a manner that each person influences and is influenced by each other person.[2]

It is important to note that interaction alone does not differentiate a group from a collection of people. Assume the situation where you go to an art gallery by yourself. Many other people are viewing the paintings displayed in several different rooms. As you move from one painting to the next, you interact with others—you avoid bumping into each other and you do not interfere with each other's viewing of the work on display. To that extent, you do influence each other's behavior. However, the influence is casual, temporary, and fairly impersonal. In groups, the mutual influences that result from interaction usually are deeper and more pervasive. The interactions usually are aimed at achieving some shared goal, as well as satisfying the individual members' needs. Shivers provided this definition.

> A group is made up of two or more individuals whose reactions and behavior patterns are modified because of some interpersonal relationship developed over time and created during the pursuit of some common interest, utilizing this entity to achieve satisfaction of needs.[3]

Knowles and Knowles noted that group members are interdependent in their attempts to satisfy needs. That is, "the members need the help of one another to accomplish the purposes for which they joined the group."[4]

A definition given by Potter and Anderson focused on the aspect of individual need satisfaction as well as on structure, identity, and content.

> A group refers to a face-to-face or co-acting interaction system in which successive interactions determine its structure, identity, and content, and contribute to the satisfaction of certain needs of the members of the system.[5]

Groups do develop identities. Most groups have an identifiable membership; the group's existence can be known by nonmembers, and members realize that they are members. Knowles and Knowles spoke of this last condition as a "group consciousness."[6] Groups also are structured. Structure has to do with such things as roles assumed by different members, patterns of expected behaviors or norms and ways in which the group is organized. Two terms are useful to note at this point: *role* and *norm*.

Roles are the behaviors of individual group members that come to be expected by other members. They can be behaviors related to positions, such as the chairperson or the secretary, or they can be associated with the typical kinds of behavior in which different individuals engage in the group. These include ways members contribute to the group's task. They may include such things as whether a member tends to be dominant or submissive, positive or negative.[7] Other members come to expect this kind of behavior of certain individuals, based on their past behaviors in the group. Sessoms and Stevenson noted this, and called attention to a possible problem.

> Although different individuals play different roles at different times in the group process, most become comfortable with certain roles and tend to play them more than others. Consequently, groups tend to look to certain members for certain activity. They expect John to initiate discussion, Mary to gatekeep, and Fred to summarize.[8]

> Roles are essential to good group performance, but if they are performed inappropriately they may interfere with the group's operation. There is also a danger of stereotyping people in certain roles, thereby negating their poten-

tial contribution in other roles. Who expects the clown to initiate or give pertinent facts?[9]

As indicated, roles may be associated with positions held in a group. In some groups, different positions are afforded different statuses, and different amounts of influence. Shaw described this characteristic.

> When one identifies a person's position in the group, one is at the same time identifying his [or her] relative standing with respect to such dimensions as power, leadership, and attractiveness. Status, on the other hand, refers to the evaluation of that position. It is the rank accorded the position by group members—the prestige of the position.[10]

Shaw also noted that all members of a group hold positions, and that a group's structure can be thought of as the "pattern of relationships" that exists among these positions.[11]

Norms also are the expectations members hold that are related to behavior. However, unlike roles, norms involve behaviors expected of all members. Norms are developed by a group so that members know what is expected of them. These might be thought of as standards or rules of conduct. Knowles and Knowles suggested the kinds of things that often are included.

> Which subjects may be discussed, which are taboo; how openly members may express their feelings; the propriety of volunteering one's services; the length and frequency of statements considered allowable; whether or not interrupting is permitted—all these and many more "dos" and "don'ts" are embodied in a group's standards.[12]

Norms not only help each member know what is expected; they also permit all members to anticipate the behavior of each other member, with respect to the standards that have been developed. This enables the group to function more effectively and with less confusion.[13]

Hare reviewed over 6,000 references on groups written during the period from 1898 to 1974. Based on the characteristics of groups that emerged from this review, his definition provides a useful summary.

> There are then, in sum, five characteristics which differentiate the *group* from *a collection of individuals.* The members of the group are in *interaction* with one another. They share a common *goal* and set of *norms*, which give direction and limits to their activity. They also develop a set of *roles* and a *network of interpersonal attractions,* which serve to differentiate them from other groups.[14]

The YMCA club and the staff described at the beginning of the chapter would exhibit these characteristics. In both, there is interaction among members. Members share some common goals: the planning of a canoe trip and a father-son banquet, for example. They also probably receive a variety of individual satisfactions from being part of the particular group.

In attempting to achieve the goals, and to meet individual needs, they rely on each other for help.

In each group, a set of norms could be identified. In the staff group, it is apparent that objections can be voiced. No doubt, there are some accepted ways in which members can do this. In the club group, it is OK to be noisy and energetic.

Roles also could be defined. The leader and the secretary both engage in behaviors associated with their "official" positions. Perhaps, one staff member tends consistently not to initiate behavior but to support the suggestions and ideas of others. Maybe one of the boys tends to dominate the other club members in most discussions and activities. The positions associated with these role behaviors stand in some kind of relationship to each other, and this can be thought of as the structure of each of the groups.

Finally, the conditions of identity are present. The club is an identifiable group; so is the staff. Symbols such as jackets and emblems may contribute to this identity.

GROUPS IN RECREATION AND PARK SETTINGS

As suggested earlier, recreation and park personnel relate to a variety of different groups. One general type of group is made up of *participants*. The YMCA club is an example. So is the Cub Scout troop described at the beginning of the last chapter. Another kind of group is the *functional group*. An example would be the professional society's legislative committee mentioned in the last chapter. Included in this category also would be agency staff groups and community groups devoted to the accomplishment of some specific task or tasks. In groups of participants, the members come together to engage in recreation behavior. Functional groups exist to achieve some purpose other than the direct satisfaction of members' leisure needs. The two categories are not mutually exclusive. If the YMCA club members decide to clean up a section of the river while canoeing down it, they will be accomplishing a purpose beyond having fun. The legislative committee chairperson might see his involvement with that group as a leisure experience as well as a professional responsibility. He may derive satisfactions similar to those he experiences in activities which are more clearly recreational. For many people, community service *is* leisure activity. Nonetheless, the general distinction between participant groups and functional groups is useful in understanding the types of groups with which recreation and park personnel work.

Participant Groups.   There are many different kinds of participant groups. Some of these are activity oriented; that is, they focus on shared interests and the enjoyment of some particular activity. The great variety of special-interest clubs, such as model railroad clubs, ski clubs, great books discussion groups, and power boat associations are examples. In many respects, sports teams are groups—groups that have an activity emphasis. Other participant groups are oriented directly toward learning, such as square dance workshops, ceramics classes, and soccer clinics. Not all classes become groups in the sense of the characteristics described earlier, but many do. In other groups, the focus is on sociability—the enjoyment of other persons in the social sense. Older adult groups, teen clubs, and "parents-without-partners" types of groups are examples. A fairly specialized type of participant group is one concerned with the personal growth of members. These groups might be found in leisure counseling or in programs designed to develop self-awareness, confidence, assertiveness, or some other personal trait.

Again, these categories are not mutually exclusive. Activity of some kind probably would be involved in all of them. Similarly, any time people meet together regularly, some sociability probably will be evident. Learning also is very likely to occur, at least to some extent, in all types; and learning may result in personal growth. The differentiations are a matter of relative emphasis.

Functional Groups.   Groups in the functional category exist primarily to accomplish tasks. This is not to say that they do not serve to meet the individual needs of members. They do this to varying degrees; but their stated or "public" purposes are to do a job that is seen as needing to be done. An agency staff is a group. In a large agency, there may be many groups within the overall collection of employees. In a metropolitan area, the staff members at each different recreation center constitute a group. Lifeguards and instructors at a swimming pool are a group. There is a variety of citizen groups, related to leisure services, that function primarily to accomplish some task. Recreation and park commissions, citizen advisory committees for the promotion of certain events or for fund raising and boards of directors of nonprofit agencies are illustrations. All of the committees that carry on the work of professional societies also are examples. These include such groups as nominations committees, conference planning committees, accreditation teams, and legislative advocacy bodies.

Additional types of groups, that focus on getting work completed, are those community-wide groups with which recreation and park personnel frequently are involved. Often interagency committees will be formed to address some specific social problem area. For example, selected staff from the municipal recreation and park department, the police department, the local school district, the county health department, and the probation department may come together to develop recommendations for reducing disruptive juvenile behavior in a community. Representatives from different area churches and several public social service agencies might meet in response to a community's wish to analyze the needs of older adults.

Shivers observed that there are three general types of groups: (1) "primal" groups in which membership is involuntary and that are not formed around a common interest or need (for example, the family), (2) groups that come together rather spontaneously and by mutual consent, and (3) groups that are purposefully and deliberately created.[15] Recreation and park personnel usually work with deliberately created groups, such as the groups described earlier. They would be brought into existence by some agency, organization, or group of people; they would result from planning and conscious effort. However, some of them would have many of the characteristics of groups formed spontaneously (such as greater informality, fewer hierarchal relationships, and more emphasis on sociability). In fact, some groups might start on the basis of mutual consent and later be deliberately incorporated into an agency's areas of responsibility. For example, a group of older adults who get together as friends might eventually develop a structure; the group might in time expand its membership and ask for city sponsorship as a senior citizens club.

Recreation and park personnel relate to the types of groups mentioned earlier in various ways. In some groups, they will be leaders. In others, personnel will be expected to teach. In other group settings, workers might be most effective as resource persons. And, of course, in some groups, personnel will serve as members, and will carry out responsibilities similar to other members. In whichever of these capacities park and recreation personnel find themselves operating, a knowledge of group properties and processes will help them to be more effective.

GROUP PROPERTIES

Assume that you have just been employed as the associate executive director of a federation of conservation and outdoor recreation associations. Assume also that you have been assigned the responsibility of being the staff liaison to six of the associations, and that the executive director has suggested that you become acquainted with the different clubs, and get to know something about them. What can kinds of things could you get to know?

The basic characteristics of groups, discussed earlier in the section on definitions, provide you a beginning.

Goals.   You might find out something about the goals of the different groups. You could assess the degree to which these goals are clearly defined, and the degree to which they are known and supported by all members of the group. You could determine how general or how specific the different goals are.

Interaction Patterns.   The interaction patterns in the various groups would be another type of information you could gather. Do all members participate equally or are some individuals more dominant or active than others? If the group has a leader, what is his or her style and how does this influence within-group interactions? This kind of information could be obtained by observing the groups in action.

Structure.   Observations also would tell you something about how the groups are structured. What different positions seem to be apparent in the different groups? What types of roles do people carry out in these different positions? How are these positions related to one another? That is, how are the groups organized?

Group Norms.   You might also get a feeling for the norms, or standards, in the various groups. Observation might give you some clues about the types of overall behaviors that are permitted or discouraged.

Knowles and Knowles spoke of these five kinds of information as properties of groups. They suggested several additional properties.[16]

Backgrounds.   Each group may have different backgrounds of experience as a group. The backgrounds of the individual members who comprise the group probably will be different. In addition, their collective past experiences, during the life of the group, will differ from the collective experiences of other groups. These past experiences can influence the present and future actions of the group, as individual member behavior can.

Group Friendships.   Because of different backgrounds, groups may differ in the friendships, or *sociometric patterns*, that develop. Often in groups, some members will develop closer ties with other members, and some individuals will remain more isolated. These patterns develop on the basis of interpersonal attraction—of members liking one another.

Intimacy.   The extent to which there is overall attraction among members and to which individuals are familiar with personal details of each other's lives, has been referred to as the degree of intimacy that is present.[17] In a group in which intimacy has developed, members feel close to one another and feel more secure in engaging in self-disclosure and feedback.

Atmosphere.   Related somewhat to friendship patterns and intimacy is the social climate or atmosphere of the group.

> Although atmosphere is an intangible thing, it is usually fairly easy to sense. In the literature it is often referred to as the "social climate" of the group, with such characterizations as "warm, friendly, relaxed, informal, permissive, free," in contrast to "cold, hostile, tense, formal, restrained."[18]

This condition also is related to the *hedonic tone* of a group—the pleasantness of agreeableness of the group experience for members.[19]

Cohesion.   Another group property, cohesion refers to the degree to which the group is unified—how well it "sticks together." Knowles and Knowles commented on the symptoms of low cohesion.

> Symptoms of low cohesion include *sub rosa* conversations between pairs of members outside the main flow of the group's discussion, the emergence of cliques, factions, and such sub-groupings as the "old timers" versus the "new comers," the "conservatives" versus the "liberals," and so on.[20]

Cohesion is related to *viscidity*—the ability of the group to work together as a unit.[21]

Permeability and Potency.   Two other characteristics are useful in developing understandings about specific groups: permeability and potency.[22] *Permeability* refers to how easy or how difficult it is for new members to be assimilated into a group. *Potency* is the strength of the influence that a group has on its members. In many ways, the potency of a group is determined by the degree to which the characteristics that define a group are in evidence. These characteristics are interaction, identity, shared goals, norms and interdependence in the satisfaction of needs. Groups in which interactions are more frequent or more intense will have greater potential for influencing members.

Similarly, when members identify more strongly with a group, the potency of the group will be greater. If the shared goals that the group is pursuing are of great importance to members, the group will have greater potency than if the goals are less important. Groups in which the standards for member behavior are clear and more directly enforced will exert more influence than those groups in which the rules of conduct are more vague and more subtly applied. Perhaps most important as a determiner of potency is the degree to which the group experience contributes to the satisfaction of the needs of individual members. The more satisfaction members receive from being in the group, the more likely that they will be influenced by the group. In fact, in those groups where membership is voluntary, unless members feel that their needs are being met rather consistently, they probably will leave the group.

Psyche and Socio.   There are two additional aspects that help us to understand groups in general, as well as to identify differences from one group to another. These two aspects are referred to as the psyche dimension and the socio dimension. The *psyche* dimension is the part of group interaction that is concerned with the enjoyment of relationships among members in the social sense; the *socio* dimension is concerned with accomplishing some specific purpose or task. These two dimensions can be observed in most groups in differing degrees; some groups will be almost entirely focused on task activities, such as a city council or a citizens committee formed to work for the passage of a park bond election. Even in these groups, the psyche dimension usually is present. It is almost inevitable that council or committee members will develop at least casual friendships within the group, and that some satisfaction will result from interactions not directly related to the task. Similarly, the socio dimension frequently can be observed in what appears to be strictly an informal socially oriented group. It often happens that when several friends get together over an extended period of time, someone will think of a project to undertake, like a neighborhood improvement project or a fund-raising event for a worthy cause. Knowles and Knowles commented on the presence of both dimensions in groups.

> Most groups need the psyche dimension to provide emotional involvement, morale, interest, and loyalty; and the socio dimension to provide stability, purpose, direction, and a sense of accomplishment. Without the dimension of work (socio) members may become dissatisfied and feel guilty because they are not accomplishing anything; without the dimension of friendship (psyche) members may feel the group is cold, unfriendly, and not pleasant to be with.[23]

It is interesting to note that these two dimensions are related to two general leadership activities that are seen by members as evidencing leader effectiveness. Leaders who contribute to viscidity (the group's ability to work together as a unit) and to hedonic tone (the pleasantness of the group experience) are perceived as being effective. This condition was discussed in Chapter 5. Contributions to viscidity are related to the socio dimension; those leader behaviors which contribute to hedonic tone are related to the psyche dimension.

Synergy.   Shaw described two aspects of "synergy" that are related to the socio and psyche dimensions.[24] *Synergy* is the total amount of energy brought to the group by its individual members; it is the collective energy available for group activities. Some of this energy is devoted to establishing and maintaining group cohesion and harmony. Shaw identified this as *maintenance* synergy. What is left over is termed *effective synergy*—energies that can be devoted to the task on which the group is working. Shaw observed that the maintenance needs of the group are served first, since the satisfaction of these needs is necessary for the continuation of the group as a group.[25]

Content and Process.   Two other aspects of group behavior also can be defined: content and process. *Content* is the task on which the group is working; it is the subject of group interaction. *Process* is the interaction itself—the ways in which the group attempts to accomplish the task. At first glance, it might seem that these are the same as the socio and psyche dimensions. They are related but they are not exactly the same. The socio dimension is the task accomplishment dimension, and of course the task is the content. However, in some groups the content will be social, such as at a party or picnic. The process here would be the social interactions that permit group members to enjoy each other as persons. In a bond election committee, the content would be the task of promoting the park issue and the successful passing of the bond. In this case, the processes would be directed toward accomplishing these objectives.

Environments.   Shaw provided a useful concept that also contributes to an understanding of the different properties or dimensions of a group.[26] He noted that groups are influenced by the environments within which they exist. These include a physical environment, a personal environment, a social environment, and a task environment. The *physical* environment is comprised of such things as the nature of the facility where the group is meeting, table arrangements, heating and lighting. The *personal* environment includes the unique characteristics that each member brings to the group. The patterns of interaction that develop as the group meets or works together constitute the *social* environment; and the *task* environment includes factors associated with the characteristics of the specific task on which the group is working. The environments are not mutually exclusive; any one can influence another. Together they form the complex, overall environment of the group. And, of course, the group exists within the larger environment of the organization and society with which it is associated.

GROUP DEVELOPMENT

Groups exist over different periods of time. Groups come into being, and eventually they dissolve. Some small organizations, which might be thought of as groups, have existed for long periods of time, and they probably will continue on almost indefinitely. For example, the YMCA mentioned at the beginning of the chapter may have had a group of professional staff members for the past thirty years; and it may continue to have one for an indefinite future period. However, this group might be a succession of different groups rather than one continuing group. As staff members come and go, the composition of the group might be changed so much that the modified collection of individuals really is a new group.

Stages of Development.   During its existence, a group changes or develops. Several stages can be identified. Stanford's concept provides a useful framework for understanding these stages.[27] He observed that in some ways group development proceeds naturally and predictably even without interventions on the part of the leader.

> The concept of group development emerged originally from observations of the changes that occurred naturally in groups over time. Researchers noted that even when the leader made no attempt to intervene in the developmental process, most groups moved through fairly predictable stages—the more successful groups moving further, the less successful ones becoming arrested in early stages.[28]

However, in many groups leaders do intervene, especially in recreation and park settings, as well as in the educational settings from which Stanford was writing. He suggested that the natural processes of group development, modified by the interventions of a leader (teacher) who is attempting systematically to facilitate group functioning, lead to five fairly predictable stages. The first of these is the *orientation* stage. When people first come into a group, they usually want to know what the experience will be like, what is likely to happen to them. People want to know what will be expected of them. They want some assurance that the experience will not be unpleasant. They also want to know who the other people are, to know something about them.

After group members have these questions reasonably well answered, the group usually moves into the second phase, *norm setting*. Norms were defined earlier as the behavior established by the group. Some groups develop these standards directly and openly; other groups establish them more subtly. They relate to such things as how members interact with each other: what kind of behavior is permitted and what is not. During this stage the group begins to develop ways of working together. Norms are developed that relate to decision-making and coping with conflict.

Conflict often is present in group interaction. Orientation and establishment of group norms, in some ways, set the stage for conflict to occur. When people know what is expected of them and they have become more familiar with other members, they feel more free to communicate openly. This leads to the possibility that divergent ideas and opinions will be expressed and that there will be disagreements. Openness also leads to the possibility that feelings will be expressed, making conflict more apparent. So the third stage of group development involves the expression of conflict and the development of ways of *coping with conflict*.

Once members are relatively able to do this, and after norms and ways of working together have been established, a group enters a *productive* period. This is the fourth stage. Stanford noted that this stage is characterized by the group's ability to accomplish tasks and to provide for the maintenance of appropriate interpersonal relationships among members.

> An especially important characteristic of the Productivity Stage is that the group's attention seems to alternate between the task at hand and the interpersonal needs of members.[29]

This condition is congruent with the earlier discussion of the socio and psyche dimensions of a group. Stanford observed also that increased intimacy between group members often occurs during this stage; individuals are more willing to self-disclose appropriately and they are more receptive to feedback from other members.

The final stage is the *termination* of the group. This stage may be quite short and uneventful, or it may take considerable time. In groups that have developed a mature productive stage, there will be much interaction among members, from which individuals will receive satisfaction. Therefore, an awareness of the concluding of the group's work and the probable ending of associations among members often creates a period of anxiety. Stanford called this "termination anxiety."[30] He identified several symptoms: increased conflict, a breakdown of the group's ability to work together, and lethargy or frantic efforts to get as much as possible accomplished in the time remaining.

Stanford suggested that this progression—orientation, norm setting, coping with conflict, productivity, and termination—may be arrested at any point. That is, the group may not develop or mature because it is unable to develop the means necessary to accomplish the purposes at any particular stage.

Bradford also suggested that, as a group matures, the completion of one stage creates the conditions for moving into the next stage. His concept assumes that there are

> . . . phases or major problem areas in the continuing life of a group, with each problem area, when adequately resolved, creating improvement in internal group functioning and consequent productivity.[31]

He identified four different phases of group development: the *initial formation and movement* of the group, *encountering and confronting a problem, solving the problem* through cooperative action, and *reorganization of group structure and function.*[32]

The first phase is similar to stages one and two in Stanford's scheme (orientation and norm setting). Bradford suggested that until this phase has been satisfactorily accomplished the collection of people who are meeting together are not really a group.

The encountering-and-confronting-problems phase parallels Stanford's coping-with-conflict stage. Bradford cautioned that group development can be arrested easily at this point.

> The most destructive situation that can occur after a group has achieved trust among members and is functioning effectively is to reach such harmony that no difficult problem or disagreement confronts the group. If this happens, the mood and purpose of the group is to maintain peace and harmony at the cost of productivity and growth.[33]

The third phase, solving problems through cooperative action, and the fourth phase, involving a restructuring so that the group can move forward, influence the productivity of the group. In that sense, they are related to the fourth stage of Stanford's concept of group development.

Bradford suggested that the four phases, which he defined, occur in cyclical fashion.

> Groups seem to go through these phases over and over again; each time, hopefully, at a slightly deeper level. In a sense, a group reforms each time it meets. Intervening events for the individual members, new expectations, problems or pressures from outside sources, subgroup cliques, rumors and gossip—all conspire to create a new group at each meeting. Absent or new members produce a new set of interrelationships, and sociometric choices may change. Hence, observing a group's phases of behavior is a matter of examining a process of continuing dynamic change.[34]

Obstacles to Group Development.   Bennis and Shepard's theory of group development[35] focused on the obstacles that groups overcome in their progress toward effective functioning. These obstacles are barriers to open communication between members and to group processes for arriving at consensus among members. They are the results of two major areas of uncertainty that must be reduced if the group is to move ahead. One of these areas is the orientation that group members have toward authority; the other is the orientation members have toward each other. These two areas of uncertainty define the two major phases a group moves through in its development. In the first phase members are preoccupied with working out dependency relations with the authority figure in the group. In the second phase their main concern is the personal relations among members.

Dependence on the Leader.   Each phase is comprised of three subphases. In phase one, as the group works out uncertainties about authority relationships and power, members move from a general submissiveness (subphase 1) to a general stance of rebelliousness (subphase 2), and then to a resolution of the uncertainties about power in the group (subphase 3). In this resolution of the dependency or authority problem, group members typically come to accept responsibility for what happens in the group. Bennis and Shepard stated that the successful completion of this subphase means autonomy for the group. It is no longer dependent upon the leader; and the leader is no longer seen as either the protector of the group or a manipulator or exploiter.[36]

Relationships in the Group. When these conditions are present, the group moves into the second major phase, in which members are preoccupied with relationships among individuals. The authors identify this phase as one of "interdependence," as compared with the dependence that characterized the earlier phase. In the first of the next three subphases, (subphase 4), the emphasis is on harmony within the group. Having worked out problems of independence in phase one, members enjoy and wish to preserve the resulting sense of groupness. However, individual identities and needs often are made secondary to group harmony. Therefore, this subphase frequently does not last long. The group moves into a period of relative disenchantment (subphase 5). Typically, two subgroups form: one that resists any further involvement, and one that continues to press for group solidarity. The condition that enables the group to come back together again, and to move ahead, is one in which the group perceives an overriding need to accomplish a task. Often this need is intensified if the group is about to terminate. When this happens, the group moves into subphase 6, the final subphase, which the authors labeled "consensual validation." They listed the characteristics of this stage in group development.

1. Members can accept one another's differences without associating "good" and "bad" with the differences.
2. Conflict exists, but is over substantive issues rather than emotional issues.
3. Consensus is reached as a result of rationale discussion rather than through a compulsive attempt at unanimity.
4. Members are aware of their own involvement, and of other aspects of group process, without being overwhelmed or alarmed.
5. Through the evaluation process, members take on greater personal meaning to each other. This facilitates communication and creates a deeper understanding of how the other person thinks, feels, behaves; it creates a series of personal expectations, as distinguished from the previous, more stereotyped role expectations.[37]

The authors noted that any one group may never reach this final subphase. The group may become arrested at an earlier point, and may not be able to overcome the obstacles to moving ahead.

Bennis and Shepard provided a useful summary of what happens during the course of a group's development.

> The group in Phase I emerged out of a heterogeneous collectivity of individuals. The individual in Phase II emerged out of the group.[38]

Bennis and Shepard's theory pertains particularly to training groups—groups that are formed for the purpose of letting members experience the processes and dynamics which are involved. However, the theory has applicability to other types of groups. Members in any group must deal, to some degree, with questions of power and dependency and with concerns about relationships among members. The various stages can be observed, in varying forms, in many groups with which recreation and park personnel work. If these groups are to be most effective, each member must develop a sense of responsibility for what happens in the group (subphase 3). Also, members must develop relationships with each other that are appropriate to the needs of the group as well as to the needs of the individuals who compromise the group (subphase 6).

A Composite View.   While the concepts presented by Stanford, Bradford, and Bennis and Shepard are different in various ways and similar in others, overall they suggest some major aspects of group development. We would expect to find these in the types of recreation and park groups described earlier. The state professional society legislative committee, mentioned in Chapter 5, provides an illustration.

1. *Initial Orientation.* During the first meetings of the committee, following appointment of the members by the society's president, it probably will be possible to observe an orientation period. Appointees will want to get acquainted with each other, and they probably will want to know some things about what will happen during committee meetings, especially what will happen to them. Different members will have different levels of interest in knowing others, and different needs for finding out something about what the group experience will be like. Whatever these differences may be, members must have some answers to their initial questions, and they must develop at least beginning relationships with each other, if the collection of appointees is to become a group.

2. *Initial Development of a Functioning Group.* A period of developing working procedures and furthering relationships between members probably will follow the initial orientation phase. The committee probably will have "organized" at one of the initial meetings. The chairperson and a secretary will have been selected, and some decisions will have been made about how meetings will be conducted (including such matters as whether or not minutes will be kept, how items will be developed for agendas, and where and when meetings will be held). However, the details of this tentative organization will be developed and implemented over several subsequent meetings. In addition to these "official" acts, norms will be established, subtly or directly, that define expected behavior for all members. Different roles for different members will begin to evolve.

Individuals on the committee may exhibit variations in their reactions to the chairperson; some oversubmissiveness or overrebelliousness may be evident. These problems will have to be worked out by the group if the committee is to function most effectively. However, the development of norms and roles makes the group a safer place for members. The behaviors of other members are more predictable; therefore there is less uncertainty and more trust within the group. This promotes interaction. Increased interaction strengthens the identification of members with the group. Individuals develop a sense of responsibility for the group as well as for their own behaviors. During this phase, the phenomena that Bennis and Shepard observed will occur: The group (committee) will develop from the collection of individuals appointed by the president.

This period might be seen as an extension of the orientation stage or as an overlapping period. At the first meeting of the committee, many things will be done that relate to the continued development of the group. On one hand, as suggested, officers may be elected or appointed. The process of norm establishment and role definition will begin; and relationships between members will be initiated. On the other hand, the questions that members bring to the initial meetings—about who the other people are and what will happen in the group—will continue to arise even after the initial orientation phase.

In this second phase, members probably will have a heightened awareness of identity with the group. As members become more responsible for the group experience, they may make a considerable effort to avoid conflict. A "trouble-free" period, varying in length from group to group, may occur. However, problems that challenge the group harmony will arise. These initiate a third major phase.

3. *Confronting and Solving Problems.* The problems with which groups must deal have to do with both content and processes. Some are associated with the tasks the group is trying to accomplish: The legislative committee may be having difficulty getting an appointment with a key legislator. There may be differences of opinion between the committee and the society's board of directors about the relative importance of various bills. Other problems are related to group processes: Conflicts may arise between members over such issues as how committee decisions will be made, or the frequency with which meetings will be held. Certain members may become disinterested and cease to participate. One individual may attempt to use the committee as a forum for promoting his candidacy in an upcoming society election of officers. Other members may begin to feel that committee meetings are taking too much time, that the results of the committee's work are not worth the effort, or that the job is too big. Issues associated with processes influence the ability of the group to deal with content matters.

These types of concerns are related to three general categories of problems, identified by Bradford, Stock, and Horwitz as the ones that are most commonly found in groups: conflict or fight, apathy and nonparticipation, and inadequate decision making.[39]

To continue to function effectively, groups must confront these problems and find ways to solve them. They must develop processes that contribute to the accomplishment of goals and that do not detract from the needs of individual members. This may mean a restructuring of some of the procedures or a modification of some of the norms established in the initial development phase. The group also must find ways of maximizing the contributions of individual members. This problem-confronting and problem-solving cycle will occur repeatedly as the group encounters each new problem or set of problems.

These three stages probably will be evident, to varying degrees, in most groups. However, a group's progress toward full functioning may be arrested at any point because of its inability to solve the problems confronting it or to create the conditions necessary for growth.

Finally, the group may terminate at some point. This phase may produce the various kinds of termination anxieties described by Stanford.[40]

As suggested earlier, the phases overlap somewhat. They might be represented symbolically, as shown in Figure 6-1.

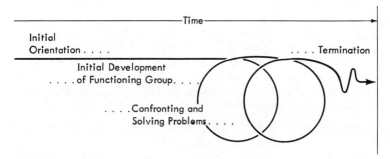

6-1 A representation of group development.

INDIVIDUAL BEHAVIOR IN GROUPS

A group is more than simply a collection of individuals. It has a history, a set of norms, a social climate, decision-making processes, and other properties that exist beyond the characteristics of its members. In fact, the group has a personality. The term *syntality* is used to express this dimension.

> Syntality is defined as the personality of the group, or, more precisely, as any effect that the group has as a totality. It is that which makes the group a unique entity.[41]

While the group has an identity of its own, it is made up of individuals. Group processes result from individual behavior. We cannot understand a group fully without developing some understandings of the behaviors of its members. To do this, we need to be aware of some typical behaviors in groups, and we need to know something about the factors that influence individual behavior in groups.

The Influence of Personal Characteristics. The generalizations about behavior suggested in Chapter 3 apply to the actions of individuals in groups. People do not leave their personal characteristics behind when they join a group. They bring all of their attitudes, interests, skills, past experiences, and self-concepts with them. Their behaviors are a function of their perceptions in the group setting just as they are in other settings. Members are motivated by personal goals as well as by the goals of the group; these personal goals often exist outside of group interactions but they influence the behavior of the individuals in the group. The ideas about conflict and level of aspiration, discussed in Chapter 3, apply to individual goal-seeking in groups, as well as in nongroup situations. The individual comes to the group as a total person. He will be influenced by other people in the group, and in turn, he will exert influences on their behavior. All of the members, to different degrees, will exhibit behaviors that are the results of the group experience. However, these behaviors are conditioned by all of the personal characteristics of each member.

The Influences of the Group.   Several general influences of groups on the behaviors of individuals have been suggested in psychological literature.[42] One of these is the stimulation of individual energy and activity that Allport termed *social facilitation*.[43] Another is pressure to conform.

The notion of social facilitation has been questioned.[44] Studies carried out more recently than the work of Allport suggest that it is not a principle that can be generalized to all groups. However, under certain circumstances, the group may serve to stimulate individual productivity. An example is a "brainstorming" session, where group members are encouraged to produce as many solutions to a specific problem as possible in a set period of time. Here, the ideas of one member stimulate the ideas of other members. Another illustration would be group encouragement to do something which the individual would not attempt without such encouragement, for example, trying a new skill (such as singing, public speaking, or roller skating). In this sense, social facilitation may be a form of response to group pressures to conform. If the group norm is to participate actively in group problem-solving sessions or to try new activities, individuals may engage in these behaviors more as a matter of conformity than stimulation.

Sessoms and Stevenson suggested that groups may encourage or inhibit the participation of any one individual. Members tend to be stimulated to participate most when three conditions are present:

> Personal confidence, the presence of trust as opposed to threat in the tone of the group, and the positive encouragement of other members all increase the chance of positive participation.[45]

Groups also exert subtle and direct pressures to conform on individual members. This may result from the establishment and enforcement of relatively well defined and rather stable norms. It may be a more generalized result of individuals behaving so as not to seem different from other members or because of a desire to be accepted and liked in the group.

In his review of research on conformity in groups, Hare identified four major types.[46] One is *convergence*, where a member interprets facts similar to the way they are interpreted by other members. Another is *compliance,* in which the individual's behavior is modified because of another member's authority in the group. *Conformance* is where a member conforms because of attraction to the group and the adoption of its values. Hare termed the fourth type *consentience,* where the individual assimilates group values and then is influenced by the internalized states that are produced. Hare suggested that there are factors that influence the strength of a conforming influence

> The factors which influence the general tendency to conform are found in the *object* about which the judgment is to be made, in the *subject* who is making the judgment, and in the *situation.* The subject will conform more to group opinion when the object to be judged is ambiguous, if he must make his opinion public, if the majority holding a contrary opinion is large, and if membership in the group is highly valued. A minority view will prevail if the minority has high status, through power, popularity, or expert knowledge.[47]

Consistent with this last idea is the notion that group members who do not conform "earn" the right to do so if their individuality contributes to the group in some way—that is, if their nonconformity is valuable to the group.[48]

Related to the issue of conformity is the concept of *reference groups.* The basic idea of a reference group is that an individual behaving in one group setting may be influenced by values and attitudes that are dominant in another group of which he also is a member. For example, assume that a person is an active member of the Sierra Club, an organization strongly committed to conservation and environmental protection. Suppose also that the individual has been appointed to a citizens' committee charged with making recommendations, to a district office of the Bureau of Land Management, about off-road vehicle use in desert areas administered by the BLM. The person's actions in the citizens' committee probably will be influenced by the values and attitudes he brings with him from his Sierra Club affiliation. Knowles and Knowles spoke of reference groups as *invisible committees* and as *associational forces.*[49]

While a conforming influence is observable in most group situations, the precise nature of the influence of groups on individual behavior generally is difficult to describe. The personal characteristics of each individual member, variations in group properties such as structure and communication networks, and different leadership styles may lead to different kinds of influence.[50]

Whatever the nature of the specific influences of a specific group on an individual, the strength of those influences will depend upon the degree to which the defining characteristics of the group are evident. As indicated earlier in the chapter, in those groups in which there is more interaction among members, where shared goals are clear and strongly supported, where there is interdependence in the meeting of group and individual needs, where members adhere closely to norms, and where strong identities with the group exist, group influences on individual behavior will be more potent. Also, the potency of influence may vary from member to member in any one group for the same reasons.

Some Typical Individual Behaviors in Groups. Bennis and Shepard suggested some characteristic behaviors in groups.[51] Some members typically engage in behaviors that can be labelled *dependent*—behaviors that indicate an acceptance of and security in leader authority and group structure. Other behaviors, called *counterdependent,* are typical of members who find less comfort in these factors. Another dimension is related to intimacy between members.

> Members who cannot rest until they have stabilized a relatively high degree of intimacy with all the others are called "overpersonal." Members who tend to avoid intimacy with any of the others are called "counterpersonal."[52]

Still other members exhibit behaviors that are neither dependent nor counterdependent, nor overpersonal or counterpersonal. These members are called *unconflicted* or *independent.* Bennis and Shepard indicated that these individuals often are responsible for the group moving forward through the various stages of development.

Benne and Sheats presented a "classification of member roles" that covers typical individual behaviors in groups.[53] These roles are seen as behaviors or functions that help a group develop and function effectively. This position is synonymous with the concept of leadership as a function of group interaction.

> No sharp distinction can be made between leadership and membership functions, between leader and member roles. Groups may operate with various degrees of diffusion of "leadership" functions among group members or of concentration of such functions in one member or a few members. Ideally, of course, the concept of leadership emphasized here is that of multilaterally shared responsibility.[54]

Three categories of member roles or behaviors were identified: (1) task completion, (2) group building and maintenance, and (3) the satisfaction of individual members' needs. Included in the task category are such behaviors as initiating, seeking opinions or information, giving opinions and information, elaborating and coordinating. The group-building-and-maintenance category includes such behaviors as encouraging, compromising, mediating, and following. The individual-need-satisfaction category includes behaviors that do not contribute to group effort or maintenance: expressing aggression, dominating, seeking recognition, and blocking group action are examples.[55]

These self-centered types of behaviors have been called *nonfunctional.* They are nonfunctional in that they do not contribute to the progress or welfare of the group. However, they *are* functional in terms of the needs of the individual. They pose problems for the group that should be dealt with and not suppressed. If they are suppressed, the persons who are engaging in them may withdraw from the group. Benne and Sheats pointed out another disadvantage—if self-centered behaviors are suppressed the group will lose an opportunity to use these nonfunctional actions as part of a process of group self-diagnosis and correction.[56]

GROUP EFFECTIVENESS

As suggested earlier, groups are abundant in the field of leisure services. Moreover, they are evident in almost all aspects of everyday life. Legislative processes in our Congress are enabled by committee actions, businesses operate on the basis of the decisions of boards of directors, and city councils set policies for the operation of municipal governments. The list of examples could go on endlessly.

That groups are so pervasive frequently causes us to question their effectiveness. Perhaps this is because some groups are ineffective, and because we sometimes use groups inappropriately; that is, we use them when an individual might be better suited to the task. Take, for example, the YMCA staff meeting described at the beginning of the chapter. Assume that the board of directors has asked the executive secretary to develop a master plan of the agency's expected growth during the next ten years. The plan is to include projections of services and financial needs. This would be an extremely important report, and the executive secretary would want to go about completing it in the best possible way. One decision he would have to make is whether to ask one person to do the work or to assign it to a staff committee. In making this decision, he would need to raise the basic question, Which alternative will lead to the best result? The question could be raised by any supervisor or administrator who is responsible for achieving results through other people's work.

Who Is Best for the Job—a Group or an Individual? The answer to this question must be qualified. It depends upon the nature of the task, and upon the capabilities, motivations, and characteristics of the people involved.

Groups do have the benefit of greater resources. Theoretically, five people should be able to generate more ideas, more solutions to a problem, than one person. Collectively, five people should have a greater variety of skills and knowledges that are relevant to the task at hand. Groups also have the advantage of being able to divide a task.

Collins and Guetzkow indicated that greater resources is one of three basic advantages that groups have over individuals.[57] The other two are *social motivation* and *social influence*. Social motivation involves the idea that a person may work harder or be a more effective group member because of the rewards that such behaviors produce from other members. These rewards include such things as recognition, praise, and status. Collins and Guetzkow refer to these as *social motives*. Social influence is related somewhat to the resources of the group; more specifically, it has to do with the group's uses of its resources. Here, resources refer to the skills and knowledges of members. The group member who has sound ideas and who has made good contributions to the group in the past tends to have greater influence. Therefore, the contributions of such a person are more likely to be accepted.

Both social motivation and social influence can serve as advantages for groups. If members work harder, more carefully, or more creatively because of the social rewards they receive, the overall group performance should be greater, more accurate, or more creative than if people worked individually. If members who usually have good ideas are listened to more seriously or have more influence in the group, again group performance should be improved.

However, Collins and Guetzkow cautioned that these outcomes do not always happen.[58] The presence of other people, instead of being socially rewarding, may constitute a threat and lead to defensive behavior (to avoid embarrassment); or it may be distracting and lead to lowered productivity. Also, groups can become overreliant on members who have made good contributions in the past. This may lead to inappropriate dependence on a few individuals and to the possible failure of other members to make their fullest contributions.

Hall reported an interesting study that suggested that in problem-solving situations groups are more effective than individuals, and that this effectiveness can be improved by helping the groups develop consensus-achieving techniques.[59] He developed an exercise in which participants were asked to assume that they had crash-landed a spaceship on the moon. They were given a list of equipment and supplies salvaged from the ship and were asked to rank the separate items (such things as oxygen tanks, food concentrate and signal flares) according to their importance for survival on a hike back to the mother ship.

Participants ranked the equipment first as individuals, then as a group. Rankings were compared with answers provided by experts from the National Aeronautics and Space Administration. Hall concluded that groups consistently performed better than individuals. Moreover, he found that groups that were instructed on how to achieve consensus (for example, how to make full use of the resources of all members, and how to resolve conflicts effectively) performed better than groups that were not.[60]

It appears on one hand that groups have advantages over individuals if the task requires the generation of considerable data or ideas, the confirmation or cross-checking of these ideas or data, or the utilization of a variety of skills. On the other hand, if synthesis of data is needed, or if the problem is one of gaining overall insight into the meaning of the data, an individual may be more effective.[61] In the YMCA report on future services and financial needs, this would suggest that the staff (as a group) be involved in generating relevant data, but that one person be assigned the responsibility to pull the data together, make some tentative judgements about what it all means, and then write a draft of the final report.

If the executive secretary adopted this plan, he probably would wish to maximize the effectiveness of the staff working together as a group.

Conditions That Contribute to Group Effectiveness.   At the beginning of the chapter, several characteristics that define a group were described. These included interactions among members, shared goals and norms, interdependence of members in the meeting of individual and group purposes, and a sense of identity. Later in the chapter, I suggested that the influence of a group on any individual member is determined by the strength of these characteristics. For example, the more members interact in a group, the more the group will influence individual members. Similarly, the stronger these defining characteristics, the more effective a group will be, in terms of both task success and member satisfaction.

Appropriate interaction among members helps a group achieve its goals. A group in which these goals are clear, and are supported by all members, will be more effective. This success contributes to the satisfactions of members and to their sense of independence. If group norms are well defined and respected, the group will be able to function more effectively. Members will know what is expected in terms of behaviors in the group, and there will be less ambiguity. Members can be more free in their interactions. Of course, if the norms are inappropriately restrictive, they may detract from the group's effectiveness. All of these conditions (interaction, shared goals and norms, and interdependence) usually will be greater in those groups in which members identify strongly with the group. In other words, identity also contributes to effectiveness.

An effective group might be thought of as a "healthy" group—one which continues to grow. Gibb and Gibb provided a very useful concept of the differences between healthy, growing groups and groups that are stagnant.[62] The authors noted four ways in which groups differ. These are (1) the degree to which trust exists among members, (2) the presence and usefulness to the group of a feedback system, (3) the degree to which member behavior is directed toward group goals, and (4) the amount of interdependence among members.[63] Feedback means open communication between members. It permits the group to be aware of the feelings and reactions of individual members and to assess the effectiveness of group actions and procedures. Interdependence often is facilitated by organization, that is, by the development of a system of norms, roles, and procedures that enables members to relate more appropriately to each other.

Gibb and Gibb contended that reciprocal trust among members is the key factor.

> Trust is the pacemaker variable in group growth. From it stem all the other significant variables. That is, to the extent that trust develops, people are able to communicate genuine feelings and perceptions on relevant issues to all members of the system; they are able to communicate with themselves and others to form consensual goals; and they can be truly interdependent.[64]

The authors see the four factors as a hierarchy. Valid feedback can occur only if trust exists between members. The definition of goals that generate the support of members requires relevant feedback. And the development of appropriate norms and structures is based on a clear identification of goals.[65]

Shepherd, describing the "features of a successful group," focused on some of the same factors defined by Gibb and Gibb. He defined five features—(1) the presence of clear group objectives with which the personal objectives of individual members are compatible; (2) a clear differentiation in the roles of members, including the identification of "official and unofficial" leaders; (3) shared norms and values; (4) free communication that permits the ideas and feelings of each member to be expressed; and (5) sufficient heterogeneity among members to provide for "diverse skills, experience and interest," (but not so much heterogeneity that agreement on goals and processes is difficult to achieve).[66] Shepherd observed that these factors lead to group cohesiveness and productivity.[67]

Knowles and Knowles also noted the contributions of clarity of goals and appropriate structure to group effectiveness. They suggested that, in effective groups, members agree on goals and on the processes used to reach these goals, and that the processes used are appropriate for the group's "task and stage of development".[68] They also noted that the availability of appropriate resources (such as a budget, staff time, and information) influences group effectiveness.

In summary, effective groups are ones in which members know and agree upon what it is they want to achieve. They develop appropriate processes for working together so that the diverse talents of each person can be used. These conditions are encouraged by trust among members and by open communication.

Group Problems. Unfortunately, the conditions that contribute to effectiveness are not always present. You will remember that a group's development might be arrested at some point. In such cases, the group fails to mature and so is less effective than it would be otherwise. Also, groups may experience problems that can impede development, either permanently or temporarily.

As indicated earlier, Bradford, Stock, and Horwitz identified the three kinds of problems most often encountered by groups: conflict within the group, apathy or lack of participation by members, and the inability of the group to make satisfactory decisions.[69]

The authors noted several signs of conflict: disagreement among members, attacking ideas before hearing them fully, refusing to compromise, impatience within the group, and tension. They suggested several possible reasons for this conflict.[70] First, group members may feel that their task is unachievable and that they are unable to meet expectations. Second, members may be overly concerned about personal power and status. Third, members may have greater loyalties to other, competing groups; these feelings may lead to resistance and lack of cooperation. Fourth, members may clash when they are working hard at a task with which they are deeply involved; they may disagree about procedures and plans or may become impatient or irritated when other members fail to see the logic of their suggestions and ideas. This kind of conflict can be useful if it is recognized for what it is.

Sessoms and Stevenson noted the possible benefits of conflict within a group.

> Conflict is natural and healthy. Properly handled, it aids in clarifying the issues, brings solutions into focus, and stimulates action. It is essential to creativity and production. . . . Misused, however, conflict can be fatal to the group's life.[71]

This view is congruent with the suggestion in Chapter 4 that interpersonal conflict is inevitable, and that it should be recognized and managed rather than ignored.

Sessoms and Stevenson offered some strategies for dealing with conflict in a group.[72] Basically, they suggested that "win-lose" solutions be avoided, and that attempts be made to find answers to problems that are mutually acceptable to those who are involved. This is similar to Gordon's "no-lose" approach,[73] presented in Chapter 4.

Apathy shows up in a group as boredom, indifference and lack of enthusiasm for the task at hand, unsatisfactory task achievement, and complete failure to participate. Bradford, Stock and Horwitz identified these possible reasons. The group's task may not seem important to members. Or it may be important to them, but because members are afraid of failing, or of being punished or embarrassed, they avoid the task. They may not have developed appropriate methods of working on the task and so sense a futility about trying. They may feel they have no real influence on decisions that are made, or that the decisions they do make are unimportant. They feel powerless. Sometimes a long-term, continuing conflict among a few dominant members can seem overwhelming to less dominant members, who feel unable to solve or reduce it.[74]

The inability of a group to make appropriate decisions is evident in decisions that are made too rapidly or not at all. The group may not be sufficiently aware of the decisions that must be made, or they may be uncertain about what will constitute a decision (such as agreement by the majority, a unanimous vote, or pronouncements by the leader).[75]

The problems groups encounter may arise from the behavior of one member. Dutton, Seaman, and Ulmer spoke about problems with individuals. They discussed the influence on the group of "over-participants, under-participants, and anti-participants."[76] The overparticipant is a member who talks to such an extent that other members are deprived of opportunities to participate. Often, the contributions of the overparticipant are not relevant to the task. Underparticipants do not make the contributions to group life and activity that they are capable of making. They might be shy, or bored, or unmotivated. When a group is apathetic, there probably are many members who are underparticipants. Antiparticipants are members who argue, or complain, or wander off the subject so much that group progress is impeded. The antiparticipant might be an individual who takes advantage of the group discussion to seek personal advice.

Sessoms and Stevenson noted that problems often stem from the failure of the group to satisfy or deal with the ego needs of individual members (needs for such things as recognition and praise).[77] They observed that group problems can arise also from the formation of cliques within the group or from inappropriate processes (such as moving too fast, pressuring members for agreement and conformity, and failing to establish feedback mechanisms).

Helping Groups Function Effectively. The chapter began by observing that recreation and park personnel invariably work with groups. It might also be said that groups invariably encounter problems. To varying degrees, these problems cause them to function less effectively than they otherwise might. For these reasons, it is important that recreation and park personnel be able to help groups function efficiently. How can this be done?

First of all, it is well to remember that the group itself must take responsibility for its own actions and progress if it is to grow and become more efficient. If the leader assumes all responsibility for improving group effectiveness, group members are denied opportunities to learn and to develop needed skills. A group that is overly dependent upon a leader probably will never reach its full potential. However, appointed and elected leaders do have responsibilities to help their groups become as effective as possible.

There are some generalizations about helping groups become more effective. If you can assist the group to clarify its goals or to develop better ways of working together, you will have enabled it to become more effective. If you can facilitate the group's successful development, through the stages described earlier, the group will be more effective. If you can assist individual members to behave more appropriately, you will have helped the overall group. And if it is within your ability to provide the resources needed by the group (such as facilities and supplies), and you do so, you will have added to the group's effectiveness. All of these are ways in which leaders can help.

Also, the factors described in Chapter 5 that make for effective leadership tend to contribute to group effectiveness.

Probably the most important thing a leader can do to help a group become more effective is to facilitate the group's ability to develop and use feedback mechanisms. The group needs to know how it is doing in accomplishing its goals. Bradford, Stock, and Horwitz suggested that there are three basic aspects to the process of a group becoming more effective.[78] Information is needed about such things as (1) the degree to which the group seems to be moving toward its goal, (2) whether or not the group appears to be using appropriate methods, and (3) the levels of participation of the various members. This information needs to be reported to the group. Based on what is reported, the group needs to diagnose its situation and make decisions for appropriate changes.[79]

The leader can function as an observer of the group, and can report his or her observations. One disadvantage of this approach is that it may detract from the leader's other responsibilities and may make the group more dependent upon the leader. However, since facilitating group effectiveness probably is the leader's most important function, this disadvantage may be completely acceptable. Marram reinforced the idea that the leader has a basic responsibility for observing and reporting group progress.

> The group should be able to rely on its leader to keep them on track toward successful accomplishment of their goals. As an observer—not a member— the leader is in a key position to oversee group growth and continually measure the group's progress toward its goals.[80]

Bradford, Stock, and Horwitz identified other alternatives.[81] One is for a member of the group to be appointed to serve as observer and perhaps to rotate this assignment. Second, this observer and the leader might jointly assume responsibility for collecting and reporting information. Third, all members of the group, including the leader, can be responsible for the feedback process. This has the advantage of placing the responsibility on the total group, but the possible disadvantage of so diffusing the responsibility that feedback may not occur systematically.

Once information is collected, it must be shared with the group. Bradford, Stock, and Horwitz called attention to some principles of providing appropriate feedback to the group.[82] These are similar to the suggestions for giving constructive feedback to an individual that were presented in Chapter 4. The information shared should be relevant to questions of group efficiency, stated so as to be nonthreatening to individual members of the group, and adjusted so that the amount of information provided at one time is not too much for the group to use.

Once information is gathered and shared, the group must analyze it. Two basic questions must be asked: What caused the events to happen that were observed? What changes will allow the group to be more efficient in the future? Based on the answers, decisions for action must be made. Bradford, Stock, and Horwitz saw this analysis and decision stage as a critical one.

> Unless the members are able to gain new insights into the functioning of the group, and are able to find new ways of behaving, the group will not improve its processes and continue in its growth and development.[83]

The leader has a responsiblity to help the group use the information that has been gathered to change to become more effective.

Marram defined four basic functions of leaders that aid group effectiveness: (1) to help members meet individual needs, (2) to help maintain a group atmosphere in which members are free to participate fully, (3) to facilitate group growth, and (4) to facilitate the growth of individual members in the group setting.[84] Out of these general functions grow several "leadership interventions"—specific actions taken by a leader.[85] While Marram's discussions are directed toward the field of nursing, the interventions which she presented are useful things a leader can do to help a recreation and park group become more effective.

Assume the situation described at the beginning of the chapter, where a YMCA program secretary is working with the members of his staff. Marram's interventions would suggest the following activities by the program secretary as he works with his staff on their continuing concerns: He will make sure they are aware of and understand their objectives. As they meet to work on these objectives, he will manipulate the physical environment and organizational details to maximize their opportunities for productive interaction. He will provide an adequate meeting room, needed information, stenographic help, and information about the responsibilities of the different members. He will set, or will help the group to set, appropriate meeting times and dates. He will help to stimulate interaction between members of the group by encouraging specific individuals and asking relevant questions. He will encourage staff members to share their problems and to learn from one another. He may consult with individuals whose behaviors in the group detract from the group's ability to be productive, either talking to an individual privately or helping the group itself relate differently to one member.

The secretary will try to schedule staff meetings for times when unproductive anxieties are reduced or eliminated. Some tension may be useful, but too much can be damaging. Staff members should feel free to express opinions and suggest ideas without being embarrassed or unfairly criticized. They should not have to worry about what is going to happen to them in the meeting.

The secretary will be clear himself about his own theories of how groups operate and about his expectations, and he will communicate these to the staff as it is appropriate. He will observe group performance and report his impressions. Periodically, he will summarize the progress the staff has made.

These activities, based on Marram's interventions, do not mean that the leader is solely responsible for the group's effectiveness. If the group does not take responsibility for its own functioning, the members are unlikely to grow. But there are specific things that a leader can do to help a group improve its own functioning.

Patch suggested that the interventions a group leader uses fall into one of three categories: (1) process interventions, (2) task interventions, and (3) environmental intervention.[86] *Process* interventions include such things as asking openended questions to stimulate thought and interaction, confronting group members whose behavior is detrimental to the group, and modeling desirable behaviors such as appropriate self-disclosure. *Task* interventions are activities such as identifying resources available to the group, helping with goal clarification, and time keeping. Activities such as adjusting heat and light, arranging seating, and controlling noise are *environmental* interventions.

Patch noted several criteria that a leader can use in selecting specific interventions.

1. The intervention should be based on a clear understanding of why it is being used and of the purpose the leader hopes to accomplish.
2. The leader should be sure that the motive for selecting the intervention is appropriate to the situation.
3. The intervention should be congruent with the norms and history of the group.
4. The possible consequences of the intervention should be considered and should be acceptable.
5. The timing of the intervention should be appropriate.
6. The intervention should be selected only if the leader is reasonably confident that he is able to carry it out.
7. The intervention should be selected that is focused most directly and is most simple, yet that will accomplish the leader's purpose.[87]

The criteria cannot be applied mechanically; nor is the intervention process itself mechanical. Instead, the leader makes decisions and acts in the ongoing flow of interactions within the group. Sometimes there is time for considerable thought about the best action to take; at other times, the leader must respond very quickly.

SUMMARY

A group is a collection of individuals who interact with each other in the pursuit of shared goals. As they interact, they develop sets of norms and roles, or expected behaviors. They develop an identity.

Recreation and park personnel work with two basic categories of groups: groups of participants, and groups that meet to accomplish some purpose (other than the enjoyment of free time). A recreation and park staff would be included in the latter category.

Groups exhibit different characteristics or features that can be observed or studied. These include the goals of the group, the ways in which members interact with each other, the way in which the group is organized, the group's history, the ways in which members are expected to behave, and the group atmosphere or social climate. Groups also exhibit a socio dimension (a work orientation) and a psyche dimension (the relationships among members). Two additional aspects are the content or task on which the group is working, and the process that is used to accomplish the task.

Different theories have been advanced on the ways in which groups develop. A composite of these theories suggests that there is an initial orientation period during which members get to know one another and become familiar generally with the task and what is expected of them. Next, the group develops its ability to function. It may elect or appoint officers; it establishes norms; and the members develop techniques for working together. Eventually, conflicts or problems arise, which are confronted and solved. Finally, the group terminates. These different stages may not be completely separate phases; probably there will be overlap. Also, development may be arrested at any stage, and the group may fail to develop further.

Individual behavior in groups is influenced by the personal characteristics and background of the individual member, as well as by the overall influence of the group itself.

Several factors contribute to the effectiveness of a group. These include the degrees to which members are aware of and support group goals, the degrees to which members agree upon methods of reaching these goals, the degrees to which they are able to work together, the amount of trust that exists between members, and the ability of the group to develop and use feedback mechanisms.

Groups do encounter problems, such as conflict or apathy among members, and procedural difficulties such as ineffective decision making. It is most appropriate for a group to solve its own problems, since this leads to growth and avoids dependence on a leader. However, leaders have responsibilities to help groups grow and to become more effective. In general, they can do this by helping the group to sharpen its awareness of its goals, to develop the abilities of its members to work together, and to increase trust among members.

Groups also need to develop ways of collecting information about how well they are progressing, and of using this information to make appropriate changes in member behaviors or overall procedures. The leader can facilitate this process.

REVIEW QUESTIONS

6-1 In what ways does a group (as discussed in this chapter) differ from a collection of people who happen to be together in one place at the same time?

6-2 How do groups differ, one from another? That is, in what different ways might one group be different from another group?

6-3 What are the different stages groups seem to go through, as they develop or exist over a period of time?

6-4 What are the characteristics of an effective group?

6-5 Groups frequently encounter problems that interfere with their effectiveness or their abilities to function. What problems are these? What can be done by the group leader to overcome these problems?

6-6 What are typical individual behaviors in a group? How do these contribute to—or detract from—the functioning of the group? In what ways might the group exert influence on the individual members?

TO DO

6-A On a sheet of paper, write the different properties of groups (such as social climate, structure, interaction, patterns, and others). List these down the left-hand side. Then draw a vertical line near the center of the page, dividing the blank part of the paper in half. This creates two vertical columns. At the top of each column, write the name of a group to which you belong. Now, write down a few adjectives or nouns in each column, adjacent to each property that describes the two groups. Then, look back over the page, and write a paragraph that compares and contrasts the groups. How are they different and how are they alike?

6-B Observe a group in action. It could be the meeting of a club, or a committee, or a group such as a city council. Think about answers to the following questions as you watch:

1. At what stage of development does the group seem to be?
2. Does the group seem to be encountering any problems related to processes? If so, and if you had the opportunity to do so, how could you help the group overcome the problem and move ahead?
3. What individual behaviors can be observed in the categories of task completion, group building and maintenance, and non-functional? For this question, write down the names of members (or identify them by some other means) on the left side of a piece of paper. Then

make three vertical columns—one for each category of behavior. As you observe the interactions, put a check mark in the appropriate column after the person's name who engaged in the behavior (as you see it happen). Later, as you look over the check marks, note which behaviors were more frequent. Did any individual tend to engage in one category of behaviors more than either of the two categories? Did different individuals tend to engage consistently in different behaviors? Did some behaviors tend to come earlier in the meeting than others?

6-C   Sometime as you are participating in a group to which you belong, be aware of your own behavior. What types of behaviors do you typically exhibit? That is, in what category (or categories) do your behaviors tend to fall? If you tend to do just one or two different things in a group, try some new ways of interacting with other members or of contributing to the group's task.

END NOTES

1. For a discussion of different categories of definitions, see Marvin E. Shaw, *Group Dynamics: The Psychology of Small Group Behavior* (New York: McGraw-Hill Book Company, 1971), pp. 5–9.

2. Shaw, *Group Dynamics*, p. 10.

3. Jay S. Shivers, *Recreational Leadership: Group Dynamics and Interpersonal Behavior* (Princeton, N.J.: Princeton Book Company, 1980), p. 119.

4. Malcolm Knowles and Hulda Knowles, *Introduction to Group Dynamics* (New York: Association Press, 1959), p. 40.

5. David Potter and Martin P. Anderson, *Discussion: A Guide to Effective Practice*, 2nd ed. (Belmont, Calif.: Wadsworth Publishing Company, 1970), p. 12.

6. Knowles and Knowles, *Introduction to Group Dynamics*, p. 39.

7. A. Paul Hare, *Handbook of Small Group Research*, 2nd ed. (New York: The Free Press; A Division of Macmillan Publishing Co., Inc., 1976), p. 151.

8. H. Douglas Sessoms and Jack L. Stevenson, *Leadership and Group Dynamics in Recreation Services* (Boston: Allyn and Bacon, Inc., 1981), p. 69.

9. Sessoms and Stevenson, *Leadership and Group Dynamics*, p. 69.

10. Shaw, *Group Dynamics*, p. 241.

11. Shaw, *Group Dynamics*, p. 234.

12. Knowles and Knowles, *Introduction to Group Dynamics*, p. 46.

13. Shaw, *Group Dynamics*, p. 247.

14. Hare, *Handbook of Small Group Research*, p. 5.

15. Shivers, *Recreational Leadership*, pp. 125–28.

16. Knowles and Knowles, *Introduction to Group Dynamics*, pp. 41–50.

17. John K. Hemphill and Charles M. Westie, "The Measurement of Group Dimensions," *Journal of Psychology* 29, (April 1950): 327.

18. Knowles and Knowles, *Introduction to Group Dynamics*, pp. 45–46.

19. Hemphill and Westie, "The Measurement of Group Dimensions," p. 327.

20. Knowles and Knowles, *Introduction to Group Dynamics*, p. 45.

21. Hemphill and Westie, "The Measurement of Group Dimensions," pp. 327–28.

22. Hemphill and Westie, "The Measurement of Group Dimensions," p. 327.

23. Knowles and Knowles, *Introduction to Group Dynamics,* p. 51.

24. Shaw, *Group Dynamics,* p. 24. Shaw's comments are based on ideas developed by Raymond B. Cattell in "Concepts and Methods in the Measurement of Group Syntality," *Psychological Reveiw* 55, no. 1 (January 1948): 48–63.

25. Shaw, *Group Dynamics,* p. 24.

26. Shaw, *Group Dynamics,* pp. 117–18.

27. Gene Stanford, *Developing Effective Classroom Groups: A Practical Guide for Teachers,* (New York: Hart Publishing Company, Inc., 1977), pp. 27–33.

28. Stanford, *Developing Effective Classroom Groups,* p. 280.

29. Stanford, *Developing Effective Classroom Groups,* pp. 251–52.

30. Stanford, *Developing Effective Classroom Groups,* pp. 265–68.

31. Leland P. Bradford, "Group Formation and Development," in *Group Development,* 2nd ed., ed. Leland P. Bradford (La Jolla, Calif.: University Associates, 1978), p. 4.

32. Bradford, "Group Formation and Development," in *Group Development,* 2nd ed., p. 4.

33. Bradford, "Group Formation and Development," in *Group Development* 2nd ed., p. 8.

34. Bradford, "Group Formation and Development," in *Group Development* 2nd ed., p. 4.

35. Warren G. Bennis and Herbert A. Shepard, "A Theory of Group Development," in *Analysis of Groups: Contributions to Theory, Research and Practice,* ed. Graham S. Gibbard, John J. Hartman, and Richard D. Mann (San Francisco: Jossey-Bass Publishers, 1974), pp. 127–53.

36. Bennis and Shepard, "A Theory of Group Development," in *Analysis of Groups,* pp. 140–41.

37. Bennis and Shepard, "A Theory of Group Development," in *Analysis of Groups,* p. 149.

38. Bennis and Shepard, "A Theory of Group Development," in *Analysis of Groups,* p. 153.

39. Leland P. Bradford, Dorothy Stock, and Murray Horwitz, "How to Diagnose Group Problems," *Adult Leadership* 2, no. 7 (December 1953): 12.

40. Stanford, *Developing Effective Classroom Groups,* pp. 265–68.

41. Shaw, *Group Dynamics,* p. 23.

42. For example, see William W. Lambert and Wallace E. Lambert, *Social Psychology* 2nd ed., (Englewood Cliffs, N.J.: Prentice-Hall, Inc., 1973), pp. 123–33.

43. This concept, defined by F. H. Allport, is discussed in Lambert and Lambert, *Social Psychology,* pp. 123–24.

44. Lambert and Lambert, *Social Psychology,* p. 124.

45. Sessoms and Stevenson, *Leadership and Group Dynamics,* p. 99.

46. Hare, *Handbook of Small Group Research,* p. 58.

47. Hare, *Handbook of Small Group Research,* p. 58.

48. This idea is developed in E. P. Hollander, "Conformity, Status, and Idiosyncrasy Credit," *Psychological Review* 65, no. 2 (March 1958): 117–26.

49. Knowles and Knowles, *Introduction to Group Dynamics,* pp. 35–36.

50. For a discussion of conformity and the personal characteristics of group members, see Lambert and Lambert, *Social Psychology,* pp. 127–30.

51. Bennis and Shepard, "A Theory of Group Development," in *Analysis of Groups,* pp. 130–32.

52. Bennis and Shepard, "A Theory of Group Development," in *Analysis of Groups,* p. 130.

53. Kenneth D. Benne and Paul Sheats, "Functional Roles of Group Members," *The Journal of Social Issues* 4, no. 2 (Spring 1948): 41–49.

54. Benne and Sheats, "Functional Roles of Group Members," *The Journal of Social Issues,* p. 41.

55. Benne and Sheats, "Functional Roles of Group Members," 42–46.

56. Benne and Sheats, "Functional Roles of Group Members," 45.

57. Barry E. Collins and Harold Guetzkow, *A Social Psychology of Group Processes for Decision-Making* (New York: John Wiley & Sons, Inc., 1964), p. 52.

58. Collins and Guetzkow, *A Social Psychology of Group Processes for Decision-Making,* pp. 36–37, 41–42.

59. Jay Hall, "Decisions, Decisions, Decisions," *Psychology Today* 5, no. 6 (November, 1971): 51–54, 86, 88.

60. Hall, "Decisions, Decisions, Decisions," p. 88.

61. Joseph Luft, *Group Processes: An Introduction to Group Dynamics,* 2nd ed. (Palo Alto, Calif.: National Press Books, 1970), p. 30.

62. Jack R. Gibb and Lorraine M. Gibb, "The Group as a Growing Organism," in *Group Development* 2nd ed., ed. Leland P. Bradford (La Jolla, Calif.: University Associates, 1978), pp. 104–16.

63. Gibb and Gibb, "The Group as a Growing Organism," pp. 106–7.

64. Gibb and Gibb, "The Group as a Growing Organism," p. 107.

65. Gibb and Gibb, "The Group as a Growing Organism," p. 107.

66. Clovis R. Sheperd, *Small Groups: Some Sociological Perspectives* (San Francisco: Chandler Publishing Company, 1964), pp. 122–24.

67. Shepherd, *Small Groups,* p. 124–25.

68. Knowles and Knowles, *Introduction to Group Dynamics,* pp. 61–62.

69. Bradford, Stock, and Horwitz, "How to Diagnose Group Problems," p. 12.

70. Bradford, Stock, and Horwitz, "How to Diagnose Group Problems," pp. 12–13.

71. Sessoms and Stevenson, *Leadership and Group Dynamics,* p. 174.

72. Sessoms and Stevenson, *Leadership and Group Dynamics,* pp. 174–79.

73. Thomas Gordon, *Leader Effectiveness Training* (New York: Wyden Books, A Division of P.E.I. Books, Inc., 1977) pp. 175–90, 193–98.

74. Bradford, Stock, and Horwitz, "How to Diagnose Group Problems," pp. 14–15.

75. Bradford, Stock, and Horwitz, "How to Diagnose Group Problems," p. 16.

76. M. Donnie Dutton, Don F. Seaman, and Curtis Ulmer (eds.), *Understanding Group Dynamics in Adult Education* (Englewood Cliffs, N.J.: Prentice-Hall, Inc., 1972), pp. 51–53.

77. Sessoms and Stevenson, *Leadership and Group Dynamics,* p. 172.

78. Bradford, Stock, and Horwitz, "How to Diagnose Group Problems," pp. 16–19.

79. An excellent collection of scales and questions used for gathering information about group performance and member involvement is provided in George M. Beal, Joe M. Bohlen, and Neil Raudabaugh, *Leadership and Dynamic Group Action* (Ames, Iowa: The Iowa State University Press, 1962) pp. 289–341.

80. Gwen D. Marram, *The Group Approach in Nursing Practice* (St. Louis: The C. V. Mosby Company, 1973), p. 143.

81. Bradford, Stock, and Horwitz, "How to Diagnose Group Problems," p. 17.

82. Bradford, Stock, and Horwitz, "How to Diagnose Group Problems," p. 19.

83. Bradford, Stock, and Horwitz, "How to Diagnose Group Problems," p. 19.

84. Marram, *The Group Approach in Nursing Practice*, pp. 131–33.

85. Marram, *The Group Approach in Nursing Practice*, pp. 133–44.

86. Glenn Patch, Lecture given at National Institute of Drug Abuse Short-term Client Counseling Workshop, California State University, Chico, California (August 1977).

87. Patch, NIDA Short-term Client Counseling Workshop (August 1977).

chapter 7

Teaching and Learning

PREVIEW

One specific type of group with which recreation and park personnel work is an instructional group; that is, with a collection of people who are attempting to learn something. In these settings, the responsibilities of personnel are somewhat different.

Leisure service staff do teach in a variety of situations. The most common one is where participants wish to learn more about a specific recreation activity, such as bridge, cross-country skiing, or square dancing. Personnel also teach other staff members, frequently in in-service training sessions or workshops of various kinds. Often, teaching occurs in a group setting, as suggested earlier. However, it sometimes is a one-on-one effort.

In this chapter, attention will be given to how people learn, and to what recreation and park personnel do when they teach.

A general teaching model will be presented. Three basic categories of learning will be examined, and some specific teaching suggestions related to each of these categories will be discussed.

Effective teaching requires planning, and planning requires the definition of objectives and the evaluation of how well learning has progressed. These elements also will be discussed in this chapter.

Finally, the matter of discipline problems will be examined. Effective instructional techniques will minimize problems with disruptive behavior. However, these occur occasionally even in sessions that are well-planned and conducted. Suggestions will be given for preventing such behavior, and for dealing with it when it occurs.

In this chapter, various terms are used that are associated with teaching and the field of education—terms such as teacher, learner, learning domains, and disci-

pline. As you read the chapter, keep in mind that the terms are applicable to recreation and park situations. Recreation personnel are teachers. Participants in our programs and users of our parks often learn new things; when they are doing so, they are learners. The settings within which we teach usually are less formal than educational classrooms. However, the processes of instruction and learning are similar.

The therapist stood waist deep in the center's swimming pool, her hand lightly supporting the twelve-year-old boy floating on his back. The boy was blind. When the boy regained his feet, the therapist described the arm movements used in the elementary backstroke; and she guided his arms through several strokes to give him a feeling for the movement pattern. In other parts of the pool, volunteers were working with other blind children.

Later, the therapist met in one of the center's classrooms with the volunteers. The meeting was the fourth in a series designed to improve the effectiveness of the volunteer instructors. The therapist was presenting some ideas on the emotional needs of the blind; she outlined her main points on the blackboard at the end of the room.

Recreation and park personnel frequently do engage in instructional activities. The incidents described above illustrate two basic types of situations within which these instructional activities fall. One of these is when personnel work with the users of agency services. Teaching swimming to children, folk dance steps and patterns to senior citizens, tennis strokes to young adults, and craft techniques to adolescents are all examples of skills that we teach to users. The list could be expanded to include skills from all of the major program areas, including sports, the arts, and outdoor recreation. We also teach certain knowledges about these skills: the rules of the game of tennis, information about water safety, and the historical and cultural background information of different folk dances.

We sometimes teach things unrelated to activity skills. The resident camp director who helps children learn about local plant species and wildlife is teaching. While the information the children learn probably makes other camp activities, such as day hikes, more enjoyable, the knowledge does not relate directly to the activity.

Recreation and park personnel also are concerned with the development of certain attitudes on the part of participants. Rangers and interpreters try to instill attitudes related to appropriate uses of our parks and natural areas, and to environmental concerns generally. Leaders in youth organizations, such as the Boy Scouts and the Y.W.C.A., work at the development of certain values which are part of the organizations' creeds or ethics. Recreation therapists also often spend considerable time encouraging handicapped persons to develop attitudes toward leisure that will help them to live more fully. All of these people are teaching in the broad sense of the term.

A second basic type of instructional situation is where recreation and park personnel, who have responsibility for supervising other workers, provide staff training or in-service training. This training might be conducted formally, in a typical classroom setting or it might be quite informal, often one-to-one. The objectives usually include orienting new workers to their jobs and agencies and helping staff members improve their effectiveness.

In both staff training situations, and in those situations involving the users of agency services, personnel attempt to create learning conditions and experiences.

WHAT IS LEARNING?

Learning, like any human activity, is an experience. It is the experience of being in an environment, and interacting with the elements of that environment. One of the elements often is an instructor or someone who engages in teaching. In the swimming example, at the beginning of the chapter, the twelve-year-old was in an environment that included the water in the pool, the pool itself, the heat and noise level in the room, other swimmers, and the therapist. The swimmer was interacting with the therapist—responding to suggestions made by the therapist, asking questions of her, and telling her how he was feeling about his attempts to learn the stroke. She was responding to his attempts and to his questions. Each one's behavior was influenced by the other person. The learning that took place was due partly to this interaction.

However, an instructor does not have to be present for learning to occur. A child who jumps into the shallow end of a swimming pool for the first time learns many things about water, even though there is no interaction with an instructor. For example, water may make you cough if it gets in your mouth or nose; your body feels lighter in it; and things look different under water. Interaction still takes place. That is, the learner is involved with the environment, in some way; he is experiencing it. Park interpreters often create or manipulate certain elements in environments so as to encourage learning in the absence of a formally designated instructor. Self-guiding nature trails, with brochures and signs, are intended to teach something as well as to help the user enjoy the resource. Exhibits in visitors' centers have the same purposes. In these cases, the interactions that contribute to learning are observing, reading, listening, touching, and smelling.

The ongoing interactions with a teacher, or with certain other elements of the environment, might be thought of as a learning process. The process teaches a person something that he did not know before, helps him to do something that he could not do previously, or changes the way he feels about someone or something.

TYPES OF LEARNING

The things people learn can be categorized into *learning domains*. These domains are groupings based on the nature of the changes which take place in the learner. In a sense, they are categories of outcomes of learning.

Several different learning domains have been identified.[1] The three most common ones are (1) the cognitive domain, (2) the affective domain, and (3) the psychomotor domain.

The Cognitive Domain. Cognitive outcomes generally are related to information (knowledge) and concepts. Within the domain, many subcategories can be defined. Different investigators have described different categorizations. Perhaps the most widely known and used is a taxonomy developed by Bloom.[2] Bloom felt that the cognitive domain was comprised of three major subcategories: (1) specific information (facts and terminologies), (2) processes for dealing with specific information, and (3) universals and abstractions. For each of these subcategories several more definitive classifications exist.[3]

Davis suggested a categorization similar to Bloom's.[4] He theorized that knowledge could be broken into two broad types: (1) that in which recall is emphasized, and (2) that which involves "effective thinking." In *recall,* the learner is expected to be able to reproduce information. In the illustration of the therapist working with the volunteers, she (the therapist) was teaching something about the emotional needs of the blind. She might expect that a volunteer who had learned these needs would be able to list them on a written examination or to discuss them, if called upon to do so in the group meeting. In a sense, these emotional needs of the blind are pieces of specific information. Knowledge of the different types of swimming strokes, the depth and temperatures of the pool water, and the names of individual participants are also specifics.

In most recreation and park situations we are concerned with practical application of knowledge. In recall, application is not emphasized. However, Davis's second major type of learning does involve *use of information.* He labelled this type "effective thinking," and suggested that two subtypes were included: (1) critical thinking, and (2) problem solving.[5] He observed also that problem solving is based on critical thinking. In critical thinking, the learner is expected to draw generalizations from specific information, to apply principles, and to interpret data or to provide logical conclusions or proof based on specific data. In the volunteer example, the learners might be expected to develop general principles about working with blind youngsters, based on a knowledge of their emotional needs. Or, they might be expected to show, logically, the relationships between the needs of the blind and the potential contributions of a swimming program. They might be asked to review demographic information about the blind in their community and to justify the need for the swimming program.

These activities are related closely to problem solving. This type of learning is characterized by the ability to identify a problem, to define various alternatives, to assess the probable consequences of each alternative, and to select the most appropriate one. Here, the volunteers might be expected to plan a full swim program for blind youngsters or to devise a method for publicizing or funding such a program.

Another aspect of the cognitive domain is the area of concepts. A *concept* is a set of information about something. Klausmeier, Ghatala and

Frayer said it this way:

> We define a concept as ordered information about the properties of one or more things—objects, events, or processes—that enables any particular thing or class of things to be differentiated from and also related to other things or classes of things.[6]

The term *swimming pool* involves a concept. When we think of pool we usually think of a concrete structure that holds a body of water; the water usually is filtered and chemically treated. Typically, the pool has a fence around it or is enclosed in some manner. We might all think of different sizes and shapes of pools, and the specific details may vary. However, when someone says *swimming pool,* we know generally what that person means. Similarly, we have concepts about such things as blindness, volunteers, and therapists. These terms suggest characteristics to us that define what blindness is, what a volunteer is, and what a therapist is. There will be differences in meaning from one individual to another, but to the extent that our experiences are similar, we will still have similar ideas about the concept. A concept stands for something. It is a word symbol that summarizes the properties or characteristics of something. In this sense, concepts allow us to communicate with each other. Concepts are used in critical thinking and problem solving. In part, they are the abstractions and generalizations that enable us to work with information. Like knowledge, there are different categories or levels of concepts.[7]

Principles express the relationships between concepts.[8] A principle, like a concept, is a mental construct. It is a word or collection of words that describe a relationship. The relationship can take several forms.

One of these forms is *cause and effect,* in which one thing (identified by a concept) is thought to cause another thing. For example, encouragement from a swimming instructor usually causes most children in swim lessons to try harder. Kicking the feet, when in water and in a prone position, usually causes the body to move forward.

Another form of relationship involves *probability.* Probabilities enable us to make predictions. It is probable, for example, that most children will be anxious and excited the first time they get into a swimming pool. It is probable that most volunteers will be satisfied to see the blind children, with whom they are working, progress in their swimming abilities.

Closely related to probability is *correlation,* when two events happen together. One does not necessarily cause the other, however, as in the cases of cause and effect. As an illustration, there may be a correlation between the amount of time children spend practicing swimming and the speed at which they progress.

All of the above types of learning are related to "knowing" something. From the learner's standpoint, mental or intellectual processes are involved. The two major types of learning in this cognitive domain are the recall of information and the use of knowledge (which includes recall of specific information). Recreation and park personnel primarily are concerned with teaching for the use of knowledge.

The Affective Domain.   The affective domain includes such things as attitudes and values—things in which feelings are evident. An *attitude* is an emotional condition within a person that influences that person's acceptance of or attraction to other people, things, or ideas. One of the blind youngsters enrolled in the swimming program may have the feeling that adults are not to be trusted. This is an attitude that may influence how the child feels about the therapist, and accordingly, how he behaves in the swim lessons. He may also have some attitudes about new experiences, such as the swim lessons; these may also influence his behavior. Similarly, the attitudes the adult volunteers have about children, about blindness, and about their own responsibilities will influence how they work with the children.

Attitudes involve information, emotion, and behavior. The child who feels adults cannot be trusted has some information about adults. It may or may not be accurate, but the child no doubt takes it to be correct. He also has feelings toward adults—in this case, feelings about the trustworthiness of adults. This is the emotional dimension, the dimension that most characterizes the affective domain. His knowledge, as he perceives it, and his feelings influence his behavior. He may seek to avoid adults as much as possible, or he may engage in various kinds of testing behavior to confirm his feelings.

Attitudes vary in both intensity and direction. Some attitudes we hold more intensely than others. *Direction* has to do with whether our feelings are favorable or unfavorable, that is, whether we tend to approach or avoid a person or object. These ideas of intensity and direction can be found easily in any controversial issue. The issue of wilderness is an example. Some people believe that the federal government should set aside more wilderness areas—areas where land and forest areas are preserved in their natural states that are accessible only on foot or on horseback. People who feel this way have a favorable attitude toward wilderness. Others hold unfavorable attitudes toward the preservation of natural areas. These people believe that the creation of such areas "locks up" needed timber and mineral resources or that they serve only a small percentage of the population because they are accessible only by nonmotorized means. Positive or negative, these feelings are directional.

Within either position, there are many variations of intensities. Some people hold strongly positive or strongly negative views. These are the individuals who might work actively for or against the creation of new wilderness areas, contribute money and time to voter campaigns, write letters to legislators, and speak to various groups and organizations for or against the issues. Those whose attitudes are held less intensely might do no more than take the time to vote, or to speak to a few friends about the issue.

We expect an individual's behavior and attitudes to be consistent. An avid backpacker would be unlikely to have antiwilderness feelings; and we do not expect a person who strongly believes in wilderness to work for a lumber company that advocates opening up more forest areas to timber cutting. This congruency between attitudes and behavior, though, is not automatic; people's behaviors do not always match the attitudes they say they hold. However, if we know a person's attitudes about something, we can predict something about the individual's behavior.

Values, like attitudes, influence our behavior. Values tend to be more general than attitudes, and they tend to involve fairly strong, positive feelings. The therapist might value the right of people to be self-determining. This value would influence how she structures programs for the blind, and how she relates to the volunteers. One of the volunteers might value the preservation of wilderness areas. Knowing this, we might guess that she likes to hike or backpack, that she is a member of the Sierra Club, or that she would be less likely to vote for a candidate for the U.S. Senate who advocates the issuing of permits for commercial developments in certain existing wilderness areas.

While the actions of the individual described above are influenced by the information she possesses, her feelings probably are the keys to understanding her behavior. This emphasis on feelings is the central characteristic of the affective domain.

The Psychomotor Domain.   The central characteristic of psychomotor outcomes of learning is skilled performance—the ability to engage in some activity.

Recreation and park personnel teach a wide array of psychomotor skills. We teach the people who use our services to play basketball, to watercolor, to paddle canoes, to carve wood, to play guitars, to square dance, and to do countless other activities. We teach our staff members such skills as running a power lawn mower, operating a swimming pool filtration system, and using a ditto machine.

These skills involve mastering the component movements and sequencing these movements into a coordinated act. For example, if the blind boy with whom the therapist is working is to be able to swim the elementary backstroke, he must learn the various components of the stroke: the proper body position, the kick, and the arm strokes. He also must learn to perform the kick and arm strokes in the correct sequence and with the right timing so that he moves through the water. That is, he must master the coordinated skill.

Skilled performance is based on the learner's image of how to do the activity. The blind youngster must have a mental image of how to perform the elementary backstroke. This image is the "plan" that was discussed in Chapter 3. Klausmeier and Goodwin spoke of this image as "an internal model for performance."[9] For the blind youngster, this internal model might be based on how it feels to do the stroke.

We all develop, often with the help of instructors, cues that contribute to our models of how to perform certain skills. Some of these are cues related to how it feels to engage in the skill; they are *kinesthetic* cues. Other cues are *visual*—how it looks when the skill is performed, how the arms are moved in the elementary backstroke, for example. Still other cues are *auditory*. We often use auditory cues in the operation of equipment. The sound of a table saw tells the hobby woodworker whether or not he is moving the wood through the saw too rapidly. Musical skills, of course, nearly always use auditory cues; the rhythm guides a dance step, and the sound of a strummed chord on a guitar confirms one's proper finger positions.

A *feedback-and-correction* process is used in skilled performance. This is the process of knowing what you want to do, perceiving cues that guide your performance, and then modifying (or continuing) action on the basis of how the performance matches the cues. Assume, for example, that a person is attempting to "throw" a simple clay bowl on a potter's wheel. She has a mental image of what she wants the bowl to look like. As she brings up the walls of the bowl, using her fingers and thumbs on the rotating clay, she can match what she sees on the wheel with her mental image. This may suggest changes in how she is holding her hands, or how rapidly she is working the clay. She may also know what it feels like to bring up the clay sides of the bowl. This is a kinesthetic sense involving muscle tension, the movement of body parts (arms and hands, in this case), and the relationships of body parts. In addition, an instructor might provide some auditory cues by offering verbal suggestions.

In most psychomotor skills, the various components are performed in a sequence, a proper sequence for the particular skill. A golf swing, for example, involves initiating the backswing, cocking the wrists on the way back, clearing the hips at the start of the downswing, uncocking the wrists, and following through—in that order. Completing one component becomes a cue for beginning the next component. In this way, the movement becomes coordinated.

Different levels of performance (learning) can be identified in many psychomotor skills. These often are spoken of as beginning, intermediate, and advanced levels.

The characteristic of all psychomotor skills is movement. In some skills such as swimming and golf, the movement is obvious. In others, such as reading and handwriting, the movement is less obvious. Psychomotor skills are not comprised of movement alone, however. Perception is involved. So is cognition (thinking). The golfer uses different strokes based on his perception of the distance to the green and the lay of the ball. He also knows the typical flight paths of balls properly hit with different clubs. Attitudes also may be involved. One golfer may be a very conservative player, shooting around hazards rather than attempting to go over. Another may play much more aggressively. The differences might, in part, be attributed to the golfers' feelings about the game, about themselves, or about the importance of winning.

This blending of one domain into the others is found frequently. Learners often develop attitudes (affective domain) about the information (cognitive domain) they are attempting to learn. In fact, the teacher usually accepts responsibility for encouraging the development of appropriate and related attitudes when teaching for outcomes in the cognitive and psychomotor domains.

HOW DO PEOPLE LEARN?

There are many theories of how learning occurs, and what happens inside the learner. Volumes have been written about these theories. However, it is possible to provide a brief overview of major points of view.

In a general sense, learning is behavior. What we know about behavior is applicable to learning. Broadly, learning involves the individual "behaving" in a certain environment. Another way of saying this is that the individual experiences something. The various major theories that exist deal more specifically with the nature of the behavior or the experience.

As noted in Chapter 3, there are two primary schools of thought in explaining behavior: the behaviorist tradition and the humanist tradition.[10] Several learning theories are derived from these two general systems of thought.

The Behaviorist Tradition. Theorists in this category explain learning in terms of stimulus and response linkages. The focus is on observable events—events in the environment that stimulate an individual to respond and the responses made by the individual. People learn, according to this position, by making associations between events (stimuli, their responses, and the consequences of their responses). For some theorists, the condition that causes learning is the occurrence of two events in close time proximity. For example, a bowler might observe that if she rotates her wrist inward when releasing the ball, the ball curves in its path toward the pins. She "learns," by associating these events, that rotating the wrist produces a curve. This point of view has been referred to as the *contiguity version* of association.[11] Assume that a camp counselor is taking a group of third grade children on a nature hike. Periodically, the counselor points out a particular plant species—manzanita, for example. Each time manzanita is pointed out, the counselor names it. The children associate the name with the characteristics of the bush; they learn what manzanita is. This involves the process of discriminating the characteristics of manzanita from the characteristics of other plant species.

Another version of association has been termed the *reinforcement version*[12]; the term *operant conditioning* also has been used.[13] From this point of view, learning occurs when an individual associates a response either with receiving a reward or with the removal of a punishing condition. The reward (or removal of a punishing condition) "reinforces" the response. Therefore, it is learned. This point of view is concerned with the kinds of reinforcements given, when they are given, and under what conditions. Assume the bowling illustration used above. If the bowler's first curve ball knocked down all of the pins, we could say that she had received positive reinforcement. Similarly, a compliment on the curve from a friend probably would provide positive reinforcement. Or assume that she rolled a curve after rolling several straight balls. If a friend had been teasing the bowler about her inability to roll a curve, stopping the teasing after the first curve could serve as reinforcement. In the manzanita example, positive reinforcement could consist of the camp counselor's praising the children each time they made a correct identification.

The basic characteristic of both the versions described above, and of the behaviorist tradition generally, is a focus on *observable events:* stimuli and responses. Primarily, learning is seen as the result of the individual responding to stimuli.

The Humanist Tradition.   The humanist tradition focuses primarily on the individual. Central to theories in this tradition are the internal states and processes of the learner. For the most part, they are not directly observable. Instead, we infer them from an individual's behavior or from what the individual says. Involved are such things as the way an individual perceives the environment: how he or she thinks and feels about it. These are personal meanings, past experiences, and ways of organizing information that are unique to the individual. Humanists do not deny the effects of stimuli and the presence of observable responses. Instead, they contend that the internal processes and states of the individual "mediate" between stimuli and responses.[14] That is, one individual might perceive a stimulus differently from another individual; as a result, the two persons' responses to the same stimulus might be different. Also, the individual does not simply react to stimuli or elements in the environment. Rather, the learner frequently takes an active, seeking role. There is a "processing" of what is perceived. The individual thinks, organizes, analyzes, and solves problems. It is in this way that learning occurs.

Consider the nature hike example given earlier. Assume that the counselor, leading the hike, wished to teach the campers something about the relationships of vegetation and water. To do so, he takes the group to a stream near camp, where trees and bushes grow abundantly near the water, but thin out on the small ridge behind the stream. Some children might learn that plant growth depends upon water simply by seeing the stream and vegetation and hearing the counselor explain the situation. Other children might learn best by digging at the soil near the stream and on the ridge, and observing the different amounts of moisture. Some might have helped with watering the lawn or houseplants at home; for these children, the idea of water helping trees and shrubs grow might fit easily into existing knowledge. Each child is unique in terms of self-concept, views of the world, motivations, and general past experiences. Therefore, the experience of being at the stream with the counselor, will have different meanings for each child. Each may learn something different, or learn it in a different way. The children will interact with the environment. They will try to make new information fit what they already know; they will change and grow as they adjust to new awarenesses about themselves and their environments. It is this influence of the individual that is characteristic of theories in the humanist tradition.

A Blending of the Major Views.   As mentioned above, humanists do not deny stimuli and responses. Neither do behaviorists ignore completely the influences of the learner. The difference is a matter of emphasis.

There are authors who find a blending of the two major points of view to be appropriate. Clayton presented a very useful model of learning that is based on both stimulus (S) and response (R) variables, and the internal characteristics of the learner. Clayton termed these characteristics "O variables," or variables of the organism. He noted that

> Any stimulus or set of stimuli to which the organism is sensitive can become part of the learning situation. . . . The individual sees, hears, touches, and manipulates the objects in his environment in order to sense them. In general, multisensory stimulations provide more opportunity for learning than does stimulation by a single mode.[15]

The learner perceives the stimuli, gives meaning to them, and responds to them in terms of their importance to him. The learner's response is a necessary condition of learning. "Learning depends upon what the learner does. It is his response to the situation that makes further change possible."[16] The response includes "overt, observable behavior," as well as emotional reactions.

Clayton expressed the interacting relationships of the S, O, and R variables and the learning process in this way.

> In a learning situation, the learner's immediate organization impels him to perceive certain aspects as being more significant than others, and he reacts to these aspects in some way. The response has certain consequences for him; it affects him in some way and produces some change in the structure. . . . To some extent, the individual learner has changed and now moves on to a new situation with a different potential for response.[17]

The model of behavior discussed in Chapter 3 might be thought of in terms of learning; and it accounts for considerations of stimulus, response, and organism variables. In this model, an individual in a situation is motivated to reach or obtain a goal. The individual develops a plan for reaching the goal, responds on the basis of the plan, and perceives the consequences of the response. Success in achieving the goal tells the learner that the particular plan and the particular response were appropriate. The individual learns from experience that the plan works. For example, the blind youngster mentioned earlier will develop a mental image of how to do the elementary backstroke or a feeling about how to do it. The therapist will help him develop a plan. If he is successful when he responds on the basis of the plan—if he swims—he will have learned, at least in part, how to do the stroke. As he practices, he will strengthen this learning. If he is unsuccessful, he may try a different plan, leading to a different response. The elements of stimuli (such as the suggestions of the therapist and the physical elements of the pool) and response (the youngster's attempts to do the stroke) are present. These are influenced by the learner's own individual characteristics, or "O variables" (such as his coordination, attitude toward learning, lack of fear of the water, energy level, and other factors).

The nature hike example also illustrates these elements, and the behavior model. Assume that a hiker wishes to identify a manzanita bush correctly. The individual has a plan for how to do this—an image of what the bush looks like. At the next likely looking bush along the trail, she says to the counselor, "I think that is a manzanita bush." If the counselor indicates that it is, she learns that the identifying characteristics she had in mind are correct. Or, if incorrect, she learns this. Again, stimulus, response and organism variables are involved.

Some Additional Considerations.   In many ways, learning is the development of meaning. It is what happens when new information "makes sense"—when we understand something or see how it fits in with what we already know. Often, it involves finding out that information or a skill is useful to us. Meaning contributes greatly to learning. Learning to identify manzanita might be challenging, fun, or rewarding if we are praised for doing so. However, learning to identify and to avoid poison oak would have more meaning for most hikers.

Direct experience tends to promote learning more than do contrived or vicarious experiences. Actually seeing a poison oak plant teaches one more than reading about it. Being exposed, by contact, to the plant and developing the itching and irritation that result might be the most direct experience. Obviously, however, these disadvantages make this an unwise choice.

Often it is impossible or impractical to use direct experience. Instructors, therefore, are concerned with transfer. How can we maximize the probability that something learned in an artificial situation will be applicable in (or will transfer to) a real situation? Learning does seem to be more specific than we once thought. However, the transfer of information or skill from one situation to another appears to be facilitated if there are identical elements in the learning situation and in the actual situation. The identical elements might involve processes, principles, skills, or knowledge.[18] Transfer is facilitated also if the instructor conscientiously points out transfer possibilities, and encourages the learner to apply new information and skills to other situations.

Imitation also helps. We often learn by observing someone else and then imitating that person's behavior. This aspect of learning is most useful in learning psychomotor skills. When an instructor demonstrates a skill, one of the primary intents is that students will imitate his or her performance. Less apparent, but equally important, is the use of imitation in the affective domain. We adopt many of our attitudes from other people, who serve as models for us. In part, this is why youth-serving agencies such as Boys Clubs and the YMCA usually expect staff members and volunteers to exemplify those values of the particular agency's creed or ethic. What seems to happen is that the learner adopts "trial" attitudes from other respected individuals. If the trial attitude pays off (rewards the learner), then the attitude is strengthened and eventually learned. More precisely, if the behavior which is based on the trial attitude pays off, the attitude is strengthened.

WHAT IS TEACHING?

Essentially, teaching is creating or manipulating environments so that students (participants or staff) have experiences that contribute to learning. The therapist does this by creating an environment that encourages blind youngsters to experience swimming. As mentioned earlier, this environment includes the various pool elements (water, kick boards, deck and lane markers), instructors, and other swimmers. The therapist manipulates these elements; she uses them, and her own skills, to provide the opportunity for learning. Similarly, in the classroom with volunteers, she uses the blackboard, lighting, chairs, tables, and her own voice and personality to create a learning opportunity.

It is not entirely correct to say that the teacher creates the environment within which learning opportunities occur. The teacher has a major responsibility to see that this happens. Actually, however, the environment is created by the teacher *and the learners.*

> We think of teaching as a process by which teacher and students create a shared environment including sets of values and beliefs (agreement about what is important) which in turn color their view of reality.[19]

Teaching involves interacting with the learner. More specifically, it involves a teacher interacting with students, with the intent to cause learning to happen. That is, the teacher does something with the expectation that this something will cause students to behave—to think or act. The therapist says to the blind youngster, "Pull your hands up along your sides, then push them out, and sweep the water toward your feet," expecting that the learner will attempt the armstroke used in the elementary backstroke. The camp counselor may put up some signs along the nature trail, with the expectation that campers will read them as they hike along the trail.

In teaching, the instructor assesses the student's condition. This includes the student's readiness to learn, and his or her present knowledge or level of skill. If the teaching involves a direct interaction, the assessment includes the student's response to the most immediate past behavior of the teacher. The teacher perceives the student's response and assesses the student's interest and understanding. This leads to the next teacher behavior, that is, to the teacher's response. The learner assesses this and, in turn, responds. This repetitive sequence has been called the *teaching cycle.*[20]

Remember, however, that the teacher need not be present for learning to occur. The camp counselor setting up a nature trail is teaching. He may not be on the site when campers use the trail; but he has created a learning opportunity by manipulating the resources that he has available: the natural environment, appropriate signs that identify plants and trees, and, perhaps, descriptive brochures. Students interact with these elements; they may read them, think about them, and talk about them.

The act of teaching includes planning, preparation, and evaluation. When we teach, we need to know whether or not someone is learning. We need to know how effective our efforts are. This information helps in the planning of further teaching attempts.

Teaching also includes what has been called *classroom management.*[21] This aspect involves such things as organizing students into appropriate groups, handling transition from one activity to another, and dealing with student behavior that detracts from planned experiences.

A TEACHING MODEL

As there are many different learning theories, there also are many different models of teaching.[22] These models are descriptions of the teaching process, the steps involved, and the sequences in which the steps usually occur. Models either are based on a theory of learning, or on some assumptions about the learning process. Different models suggest different roles for teachers, and different activities on the part of students.

Joyce and Weil presented sixteen different teaching models. The authors explained that no single model is superior to another. Based on a review of research on the comparative effectiveness of different teaching approaches, they concluded that

> Although the results are very difficult to interpret, the evidence to date gives no encouragement to those who would hope that we have identified a single reliable, multipurpose teaching strategy that we can use with confidence that it is the best approach.[23]

It does seem possible, however, to identify a general model, based on the major activities of the teacher, which is broadly applicable. The following elements are included:

Definition of Goals or Objectives. This may be done by the teacher, by the students, or as a task shared by both teachers and learners. The goals or objectives might be predetermined, or they might emerge, or be "discovered," in the course of the activity. Different goals or objectives might be defined for different learners. By whatever means these are identified, they serve the purpose of guiding the learning experience; and they provide the criteria for evaluating the effectiveness of teaching or learning.

Assessment of Learners. The teacher will be able to function most effectively, in most teaching strategies, if he or she has a good awareness of the learners. Knowledge of their wishes and interests, their present levels of learning (in the particular subject area or skill being attempted), and their readiness to learn (in terms of physical and attitudinal factors) contribute greatly to the teacher's effectiveness. In most recreation and park situations, teachers learn these things about students by observing them, talking with them, and reviewing any past experiences with them (as students in previous learning situations). In some cases, records might be available, such as test scores or other written information.

Planning. Based on a knowledge of the learners, including an awareness of what they wish to achieve, the teacher makes some decisions. In making these decisions, the teacher also considers agency purposes and objectives.

The decisions have to do with such questions as, What will be taught? What methods will be used? What will students be expected to do? What resources will be needed? How will learning be evaluated? In answering these questions, alone or with students, the teacher is engaging in planning.

Involvement of Students in Activity. People learn by doing something, by engaging in activity. This is experience. On one hand, teachers frequently take a direct role in involving students. They plan the activity and they guide student responses. On the other hand, the students might initiate and direct the activity with the teacher taking the less-direct role of an encourager and facilitator. Or the teacher may create the environment that encourages student activity, but not be present when the activity takes place, as in the nature trail example mentioned earlier. In either case, this is the *interaction* phase discussed previously. The learner interacts with the teacher or with certain other elements in the environment.

As a part of this phase, the teacher might engage in activities intended to motivate learners to participate (and learn). Also, during this phase, the teacher may explain and demonstrate. Lectures or audiovisual resources might be used.

Monitoring also may occur. This happens when the teacher observes the learner's activity and helps the individual assess or evaluate her performance. For example, a beginning golfer often is able to hit the ball reasonably far. However, she may be using incorrect form, making progress beyond a certain point unlikely. In this case, the feedback from the learner's own perceptions might be very positive. The ball is hit; it travels fairly straight and far; the technique must be good. However, the instructor who is monitoring the performance can observe flaws in form that are not apparent to the learner. And, the instructor can help the learner make appropriate adjustments.

Evaluation. Evaluation informs both the learner and the teacher. The learner receives feedback about his or her performance. This kind of feedback may come from the learner's own perceptions or it may be provided by the teacher. Evaluation also helps the instructor assess teaching effectiveness. The quality or extent of student learning gives the teacher a base for future instructional efforts. Evaluation enables more realistic planning.

Evaluation by teachers can take many forms. Written examinations are used to assess learning in the cognitive domain. In selecting alternatives, the teacher may use an objective test, such as multiple choice, true-false, matching, or fill-in. These typically require a specific response. They are called *objective* examinations because they require relatively little interpretation of the responses by the teacher. Theoretically, then, the perceptions and biases of the teacher are minimized.

The other general type is an *essay* examination. In this type, the learner is asked to answer questions in a narrative or descriptive fashion. Here the subjective interpretation of the teacher is more of a factor. Both types have their advantages. Good objective questions are more difficult for the teacher to develop, but they are easier to grade. Essay questions can be developed more rapidly; however, considerably more time must be devoted to reading them. Teachers often use a combination of both types. This may provide a better picture of what students have learned, since individuals respond differently to the two types. Some students find it easier to complete an objective test; others prefer an essay.

The teacher may elect to use an oral examination.

Evaluation of skill learning usually takes the form of observation. The teacher watches the student perform, and judges the learning that has occurred.

Evaluation in the affective domain is somewhat more difficult. Since attitudes and values influence behavior, some inferences about attitude or value changes can be made by observing behavior. Also, we can ask learners about their feelings, interests, and opinions. In this way, some assumptions about the attitudes and values which have been developed, or modified, can be made. Sometimes, rating scales are used, in which respondents are asked the degree to which they agree or disagree with a statement (for example, strongly agree, agree, uncertain, disagree, strongly disagree). These can be used to infer changes in the affective domain.

In addition to making decisions about the form of the evaluation (objective, essay, or combination), the teacher must decide the basis for the evaluation. Will the performance or responses of the learner be compared to some standard or ideal performance or to the performances of other students? In a *criteria-referenced* evaluation, a standard is defined and the performances of individual students are compared to this standard. An example is the progression of standards in swimming (from beginner to advanced), set by the American Red Cross. The learner is evaluated in terms of the ability to perform any given stroke; often distances are prescribed. Another example could be the expectations of the therapist who teaches volunteers about the emotional needs of the blind. If she expected each of the volunteers to be able to complete a written test with a score of 70 percent or better, she would be setting a criteria-referenced standard. She might decide, instead, to see how the responses of any one volunteer compare with the overall performance of the group. This would be a *norm-referenced* approach. Criteria-referenced evaluation generally is more applicable in recreation and park settings. In these settings, usually we are more concerned about students knowing something, or being able to do something; we rarely are interested in giving grades, so comparative performances are of less interest.

This general model of teaching might be summarized symbolically as shown in Figure 7-1. This model is congruent with the general scheme of behavior presented in Chapter 3 and discussed earlier in this chapter. The teacher helps students define or clarify goals and objectives, facilitates their development of plans for responding, involves them in activity, and assists them in perceiving accurate feedback from their responses.

INSTRUCTIONAL GOALS AND OBJECTIVES

When recreation and park personnel attempt to teach, they have certain goals and objectives in mind. For instruction to be most effective, these goals and objectives should be clearly defined. When it is clear what you want to accomplish, it is easier to plan, to "keep on target," and to evaluate what you have done.

The kinds of things that recreation and park personnel want to accomplish when they teach can be stated in varying degrees of generality.

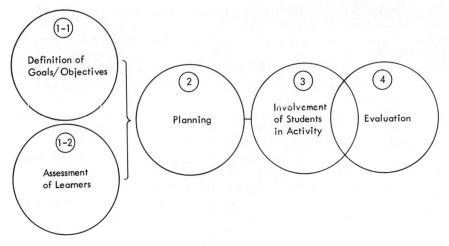

Figure 7-1 A general model of teaching.

Goals tend to be more general; objectives grow out of goals, and are more specific. The overall goal of the therapist providing instruction for the volunteers who work with the blind youngsters might be stated something like this: "To help the volunteers become more effective in their work with blind children in the swimming program." Her objectives for the particular session on emotional needs might include:

1. To identify the general nature of emotional needs; what emotional needs are, and the ways in which they influence development and behavior.
2. To show the ways in which these needs are the same or different for blind children, and to define the possible influences of blindness on the ways individuals seek to meet their needs.
3. To illustrate methods of working with blind children, in a swimming program, which will be most effective in helping these children meet emotional needs.

These objectives, and the general goal, are stated in terms of what the therapist wishes to accomplish. They could also be stated in terms of changes in the volunteers. For example, the general goal could be "to become more effective in teaching blind children to swim." The third objective could be "to be able to use different methods of teaching to contribute to the emotional needs of blind children."

As suggested above, goals and objectives help the teacher plan effectively. If you know what it is you want people to learn, you can do a much better job of deciding how you want to teach. Also, you can evaluate more accurately the degree to which learning has occurred. If recreation and park personnel can specify what they want to teach, in terms of learned behavior, it will be easier for them to evaluate.

Mager noted that an instructional objective is a written or verbal description of a teacher's intent. He stated that the objective will communicate this intent to the degree that you as the teacher have "described what the learner will be DOING when demonstrating his achievement and how you will know when he is doing it."[24] Mager contended that useful instructional objectives have three components.

1. A description of the learner's *behavior,* which will be evidence that desired learning has occurred.
2. A definition of the *conditions* under which the behavior will occur.
3. A statement of the *criterion* or standard that will be used to judge performance.[25]

Following are examples: At the conclusion of the series of twenty swim lessons, and in the shallow end of the pool (*conditions*), the learners will be able to swim without assistance (*behavior*) from one side of the pool to the other, using any one of the strokes taught, without stopping or touching the bottom (*criteria*). After a lecture or discussion on emotional needs, given a written examination (*conditions*), the volunteers will be able to list the emotional needs of the blind (*behavior*) with an accuracy rate of at least 80 percent (*criterion*).

These two examples are related to the psychomotor and cognitive domains. An example from the affective domain is related to the attitude of a willingness to work with the blind. Given the opportunity to do so, without specific encouragement from the therapist or promise of other reward (*conditions*), volunteers will spend extra time beyond the regular period (*criterion*) helping the learners improve swimming skills (*behavior*). In this example, the attitude is inferred from observed behavior.

Specifying instructional objectives, using the three components, helps the learner know what is to be accomplished. This makes for more efficient learning and contributes to more favorable attitudes on the part of the student. However, it is not possible or necessarily desirable to state all objectives in such terms. For example, objectives related to creativeness and self-expression in the arts may be difficult to write specifically in terms of conditions, behaviors, and criteria. The approach to writing objectives that seems most useful is to develop them as specifically as possible, considering the specific subject and learning domain, and the overall goals from which the objectives are derived. The purposes of objectives should be kept in mind. They are to facilitate teaching and learning; however, they should not become ends in themselves. That is, the teacher should not feel restricted to teaching only what can be reduced to specific objectives. Also, objectives should not restrict the learner's opportunities for exploration and discovery.

An additional point is of central importance. The learner should be involved in the development of the objectives which are to be pursued; at the very least, the learner should be aware of and approve of them. This notion is applicable to teaching situations involving both users of agency services and staff members. And it is consistent with a humanistic approach to working with people.

SPECIFIC METHODS IN THE COGNITIVE DOMAIN

The general model of teaching presented earlier is applicable to the cognitive domain as well as to both the affective and psychomotor domains. There are, however, some specific methods that seem most appropriate to promoting learning in the cognitive area.[26] The ones that appear to be most applicable to recreation and park settings are discussed in this section.

Help Learners Discover Personal Meaning in Information and Concepts. Meaning is a highly personal matter. We interpret new information on the basis of our own perceptions. These are influenced by such personal characteristics as self-concepts, attitudes, biases, and needs. What we perceive is reality for us; we assume that it is the way things really are. Teachers can help students develop common meanings, but individual understandings are the basis for behavior. This means that the same information may have different meanings for different people. For example, suppose a televised weather bulletin announces that a storm is approaching a certain area, and that several inches of new snow are expected. To the skier, this information may promise a good day in new snow. To the recreational pilot, the information may mean a cancelled or postponed flight. Both probably are very attentive to the announcement. To a person confined at home, recuperating from recent surgery, the announcement may be meaningless; he may pay little or no attention to it. Many educators believe that we learn only that which has, or comes to have, personal meaning for us. Combs and Snygg provided this observation.

> It is only when events are perceived as having some important relationship to self that they are likely to produce much change in the individual's behavior.[27]

Combs, Richards, and Richards related this phenomenon to the process of learning and teaching.

> This discovery of the personal meaning of ideas, values, experiences, or the accumulated culture of the race is the very essence of learning and the art of teaching is in helping people to make this discovery.[28]

This seems to suggest that teachers should help students realize how the information which is being taught is related to them. What are the personal benefits of learning it? How will it help them achieve their purposes? This requires that the teacher have sufficient information about the students, to be able to make reasonably accurate inferences about their interests and needs.

In Teaching New Information, Build on What Learners Already Know. This suggestion is related to the idea of helping learners discover personal meaning. It also is based on the belief that new information will make more sense if it is related to the person's existing knowledge. It fits in. It becomes part of what is already known. The park maintenance person who has a basic knowledge of small, internal combustion engines will be more able to learn the technical, informational aspects of repairing and maintaining a new power mower than will another staff worker who does not have the background information. However, the advantage is more than the possession of prerequisite knowledge. It also has to do with confidence. If the new information makes sense, the learner will approach the learning task with greater confidence. This suggestion requires teachers to know, or to find out, what their students already have learned.

If the material to be learned is so new or unique that no relationships with existing knowledge can be established, an *advance organizer*[29] can be used. This is brief, introductory material that provides a framework upon which new and more detailed information can be built. This material might take the form of an outline of major concepts and ideas, a brief summary of these concepts and ideas, and a short statement of the ways in which they are related. The short introductions at the beginning of each chapter in this text serve advance organizer functions.

Arrange Material to Be Learned into Appropriate Units. This suggestion has to do with both amounts of information to be learned and the grouping together of similar information. People seem to learn best when they experience some kind of closure, when they sense accomplishment or completion of some phase of a task. This suggests that teachers break information down into units (or subunits) that students can learn in a reasonable length of time. For example, the information needed to operate a swimming pool is complex when taken in its entirety. However, there are logical subunits that can be taught, including such elements as the filter system, the chemical treatment of water, general pool maintenance and sanitation, the patron processing system, the protection of patrons (guarding procedures), and the handling of money from pool admissions. Any one of these subunits could be broken down further.

In general, the younger the students, the smaller the learning units should be. However, there is considerable variation within any particular age group in how different individuals learn. The teacher should consider the nature of the information to be taught, and should know the students with whom he or she is working, as well as the material.

In addition, learning is facilitated when similar pieces of information are presented together in one unit. Generally, the less homogeneous the information, the more difficult it is to learn. However, in learning concepts, it is easier for students to identify examples if the characteristics are widely dissimilar.

Arrange Information to Be Learned in a Logical Sequence. There are three aspects to this suggestion. First, build on already existing knowledge, as discussed earlier. Second, develop a foundation (prerequisite information) on which later knowledge can be built. In learning how to play chess, the beginner must learn the basic moves of each piece before he can learn any strategies of play. Third, move from simple to more complex information.

There is one qualification for all three of the above. The interest of the student is a key factor in learning. Student interest may not follow a logical sequence. The chess student may want to know an opening move, even before he understands the moves of all of the pieces. The teacher should be sensitive to student interest. Occasionally, a departure from the logical sequence might promote learning.

Provide Feedback for Learners.   This suggestion is applicable to the affective and psychomotor domains, as well as to the cognitive domain.

Appropriate feedback gives the student an idea about how well he is progressing. It lets the learner know where corrections are needed, and it reinforces learning. The feedback might be in the form of comments from the teacher, or it might involve the results of written tests or examinations. Or, the student might receive feedback as he uses the new information he has learned.

Give Learners Opportunities to Use New Information or Concepts.   As suggested earlier, using what has been learned provides appropriate feedback. If the practice, or use of knowledge, can be done in actual situations, this helps the learner develop personal meanings. It also provides motivation for further learning.

SPECIFIC METHODS IN THE AFFECTIVE DOMAIN

Attitudes and values develop through conditioning and association, by observing and imitating others, and by being exposed to logical persuasion.[30] These three general sources of learning in the affective domain suggest several specific methods.[31] The following seem most applicable to recreation and park settings.

Identify the Attitudes or Values to Be Developed.   It is more difficult in the affective domain than in the cognitive and psychomotor domains to state objectives in behavioral terms. However, it is no less important in the affective domain for the teacher to be clear about what is to be taught and for the learner to know what is to be learned.

Provide Appropriate Information.   As indicated earlier, the attitudes we have about any particular object (or concept or person) include both knowledge and feelings. Our knowledge may be inaccurate, but it influences our feelings nonetheless.

If a person has no existing knowledge about and feelings toward something, providing information about the object (or concept or person) may contribute to the development of an attitude. For example, if a group of fifth-grade children knew nothing about the concept of wilderness, providing information about the benefits of preserving land in its natural state probably would encourage favorable attitudes toward wilderness. At least, it would encourage the development of favorable tentative attitudes. This would happen if the children respected the source of information (the teacher, or sources used by the teacher such as printed materials and films). If the individual experiences of the fifth-graders supported these tentative attitudes, they would be strengthened.

On the other hand, if a person already has an attitude about wilderness, information may not change that attitude. Change depends on the strength of the existing feelings. Strongly held attitudes will be less likely to change—in fact, be quite unlikely to change—on the basis of new information. If a person who strongly values wilderness hears information contrary to his beliefs, he may discredit the source or modify his perception of the information so as to make it congruent with his beliefs. However, if the new information comes from a highly creditable or respected source, it might contribute to modification of existing attitudes.

Exemplify the Attitudes or Values to Be Developed.   Frequently, people adopt tentative or "trial" attitudes by imitating others they respect. People who are the sources of the trial attitudes often are called *identifying figures.* Again, these trial attitudes are either reinforced or rejected on the basis of experience. One way, then, of teaching attitudes and values is to provide appropriate models—personnel (instructors, leaders, supervisors, and others) who demonstrate the desired attitudes and values.

It is important to emphasize that for trial attitudes to develop, the model must be respected. A leader who is not respected by the adolescents who participate in the city's teen program probably will not become a model for many of the teens. The supervisor who has not developed rapport with staff members probably will be ineffective in influencing their attitudes, at least their attitudes toward those efforts with which the supervisor is identified. This matter of respect or rapport is basic to the idea of an identifying figure. The learner must identify with the model.

Groups often serve as models. Members frequently adopt the dominant attitudes and values held by the overall group. *Reference groups* are groups to which members look for tentative feelings about issues and ideas. Group process also influences attitude development. Research suggests that information discussed in a group has greater impact than information given without discussion. Also, decisions reached through group interaction are supported more strongly; this suggests the presence of stronger beliefs or feelings.[32]

Reinforce Behaviors that Are Based on Desired Attitudes and Values.   The instructor can reinforce trial attitudes and encourage the development of values by rewarding learner behaviors that reflect these attitudes and values. Probably the most potent type of reward is praise or recognition. As an example, suppose a camp counselor wanted to develop camper beliefs in the benefits of not littering. If the counselor expressed appreciation when the campers picked up litter in the camp area, or on the trail, and if the campers identified with the counselor, the attitude would be encouraged.

Pleasant experience related to the object or person involved will also contribute to the development of positive attitudes. Conversely, unpleasant experience usually leads to unfavorable attitudes. When recreation and park personnel help participants have pleasant experiences, they are nurturing positive attitudes. If the blind swimmers enjoy their swimming lessons, there is a much greater chance that they will develop positive attitudes toward safe and enjoyable use of the water than if their experiences are unpleasant. The contribution of pleasant experiences to positive attitudes suggests that teachers create opportunities for learners to "practice" these attitudes. That is, learners should have opportunities for engaging in behaviors based on the attitudes.

SPECIFIC METHODS IN THE PSYCHOMOTOR DOMAIN

Since learning psychomotor skills usually involves information and attitudes the specific suggestions discussed earlier in the chapter generally are applicable here also. There are some additional considerations that promote the learning of skill.[33]

Demonstrate and Explain the Skill to Be Learned. Demonstration and explanation of the skill to be learned help to create interest on the part of the learner. However, the primary reason for demonstrating and explaining a skill is to enable the learner to develop a plan (a mental image) of how to perform the skill. A major part of this plan is the perception of visual cues. In demonstrating, the teacher is, in effect, saying, "This is how it looks when you perform this activity." The explanation also helps the learner. Given during the demonstration, the explanation contributes to the learner's plan. The explanation given later during practice periods provides auditory cues. During later practice, the learner may use these visual and auditory cues to develop kinesthetic cues (or a feeling for how to perform the skill).

Because the demonstration is focused on helping the learner perceive cues, the teacher should analyze the particular skill being taught prior to demonstrating it, so that the various components of the skill can be differentiated. In swimming, this often is called "breaking the stroke down." The teacher should know the different parts of the skill (such as body position, arm stroke, kick, breathing and coordination). In the demonstration and explanation, cues for these various parts can be provided.

It is not necessary for the teacher to do the actual demonstration. Doing so contributes to the students' confidence in the teacher—if the teacher can perform the skill adequately. However, it sometimes is better to use an aide or an advanced student for demonstrations. This enables the teacher to give full attention to the explanation. It often puts the teacher in a better position to sense student reactions and to respond to questions.

Provide Appropriate Practice Periods. Obviously, if students are to learn a skill they must have the opportunity to try it. In setting up practice periods, the teacher must decide how long each period is to be and how the periods will be spaced. There are two general approaches: *distributed* practice and *massed* practice. Distributed practice involves shorter practice periods spread over a longer span of time; while massed practice involves longer individual sessions. Assume that a total of twenty hours was to be devoted to the swim program for blind youngsters. Arranging for forty half-hour sessions would be a distributed approach. Ten two-hour sessions would be a massed approach. The nature of the skill being taught and the maturity of the learners influence which approach is more appropriate. Any one practice period must be long enough to permit student improvement in the skill, but short enough to avoid fatigue or boredom. The time between periods should not be so long that too much is forgotten from one session to the next. Some skills require longer practice periods, simply because of the time involved. Also, mature students can benefit more from longer periods than can less mature learners. In general, however, distributed practice is more appropriate.

Another decision is whether the skill is to be practiced in its entirety, or if emphasis is to be on the various parts. There are three general approaches: the *whole* method, the *whole-then-part* method, and the *progressive part* method. In the whole method, the skill is practiced in its entirety. In some skills, this is necessary. The forward roll in gymnastics and the back dive in aquatics are examples. In the whole-then-part method, the learner tries the whole skill, then concentrates on those parts where improvement is needed. There are two advantages to this approach. Usually, learners are eager to try the whole skill; they want to try to swim, or shoot the bow and arrow, or paint a picture. Letting this happen capitalizes on student motivation. Also, when students have a chance to try the entire skill, it becomes apparent both to them and to the instructor which parts need to be improved. In the progressive part method, each succeeding skill is built upon the prior one; the student learns the first in the sequence, then progresses in turn to each successive part. In the beginning swimming lessons, for example, the student first becomes adjusted to the water, then learns to float, then glide, and so on. This method has all of the advantages identified in the section on sequencing (see the discussion of specific methods in the cognitive domain). It also is very workable with large groups of students, though some provision to assess individual progress is desirable. Otherwise, it is difficult to account for individual differences in rates of learning.

In considering learning rates, it is useful to be aware of *learning progressions*. A typical one, somewhat exaggerated and with the irregularities smoothed out, is shown in Figure 7-2. Generally, one can expect student progress to improve with additional practice. However, the rate of progress usually is not even. "Plateaus" tend to be evident in most cases. These are flat spots in the learning progression, denoting periods when no advancement is apparent. They are to be expected. In fact, learning may be occurring as the student tries changes in form or adjusts to greater complexity. Or the plateau may be due to boredom, fatigue, or the use of inadequate cues.

A general suggestion for arranging practice periods is to provide for practice in the actual situations in which the skill will be used or, if that is not possible, to duplicate the actual conditions as closely as possible.

Provide Feedback for Learners.   As noted in the section on methods in the cognitive domain, feedback reinforces learning. This is especially true in the psychomotor domain. Practice enables feedback and correction.

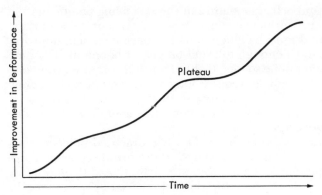

Figure 7-2 A typical learning progression.

In many skills, the learner will perceive results from the performance itself. In other words, in some activities it is easy to see how you are doing. The result of shooting an arrow at a target is seen immediately. The shape and wall thickness of a bowl thrown on a potter's wheel can be discerned the moment it is thrown. But there are other skills in which results are not so easily perceived. Until one develops the "ear" for it, it is difficult to know exactly how an F-chord, fingered and strummed on a guitar, is incorrect. The breast stroke kick cannot be seen easily by the performer; even if he makes progress through the water he may be performing the kick incorrectly. In golf, a beginner might hit a wood shot reasonably straight for eighty or ninety yards, and thus assume that he is performing the stroke properly. However, the form being used may be such that further improvement will be unlikely. In these cases, it is important for the teacher to monitor the student's practice and to provide feedback.

In providing feedback, it is an advantage for the teacher if the learner's level of aspiration can be identified and kept in mind. This concept was discussed in Chapter 3.

MANAGING THE LEARNING ENVIRONMENT

In the overall sense, teaching involves creating or manipulating environments within which students can learn. The major aspect of teaching is interacting with students or providing situations where students interact with other elements of the environment. There is, however, an additional aspect to which the teacher must attend. This aspect includes teacher activities that are not directly part of the interaction process. Involved are such things as organizing a group of students so as to facilitate learning activity, accomplishing transitions from one learning activity to the next, distributing and collecting materials used by students, and preparing or obtaining appropriate audiovisual resources.

HANDLING DISCIPLINE PROBLEMS

An additional consideration in classroom management is controlling or preventing disruptive behavior. Discipline in recreation and parks is less of a problem than it is in other situations, since users of leisure services participate voluntarily and tend to be highly motivated. Also, well-planned learning experiences that appeal to the needs and interests of students minimize the probability of problems. However, disruptive behavior can occur. For example, assume that you are teaching a watercolor class for a group of fifth-graders at a recreation center. One of the girls continues to disrupt the class by poking her neighbors when they are painting, by flicking paint at others in the room, and by talking when you are giving instructions. This may happen even when the class has been well planned and normally runs smoothly. And it may be sufficiently disruptive that you have to do something about it.

The ideal situation would be for students to be responsible enough for their own behaviors that classroom disruptions would not be a problem. One facet of handling problems is to help students grow in their abilities to do this, to be responsible and to discipline themselves. Often this can be facilitated by giving responsibility, by expecting good behavior, and by helping students experience success so that recognition comes from accomplishment rather than misbehavior. It would be unrealistic, though, to believe that this ideal can be achieved at all times. Occasionally, more immediate means of coping with discipline problems are needed.

Canter and Canter developed a system for classroom teachers based on what they called "assertive discipline."[34] Used widely in both elementary and secondary schools, this method seems applicable to recreation and park settings. It is characterized by several basic premises. These can be stated in recreation terms, approximately as follows:

1. *Recreation leaders have needs and rights.* If you were teaching the watercolor class described earlier, you would have a right to be free to carry out your responsibilities without having to devote excessive time to controlling disruptive behavior. You would have the right to a comfortable relationship with participants. And, you would have the responsibility to create an environment that is conducive to the well-being of all the members of the class. It is reasonable to expect that students should not infringe on these rights.

2. *Participants can behave.* Disruptive behavior is not inevitable. Canter and Canter describe several potential sources of behavior problems that teachers feel are difficult to handle. They include such things as emotional problems, peer pressure, poor parenting, and poor home and neighborhood environments.[35] Teachers often lack confidence in their abilities to do anything about classroom behavior because of their inability to deal with the perceived sources of the problems. The authors noted, however, that children often misbehave not because they have to but because they want to.

All of these are *real problems* that can affect the behavior of children and make it more difficult for them to behave appropriately. But, these problems do not prevent the teacher from being able to influence the child's behavior, given the right methods. Children with these problems *can* behave, when they want to do so: they *choose* not to behave. In other words, they won't behave.[36]

You might believe that the fifth-grader in your watercolor class misbehaves because her parents are divorced, her mother works, and she spends a lot of time alone and without adult guidance or affection. Canter and Canter would suggest that this situation might make it more difficult for her to behave, but not impossible. It is fair and reasonable for you to expect good behavior, assuming that you create the conditions to facilitate it.

3. *The rights and needs of leaders and the welfare of participants are served best if leaders are appropriately assertive.* Disruptive participant behavior detracts from your needs and infringes on your rights. It also infringes on the rights of other participants by interfering with their learning or their enjoyment. In some cases, it may endanger them—for example, pushing and tripping in a low-organized game, or ducking and splashing in swim lessons. Appropriate assertive behaviors by leaders help children grow in their abilities to respect the rights of others.

a. *Leaders who are appropriately assertive set appropriate limits on children's behavior.* They make certain that participants know what is expected of them, what behavior is acceptable and unacceptable. Setting limits involves requesting the desired behavior, and knowing what you will do if the participant does not comply with the request. If you can cause the desired behavior to happen without making a demand, it is preferable to do so. You might ask the girl in the watercolor class to stop bothering others, or you might send an "I-message." "I want you to stop bothering the boys and girls near you." Usually in leisure settings, children will respond to such requests. It might be necessary for you to demand the behavior. However, children usually are less responsive to demands than to requests, and demands imply a consequence.[37] The implication is that if the participant doesn't change her behavior you will do something. Therefore, if you make a demand you should be prepared to carry through with the consequences—and the participant should know what those consequences are. In a sense, students are given a choice—to behave or to accept the consequence. The leader promises rather than threatens. The promise is that the consequence will occur if the participant chooses to misbehave.

Canter and Canter noted that children need to have limits set. They suggested that to permit children to engage in disruptive behavior is a threat to their own well-being as well as to the welfare of other children.[38] Again, this generalization seems applicable to recreation and park settings. The fifth-grader will hardly grow in self-discipline if no limits are set on her behaviors—if she does not know what is unacceptable and what the consequences are if she does not behave.

b. *Assertive leaders also consistently and systematically reinforce good behavior*, with praise or with some other appropriate recognition. In addition to needing to have limits set, children and youth need approval and recognition from adult authority figures. Canter and Canter observed that teachers frequently spend considerable time responding to behavior problems, but relatively little to good behavior.[39] They contended that rewarding good behavior encourages children to learn that good behavior pays off. Also, responding only to negative behavior may suggest to children that they can get your attention only by misbehaving.

> All children want your attention! If they feel they can't get it by being "good," then they will try to get it by being "bad." If you recognize and respond only to their negative behavior, the children will continue to act up in order to receive the attention from you that they can.[40]

Focusing on positive behavior makes relationships with participants more pleasant, for you and for them.

Nonetheless, both appropriate consequences and positive reinforcements are needed for effective discipline. What are these, and how can they be selected?

Canter and Canter suggested that teachers plan for which consequences and reinforcers will be used.[41] They recommended consequences such as "time out" or isolation, removal of privilege, and informing parents of the child's disruptive behavior. In the case of the watercolor class, isolation would be moving the child to another part of the room and requiring her to sit and not participate for a reasonable length of time (ten minutes, for example). Removal of privilege might be not permitting her to participate in a coming field trip to an art gallery. It is important, of course, that the privilege removed be something that the child values. However, it should not be something that denies her necessary learning experiences. Consequences should not violate the child's best interests. The assumption in the selection and use of a consequence is that the behavior that led to its use is self-destructive. Therefore, if the the use of the consequence causes the behavior to stop, the child's best interests are served. If the child's best interests are not served by the consequence, it should not be used.

Canter and Canter presented criteria to consider in choosing which consequence to use.[42] It should be something you feel comfortable using and are willing to follow through with. It should not be harmful to the child, but it should be something she does not like. To be effective, a consequence should be presented as a choice the child can make (to behave or accept the consequence). It should be carried out as closely as possible to the time the child makes the choice not to behave; and, it should be carried out "in a matter-of-fact manner," with as little display of emotion by the teacher as possible.

Finally, consequences should be applied consistently. The child should realize that when she chooses not to behave, her choice will lead to a consequence. In recreation and park settings where participation is voluntary, it seems especially important that the consequence seem fair to the child. Also, it should not be so severe that the child loses hope for future participation. For example, excluding the girl from the watercolor lesson for ten minutes probably will seem fair and reasonable to her, even though she may not like it. Excluding her for two days probably would seem so long to her that she might drop out of the lessons completely. This suggests that the consequences should fit the misbehavior; minor disruptions should lead to relatively light consequences. However, there does not seem to be consensus on this approach. The assertive discipline method is based on the idea that consequences are known to children, and are consistently applied when they choose to misbehave. Consistency is important. Matching the consequence to the misbehavior makes it difficult to define in advance what will happen; therefore the opportunity for children to choose to behave or not is minimized. And the element of consistency is reduced.

Canter and Canter suggested that teachers use a series of consequences, ranging from relatively light to more severe.[43] When a child chooses initially to misbehave, the consequence should be relatively light; as the misbehavior continues, the consequences should become more undesirable *as seen by the child*. Perhaps the first time the girl fails to respond to your request, and continues to bother her neighbors, you might move her to an area apart from the other children (but still within the classroom where you can observe all the participants), and let her continue her activity there. If, after she returns to the regular group, she continues to engage in disruptive behavior, you might require her to sit and not participate for ten minutes. If this consequence does not lead to the desired behavior, you might increase the "time-out" period to thirty minutes. The next consequence might be to call her parents and discuss her misbehavior; the result of this discussion might be that she would not be permitted to return to the lessons during the current session. However, she should not be sent home until the time the class regularly ends or without discussing the matter with the parents. You are responsible for her until the class is over, and the parents are expecting that she will be in the class until it is finished for the day.

The authors suggested that the plan for consequences include a "severe clause"; in this case, if the initial misbehavior is serious enough, the child's parents might be called immediately.[44]

Canter and Canter's method includes the provision that the teacher seek help from the principal and parents as needed. In recreation and park settings, this might mean involving a supervisor if the leader needs assistance and, as suggested, it might be appropriate to involve the parents.

Probably the most important positive reinforcement is praise—verbal recognition of good behavior. Canter and Canter noted that with some students, especially teen-agers, such praise might be embarrassing if given in front of others; in such cases, verbal recognition might be best if given privately.[45] Other types of positive reinforcements include notes or phone calls to parents, awards, and special privileges of various kinds.[46]

The "assertive discipline" approach, as applied to a leisure setting, might be summarized in this way: Leaders should assert their rights to appropriate participant behavior. This can be done most effectively by making sure that participants know what behaviors are acceptable, and what the consequences will be if they choose to misbehave. Consequences, if needed, should be applied consistently and without hostility. The consequences should be selected in terms of the best interests of the participant and the ability of the leader to carry them out. Positive behavior also should be recognized consistently.

The assertive discipline approach was designed for use in classroom settings. It seems applicable also to nonteaching situations. Assume that you are a lifeguard on duty at a swimming pool A teen-ager is running on the deck. Pool rules, posted clearly in the locker room and on deck, prohibit running. You blow your whistle and motion the adolescent over to the guard stand. You quickly explain the reasons for not running and ask him to stop the behavior. If he is a newcomer at the pool, you might quickly explain the consequences; if he is not, he no doubt will know them from his own past experiences or the experiences of friends. Several minutes later, he is running again. You blow the whistle, call him over, and ask him to sit down on the deck for ten minutes. If he is caught running a third time, the "time-out" period might be thirty minutes. For subsequent infractions, you might expel him from the pool for the day. As mentioned earlier, it might be advisable to have him sit down until you rotate off the guard stand, then phone his parents to indicate what you are going to do. It depends upon the age of the child and when he normally would leave the pool. It would not be appropriate to send a six year old home when the parents expect him to be at the pool until four, for example. It might be quite appropriate to exclude an older adolescent from the pool without notifying parents, since he probably has much more independence in terms of coming and going.

Dreikurs and Cassel provided another approach to discipline that is also useful for recreation and park personnel.[47] Their methods are especially applicable in working with younger children (up to about ten years of age). They pointed out the disadvantages of using rewards and punishments to obtain desired behavior and suggested that a democratic approach to discipline is more effective. They noted that punishments lead to retaliation, and that rewards, if they are perceived as bribes, suggest to children that we do not trust them.

> The principle of reward and punishment must be abandoned. But this does not mean embracing a "permissive" attitude; this would only create chaos and anarchy. Instead choose democratic methods which are based on the recognition of mutual equality, mutual respect, and order in the classroom.[48]

Dreikurs and Cassel talked about "logical consequences" and "natural consequences."

> *Logical* consequences, structured and arranged by the adult, must be experienced by the child as logical in nature. He will see the consequence of his behavior by experience and will learn from it. . . .

Natural consequences are based on the natural flow of events and are those which take place without adult interference.[49]

In the watercolor class illustration, it might or might not seem logical to the child that the leader moves her away from the other participants. It is possible for a child to see something as logical but not to like it. A natural consequence, occurring without the leader's involvement, might be that the older children move away from her, or that they retaliate and begin teasing or bothering her. This might cause her to stop her misbehavior, or it might lead to further disruption of the class. In either case, she might learn that other people do not like her misbehavior. In the swimming pool example, a natural consequence of running on the deck might be slipping and injuring oneself. The teen-ager probably would learn from this experience not to run on pool decks. However, in this case, the consequence can lead to injury; the probable learning is not worth the hazard.

The generalization that we can draw from Dreikurs and Cassel's suggestions is that if children perceive the undesirable consequences of their behaviors as either logical or natural, they will learn not to engage in such behaviors, and the feelings they have toward the teacher (leader) will be less negative and more appropriate for their growth in self-discipline. The authors observed that logical or natural consequences are not possible in all situations.[50] If, however, adults are sensitive to the advantages of them, they will be more likely to avoid actions that are seen by the child as bribes or punishments.

Dreikurs and Cassel identified four goals younger children seek by misbehaving: attention getting, power, revenge, and display of inadequacy.[51] In *attention getting,* the child is not receiving recognition for positive behavior and seeks it instead by misbehaving. The teacher's action in such cases is to consistently provide recognition for good behavior, and to give attention as often as possible, even if the child does not appear to be seeking it. *Power seeking* can be active or passive. The active child might be rebellious or openly disobedient; the passive youngster might do nothing at all. The suggested teacher response is to attempt to redirect power seeking into positive channels. Give responsibility, and recognize the good work the child has accomplished. The child who seeks *revenge* often feels like hurting others, including the teacher, because he has been hurt by others. The authors observed that it is difficult to work with this type of a situation and that outside help sometimes is needed in addition to what the teacher might do. An appropriate response is to attempt to show the child that he is liked by others, to be empathetic, and to not feel personally hurt by the child's behavior. The child who displays *inadequacy* has given up hope and expects to fail; he therefore participates very little. The most effective teacher response is to provide encouragement, especially when the child makes mistakes.

These goal-seeking behaviors often occur in a predictable sequence. Active or passive constructive attention getting, if not successful, leads to destructive attention getting. This may lead to power and revenge, or to displays of inadequacy.[52] Adult responses often reinforce the misbehavior.

Failing to recognize good behavior, we respond to the attention-seeking misbehavior; therefore, we reinforce the misbehavior. We feel threatened by children's expressions of power, so we use our own power to control them. This tends to convince children that power works. When children seek revenge, teachers are apt to punish them and intensify their desires to strike back. Finally, we tend to give up on children who display inadequacy; in so doing we confirm their perceptions that they cannot achieve success.

The authors pointed out that adults will be more effective if they recognize children's motives. They suggested that we carefully observe their behavior and be sensitive to our own reactions. If we feel annoyed by the misbehavior, it is likely to be attention seeking. If we feel threatened, power probably is involved. Feelings of being hurt suggest revenge, and helplessness is an indication of displays of inadequacy.[53]

A basic premise mentioned earlier is the assumption that children can behave, but that when they misbehave, they choose to do so. This is an appropriate assumption to make. However, it does not mean that you should be insensitive to underlying causes such as poor health and family problems. While these problems probably are beyond your ability to solve, you might be able to get assistance for the child through appropriate referrals. Or you might be able to help the child become more effective in coping with problems. And you can always be empathetic. You can do these things and still set limits and provide positive reinforcements that encourage children to choose to behave in spite of problems. By doing this, you will be helping them grow.

Some underlying causes of discipline problems may be things you can minimize or eliminate. You can plan programs or classes that are interesting and appealing to participants. Poorly planned programs and disinterested participants can be major sources of disruptive behavior. You can check your own perceptions of the children with whom you are working. Insensitive teachers and leaders also are sources of problems. You might be picking on particular individuals because of your own biases or expectations. First noted that if teachers are unfair or inconsistent in setting limits, children respond negatively.[54] She also observed that lack of sensitivity to children's uniqueness frequently leads to disruptive behavior.

> Teachers who fail to treat all children with sensitivity can expect to get more than the usual number of angry, acting-out responses from children. Youngsters whose poverty is unwittingly singled out for notice, whose nonstandard English is attacked, or who experience repeated put-downs resulting from racial, religious, economic or life style differences find their self-esteem eroded and respond in one of several negative ways: by striking back in anger, by withdrawing safely out of harm's way or by attempting to triumph in games of testing, manipulation and power which pit child endlessly against adult.[55]

The task is to try to eliminate those causes of misbehavior over which you have some control, to be sensitive to the influences of those which are beyond your control, and to consistently and fairly set limits and provide reinforcements that encourage acceptable behavior.

Handling discipline problems probably will be a relatively minor responsibility for most recreation and park personnel; yet it is an important one. Disruptive behavior in a classroom or in any program, if not dealt with, can diminish the value of experiences for participants and result in leader or teacher frustration. The matter should be kept in perspective, however. For one thing, you will have to decide what you consider misbehavior (perhaps you can do this cooperatively with participants). In formal classroom settings, it often is difficult to determine which problems are discipline problems and which are not.[56] For example, is talking during class misbehavior? Is tardiness? In recreation and park programs it may be more difficult to decide. Our expectations for participant behavior should be realistic. We need to guard against creating problems where none exist. The criteria for judging whether a child's actions are problems should be:

1. Does the behavior disrupt the program so that the experiences of other participants are lessened?
2. Does the behavior detract from your ability, as the leader, to meet your responsibilities?
3. Is the behavior contrary to the best interests of the child?

If the answer to all of these questions is No, it is probable that no discipline problem exists. This is not to suggest that we ignore misbehavior, or that we fail to assert our rights as leaders and teachers; but it does mean that we adopt realistic standards.

A second aspect of keeping things in perspective is to recognize that your classroom or program will not be perfect all the time. Disruptive behavior probably will occur in spite of your preventive efforts, and your methods of handling discipline may not be effective at all times. That does not necessarily mean that you or your programs are failures. Handling discipline problems is a matter of knowing the behaviors you want from participants, using the methods available to you as effectively as you can,[57] and not worrying needlessly about unachievable objectives. First concluded, "It is more productive to spend one's energies wrestling expectations into alignment with reality than wrestling reality into line with unrealistic expectations."[58]

The two methods of working with behavior problems, described in this section, suggest some ways of working with students in recreation and park settings. The assertive discipline approach places the teacher or leader in a more direct role as a limit-setter and provider of consequences and positive reinforcements. Dreikurs and Cassel's approach emphasizes the contributions of logical and natural consequences to the growth of children's ability to discipline themselves. Canter and Canter's techniques are useful with participants up through the high school years; the methods proposed by Dreikurs and Cassel, as described here, are more appropriate with younger children. Neither method is addressed to disruptive behavior on the part of adults, or to criminal or violent behaviors. (These matters are discussed in Chapter 9.)

The overall objectives in handling discipline problems, in or out of instructional settings, are to assure positive leisure experiences for all participants and to help individuals grow in their abilities to meet their own needs with consideration for the needs of others.

SUMMARY

Recreation and park personnel teach in a variety of situations, involving both participants and staff. In doing so, they attempt to promote learning in the cognitive domain, the affective domain, and psychomotor domain. Learning in these three domains can be thought of as a change in the learner's ability to behave—to think, to feel, to perform. Recreation and park personnel who teach bring about these changes through various teaching methods, depending upon the subject being taught, the nature of the learners, and the perceptions of the teacher. A general teaching model can be described that includes defining objectives, assessing the learners, planning and making decisions about specific methods, involving students in activity, and evaluating both student progress and teaching effectiveness.

Staff members who teach also are responsible for managing the learning environment. This includes handling discipline problems that might occur, by setting limits, providing positive reinforcements, and encouraging self-discipline.

REVIEW QUESTIONS

7-1 Two major views on how people learn were presented in this chapter. How can these two views be blended into a composite explanation? In what ways is this composite similar to the model of behavior presented in Chapter 3?

7-2 What kinds of activities do leisure service personnel engage in as they teach? What are the general steps in the teaching process?

7-3 What illustrations can you give of the things that might be taught in each of the three learning domains?

7-4 In what ways might your teaching methods differ in each of the three domains? That is, what specific techniques seem especially applicable in each?

7-5 What are the characteristics of an instructional objective that is written appropriately?

7-6 What is meant by the term *discipline*? In what kinds of situations might recreation and park personnel be concerned about discipline? What general methods are effective in these situations?

TO DO

7-A Look back over the list of your own recreation behaviors, that you wrote down in item 3-A (Chapter 3). Pick two of those activities and for each answer the following questions:

1. What aspects of this activity could be considered in the cognitive domain? Are there aspects that are in the affective domain? Does the activity involve motor skills?

    2. How did you learn this activity? Try to remember such details as: how old you were, where you were, from whom you learned the activity, and what that person did.

7-B When you have some free time, try something new, some recreation activity that you have not done before. Something that you can do without much expenditure of time or money is preferable (for example, playing a new electronic game, completing a new craft project, learning a new song, shooting baskets in the gym, or trying miniature golf, if these are new activities). Before you engage in the activity, write an instructional objective for what you are about to do. As you engage in the activity, try to be aware of these things:

    1. How does what you are doing match the general model of behavior presented in Chapter 3?
    2. Are you using cues of any kind (visual, auditory, or kinesthetic)? Is the process of feedback and correction involved?
    3. Which different learning domains are involved?

7-C If you are taking a class at the present time, observe what the teacher does as well as what is being taught. Try to be aware of the specific methods used by the teacher.

END NOTES

1. Nelson F. Dubois, George F. Alverson, and Richard K. Staley, *Educational Psychol ogy and Instructional Decisions* (Homewood, Ill.: The Dorsey Press, 1979), pp. 138–39.

2. B. S. Bloom, ed., *Taxonomy of Educational Objectives. Handbook I: Cognitive Domain* (New York: David McKay Company, Inc., 1956).

3. For examples, see Herbert J. Klausmeier and William Goodwin, *Learning and Human Abilities: Educational Psychology* (New York: Harper & Row, Publishers, 1975), pp. 247–50.

4. Robert A. Davis, *Learning in the Schools* (Belmont, Calif.: Wadsworth Publishing Company, Inc., 1966), pp. 11–20.

5. Davis, *Learning in the Schools,* pp. 15–16.

6. Herbert J. Klausmeier, Elizabeth Schwenn Ghatala, and Dorothy A. Frayer, *Conceptual Learning and Development: A Cognitive View* (New York: Academic Press, Inc., a Subsidiary of Harcourt Brace Jovanovich, Publishers, Inc., 1974) p. 4.

7. Klausmeier, Ghatala, and Frayer, *Conceptual Learning and Development: A Cognitive View,* pp. 12–21.

8. Klausmeier and Goodwin, *Learning and Human Abilities,* pp. 272–74.

9. Ibid., p. 335.

10. Arthur W. Combs, Donald L. Avila, and William W. Purkey, *Helping Relationships: Basic Concepts for the Helping Professions* (Boston: Allyn & Bacon, Inc., 1978), pp. 106–11. See also Dubois, Alverson, and Stakey, *Educational Psychology and Instructional Decisions,* pp. 39–41.

11. Dubois, Alverson, and Staley, *Educational Psychology and Instructional Decisions,* p. 53.

12. Ibid., pp. 51–53.

13. Klausmeier and Goodwin, *Learning and Human Abilities,* pp. 25–26.

14. Thomas E. Clayton, *Teaching and Learning: A Psychological Perspective* (Englewood Cliffs, N.J.: Prentice-Hall, Inc., 1965), pp. 55–56.

15. Clayton, *Teaching and Learning,* p. 39.

16. Ibid., p. 42.

17. Ibid., p. 42.

18. Ibid., pp. 86–87.

19. Bruce Joyce and Marsha Weil, *Models of Teaching* (Englewood Cliffs, N.J.: Prentice-Hall, Inc., 1972), p. 3.

20. B. Smith, "A Concept of Teaching," *Teachers College Record* 61, no. 5 (February 1960): 234–35.

21. Bryce B. Hudgins, *The Instructional Process* (Chicago: Rand McNally College Publishing Company, 1971), pp. 20–23.

22. For examples, see Joyce and Weil, *Models of Teaching.* Also, John P. DeCecco and William R. Crawford, *The Psychology of Learning and Instruction,* 2nd ed. (Englewood Cliffs, N.J.: Prentice-Hall, Inc., 1974), pp. 8–21; and Clayton, *Teaching and Learning,* pp. 13–20.

23. Joyce and Weil, *Models of Teaching,* p. 4.

24. Robert F. Mager, *Preparing Instructional Objectives* (Palo Alto, Calif.: Fearon Publishers, 1962), p. 53.

25. Mager, *Preparing Instructional Objectives,* pp. 10–14, 25–27, 44–46.

26. Klausmeier and Goodwin, *Learning and Human Abilities,* pp. 259–66. See also Dubois, Alverson, and Staley, *Educational Psychology and Instructional Decisions,* pp. 328–47.

27. Arthur W. Combs and Donald Snygg, *Individual Behavior: A Perceptual Approach to Behavior* (New York: Harper & Row, Publishers, 1959), p. 147.

28. Arthur W. Combs, Anne Cohen Richards, and Fred Richards, *Perceptual Psychology: A Humanistic Approach to the Study of Persons* (New York: Harper & Row, Publishers, 1976), p. 204.

29. Klausmeier and Goodwin, *Learning and Human Abilities,* pp. 42–43.

30. Dubois, Alverson, and Staley, *Educational Psychology and Instructional Decisions,* p. 311.

31. Klausmeier and Goodwin, *Learning and Human Abilities,* pp. 374–82; Dubois, Alverson, and Staley, *Educational Psychology and Instructional Decisions,* pp. 310–18.

32. Klausmeier and Goodwin, *Learning and Human Abilities,* p. 380. See also Dorwin Cartwright and Alvin Zander, eds. *Group Dynamics: Research and Theory,* 3rd ed. (New York: Harper & Row, Publishers, 1968), p. 53; and Alberta Engvall Siegel and Sidney Siegel, "Reference Groups, Membership Groups, and Attitude Change," in Cartwright and Zander, *Group Dynamics,* pp. 74–79.

33. Klausmeier and Goodwin, *Learning and Human Abilities,* pp. 344–52. See also Dubois, Alverson, and Staley, *Educational Psychology and Instructional Decisions,* pp. 318–27.

34. Lee Canter with Marlene Canter, *Assertive Discipline: A Take-Charge Approach for Today's Educator* (Los Angeles, Calif.: Canter and Associates, Inc., 1976).

35. Canter with Canter, *Assertive Discipline,* pp. 46–49.

36. Ibid., p. 49.

37. Ibid., pp. 72–73.

38. Ibid., pp. 92–93.

39. Ibid., p. 118.

40. Ibid., p. 119.

41. Ibid., p. 136.

42. Ibid., pp. 94–95.

43. Lee Canter and Associates, *Assertive Discipline: In-Service Workshop, Teacher's Packet* (Los Angeles, Calif.: Canter and Associates, 1979), p. 5.

44. Ibid., p. 5.

45. Canter with Canter, *Assertive Discipline*, p. 122.

46. Canter with Canter, *Assertive Discipline*, pp. 124–25.

47. Rudolf Dreikurs and Pearl Cassel, *Discipline Without Tears* 2nd ed. (New York: Hawthorne Books, Inc., 1972).

48. Dreikurs and Cassel, *Discipline Without Tears*, p. 61.

49. Ibid., p. 62.

50. Ibid., p. 63.

51. Ibid., pp. 34–41.

52. Ibid., p. 40.

53. Ibid., pp. 34, 40–41.

54. Joan M. First, "Expectations," in *Everybody's Business: A Book About School Discipline*, ed. Joan McCarty First and M. Hayes Mizell (Columbia, S.C.: Southeastern Public Education Program, 1980), p. 18.

55. First, "Expectations," in *Everybody's Business*, p. 19.

56. Joan M. First and M. Hayes Mizell, "Perspectives," in *Everybody's Business*, p. 5.

57. An excellent summary of forty-seven different approaches used by schools to improve discipline is provided by W. W. Wayson and Gay Su Pinnell in *Everybody's Business*, ed. First and Mizell, pp. 27–44. The essential nature of each method and advantages and disadvantages are described. Many of the methods have potential applicability in leisure settings.

58. First, "Expectations," in *Everybody's Business*, p. 25.

chapter 8

Referral and Advocacy

PREVIEW

In the processes described thus far (leadership, working with groups, and teaching), recreation and park personnel work directly with the users of leisure services or with staff members in the agencies that provide the services. In this chapter, two processes are discussed in which the primary contacts are with people other than participants or leisure agency staff. These are the processes of referral and advocacy.

In referral, individuals who have needs that cannot be served adequately by the recreation and park agency are referred to other agencies that can provide the needed help. In some cases, the need is for a special type of leisure service not offered by the referring agency; in others, the individual is experiencing a nonleisure problem which limits his ability to enjoy free time fully.

In advocacy, recreation and park personnel seek to bring about changes in community conditions that are barriers to participation. In these cases, the sources of the problems are such things as restrictive agency policies, lack of needed services, unequal access to opportunities and other limiting factors.

Referral is considered first. The conditions under which referrals are indicated are discussed. Agencies to which referrals can be made are described; and information is provided on ways to find out about the existence of, and nature of, these agencies. Ways are presented of developing agency contacts that facilitate referrals. Attention is given to the question of when referrals should be made. Finally, the referral process itself is described.

Advocacy is then considered. The concept is presented, and some reasons are given why it is appropriate for recreation and park personnel. Following this, various advocacy methods are described. A section is included on influencing legislative processes.

The teen-ager was pregnant; she was frightened and she was confused. The only person she felt she could talk to was the recreation center director. She regularly attended teen functions at the center, and she had known the director for almost two years. The two of them were sitting in the director's office. The girl said that she was thinking about running away. The director listened, helped the girl explore her feelings and different alternatives; she then suggested that the girl might want to talk with a counselor at the local Children's Home Society, an agency that works with pregnant teen-agers. The director knew several counselors at the Children's Home Society and had referred girls to them previously.

The next morning the director attended a meeting of staff members from several community human service agencies. The group met regularly to talk about common problems and to share ideas. A social worker from the Family Service Agency asked the recreation center director to send a copy of the center's current program to a family he had been working with, and to follow up the mailing with a phone call to the family. The social worker felt that members of the family involved needed opportunities to meet and interact with other individuals in the community.

Recreation and park workers frequently find themselves in a position to help people, but do not feel very confident about their ability to provide the help needed. The situation with the pregnant teen-ager is an example. Another would be the case of an adolescent who has a continuing record of socially disruptive behavior. His only consistent potential support source might be the recreation agency. It is likely that his relationships with the school and with his family are not entirely adequate; if he is employed, it might be in a marginal job from which he could readily be released. His perception of the police department is probably negative. The recreation agency might be seen as the least threatening contact with society. His behavior at agency events (at the recreation center or other facility) might create problems at times, but he might relate more easily to the recreation worker than to staff in the other agencies. To that extent, the recreation worker has an opportunity to help solve the individual's problems.

This, of course, is something of a stereotyped description, but it does illustrate a common situation. Because of the relatively nonthreatening nature of recreation, users often relate to recreation and park staff more readily than to other agency workers, and they sometimes ask for help of a nonleisure nature. When this happens, recreation and park personnel have three response possibilities: (1) they can decline to help because the request is not for recreation services or is inappropriate for other reasons (it is illegal, immoral, or unethical); (2) they can accept the request as appropriate and can attempt to comply; or (3) they can refer the person making the request to another appropriate individual or agency.

As pointed out in Chapter 4, a humanistic and holistic philosophy suggests that recreation and park personnel should respond to nonleisure-oriented requests for help—if they are appropriate otherwise and if time constraints and priorities do not preclude such responses. The conditions prompting such requests might indirectly influence a person's use of free time (as in health or employment problems), and they might detract from the individual's ability to fulfill his or her potential.

Maslow's theory of motivation, discussed in Chapter 3, suggests that we must satisfy some needs before we are influenced by others.[1] The needs for belonging and for self-esteem—common motives for participation in leisure activities—generally will not influence our behavior until our physiological needs (for such things as food and shelter) and our needs for safety and security are met. For example, an individual deeply concerned about a personal health problem will be less likely to seek out satisfying leisure experiences than one who is in good health. A staff member who has severe marital problems probably will not function as effectively on the job as he would if the problems did not exist. In both examples, recreation and park personnel who work with these individuals should provide help if they can.

One kind of helping is discussed in Chapter 4. However, the kind of help needed may be beyond the expertise of the worker. Clearly, recreation and park personnel should not try to be what they are not—lawyers, physicians, social workers, counselors, and other specially trained providers of human services. But they can refer users of leisure services to other providers as opportunities to do so arise, and as they receive requests for help.

BASIC CONDITIONS FOR REFERRAL

Referral is the process of making it possible for those with whom we are working to receive help from another source, when the nature of the help they need is either outside our areas of responsibility or beyond our expertise.[2] Compton and Galaway's suggestion that social work agencies have such a responsibility seems applicable to the field of recreation and parks as well.

> Our professional commitment requires us to assume responsibility not only for our judgments and actions but for the results of our judgments and actions. If we hold ourselves out as persons concerned with the struggles of others, with problems of coping, then we must be concerned not only with offering adequate service in connection with those problems that fall within our defined "turf," but also with offering the same skilled help to enable persons to reach the proper source of help.[3]

Certain conditions are necessary for us to enable others with whom we have contact to reach the sources of help they need. First of all, we need to know where our own responsibilities for direct service end; we also need to know the limits of our abilities to provide effective and appropriate help. When these parameters are clear to us, we can be most aware of when referrals are appropriate. Second, to put someone else in contact with sources of help, we need to know the nature of the problem and something about the condition of the person who is experiencing it. Finally, we have to have an adequate knowledge of community resources that are available to which the affected person may be referred.

As suggested earlier, help is appropriate when the problems of another person are interfering with that person's free time satisfactions (or work efficiency, if the person is a staff member). If the needed help falls within our responsibilities, referral may not be appropriate. For example, an individual's inability to relate comfortably to other people might make his leisure experiences unsatisfying. If the setting within which this condition was discovered were a community recreation center, the staff member might have no direct responsibility for dealing with the problem. If the setting were a nonresident facility for the developmentally disabled, the recreation therapist might be directly responsible for contributing to the solution of the problem. Referral probably would be appropriate in the first instance and not in the second. However, other factors would have to be considered. If, at the community center, the individual with the problem did not seek help from the staff member or was unwilling to confront his problem, referral would not be advisable. In the out-patient facility, if the therapist were not skilled in helping others become more effective in interpersonal relationships, referral probably would be necessary. The decision to refer or not depends on the staff member's responsibilities and capabilities and on the awarenesses, motivations, and abilities of the person with the problem.

When a decision to refer is made, its effective outcome depends on the recreation and park worker's knowledge of possible resources to which referrals can be made.

AGENCIES TO WHICH REFERRALS CAN BE MADE

Many different organizations and agencies provide human services. Even in small towns and rural areas, various sources of help are available. Oglesby provided a useful categorization of the different types of referrals: (1) professional services, such as medical care and psychiatry; (2) community organizations such as mental health societies, associations for retarded persons, and family service associations; (3) private organizations, such as Alcoholics Anonymous and the Planned Parenthood Federation of America; and (4) religious groups, such as Catholic Charities, The Salvation Army, and Jewish Health and Welfare Agencies.[4] Oglesby noted that the categories of community organizations and private organizations are very similar, but that there is a tendency for community organizations to be supported more often through federated funding efforts such as United Crusade and Community Chest. Another category that could be added to these four is that of governmental services, such as public health departments and social welfare units.

Agencies and organizations can be thought of in terms of the problems with which they are concerned. One major grouping is comprised of those services that are health related, that deal with such matters as general medical problems, substance abuse, pregnancies, and mental health. Other types of problem-oriented services include marriage and family counseling, legal assistance, employment counseling, financial aid, food and nutrition programs, rehabilitation services, housing assistance, and educational programs.

Another way of categorizing agencies is to focus on the primary client group they serve: children's services, programs for older adults, associations concerned with individuals who have common health problems (such as cancer, diabetes and lung disease), groups that assist persons who have been institutionatized to adjust to the return to larger society, and others.

However categorized, the kinds of services offered by these types of agencies tend to be characterized as informational/educational or direct; many provide both of these. Informational/educational services are intended to help a person know more about the problem with which the agency is concerned and about the help or service that is available. Direct services involve action-oriented programs that are intended to relieve the problems that the person is experiencing. Of course, knowledge itself may do this, also. Some direct service programs are crisis oriented; they are designed to provide immediate help in emergency situations, such as when a person intends to commit suicide or has taken a drug overdose. Others emphasize ongoing help. Some agencies focus more on preventing problems; others deal more with ameliorating problems after they have developed; and many organizations are concerned with both dimensions.

HOW CAN I FIND OUT ABOUT THESE AGENCIES?

There are various ways to become aware of the resources that are available in your community or area. One excellent way is to go to a public library and ask for information about human services that are available to people in the community. Most libraries have one or more staff members who are well qualified to provide such information. The library might have a printed listing of all such agencies.

Other sources of information are county welfare departments. Every county in the United States has some unit of government that provides social welfare services, and these agencies usually have information on other available human services. A community action agency may be able to supply you with a listing of other agencies that work with people.

Frequently, communities will form interagency councils, or federations of human service agencies. These are good sources of information. Other helpful contacts include county and city planning departments, public health departments, police and sheriff's departments, public school offices, community service departments at universities and colleges, hospitals, churches, and any local federated funding agency in the community (such as United Crusade, Community Chest, and others). A good way to begin a search is to look in the phone book Yellow Pages under such headings as "Human Service Organizations," and "Social Service and Welfare Organizations."

DEVELOPING CONTACTS WITH REFERRAL AGENCIES

For recreation and park personnel who make frequent referrals, a file of agencies can be very useful. Information can be kept on 3×5 cards, or in whatever other form seems most easy and appropriate. The information should be accessible when needed, and it should be easily updated. The following information on each agency would be of potential help: the agency name, a summary of the types of service provided, the phone number and address of the agency, the hours and days of operation (and whether or not after-hours emergency services are available), and the names of contact persons in the agency. To be most useful, these cards should be identified according to the general types of problems that may be referred to the agencies they represent.

The conditions for effective referral call for more than knowing what agencies exist, and the kinds of services they provide. These, of course, are critical things to know; without them, no referral can take place. However, to be most effective you should develop some lines of communication or some initial contacts with those agencies you are most likely to use as referrals. Oglesby made this observation in discussing referral responsibilities and opportunities of ministers. It seems applicable to our field as well.

> The primary consideration is that he familiarize himself with the resources available to him for referral and establish some working relationship with these resources prior to the time they will be needed. While it is probably inevitable that some situation or problem will be brought to him which will require his making an investigation at the time of the request, his ordinary procedure is not only to be acquainted with the services and agencies in his areas, but also to know those key persons in the agencies who will be involved in the referrals. It is only from this position that he is able to know in advance the kind of help to be expected by his parishioners—and to describe with integrity the possibilities and limitations of the referral resource.[5]

Developing contacts with other agency staff members facilitates making a referral when one is necessary. It is easier to talk with someone in another agency about a specific problem situation if you have had some prior contact. Also, in making these contacts you will learn more about the agency, about what services it can—and cannot—provide.

Becoming familiar with human service agencies in your community can be enjoyable. It can not only provide opportunities for you to expand your knowledge; it also can give you the chance to let others know about the services of the agency you represent.

WHEN SHOULD REFERRALS BE MADE?

It was suggested earlier that referrals should be made when an individual with whom you are working has a problem that interferes with his or her ability to enjoy free time (or to work efficiently in the case of staff members), when the person asks for help or seems willing to accept it, when the required actions fall beyond your skills and knowledge, or when you are unable to help because of the demands of higher priorities. However, the decision to refer often is not easy. The factors upon which the decision will be based frequently do not lead to a clear choice one way or the other.

Oglesby suggested that there is the possibility for referrals to be made either too early or too late, in terms of the well-being of the person who is experiencing the problem.[6] This problem may result from the attitudes or outlook of the staff member who is making the referral. If that person lacks confidence or feels inadequate, it is possible that a referral will be made before there is sufficient opportunity to see if the relationship between the staff member and the person has a chance of contributing to the solution of the problem. Conversely, if the staff member feels that she ought to be able to handle the problem, and that to make a referral is a a sign of weakness or incompetence, then the referral might be delayed too long. Since the answer may not be clear, there is some risk. If we refer too soon, we do not fully use our own capabilities. If we delay too long, the problems of the person we are trying to help may intensify. In crisis situations, such as potential suicides, such delays can lead to unacceptable consequences. In such cases, obviously, it would be better to refer too early.

At times a person with whom you are working may have a problem that falls both within your area of responsibility and your level of expertise, but other considerations may suggest a referral. Oglesby referred to such a condition as one where a "limitation of emotional security" on the part of the staff member makes it appropriate to refer.[7] What this means is that certain emotional states of the staff member may reduce the person's effectiveness to the point where referral is necessary. For example, if you have an unresolved problem similar to the one which you are confronting in the other person's life, you might not be effective. If you are experiencing considerable stress and anxiety at the time you are trying to help, you might not be effective. If, as suggested earlier, you feel that it is necessary to "prove" that you can help, or if you are unable to accept that your efforts to help might fail, then you might not be effective.

When should referrals be made? The answer to that question is less a matter of the severity of the problem faced by the person with whom you are working and more a function of your own situation and resources. When the person asks for help or is willing to accept help but the problem does not fall within your responsibilities or expertise, or when you do not have sufficient time to help because of other, higher priority responsibilities, or when your attitudinal or emotional state is such that helping is inadvisable, then a referral should be made.

THE REFERRAL PROCESS

Before referrals can be made, there must be an expression of need. The person who is experiencing the problem must ask for help; or the staff member must be perceptive enough to pick up the clues that indicate that the person needs help and is willing to be helped. It would have been difficult for the center director mentioned at the beginning of the chapter to help the pregnant adolescent if the teen-ager had not come to her. And if the young person had not wanted to be helped, it is unlikely that the director could have done much. *But the teen asked for help.* You will remember from Chapter 4 that it is difficult to ask for help. When we do so, we have to admit to ourselves and to someone else that something is wrong. We have to admit that we are unable to handle it by ourselves. These conditions influence the referral process. There is a possibility that the person with the problem may experience negative as well as positive feelings toward the staff member making the referral.

> Being referred often carries with it elements of rejection, anger, hope, and expectation. The rejection arises when clients are unable to get help needed and wanted from the original worker and must make themselves known and understood elsewhere.[8]

The teen-ager may feel threatened when the center director suggests talking to a counselor. She may feel that the person whom she trusts (the director) is "letting her down." On the other hand, she may view the suggestion as another opportunity to receive help with the problem that frightens and confuses her. If there are negative feelings, the staff member might have the additional roles of encouraging the person to use the referral resource and of strengthening her motivation to do so. Even if the teen-ager is motivated to talk with a Children's Home Society counselor, she still may find the referral process somewhat threatening. New situations will be encountered; unfamiliar people, who may have unknown expectations, probably will cause anxiety. These feelings can occur in referral processes. However, they do not negate the value of appropriate referral, or the abilities of leisure service personnel to use the process. Brill's comment about human service workers, generally, provides a useful perspective.

> A competent worker with good knowledge of and skill in the use of referral procedures can so facilitate the process that the client can make maximum use of those aids which are available. Primarily the worker must know what is available to the client and how to help the client use it.[9]

In helping an individual use a referral resource, the staff member must make some assessment of the person's capabilities and motivations.[10] How much help will the person need in getting to and using the services of the other agency? The answer to this question will suggest answers to another question: What is the staff member's role in the process? For some people, it will be enough simply to inform them about the existence of other agencies that can be of assistance. They will have the desire and the ability to get to and use the available services once they know about them. For others, it will be necessary to go with them to the other agency and to be with them during the initial (and perhaps subsequent) visits.

Keeping in mind that the actual role of the staff member making the referral will be influenced by the capabilities of the person with the problem, the elements of the process might be described in this way.

1. *Select the referral agency.* Based on the nature of the problem, and an awareness of possible referrals, an agency is selected. The staff member has the responsibility to provide as much information as possible about the kinds of help that the person can expect from the agency. If several alternatives are possible, the person with the problem should be involved in the selection.

2. *Provide appropriate help in using the referral agency.* As mentioned earlier, some persons will need only to be informed. Others will benefit from encouragement and support. Some will need to know how to get to the agency, who to see there, and generally what to do to initiate a request for help at the new agency. In some cases, it may be appropriate to go to the agency with the person. It might also be appropriate to phone the referral agency beforehand to inform staff members there that the person is being referred. A call can facilitate referrals, especially if communication between agency staff members already has been established. Sometimes, useful information about the person being referred can be passed along. However, such a call or the forwarding of information could be seen as an infringement on the person's right to privacy. On this point, it is best to check first with the individual being referred.

Brammer suggested that written permission be obtained before releasing any information to the new agency.

> Do not release information to any referral source without written permission from the helpee or his parents in the form of a signed release.[11]

3. *Follow up the referral.* The follow-up might involve only checking with the person who was referred to see if the visit was useful and what ongoing assistance is being provided. Or it might mean contacting the referral agency. Again, however, either of those actions might be viewed as infringements, especially the latter. The value of the follow-up is to enable the staff member to be of continuing help, if it is appropriate.

In this process, it is useful for the person with the problem to take as much initiative as possible. This idea is consistent with the "growth principle" discussed in Chapter 4. It also is consistent with the basic idea of self-determination, which is basic to a humanistic approach to providing service. Similarly, the overall idea of referral is basic to the human services; it is one reflection of the linkages that connect human service agencies.

ADVOCACY IN RECREATION AND PARKS

The referral process assumes that helping services are available, someplace. It assumes that the barriers to taking advantage of those services are lack of information or inability to make use of them. However, certain conditions in communities often are themselves barriers to people's abilities to enjoy free time. For example, the absence of a public transit system can be a serious detriment to older adults who no longer drive their own automobiles, and who have no one upon whom they can depend for transportation. In such a situation, even if extensive recreational programs for seniors are provided, some individuals will not be able to use them. Architectural barriers often deny access to disabled persons. As an illustration, a multistoried recreation center with no elevator denies opportunities for use to those confined to wheelchairs. Or the problem may be agency regulations or attitudes.

Often the institutions with which local residents must deal are not even neu-tral, much less positively motivated, toward handling the issues brought to them by community groups. In fact, they are frequently overtly negative and hostile, often concealing or distorting information about rules, procedures, and office hours.[12]

Lawrence discussed the situation where the problems are community conditions rather than individual inadequacies. He suggested that a human service model that assumes that the problem originates in the shortcomings of the individual be labelled a *medical model*.[13] In this model, commonly found in health care programs, the individual's problem is identified (diag-nosed) and the solution is implemented (treatment). In these situations, direct services and referrals are most appropriate. The public-transit and architectural-barrier examples exemplify a second model, described by Lawrence.

In contrast to the defect-within-the-individual model, the *community organiza-tional model* places the defect within society—its institutions, practices, and organizational patterns. According to this model, the quality of human life services to people can be optimized most effectively by intervening at the level of social institutions and organizations.[14]

In this model, human service workers are interested in social change. One of the primary ways of affecting such a change is the use of advocacy methods.

Frequently, recreation and park personnel find themselves in situa-tions where they can work toward changing community barriers.

The speaker standing at the rostrum before the board of supervisors was losing his temper. He had been describing the need for a drug counseling center funded by the county. Several members of the board were skeptical, perhaps because they weren't convinced of the need. The recreation super-visor sat in the audience, waiting her turn to speak. Several parents of teen-agers, had asked her to speak on behalf of the drug counseling proposal. And she was convinced of the need. Staff reports consistently mentioned the drug problems at the recreation centers. She flipped quickly through the notes in her lap, and glanced over her shoulder at the group of parents who had accompanied her. As she turned her attention back to the front of the room, she heard her name called, and she rose to go to the rostrum.

Some recreation and park professionals would feel that unless the supervisor in the above situation were appearing before the board of su-pervisors as a private citizen, she might be exceeding her responsibilities as a staff member. If she later joined a protest demonstration on the lawn outside the supervisors' chambers, they would be even more convinced of the inappropriateness of her behavior. However, other members of the field would see her actions as appropriate in either case. They would base their beliefs on the position that, if the field of recreation and parks is to serve people effectively, those who work in it must do what they can to help correct conditions that keep people from living full and enriched lives. They would argue that the field needs to adopt a holistic philosophy.

Such an approach suggests that recreation and park personnel must take advocacy roles at appropriate times.

WHAT IS ADVOCACY?

Basically, advocacy is the effort of a staff member to get changes made that will benefit others that are not possible for the staff member to change directly. That is, the staff member attempts to cause other people to make changes, in their areas of responsibility, that will benefit the people for whom the staff member is concerned. In the earlier illustration, the recreation supervisor appearing before the board of supervisors did not have the resources or authority to create a drug counseling center independently and directly. Instead, she was attempting to influence the political entity that could create one. She wanted the decision-makers to take action that would benefit others. In this case, she was concerned with a group of teens in the community who had drug problems.

Concern for certain segments of society is one dimension of advocacy. Another dimension is concern for a particular individual. This dimension would be illustrated if the supervisor were to phone the director of a drug counseling center in an adjacent community to obtain permission for one specific teen-ager to be admitted to the center's group counseling program.

McCormick's definition of advocacy identified these two dimensions.

> The concept of advocacy has long been associated, in its general meaning, with the defense or promotion of a cause, and more specifically, with pleading the cause of another. In the first instance, the activities are political-social in character; in the second, they can be described more accurately as personal-social. In the political context, the objective is to bring active support to ideas and programs that will benefit society as a whole, as well as particular segments of it. . . . In the second context, the focus is on the individual in his relations with other individuals and institutions: employer or landlord, court of law or welfare agency.[15]

A statement by the National Association of Social Workers also identified these dimensions.[16] The statement noted that the concept of advocacy on behalf of a specific person is similar to the idea of a lawyer working for a particular client's interests. If the advocacy attempt is not focused on a specific individual, it tends to be focused on broader causes or proposals for change.

> This definition [focusing on causes or proposals] incorporates the political meaning ascribed to the word in which a class of people are represented; implicitly the issues are universalistic rather than particularistic.[17]

The concept of advocacy presented by Sosin and Caulum recognizes the basic components that are involved.

Central to the advocacy approach is its social interaction trait with three identifiable components: a person, group or interest to advocate for, an individual or group who performs the advocacy activity and a target who controls the decision or set of actions the advocate wants to influence. . . .

Advocacy, then, is an attempt, having a greater than zero probability of success, by one individual to influence a second individual or group to make a decision that would not have been made otherwise, when this decision concerns the welfare or interests of a third party.[18]

Embodied in this concept is the idea of a decision-making structure.

Advocacy demands a *target* of change, and a *decision-making structure* within which the attempt at influence occurs. . . .[19]

In the earlier illustration, the recreation supervisor, acting as an advocate for a group of persons (teen-age drug users), was attempting to influence the board of supervisors. The board was the target. The decision-making structure involved the interactions between the board members, and between the board and the various spokespersons for the drug counseling center.

IS ADVOCACY APPROPRIATE?

As suggested earlier, some recreation and park professionals would feel that it would not be appropriate for the supervisor to appear before the board unless she did so as a private citizen. However, most would agree that she would have a legitimate concern for drug problems among adolescents in the community in which she works. This is based on the awareness that drug problems have impacts on individuals' uses of free time, as well as on the general well-being of a community.

The bases for recreation and park personnel to be involved in advocacy are very similar to the reasons why they are involved in referral. If our objective is to enable people to make the best use of free time in enriching ways, then we need to be concerned about eliminating or minimizing the barriers that prevent it. In some cases, the barrier is the individual's inability to use existing resources. In these cases, referral is appropriate. In other situations, resources are not available or not accessible to those who need them. The lack of a drug counseling center is an example.

As suggested earlier, lack of public transportation for older adults often denies them leisure opportunities. Lack of elevators and ramps at public buildings makes access very difficult, if not impossible, for people who use wheelchairs. These facilities and resources are not accessible to such individuals. To that extent, they are not available. In these conditions, the challenge is not to provide information about resources to the would-be user or to help that person take advantage of such resources. Instead, it is to change existing conditions in ways that benefit citizens with whom we are concerned. In referral, the primary focus of our efforts is the individual with the problem. In advocacy, the focus is more upon the condition or barrier causing the problem. More specifically, the focus is on the decision-makers who can eliminate or minimize problems. The two situations are not independent; in both, the end objective is a betterment of the welfare of the individual.

A human service philosophy suggests that it is appropriate for recreation and park personnel to engage in advocacy on behalf of the citizens they intend to serve. One of the three 1974 National Position Papers of the National Recreation and Park Association was concerned with human resources. This paper confirmed the need for advocacy in our field.

> Concerned laymen and recreation and park professionals, both individually and collectively, must become advocates for meaningful recreation and park programs for all sections of society. Thus advocacy requires involvement and a responsiveness to human needs. It should be remembered that recreation experiences are only one part of man's life; man's life in its entirety must be considered when one becomes his advocate.[20]

However, advocacy has not been highly evident in our field—for the same reasons that the field of social work has not used advocacy processes more widely.[21] These reasons include the idea that an adversary or combative stance, which frequently is found in the advocacy process, is not comfortable for human service workers. Professional preparation usually does not prepare personnel for such a role. Also, such workers may find that their roles as employees may restrict their functioning as advocates. The staff member's loyalties to the individual, to the group, and to the employing agency might be in conflict. The agency may resent what it sees as inappropriate behavior by staff members. In addition, there may be ambivalence on the part of those whose cause is being advocated. All of these possibilities might be intensified because of emotional states associated with controversy.

In general, advocacy is appropriate for recreation and park workers. There are risks involved, and the worker who chooses to use an advocacy process should be aware of these risks and attempt to minimize them as much as possible. The degree of risk is related directly to the advocacy methods that are selected.

ADVOCACY METHODS

There are various types of advocacy. A recreation supervisor appears before the board of supervisors to argue for a drug counseling center. A center director writes a letter to the principal of the high school, urging that sex education be involved in the curriculum. A recreation therapist joins other therapists and disabled persons to protest the lack of wheelchair access at local theaters. A city park superintendent introduces a resolution at the annual meeting of the professional organization calling upon the state legislature to set aside additional lands at state reservoirs for campgrounds and picnic sites. The youth minister at a local church knocks on doors in a neighborhood to get signatures on petitions asking that the city council fund a youth employment program.

Types of Advocacy.   In one sense, each of the above individuals represents a special interest. When we work for a cause, the cause becomes a special interest. When we join others working for the same cause, we become a special interest group. The use of this term sometimes suggests that people who comprise special interest groups stand to gain personally from the causes they support. However, the activities of those involved in the earlier illustrations are intended primarily to benefit others.

Shivers identified several different methods used by special interest groups.[22] While he presented these from the perspective of the recreation and park administrator toward whom they might be directed, the list describes methods that might be used also by recreation and park personnel on behalf of the citizens they serve. One method is to negotiate with decision-makers, to attempt to persuade them to take the action desired. In some cases, pressure might be brought to bear, perhaps in the form of such actions as a threat to withhold votes or to create unfavorable publicity. A special interest group might attempt to win the support of a decision-maker by inviting the individual to accept some favorable recognition by the group, or to carry out a responsibility on behalf of the group (such as speaking at an annual conference). The advocating group might undertake a letter-writing campaign, hold press conferences, issue news releases, or attend hearings called by the agency that has the power to make the desired changes.

Biklen also suggested a variety of methods for bringing about desired change.[23] Like Shivers, he included such actions as negotiating with decision-makers, holding press conferences and other communication efforts, and engaging in letter-writing campaigns. He also included activities such as engaging in demonstrations or symbolic acts of various kinds (marches, sit-ins, mock awards, and other devices for attracting attention to causes), presenting demands to decision-makers (lists of grievances and statements of people's rights), and boycotts based on refusals to engage in behaviors that are normally expected and that benefit the decision-maker involved in the issue.

Biklen described several methods of presenting information to community groups to gain support: pamphlets, workshops, slide shows, speakers' bureaus, and other methods. He discussed lobbying techniques, various legal methods, and the use of model programs that are intended to stimulate desired changes. For all of these advocacy methods, Biklen presented detailed suggestions, considerations, and cautions.

Benest, Foley and Welton indicated that we can serve advocacy purposes by organizing people.

> To organize people means more than involving them in an agency's established activities. We propose that people organizing is a process by which an agency interacts with community groups in order to help them determine needs and marshall resources. For example, it is reaching out to elderly

people in need, organizing them so they can identify needs, and developing political clout to advocate for public or private resources or create self-help solutions.[24]

Godbey discussed the use of confrontation, protest and disruption as methods of influencing decisions.[25] He noted that these tactics usually serve one or more of three purposes: to express frustration, to bring issues into public view, and to obtain desired actions. His presentation and illustrations were concerned with how citizen groups might use these methods to attempt to change the policies or services of recreation and park agencies. However, they could also be used by agency personnel to advocate the causes of those they serve.

Demone and Harshbarger suggested that the different forms of advocacy fall along a continuum from less intense to more intense.

> A human services organization, or certain of its staff members, might assume the role of advocacy planner . . . advocacy litigant . . . advocacy militant . . . or the role of violent advocate. . . . Or, contrariwise, the organization may use moral suasion. Admittedly, these are oversimplified roles or types, but their purpose is to define possible points on a continuum of low to high degrees of intensity or extremism in acting out an advocacy position.[26]

The authors also suggested some caution in using certain advocacy methods. They noted that as the advocate's intensity increases, his ability to control outcomes lessens and the degree of risk increases.[27] In discussing this condition, they questioned whether a human service organization should be involved in advocacy at any level. They stated their belief that advocacy is a legitimate activity for human service agencies, but that risks are involved.

> Our feeling is that the role is both a legitimate and viable one, but one that brings with it certain risks and by definition excludes other means of social change. Consequently, an organization should be fully aware of what it is doing and not assume an advocacy posture inadvertently or because of political pressures or support that might vanish under stress of conflict. After all, organizations are made up of people. They will not work harmoniously with organizations that are attacking them.[28]

Deciding Which Type Is Most Appropriate.   If a recreation and park worker or agency determines that advocacy is needed and that it will be attempted, a decision must be made about which method to use. Biklen provided a set of general criteria for estimating which method will be successful.

> Actions will be successful or meaningful if they
> - reflect short-term and long-term goals
> - fit the circumstances of the hour
> - serve to further your goals
> - utilize the skills of your constituency

- are well planned
- meet people's expectations
- educate others
- are consistent with your values
- lead to other actions[29]

Sosin and Caulum's concept of advocacy was based on the idea that the advocacy method to use depends on the situation. Their typology of advocacy included the "target" of the advocacy attempt and the "decision-making structure." These were mentioned earlier in the chapter. The authors noted that the target (the decision-maker) may have varying views toward advocacy, the individual or organization attempting the advocacy effort, and the cause itself. The target might feel in agreement with the cause of the advocate or might feel neutral or hostile. If hostile, the target may sense an adversarial relationship with the advocate.

The perceived role of advocacy, as related to the decision-making process, also may vary. In some cases advocacy may be seen as a legitimate activity by all concerned. In other cases, it may be viewed as unacceptable, or there may be neutral feelings toward its use.[30] Sosin and Caulum contended that these factors should be considered when deciding upon an advocacy method or approach. If the target agrees with the cause, the most effective advocacy method will be providing information. If hostility exists, information alone probably will not produce the desired changes. If advocacy is seen as a legitimate part of the decision-making structure, the advocating person or agency can be very direct. If advocacy is not seen by the target as legitimate, the advocate must take more care and must consider the possible consequences.

The authors identified three levels at which changes might be sought—the individual level, the administrative level, and the policy-making level.[31] The *individual* level is focused on the needs and welfare of a specific person. If a recreation supervisor were to phone the director of a drug referral center to obtain admission for a specific adolescent who had been earlier denied, he or she would be seeking a change at the individual level. If the center had a rule of admitting only those teen-agers who were referred by a physician, and if this rule restricted access to the center for certain adolescents, the supervisor might seek changes at the *administrative* level. If the center did not serve adolescents at all, but only adults, the supervisor might aim his or her advocacy efforts at the *policy-making* level, perhaps the board of supervisors in the county that supports the center.

Sosin and Caulum suggested that if the target is in agreement with the cause, a focus on the individual level is most appropriate. Since agreement exists, the assumption is that overall policies and services also exist that can be used—if the needs of individual clients are made known. If the target is in an adversary position, the advocacy attempt will be more effective if focused on the policy-making level. Here, methods that aim at basic changes in agency services or policies will be required. If the target is neutral, it may be that needed changes can be effected by dealing with staff at the administrative level.[32]

Grosser provided several critical questions designed to help in making decisions related to advocacy and in selecting specific methods. They are:

1. What is the source of the problem?
2. What is the appropriate target system?
3. What is the objective?
4. What is the sanction for the proposed intervention?
5. What resources are available for the intervention?
6. How receptive is the target system?
7. With whom should the intervention be carried out?
8. At what level should the intervention take place?
9. What methods of intervention should be employed?
10. What is the outcome?[33]

Grosser also identified five sets of variables related to case advocacy; these include twelve major components in the advocacy process.[34] The first set of variables relates to the person or organization attempting the advocacy and the individuals who will be benefited. The second set relates to the reasons why advocacy is needed—the problem, the target of the advocacy attempt, and the objective to be achieved. The third set includes the factors that influence the method to be selected; included are such considerations as the resources available to the advocate and the views and feelings held by the target. The fourth set involves the advocacy method selected and level at which it is aimed. The final set includes different possible outcomes. Grosser suggested that there is a relationship between these various elements, that one influences or is influenced by another.

In terms of specific methods of intervention which might be selected, Grosser suggested the following: *interceding*, by making requests or pleading for a cause; using *persuasion; negotiating*, including the use of bargaining; *bringing pressure* to bear; using *coercive* techniques such as disruption and legal action; and *indirect methods* such as community organization and third-party interventions.[35] These methods appear to exist along a continuum from lesser to higher intensities, similar to what was suggested by Demone and Harshbarger.

Advocacy and Change.   The basic objective in many of the advocacy methods described is to cause changes to occur—changes that benefit an individual or groups of individuals. The types of changes include modifications in the services offered by agencies and the policies and regulations by which the agencies operate. These changes usually require changes in the behaviors of personnel who are employed in the agencies.

As pointed out in Chapter 5, people resist change. The amount of resistance is influenced by the intensity with which the old position or behavior is held and the degree to which the new position or behavior departs from the old. Organizations also resist change.

This resistance to change is found in the individual, the family, the group, the community, agencies, and institutions.[36]

Shulman believed that this resistance necessitated—and justified—the use of advocacy methods. He noted that attempts to work with agencies on behalf of those who are in need of service may not be productive.

In such situations the use of confrontation and social pressure is required. Some additional force is needed to overcome the system's resistance to change and to bring to its attention the need to respond in new ways to the client's needs.[37]

Gardner presented several strategies that have helped Common Cause bring about desired changes.[38] Common Cause, founded by Gardner, is a very large citizen organization devoted to influencing political decisions. He believes that the organization has been effective, in part, because it engages in sustained action. When a goal has been defined in terms of needed changes, the organization is willing to keep at the task on a sustained basis. Also, the action is focused. That is, the organization does not dissipate its energy and resources by undertaking too many tasks at one time. The strategy, in Gardner's words, is to "select a limited number of clearly defined targets and hit them hard."[39] A willingness to become involved with details and the "nuts and bolts" of action is important.

Significant social change is accomplished by men and women with a vision in their heads and a monkey wrench in their hands.[40]

Gardner observed that some people wish to avoid the detailed work required for change. He contended that the "high-minded" citizen often fails because of self-indulgence.

He feels so noble just "fighting the good fight" that he finds rewards even in defeat. And often he believes—if only unconsciously—that high-mindedness is a substitute for professional skill in doing battle. No wonder he loses so often.[41]

Communication is a powerful tool in bringing about change. Gardner noted the value of using mass media, letters to newspapers, conversations with friends, and other personal contacts to give exposure to needed changes.

Common Cause seeks to form alliances with other appropriate groups. Gardner indicated that this is not easily accomplished. "Organizational vanity creeps into the noblest organizations."[42] Different groups, even while interested in the same goals, have different ideas about what should be done. One specific type of alliance that may be possible, and very useful, involves staff within the institution that is the target of the change effort.

There are many public officials, elected and appointive, who want very much to improve the institutions in which they find themselves. . . .

A citizen's movement makes a grave mistake if it imagines that it is so right—and so righteous—that a working public servant couldn't possibly contribute to its store of wisdom.[43]

Gardner's comments about the ways a large citizen's organization helps to cause change seem applicable to smaller organizations and even to individual advocacy efforts.

Schaller, in discussing various dimensions of social changes and strategies for bringing them about, identified three basic approaches to "getting things done."[44] One traditional approach involves the uses of persuasion, education, or legal action. He suggested that these methods have become somewhat unpopular because they are less direct than other strategies, and they do not lead to immediate results. A second approach is to use one of the "4Cs"—coercion, co-optation, conflict, or cooperation. In co-optation, the attempt is made to "buy off" those who are resisting change. A third approach is based on the assumption that there are power structures in a community, and that changes can be brought about by organizing communities to deal with those power structures (to confront them, expand them, collaborate with them or make them more responsive or effective). This approach was mentioned earlier. In all of the approaches, there are price tags—advantages and disadvantages that must be considered in selecting one's strategy.

Conflicting Interests. In estimating the costs of any advocacy method, one consideration is the relationship of the person attempting the advocacy to the group toward which it is directed. In some cases, an advocate's interests and loyalties may conflict. If the recreation supervisor who was petitioning the county board of supervisors to start a drug counseling center were a county employee, she might have a conflict of interest. Her loyalties might be divided between the adolescents with whom she works and the county, which is the source of her employment. Moreover, the board of supervisors might feel that her appearance is totally inappropriate. In these cases, recreation and park personnel often are faced with difficult decisions whether or not they should become involved directly with advocacy efforts, especially if confrontive or pressure methods are used.

An Overview of Advocacy Methods. It is possible to draw some generalizations from a review of the various advocacy methods which have been discussed. It is important first to make a deliberate decision whether advocacy is appropriate and, if so, whether to attempt it. To make this decision most effectively, the recreation and park worker must know something about the needs and capabilities of the person or group for whom the advocacy is being considered. Information about the target, or the organization which can alleviate the problem, is also necessary. And the worker needs to assess his or her personal resources and capabilities. Having decided to use advocacy, one must then select an appropriate method. The possible approaches range, in intensity and risk, from informative and persuasive methods to confrontation and the use of power. The more intense the methods, the greater the risk of loss of control of the situation and possible rebuttal tactics by the target. The probable consequences and probable effectiveness of any particular method should be estimated as carefully as possible before any action is taken.

ADVOCACY AND THE LEGISLATIVE PROCESS

One special type of advocacy is writing letters to elected officials or appearing at public hearings held by governmental bodies in an attempt to influence legislative processes. Typically, this effort relates to case advocacy, where you wish to encourage changes in laws or the passing of new legislation that will benefit a group of people. Laws create or authorize leisure services; they enable them to be funded or financed; and they influence the ways in which they are provided. While this is especially true for public agencies, it also applies to the private sector and to commercial enterprises. All levels of government are involved—federal, state, and local. In some cases, legislation is directly related to recreation and parks; for example, state health and safety codes often specify standards for operating public swimming pools. These standards benefit the users of public pools. In other cases, laws are created that have implications for leisure services but are not specifically written with that intent. An illustration would be federal legislation aimed at assuring the rights of disabled persons to equal access to services and employment opportunities.

Usually letters are in support of or in opposition to laws that have been proposed and are in the federal or state legislative processes. An example might be a proposed state law that would require county governments to offer drug counseling services. Another example would be federal legislation that would provide grants to local governments for developing public transportation systems for older adults.

The Legislative Process. How would these laws come into being? That question can be answered by a brief review of the legislative process. Remember that in the U.S. Congress and almost all of the state legislatures there are two legislative bodies—the Senate and the House of Representatives at the federal level and comparable upper and lower houses in state governments. These bodies are made up of elected persons who represent the wishes of their constituents. Proposed laws (called *bills*) can be introduced by legislators in one body or in both bodies simultaneously. If a proposal is introduced and passed in one, it must eventually be passed by the other for it to become law.

Once the bill is introduced, it follows this general pattern: It is first given an identifying number. The first page of the bill indicates who introduced the proposed law, when it was introduced, and other pertinent information, including a summary of the proposal. The bill is read before the entire body once and is then assigned to a committee. There are standing committees in both Congress and the state legislatures. These committees, composed of legislators, each have areas of special interest and expertise. They study the proposed laws, gather background information, and hold hearings and listen to testimony on the advantages or disadvantages of each issue that is referred to them. Eventually, they send each bill back to the full body with a recommendation to pass it, or to pass it with amendments; or they refer the bill to another committee. They might hold the bill in committee; this has the effect of killing the bill. When a bill is referred back to the full body with a recommendation for passage, it is read again, debated, and then voted upon. If the bill passes, it is sent to the other legislative body where it follows a similar procedure. When both bodies pass a bill, it is sent to the president (or governor) for signature.

Letter Writing.   Writing a letter to your legislator (from your district or state) stating your feelings about an issue can be an effective advocacy technique. The Sierra Club, a national organization that actively advocates for various environmental issues, emphasized the importance of letter writing in getting bills passed or defeated.

> Lobbying refers to attempting to influence public policy—usually governmental activity. . . . The most basic lobbying technique . . . is letter writing.[45]

The Sierra Club noted that the best times to express your views are when a bill in which you are interested is being considered by a committee or when it is up for a vote by the entire body.

> When a bill reaches a critical stage in the legislative process, such as a committee hearing or a floor vote in the House or Senate, Sierra Club members are alerted and urged to contact their representatives—by writing, telephoning, visiting, or wiring. . . .[46]

You can obtain information about the bills being considered at the federal and state levels by reading newspapers or listening to news reports. Professional organizations in the field of recreation and parks usually keep in close touch with legislative actions and inform their members of pertinent legislation that is being proposed. Copies of bills can be obtained by contacting a legislator who represents you. Most have local offices, with staff members who can provide assistance.

A statement by the Honorable Morris K. Udall, chairman of the U.S. House of Representatives Interior Committee in 1977, suggested the importance placed on letters by legislators.

> I read every letter written to me by a constituent. A staff member may process it initially, but it will be answered, and I will insist on reading it and personally signing it. On several occasions, a single, thoughtful, factually persuasive letter did change my mind or cause me to initiate a review of a previous judgement. Nearly every day my faith is renewed by one or more informative and helpful letters giving me a better understanding of the thinking of my constituents.[47]

A study by Dennis suggested that letters from citizens are given high priority by governmental agencies and personnel.[48] Dennis studied the relative importance placed on various means for the expression of public attitudes and reactions by the National Park Service. He compared such sources as public hearings, media releases, demonstrations, and letters. He also considered whether the expressions of attitudes and reactions were from individual citizens or from organized groups. Results of the study indicated that the greatest importance, in terms of influences upon agency decision-making, was placed upon letters from individuals.

Congressman Udall offered several suggestions for sending letters to legislators. They should be addressed properly; the bill should be identified; the letter should be sent while the bill is being considered and in time for your legislator to take action on it; and you should be fairly brief, since legislators usually receive large amounts of mail. Letters that present your views, in your own words, are better than form letters or standard wording suggested by an organization. The reasons for your feelings should be given. Be constructive in your letter; offer positive suggestions. Rather than focusing only on what is wrong with proposed legislation, suggest a better approach. Don't abuse or threaten your legislator. Such tactics are not productive. Finally, if you agree with actions your representative has taken, communicate those feelings. Saying "well done," when it is deserved, is appreciated.[49]

Public Hearings.   Letter writing is most related to influencing state and federal legislation. On occasion, recreation and park personnel may have opportunities to appear before legislative committees to offer expert testimony on issues related to leisure services. However, this form of advocacy is more prevalent at the local level.

The legislative process at the local level basically involves the elected officials (city or town council, board of directors, or board of supervisors) who are considering the proposed law and who, after hearing public reactions, will vote to enact it or defeat it. Local laws usually are called *ordinances*. Typically, before an ordinance is passed the governing body must hold a public hearing on the issue. At this hearing, citizens have opportunities to express their feelings. The procedures to be followed in the hearing normally are explained at the beginning of the session.

Effective presentations at a public hearing should be relatively brief, and should focus directly on the issue being considered. If you are expressing your views, it is wise to be well prepared. Present the pertinent facts, as they relate to the proposed ordinance. It is appropriate to express the feelings you have about the issue, if you clearly identify them as your feelings. Do not try to represent a broader group of people than you actually do. Also, as with letter writing, it is not productive to threaten or abuse the elected officials who are holding the meeting.

Petitions.   At all levels of government it is possible to encourage the introduction of needed legislation. Such a need might be called to the attention of elected representatives through letters or direct contacts. This effort is most effective if a large number of people call attention to the need or encourage a legislator to introduce a proposed law. Frequently, petitions will be circulated for individuals to sign. These petitions then become evidence of the need for legislation. In some situations, petitions may call for a *proposition* to be placed on the general ballot. In these cases, all voters may express their feelings, and the proposition becomes law if it receives a sufficient number of votes.

Working with Legislators.   As suggested, it might be possible to obtain a commitment from a legislator to introduce legislation that you feel is needed. If you seek to bring about changes in this manner, it is important to know exactly what you want.[50] Have the necessary background information before you contact the legislator, and do not misrepresent facts. You will not be expected to write up your proposal in legal terms, but you should clearly present what you want and why your proposal is needed—in writing. Legislators represent you, and all of the rest of us who make up their constituencies. Usually there are heavy demands on their time. Your proposal will stand the best chance of being considered if it is concise and clearly understandable, and if it is clear that you have done the necessary background work. You may have the opportunity to appear before the legislative committee that will consider your proposal. The suggestions mentioned earlier about effective presentations in public hearings apply also to committee hearings. Be brief, to the point, and courteous. It will be helpful to know who the committee members are, and to have some idea about the probable feelings different legislators have toward your proposal.

REFERRAL AND ADVOCACY: TWO-WAY STREETS

Recreation and park staff use referral and advocacy processes as ways of working indirectly with people or, more accurately, as ways of working with other agency staff or legislative personnel on behalf of people. The logic for using referral processes is that people often have leisure needs, or other needs that interfere with their abilities to enjoy free time, which cannot be served by a specific recreation and park agency. In such cases, we refer people to those agencies that have the appropriate resources. The logic for using advocacy methods is that conditions often exist in communities that restrict people's participation in recreation; in these cases, we attempt to get changes made that eliminate or minimize the restrictions. In both situations—referral and advocacy—our efforts are directed toward other agencies and personnel.

At the same time, our own agency might be the target of referrals or advocacy efforts initiated by personnel in other human services or by citizens. For example, a county mental health department, which works with individuals who have been discharged recently from a state hospital, might refer someone to our agency for leisure counseling. Or a group of older adults might stage a sit-in at a local recreation center, protesting the lack of programming for senior citizens and advocating more equal consideration for the recreational needs of the elderly. Situations such as these broaden our opportunities for providing service to people.

SUMMARY

If people's leisure needs are to be served most fully, recreation and park personnel will use referral and advocacy processes.

In referral situations, we need to know the nature of people's needs, the limits of our own abilities and responsibilities, and the kinds of resources that are available and to which referrals might be made. Referrals are appropriate when a person's needs interfere with his or her use of free time, but fall beyond our own expertise or responsibility. We will be more effective in making referrals if we not only know something about other community agencies but also have developed some initial contacts with personnel in these agencies. The referral process involves three basic steps after the need has been determined—selection of the referral agency, provision of appropriate help in using the referral agency for the person being referred, and follow-up on the referral. Consistent with a general philosophy of helping people grow and become more self-determining, it is useful for individuals who are being referred to take as much responsibility in the process as possible.

In advocacy, we attempt to bring about changes in conditions that limit people's use of free time. We may work on behalf of one individual or a class of individuals. Various advocacy methods can be selected. These methods are directed toward the persons, organizations or entities that have the power to make the desired changes; they are the "targets" of our efforts. The methods range in intensity from the use of persuasion and the provision of information to confrontive strategies such as protests and demonstrations. Sometimes, causes are advocated through attempts to influence legislative processes.

The use of advocacy is not without risk. We may encounter ambivalence on the part of those whose cause we are advocating. Our loyalties to the cause we are advocating and to the agency that employs us may be in conflict. The agency may resent what it sees as inappropriate behavior on our part. The target (bureaucracy, agency, group, or individual) toward which the advocacy is directed may retaliate against the intended beneficiary.

In spite of the possible risks, most recreation and park personnel do use some forms of advocacy at various times. Typically, these fall short of strategies based on direct conflict. However, the staff member who is aware of different possible strategies and when they might be used is in a better position to act responsibly and effectively when opportunities for advocacy arise. This advantage is strengthened if the individual has thought through some of the philosophical justifications for advocacy roles and defined his or her position.

REVIEW QUESTIONS

8-1   What is the referral process? Under what conditions should this process be used?

8-2   To what kinds of agencies do recreation and park personnel make referrals? How can these potential referral sources be located? What information is useful to have about them?

8-3   How can the referral process be made most effective?

8-4   What is advocacy? When should this process be used?

8-5   Several different advocacy methods were discussed in this chapter. What are these methods?

8-6   How could you support the idea that leisure service personnel should use advocacy methods? What reasons could you give?

TO DO

8-A   Think about someone you know who has a problem of some kind (such as alcoholism, depression, unemployment, or some other problem mentioned in this chapter). If you do not know such a person, select a problem that interests you. Then find out as much as you can about how a person with this problem could be helped in your community. What agencies exist to provide assistance? What other possible sources of help might be used? Make a small file of 3×5 cards, for each agency or source of help, showing the information suggested in this chapter. Visit one of these agencies to find out more about it.

8-B   Make a list showing the names and addresses of your legislative representatives (at both state and federal levels). Also list local elected officials.

8-C   Pick some issue in which you are interested that is being considered at some level of government. If possible, select one related to recreation and parks. It could be something about environmental quality, services to special populations, or almost anything where there are different positions (controversy) or an unsolved problem or area of need. Write a letter to the appropriate elected official (or officials) expressing your position. Refer to the suggestions on letter writing in this chapter.

END NOTES

1. Abraham H. Maslow, "A Theory of Human Motivation," *Psychological Review* 50, no. 4 (July 1943): 370–96.

2. Beulah R. Compton and Burt Galaway, *Social Work Processes* (Homewood, Ill.: Richard D. Irwin, Inc., The Dorsey Press, 1975), pp. 422–23.

3. Compton and Galaway, *Social Work Processes*, p. 423.

4. William B. Oglesby, Jr., *Referral in Pastoral Counseling*, rev. (Nashville, Tenn.: Abingdon, 1978), pp. 89–102.

5. Oglesby, *Referral In Pastoral Counseling*, p. 87.

6. Ibid., pp. 29–34.

7. Ibid., pp. 52–57.

8. Naomi I. Brill, *Working with People*, 2nd ed., © 1978 by J. B. Lippincott. Reprinted by permission of Harper & Row, Inc.

9. Brill, *Working with People: The Helping Process*, p. 159.

10. Ibid., pp. 159–60.

11. Lawrence M. Brammer, *The Helping Relationship: Process and Skills* (Englewood Cliffs, N.J.: Prentice-Hall, Inc., 1973), p. 132.

12. Charles F. Grosser, "Community Development Programs Serving the Urban Poor," in Compton and Galaway, *Social Work Processes*, p. 355.

13. Mark A. Lawrence, "Developing Program Models for the Human Services," in Herbert C. Schulberg and Frank Baker, eds., *Developments in the Human Services, Volume II,* 2nd ed. (New York: Human Services Press, 1977) p. 67.

14. Lawrence, "Developing Program Models for the Human Services," p. 68.

15. Mary J. McCormick, "Social Advocacy: A New Dimension in Social Work," *Social Casework* 51, no. 1 (January 1970): 4.

16. The Ad Hoc Committee on Advocacy, National Association of Social Workers, "The Social Worker as Advocate: Champion of Social Victims," in Compton and Galaway, *Social Work Processes,* pp. 371–72.

17. The Ad Hoc Committee on Advocacy, "The Social Worker as Advocate," p. 372.

18. Michael Sosin and Sharon Caulum, "Social Work Advocacy: A Conceptualization for Social Work Practice" (Paper presented at the Annual Program Meeting of the Council on Social Work Education, Los Angeles, California, March 1980), p. 3.

19. Sosin and Caulum, "Social Work Advocacy," p. 4.

20. H. Douglas Sessoms, "The Role of Recreation in Developing and Nurturing Human Resources," *Parks & Recreation* 9, no. 2 (February 1974): 31–32.

21. Charles F. Grosser, *New Directions in Community Organization: From Enabling to Advocacy* (New York: Praeger Publishers, Inc., 1973), pp. 256, 265–66; and The Ad Hoc Committee for Advocacy, "The Social Worker as Advocate," pp. 372–73.

22. Jay S. Shivers, *Essentials of Recreation Services* (Philadelphia: Lea & Febiger, 1978), pp. 154–60.

23. Douglas Biklen, *Let Our Children Go: An Organizing Manual for Advocates and Parents* (Syracuse, N.Y.: Human Policy Press, 1974), pp. 91–126.

24. Frank Benest, Jack Foley and George Welton, "Interactive: the Leadership Rx for the Future," *Parks & Recreation* 16, no. 7 (July 1981): 38.

25. Geoffrey Godbey, *Recreation, Park and Leisure Services: Foundations, Organization, Administration* (Philadelphia: W. B. Saunders Company, 1978), p. 320.

26. Harold W. Demone, Jr. and Dwight Harshbarger, "The Planning and Administration of Human Services," in Herbert C. Schulberg, Frank Baker, and Sheldon R. Roen, eds., *Developments in Human Services,* Volume I (New York: Behavioral Publications, 1973), pp. 221–22.

27. Demone and Harshbarger, "The Planning and Administration of Human Services," *Human Services,* p. 222.

28. Ibid., p. 222.

29. Biklen, *Let Our Children Go,* p. 91.

30. Sosin and Caulum, "Social Work Advocacy," pp. 5–6.

31. Ibid., p. 9.

32. Ibid., p. 10.

33. Grosser, *New Directions in Community Organization,* pp. 272–73.

34. Ibid., pp. 267–71.

35. Ibid., p. 269.

36. Lawrence Schulman, *The Skills of Helping Individuals and Groups* (Itasca, Ill.: F. E. Peacock Publishers, Inc., 1979) p. 314.

37. Schulman, *The Skills of Helping Individuals and Groups,* p. 314.

38. John W. Gardner, *In Common Cause* (New York: W. W. Norton & Company, Inc., 1972).

39. Ibid., p. 86.

40. Ibid., p. 88.

41. Ibid., p. 88.

42. Ibid., p. 90.

43. Ibid., p. 90.

44. Lyle E. Schaller, *The Change Agent* (Nashville, Tenn.: Abingdon, 1972), pp. 120–31.

45. "Sierra Club Lobbying" (San Francisco, Calif.: The Sierra Club, 1972), p. 1.

46. "Sierra Club Lobbying," p. 1.

47. Morris K. Udall, "The Right to Write: Some Suggestions on Writing to Your Representatives in Congress," *Sierra Club Bulletin* 62, no. 2 (February 1977): 12.

48. Stephen R. Dennis, "Public Involvement in the Decision-Making Process of the National Park Service, Western Region," (Masters thesis, California State University, Chico, 1981), p. 50.

49. Udall, "The Right to Write," 12–13.

50. George Hutchison, "Successful Lobbying Techniques from a Legislator's Perspective," *California Parks & Recreation* 34, no. 4 (October/November, 1978): 33–36.

chapter 9

Using Resources: Financial and Safety Considerations

PREVIEW

In working with people, recreation and park personnel utilize various processes. Two of these, referral and advocacy, were discussed in Chapter 8. Earlier chapters were devoted to examinations of leading, working with groups, and teaching. Often those processes involve the use of various resources, such things as money, areas and facilities, and other staff members. Some special considerations in using these resources will be presented in this chapter and in Chapter 10. This chapter will focus specifically on financial and physical resources.

Adequate financing is a necessary element in the delivery of leisure services. It requires money to purchase the supplies used by recreation and park personnel. The maintenance of areas and facilities and the employment of part-time staff also involve expenditures. To make these possible, agencies develop budgets and expenditure procedures. Some agency staff members will have primary responsibilities for budget preparation and administration. Others will participate in the processes in varying ways, and all staff members will be influenced by the amounts of money that are available. You will be most effective if you are aware of the financial resources available in your agency and for your particular functions, and if you are familiar with the ways in which you can participate in budget preparation and expenditure. These matters will be discussed.

Most services provided by recreation and park personnel occur at a site, such as a swimming pool, a recreation center, a state park, or a resort. Creating these sites involves planning and financing. Again, some staff members will have direct responsibilities for planning areas and facilities. Those staff members who work directly with participants at these sites will be concerned primarily with using them to support the program activities. The processes of leading, working with groups, and teaching will be involved. One special responsibility in these uses is providing for participant safety. Two different aspects of safety will be considered—preventing accidents and minimizing participant exposure to crimes and other violent acts.

In any situation where there is a potential for injury or damages, staff members face the possibility of being sued—being held liable for their actions. This chapter also will present some information related to avoiding negligent acts.

The park supervisor took a last-minute look around the shop area and the turfed area immediately outside. Inside, the shop had been cleared to make room for ten chairs around a table and a blackboard. Partially disassembled on the table was a new power edger just purchased by the city. Four additional edgers were outside on the grass. At a side table, the light on the automatic coffeepot showed red; two dozen doughnuts sat alongside. He looked over his checklist: Park maintenance personnel had been notified of today's training session; the head office had been informed and pay for attending the session had been approved; the representative from the company that manufactures the edger was scheduled to arrive any minute; and the park superintendent had been called personally and invited to drop by. The supervisor glanced at the clock just as the first pickup truck drove into the yard.

The preschool director placed a large sheet of newsprint on the low table, in front of each of the eight small chairs. She put three large jars of finger paint in the center of the table. On pegs near the door hung several fathers' discarded shirts that served as smocks. On the rug behind the table, she arranged twelve large, lightweight, brightly colored boxes. Off the rug, in the corner, were a variety of pull-toys, smaller building blocks, and dolls. A child-sized bookshelf contained various picture books. She moved past the phonograph on her desk, and checked to see what record was on it. While there, she saw a pair of sharp-pointed scissors and put these away in the desk. Assured that enough supplies were out and ready for the youngsters, who would arrive in half an hour, she went to assign tasks to three volunteer teen-age aides waiting for her in an adjacent room.

Both the park supervisor and the preschool director are using available resources as they work with people. The park supervisor wishes to teach the proper use of power edgers to park maintenance workers. He has created a learning environment by manipulating the resources of power equipment, meeting space, blackboard, table, chairs, guest expert and staff pay (for attendance at the training session). The preschool director wants children to enjoy experiences of interacting with each other and of using different materials. She is working with the resources of paints, toys, music (phonograph and records), cardboard boxes and other similar elements, and volunteer assistants. Both of these people intend to encourage certain kinds of behaviors on the part of others (turf maintenance personnel and preschoolers), by arranging and using the resources as they are doing.

TYPES OF RESOURCES USED BY RECREATION AND PARK PERSONNEL

As indicated in Chapter 1, the types of resources used in the field of leisure services include the following: areas, facilities and supplies; other staff members; money; and laws or regulations. The park supervisor will be operating in a physical environment—the maintenance shop and the grass area outside. He will be using several power edgers. A blackboard has been set up. And, of course, there are tables and chairs and coffee and doughnuts. All of these might be considered in the category of areas, facilities, and supplies.

The preschool director also is using a variety of pieces of equipment and other materials; and she is working in a room (a facility) In both instances the expenditure of money is involved. It costs money to build facilities, to purchase equipment and supplies, and to maintain facilities once they are built. The park supervisor probably used a petty cash fund to buy the morning's doughnuts; the preschool director recently may have used a purchase order to replenish her supply of finger paints.

Certain laws will influence the actions of both of these people. At a very basic level, the services that both are providing would have to have been authorized by legislation of some kind—legislation that created the recreation and park department, defined its general structure and objectives, and enabled it to be funded on a continuing basis. Laws also regulate certain recreation and park functions. A colleague of both the park supervisor and the preschool director, the manager of the city swimming pool, must operate the pool in conformance with health and safety provisions. These usually are defined in state legal codes. The minimum number of lifeguards on duty in relation to the number of swimmers, and the qualifications of these guards, also may be prescribed by law. The lifeguards constitute another type of resource—the staff members who are involved in the delivery of leisure services. The lifeguards probably are paid. The aides who will help with the preschool program are volunteers.

USING RESOURCES IN WORKING WITH PEOPLE

The primary purpose of recreation and park personnel is to enable people to enjoy leisure experiences. They do this, in the overall sense, by working with people—the citizens they hope to serve and other staff members who are involved directly or indirectly with the delivery of services. In working with people they use such processes as leadership and teaching. Often these processes are supported by certain resources, as suggested in the examples at the beginning of the chapter. In some cases, the effective use of a process depends upon the use of resources; without the appropriate resources the process would be ineffective. The use of a blackboard will help the park supervisor explain the operation of a power edger, but the lesson could be conducted without it. It might even be possible to teach groundskeepers how to use an edger without actually having the edgers there for demonstration and practice. However, it would be more difficult and considerably less effective. For the swimming pool manager and her staff, teaching children to swim without an appropriate body of water would be almost impossible.

In one sense, manipulating resources or creating environments is, in itself, indirect leadership. Certain predictable behaviors typically result from the deployment of resources in planned and systematic manners. For example, opening up a gymnasium, turning on the lights, and supplying a basketball usually results in people playing basketball. This probability is increased if a leader is there to officiate, to keep score, or to engage in some other kinds of facilitating behavior. A well-supplied ceramic studio usually encourages ceramic activity, swimming pools prompt people to swim or to sun-bathe, and so on.

Identify Resources.   The effective use of resources involves the identification of those that currently exist and are available for use.[1] Both the park supervisor and preschool director should have developed, and kept updated, inventories of available resources, or they should be aware of these inventories if they are maintained by someone else. They should have obtained a copy of the agency budget, and should have read it and understood it, especially the sections related directly to their own operations. They should know how much money they have available and the procedures to be used in spending it. Relevant information about available resources should be communicated to their staff members. The teen-age assistants should know what supplies are available, where they are kept, and how to use them. The groundskeepers need similar information to work effectively. They need to know where fertilizers and pesticides are stored, what equipment can be used, and where it is located. It is desirable if staff members in both situations have enough information about the agency's budget to know how the funding of their particular responsibilities fit in. In the examples used here, it is probable that neither the teen assistants nor the groundskeepers will make direct expenditures from the budget. However, they will have a greater appreciation of the things their supervisor does to work within the budget if they have these awarenesses.

Recreation and park personnel also should explore possibilities for identifying, developing, and using resources not held or administered by the agency but potentially available for use. This means looking around in the community, being alert for areas and buildings that might be available. Assume that enough additional parents in the community indicated a desire for preschool experiences for their children, and that the agency decided to hold another session. Assume also that the current facility was completely scheduled, and that no space was available. The director might see if one of the rooms at the elementary school was available after regular hours. She might contact local churches for possible rooms where another session could be held. The director might appeal to those parents who have expressed a wish for the new session to donate supplies. She might contact the nearby community college to recruit additional volunteer aides.

Both the park supervisor and the director will want to help staff make the best use of available resources. Staff need to know about these; and in some cases, they need to be trained to use them effectively. The session on the proper use of power edgers was intended to do this.

Agency Policies.   Often, an agency will develop policies and regulations that are intended to facilitate or maximize the use of resources. The park department probably has a policy related to the use of department vehicles. Who is permitted to operate the vehicles, and under what conditions? Is it permissible for a groundskeeper to take one of the department's pickup trucks home after work, rather than returning it to the corporation yard? Can the supervisor loan one of the vehicles to the preschool director to pick up some supplies downtown? Some questions such as these must be decided on a case-by-case basis. However, it will be more efficient if policies or regulations can be established to provide guidelines for those questions that routinely arise. Policies and regulations will be determined at different levels in the agency. General policies, of course, are determined by the policy-making body for the agency—the city council in the park illustration. Others, more specific to department or division operations, may be made or recommended by supervisory personnel. As appropriate, staff should be involved in the development of these policies. This encourages the establishment of routine procedures that are as realistic as possible, and it leads to better staff support of them.

Evaluations.   Effective use of resources requires that evaluations be made. Are resources being used to their best advantage? Are staff assigned to responsibilities where they can be most effective? Are budgeted funds spent, in the appropriate categories, so that unnecessary surpluses are not kept, or categories are not overspent? Monitoring the use of resources permits them to be used in the best possible ways, and it provides necessary information for future planning.

WORKING WITH FINANCIAL RESOURCES

At the beginning of the chapter, a park supervisor was setting up a training session on the use of the new power edgers purchased by the city. For this session to be given, the city had to make certain expenditures. The edgers were purchased. Pay for the workers who were scheduled to attend the session was allocated. Costs were involved for lighting the building in which the session was to be conducted. The representative from the equipment company had to be notified; this meant a letter, typed by the department secretary, and perhaps a phone call. Secretarial time, paper and other office supplies, postage, and telephone expenses were involved. Other direct and indirect costs could be identified.

Money is a critical resource in recreation and park agencies. It is not important in itself, of course, but it enables the acquisition and use of other resources that, in turn, enable personnel to provide leisure services. With adequate funding, an agency can obtain the personnel, areas and facilities, equipment, and supplies needed to carry out its objectives. It can supervise personnel and provide for their professional growth. It can maintain the recreation areas and facilities. Financial resources are related directly to the other resources used by recreation and park personnel.

Each agency uses financial procedures which are most appropriate for it; therefore, there are differences. And, of course, revenue sources and budget amounts will vary greatly. Staff members should become familiar with budget amounts and procedures used in their specific agency, and especially in their particular areas of work. The purpose of this section is to present some information and generalizations which should make it easier for you to do this.

How Do Agencies Obtain Money?   The financial resources of public (governmental) agencies primarily come from taxes of various kinds: property taxes at the local level, sales taxes at local and state levels, income taxes at state and federal levels. Monies also are obtained through various kinds of grants from one level of government to another. In addition, public agencies can borrow money by issuing bonds, if appropriate approval requirements are met. Private agencies receive most of their funding either from voluntary contributions (often through such federated funding programs as the United Crusade) or from membership dues and fees. In the commercial sector, funding comes from expenditures for services made by participants; the objective, of course, is to realize a profit. In both public and private agencies, profits are not intended.

What Is a Budget?   Agencies make estimates of the amounts of money that they expect to receive. They also decide how they want to spend this money. In essence, they identify their goals, and decide how the available revenues can be used most effectively to meet these goals. In that sense, a budget is a plan.

> The budget should be thought of as a management plan through which a work program or project is outlined, including the financial details and schedules necessary to achieve certain pre-determined goals.[2]

Budgets can be made for specific programs, as well as for overall agency services.

A budget enables an agency to assign costs to services and to know what services can be offered. It permits choices to be made among different services, if all cannot be funded. It provides a systematic way for the agency to keep records of expenditures; these records, in turn, permit reviews to assure that expenditures were made properly. The budget also is a device for informing the public or the constituency of the agency about the amount of money to be spent by the agency and the purposes for which it will be spent.[3] In most cases, budgets must be approved by the elected body that represents the people who are served by the agency. For example, the city council would have approved the park department's budget. In the YMCA in the same community, the board of directors would have approved the Y's budget.

Types of Budgets.   Several different kinds of budgets are used by recreation and park agencies. Their primary differences are the ways they show estimated expenditures. There are two basic formats: budgets that identify the *uses* for which the expenditures are intended (listed either by objects and services, or by programs or functions in the agency); or budgets that show both anticipated expenditures and expected *benefits or outcomes* resulting from the expenditures.[4]

Line-item and functional budgets. The first type includes *object-classifi-cation* or *line-item* budgets and *functional* budgets. An example of a line-item budget is shown in Figure 9-1. This is a hypothetical object-classification budget for the park department mentioned at the beginning of the chapter. It identifies the object or service to be purchased, and the code number or account number assigned to that specific category. For example, the maintenance workers who will be attending the training session are paid out of account number 110—"Salaries and Wages (Full Time)," in the *Personal Services* section of the budget. Calls to the company representative were part of the overall telephone bill, paid out of account number 310—"Communications." This was a *Maintenance and Operations* expenditure. The power edgers purchased by the department were authorized under account number 640—"Machinery and Equipment." This purchase fell in the *Capital Outlay* section because the mowers cost more than $100.00, had a separate identity, and had an expected lifespan (effective use period) of

Code	Object Classification	1982–83 Actual	1983–84 Budget	1984–85 Requested
	PERSONAL SERVICES			
110	Salaries and Wages (Full Time)	223,137	257,000	283,000
120	Salaries and Wages (Temporary)	6,712	7,500	8,300
130	Employee Benefits	45,969	52,900	58,300
	Total Salaries and Wages	275,818	317,400	349,600
	MAINTENANCE AND OPERATIONS			
	Supplies			
210	Office Supplies	3,391	3,800	4,200
220	Operating Supplies	42,313	46,200	50,700
230	Repair and Maintenance Supplies	23,512	25,800	28,600
240	Small Tools & Minor Equipment	1,983	2,500	2,900
	Total Supplies	71,199	78,300	86,400
	Contractual Services			
310	Communications	4,953	5,500	6,100
320	Professional Services	0	500	0
330	Transportation	634	800	900
340	Insurance	23,119	24,900	26,000
350	Utilities	8,817	9,600	10,500
360	Repairs & Maintenance	1,826	2,000	2,200
370	Rentals	318	1,600	1,800
380	Miscellaneous	325	400	500
	Total Contractual Services	39,992	45,300	48,000
	Debt Service			
510	Serial Bonds	0	0	0
	Total Maintenance and Operations	111,191	123,600	134,400
	CAPITAL OUTLAY			
610	Land	16,800	0	0
620	Buildings	0	0	0
630	Improvements Other Than Buildings	0	11,000	11,000
640	Machinery and Equipment	10,773	28,000	31,000
	Total Capital Outlay	27,573	39,000	42,000
	Total Budget	414,582	480,000	526,000

Figure 9-1   City Park Department Budget: 1983–84 (Hypothetical)

	Salaries & Wages	Maintenance & Operation	Capital Outlay	Total
Administration	53,800	19,300	0	73,100
Maintenance: Park Areas	143,200	73,010	25,000	241,210
Maintenance: City Trees	120,400	31,290	14,000	165,690
Total	317,400	123,600	39,000	480,000

Figure 9-2 City Park Department Budget: 1983–84 (Hypothetical)

over one year. Different specific criteria are used to identify capital outlay items. However, these are usually permanent structures or facilities, or items that cost over a certain amount (per unit), have an expected lifespan, and have a separate identity.[5] That is, a property number can be put on them, and they can be shown as separately identifiable items in an inventory. They are nonexpendable, in that they are not "used up," in the usual sense of the word.

Different agencies use different account numbers and classifications. The example shown in Figure 9-1 is adopted from a chart of accounts commonly used by public agencies.[6]

The budget in Figure 9-1 also illustrates the practice of showing the amount of money actually spent the previous year in each classification, the amount budgeted for this year, and the amount requested for next year.

A *functional budget* shows expenditures by operations or services in the agency. Functions, in the example of the park department, are shown in the left-hand column of Figure 9-2. This hypothetical illustration includes both functions and general categories of objects. This combination often is referred to as a *performance* budget.

Program budget. The second general type of budget is a *program* budget.[7] In this type, an attempt is made to associate costs for different programs with values or benefits received. Goals and objectives for services are identified, programs for accomplishing these goals and objectives are developed, and estimated costs for the programs are determined. Usually, the projection of costs and benefits is for a period of more than one year.

> Essentially, the program budget is a multiyear fiscal plan that articulates community goals and objectives, and designates programs and funds to meet these objectives. The budget generally includes data on operating expenditures, capital outlays, and projected program outputs.[8]

The "outputs" are the benefits or values of the programs. In the park department example, the outputs from the power edger training session might be improved worker efficiency, expressed in terms of additional footages of lawn edged per worker-hour. It would be possible in this case to establish an objective of a certain number of feet of properly edged lawn for a given time period and a given number of park maintenance workers. Outputs of the tree maintenance program might include reductions in the numbers of trees dying from disease or reductions in the number of citizen complaints about downed limbs.

The power edger training probably would be part of an ongoing, in-service training program. Overall, it would be possible to establish a per-unit cost (in this case, a per-worker cost). That is, it would be possible to know how much it costs the city to provide in-service training for each park maintenance worker. In the tree program, costs could be established per tree or on the basis of varying costs for different kinds of trees or for differing levels of maintenance. These kinds of information enable the agency, and the public, to make more informed decisions about future allocations of money.

Budget Preparation.   Most agencies establish procedures for developing the budget and a budget calendar—a timetable for planning and approving the budget.[9] This assures that the budget will be developed on time, and that adequate opportunities will be available for those who are affected to participate in appropriate ways. Usually, one person is responsible for developing a proposed budget. This person seeks requests for money for the coming year from staff members who are responsible for the various units or services in the agency. These requests are assembled, with modifications made necessary because of insufficient funds, into a *preliminary budget* by the administrator or other designated person. He or she then meets with each unit head to review the assembled budget. Based on information from these meetings, the administrator develops a budget to be presented to the agency policy-making body. In the park department example, it would be presented to the city council. Normally, the council holds one or more public hearings on the proposed budget before adopting it as presented or in a modified form. Similar procedures are followed in most agencies.

The typical staff member participates in this process by communicating realistic requests for funds to the person who is developing the preliminary budget. Assume that you are the park supervisor mentioned earlier in this chapter. The superintendent of parks asks you to submit a request for the money you will need to operate your section next year. You will have to consider ongoing programs, new programs you want to undertake, and factors such as the costs of inflation. You probably will want to get ideas from the maintenance workers who make up your staff. Since you and your staff are closest to the direct services carried out by the agency, your request is necessary for the development of a realistic budget.

Edginton and Williams suggested two techniques related to budget preparation that would be helpful for you to use.[10] One is keeping a file in which you put ideas for next year's budget as you think of them. This avoids the problem of trying to remember everything at the time the superintendent asks for your budget. The other is that you seek input from the public you serve, prior to the public hearing phase, that might help you know more about what citizens want. You might do this informally as you talk with users of city parks and listen to their reactions to present conditions and their ideas about desired changes.

You might wonder if you should ask for more money than you need, since initial requests usually seem to be reduced in the budget which finally is adopted. While it is tempting to do so, budget padding usually will result in a loss of confidence in your ability or willingness to make realistic requests.

> Unrealistic requests and padding the budget will doom the request for funds. If a budget item cannot be supported with proof of need, the item should not be proposed for consideration by the legislative body. Usually, any attempt to convince the appropriating body with false needs will breed discontent and suspicion on its part and will lead to inadequate fiscal provisions. As a result, items that are worthy of support may receive insufficient funds to meet genuine needs.[11]

How Are Expenditures Made?   As with other aspects of financial management, different agencies use different ways of making expenditures. However, some generalizations can be stated. The basic considerations are related to controlling and accounting for expenditures so that monies are used for their intended purposes.

Assume the situation of the preschool director described at the beginning of the chapter. Assume also that she wishes to purchase some additional supplies. How does she do this? First of all, she would have to know that money was available for the items she wants. This means knowing whether or not there is an account category for the supplies she needs and, if so, whether sufficient funds remain in the account to cover the expenditure. Typically, agencies compile monthly reports, showing the amount of money left in each of the budget categories. If the expenditure would be authorized, and if funds remain in the account, then she needs to determine how the monies can be spent. In many agencies, three kinds of expenditures are possible: small purchases made with "petty cash;" expenditures for capital outlay items; and expenditures for items or services that cost more than can be covered with petty cash, but less than the lower limit of capital purchases.

Petty cash.   Most agencies have a *petty cash* fund—a fund from which small expenditures can be made providing they cost no more than a set amount (for example, up to $5.00). Its main purpose is to enable staff members to buy minor supplies when the amount of the purchase is too small to justify the paperwork associated with regular expenditures.[12] The preschool director, for example, might need more construction paper to finish a bulletin board display in the activity room. She might make this purchase directly from petty cash. Even though paperwork is minimal in the use of petty cash, some basic record keeping is necessary to assure that such a fund is being used properly.

Capital account.   *Capital* expenditures, for items over a certain amount of money, usually require a bid process. That is, bids are solicited from different vendors or service contractors, indicating the amount of money each would charge for the particular item or service. Often, procedures for advertising, soliciting, obtaining, and opening bids are defined by law, especially for public agencies. The purpose of this procedure is to assure that the agency obtains an item or service of acceptable quality at the lowest price. For the purchase of the power edgers, the park department probably first decided what specifications it wanted the power edgers to meet (such things as ease of maintenance, safety features, and cutting capacity). It then obtained bids from several equipment suppliers, quoting the prices they would charge for delivering edgers that met the specifications. The department then purchased the edgers from the company that had submitted the lowest bid

Purchase orders. For purchases less than capital outlays but more than petty cash, some type of *purchase order* system usually is used. A purchase order is a written document, issued by the agency and given to a vendor, that authorizes the purchase. The preschool director might request that a purchase order be issued by the city to a local music store for the purchase of several phonograph records. The purchase order would be sent or taken to the dealer. When the preschool director received the records, she would notify the city purchasing department. The dealer also would send an invoice or a bill to the city for the records. The purchasing department would prepare a voucher—a written document that verifies that the purchase was authorized and indicates the account to which the purchase is to be charged. On the basis of the voucher, a warrant or check would be issued to the dealer. That is, the bill would be paid.[13]

Variations in these procedures are found in different agencies. In all, however, there are provisions for assuring that the purchase is authorized, that monies are available, and that the requested supplies or services are delivered; further, the procedure enables appropriate records to be kept, including the posting of the amount to the proper account. Larger agencies have purchasing agents or departments that can provide assistance in making expenditures.

Accounting. The procedures just described, and the cumulative reports that result from them, are related to the processes of accounting.

> Accounting is concerned with recording information relative to the financial operation of the department of parks and recreation. It is also involved with collecting monies, interpreting the source and use of monies, and attesting to the transactions that have taken place.[14]

The accounting procedures and the general financial management used by an agency are subject to *audit*. An audit is an examination of the agency's books to determine that funds have been handled in an authorized manner, and in conformity with the budget approved by the agency.[15] The audit usually is done by an outside accounting firm. It is called an *external* or *independent* audit to differentiate it from reviews of financial proceedings conducted by the department or agency itself.

Fees and Charges.   One of the decisions in which you might be involved is whether your agency, or your particular unit, will charge participants for the services they use. In some agencies, all services are on a fee or charge basis, especially agencies in the commercial sector. Many private agencies also rely on user fees, particularly membership fees and charges for special programs (such as day camps, swim lessons and trips). Commercial agencies structure their charges to realize a profit; private agencies operate on a nonprofit basis. Public (governmental) agencies may or may not charge fees. However, there has been an increasing tendency for them to do so.[16] When they do, they tend to charge for some services and not for others.

Why charge fees?   Particularly in the public sector, several arguments have been made for and against the use of fees. The principal reason for increasing use of fees by public recreation and park agencies is that the demand for services usually exceeds the agency's ability to fund them, and citizens are relatively willing to pay for the services they use. Receiving fees permits agencies to expand their services, and in some cases to offer programs that they would not offer otherwise. Fees permit the cost of specialized and more expensive services to be borne, in part, by the people who actually use these services. This relieves the tax burden of nonusers. Also, there is some evidence that people tend to appreciate services more when they pay user fees.[17]

But there are some disadvantages. Howard and Crompton suggested five primary ones, two philosophical in nature and three administrative.[18] Philosophically, the arguments against fees are (1) that since all citizens benefit from and need recreation, these opportunities should be funded entirely by taxes; and (2) that the use of fees discriminates against poor people. The authors noted that both of these disadvantages may be less important than they seem. It may be unrealistic to assume that public agencies should provide for everyone's needs, on a completely subsidized basis. And since poor people tend to pay larger proportions of their incomes for taxes, they might be better off to pay fees for services they desire rather than being forced to pay higher taxes to support services that they do not use. Also, it might be more appropriate to provide subsidies or fee waivers for low-income persons, rather than offering free services to all citizens.[19] Kraus reported that 43 percent of the recreation and park administrators, responding to a survey of financial trends in urban departments, used fee-waiver arrangements "to assist such groups as the elderly, young, mentally or physically disabled, and economically disadvantaged."[20] The administrative disadvantages of fees are (1) that they may be illegal, in some cases; (2) that it often is difficult to control access to services where fees are levied; and (3) that the cost of administering a fee program may be more than the revenues generated from it.[21]

Howard and Crompton also presented a rationale for charging fees based on who benefits from the services involved. They defined three categories of service—public service, merit service, and private service.[22] In public service, all citizens benefit; therefore all should support the service through taxes, but no fees should be charged. In private service, only those who use the service benefit; therefore, use fees should be charged if it is feasible to do so. In merit service, users benefit most. However, there are indirect benefits to all citizens, so it is appropriate to partially support the service with fees and partially with taxes. The authors also provided a detailed and very useful discussion of factors to be considered in establishing appropriate fees.[23] Basically, fees may be established on the basis of what comparable services would cost in other agencies, what people are willing to pay, and what the costs are for offering the service.

How to decide.   Hines suggested several basic principles for determining when fees should be charged.[24] Generally, no charges should be made for children's programs. A possible exception is the use of a small fee when special materials are involved (such as craft supplies). When the activity generates revenue for the agency from spectators, so that costs of the program are covered, no fees should be charged to participants. Examples are such activities as musical and dramatic productions, where a service is provided to the public which attends. If facilities are available (that is, are not being used for regular agency programs) these should be available on a no-charge basis to outside groups, if the group's objectives and programs are consistent with agency philosophy. Charges should be made for activities in which advanced or specialized instruction is provided, or where expensive, specialized equipment or unusual personnel requirements are involved. Frequently, fees are charged for adult activities, especially sport programs where revenues are used to cover the costs of officials and trophies.

Your Responsibility.   Regardless of the position you hold in a recreation and park agency, you probably will have some responsibility for working with a budget. You may help develop it; or you may help spend monies from it. Most certainly, you will use other resources that have been made available because of it.

You may have some specific assignment related to the management of financial resources. Whether you do or do not, your most basic responsibility is to be familiar with the operating budget of your agency: the sources from which revenues are received, the overall amounts and the amounts in those accounts that are most relevant to your unit, the procedures followed in the development of the budget, and the procedures used in making expenditures. The purpose of this familiarity is to enable you to use the financial resources available to you as effectively as possible.

MANAGING PHYSICAL RESOURCES FOR SAFE USE

In the illustration at the beginning of the chapter, a preschool director, in checking the room before the children arrived, found and put away a pair of sharp scissors. She did this to avoid a possible accident, had a child played with the scissors. In the power edger training session, one of the park supervisor's objectives no doubt is training groundskeepers to use the equipment safely.

Accidents do occur in recreation and park settings. They occur in all kinds of situations involving different staff members and users of agency services. Negley noted that over 400,000 people are injured annually in activity programs sponsored by public recreation agencies and schools.[25] Accident rates in services offered in the private and commercial sectors would add considerably to this figure. On playground equipment alone, 118,000 injuries were reported in 1974 and 1975 that required at least emergency room care; twenty-three persons died. In this particular report by the U.S. Consumer Products Safety Commission, playground equipment "ranked sixth on a list of hazardous consumer products."[26]

Recreation and park personnel have both legal and moral responsibilities to protect users of leisure services and staff members from injury, and to provide safe, hazard-free environments. To do that we need to be aware of the factors that contribute to accidents.

Factors that Contribute to Accidents.   In many cases, the natural environment is a contributing factor. A swift section of water in a river causes a canoe to overturn. A swimmer is caught in an undertow at an ocean beach. A mountain climber slips on a steep face, where the rock is loose and unstable. A backpacker is caught in an exposed position, above timberline, in a lightning storm. The list of examples could be expanded.

Poor design.   The types of developments that recreation and park agencies carry out on land and water areas sometimes are factors in accidents. An improperly laid out baseball field results in a long fly ball hitting a person in an adjacent picnic area. Improper placement of protective surfacing under a piece of playground equipment permits a child to be injured when he falls.

Poor condition.   Sometimes, the condition of the facilities causes accidents. Broken glass that has not been cleaned up in a swimming area can cause cuts. A damaged locking device on an amusement park ride fails, and several teen-agers are thrown to the ground. A piece of loose carpeting in the hallway at a recreation center causes an older adult to fall and injure herself. A burned-out light bulb has not been replaced in a center utility closet, and in the darkness the custodian hits his head on a sharp shelf edge.

Risky activities.   The types of activities in which people engage are contributors to accidents. Some activities are inherently risky. Dunn and Gulbis studied twenty-seven activities "characterized by controllable danger, excitement, or thrill to the participant."[27] The relative degrees of participant risk in these activities, as perceived by public leisure agency administrators, ranged from fairly low—such activities as judo, waterskiing, and backpacking—to high—such activities as hang gliding, parachuting, automobile racing, and "hot dogging" (snow skiing). In these types of activities, the risks are inherent in the activities themselves. They vary, of course, with the skill level and specific behavior of each participant. However, even highly skilled participants, using good judgment, are taking some risk.

Not all participants use good judgment, and not all are skilled. These factors contribute heavily to accidents.

Poor supervision.   The nature of leadership or supervision provided by recreation and park personnel is another factor. A gymnastics instructor at a youth center goes to answer the telephone while a sixth-grader is working out on a trampoline; the youngster loses her balance, falls, and is injured. A lifeguard at a swimming pool permits teens to run and scuffle on the pool deck; one slips and is hurt. A hobby shop teacher fails to teach class members safe use of a table saw, and one receives a bad cut. Again, the list of examples could be extended.

In most accidents, probably more than one of the above factors is involved. Often, it is a combination of environmental conditions and user behavior. And, more frequently than it should, staff behavior also contributes.

Minimizing Accident Potentials.   Jubenville identified the basic elements of a "hazard management" program.[28] The environment can be changed (through planning and development or modification); educational or information programs can be initiated for visitors; or use can be regulated. The author defined hazard management as

> the purposeful action taken by management to reduce the probability of injury, loss of life, or loss of property occurring to the participant from known or suspected, natural or manmade, hazards, within the recreational environment.[29]

Jubenville noted that hazard management probably will not eliminate all possibilities of accident. In fact, he contended that a hazard-free environment probably would be perceived by users as being sterile. As mentioned earlier, the risk often is an integral part of the experience, particularly in outdoor recreation activities.

The task seems to be one of minimizing the accident potentials, and avoiding risks that are not integral parts of an activity. Careful planning and persistent attention to details are required. The following staff activities contribute to creating and maintaining safe environments.

1. *Identify possible hazard areas and conditions.* The areas and facilities used by leisure service agencies should be analyzed periodically to discover possible hazards. Personnel should be alert at all times. The preschool director was alert when she discovered the sharp scissors. Recreation and park personnel who work consistently in an area or facility learn to spot conditions that need correcting. Their past experiences on site or in the facility provide a background against which they can compare current conditions. They tend to notice changes or incongruities easily, so long as they do not become complacent.

More systematic reviews should be conducted, however. The frequency depends on the potentiality of hazardous conditions occurring. Areas of possible danger should be identified and, if possible, corrected. If they cannot be corrected participants should be warned about them, or use of the area or facility should be discontinued. Changing snow conditions at a ski area provide an example. The mountain staff, or members of the ski patrol, will check the area every morning. Hazard spots, such as thin snow cover or possible avalanche areas, will be noted. If conditions warrant it, the area will be closed. Otherwise, the condition will be corrected or marked. Exposed rock areas will be identified with marker poles. Avalanche areas may be triggered purposefully before the hill opens, to relieve the danger.

The objective is to prevent accidents. If they do occur, records should be kept that indicate the exact location. This information serves various purposes. One is that, over time, the points of greatest hazard in an area can be identified. Obviously these should be corrected as rapidly as possible.

Program activities also can be analyzed to identify possible hazards. Before a new program is implemented, the agency should assess the potential exposure of participants to risk. This information, along with the usual considerations of costs and probable interest, can be used in deciding whether to offer the program.[30]

2. *Educate participants and staff for safe use.* In teaching leisure skills in which risk is involved, it is clear that safety considerations must be included. We do this routinely. We work for the development of proficiency in the activity so that hazards are minimized. This involves not only acquiring skill, but also developing appropriate knowledge and attitudes. Several national organizations, such as the American Red Cross and the National Rifle Association, provide guidelines and standards for safety in the specific activities with which they are concerned. Details can be obtained from the various organizations.

In-service training, such as the power edger session, can improve the safe operating practices of staff members. Again, skills, knowledges, and attitudes will be involved. Accident records can be used to identify training needs and to evaluate the effectiveness of training.

3. *Regulate or control use, when it is appropriate to do so.* In some cases, known hazards are such that use must be restricted. In the ski area illustration, the threat of avalanche may require that a section of the hill be closed. On those runs that are in use, ski patrol members will prevent persons from skiing too fast for the conditions. Lifeguards restrict users of swimming pools from running on pool decks, diving in shallow water, and bringing glass containers into the pool area. These actions are intended to prevent users from harming themselves or others.

4. *Keep safety considerations in mind when planning facilities.* When facilities such as playgrounds, sport complexes, and recreation centers are designed and built, thought must be given to the influence of design on safe use. During the design phase planners should consult with personnel who have had experience operating the type of facility being developed. This is true for any facility, but especially so for swimming pools, ski areas, craft shops where power equipment will be used, and other areas where there is accident potential. This assures that the facility will be functional and that it can be operated efficiently and safely.

5. *Implement appropriate maintenance practices.* Routine inspection and maintenance procedures help to prevent the occurrence of hazardous conditions. Certain pieces of equipment, or their parts, have expected lifetimes. Preventive maintenance schedules are designed to carry out routine servicing of equipment and replacement of parts before they fail.

Appropriate maintenance may involve removing part of the recreation environment. A piece of equipment on which accidents are frequent might be eliminated completely. A tree growing on a river bank in a location where large numbers of people are tempted to dive into shallow water from its branches might be cut down.

Jubenville noted the importance of developing specific guidelines for maintenance, including criteria for judging whether conditions are safe. Guidelines and criteria assure consistency in making maintenance inspections.[31] The author also indicated that records of inspections and maintenance operations performed should be kept. Such records help to protect employees and the agency from being held liable for accidents.

6. *Establish accident procedures.* Agency personnel should know what to do if an accident happens. Assume that the preschool director had not found the scissors, and that one of the children was playing with them and fell and cut himself on the arm. The wound was bleeding freely. Suppose that you were the preschool director. At that point, you would want to know exactly what to do. You would want the assurance that procedures had been thought out earlier, under nonemergency conditions. You would want answers to such questions as, What do I do first? What should I do about the injury? Who should be notified? Should I take the child home?

Your first concern probably would be to do something about the injury. Accident procedures should define what to do, and under what conditions. For the sake of the injured person, and for your legal protection and that of the agency, emergency care should be based on some proven method. American Red Cross First Aid techniques are generally accepted as standard, proven methods. These should be followed carefully; they should be carried out, but not exceeded. It is important, therefore, that personnel have current training in the administration of appropriate first aid. Van der Smissen, a recreation and park professional and a lawyer, has provided an excellent summary of principles for emergency care that contribute to the legal protection of agencies and personnel.[32]

Agency policy should indicate who is to be notified. Accident forms, standardized for the agency, should be used to record relevant details of the accident. Because of the possibilities of lawsuits arising from accidents, agencies should seek the advice of a lawyer when accident forms and other procedures are being developed.

7. *Know your responsibilities.* You should have a clear understanding of what your responsibilities are in the agency where you are working. If you are a supervisor, members of your staff also need to know their responsibilities. Obviously, if the safety of participants depends upon something you should do, or something staff members should do, this must be known. For example, if the preschool director is relying on one of the volunteer assistants to make a safety check of the room and area before the children arrive, the assistant must be aware that she has this responsibility. This example is fairly clear. In other situations, defining boundaries of responsibility may be more difficult. Assume that you are working with older adults, and that you decide to take a group to a nearby resort area. Where do your responsibilities for their well-being begin and end when you are at the resort? They are adults, and they wish to be independent. At the same time, you are the leader of the trip. In situations such as this, responsibility is more difficult to define. Even so, it is to the advantage of both staff and participants to clarify the boundaries of responsibility as clearly as possible.

You also should be aware of any laws that influence or regulate the leisure services with which you are involved. For example, state health and safety codes usually contain regulations for the operation of such facilities as swimming pools and resident camps. These should be known and followed.

LIABILITY

Another set of laws has to do with liability. These laws are based on the premise that an individual has a right to collect compensation for injuries to self or damage to property from the person or persons who caused the injuries or damages. Assume, again, that you have taken a group of older adults to a resort. Suppose that while you are there, you rent a power boat and take several of the seniors for a ride on the lake. In returning to the dock, your boat hits a rock sticking up in the lake and two of the passengers are thrown to the floor of the boat and are injured. You could be held liable. That is, you could be sued for damages if the court held that you were responsible, wholly or in part, for the accident. There are different kinds of liability. The kind involved in this case would be *tort liability*.[33] Tort liability concerns situations where the actions or wrongdoings of one person cause damages to or for another person.

Recreation and park agencies frequently *are* sued. Often these suits are judged against the agency involved, and the amounts of money that are awarded are high. Awards to injured parties of well over $100,000 are not uncommon. As a result, agency costs for insuring against liability claims have increased dramatically. Negley documented this increase for public agencies in California in 1979.

> Consider some of the following statistics: Coalinga, California, a city of about 8,000, saw premiums for liability insurance increase from $11,000 to $22,000 in one year; Fremont, California saw its rates increased from $64,453 to $225,000 in a similar one-year period; Ventura County, California is still recovering from a more than 600 percent increase that saw its premiums climb from $130,000 to $904,000 in a twelve-month span; Campbell, California saw a 256 percent increase and Bakersfield a 200 percent increase in recent years.[34]

The costs of liability insurance, based on the amounts of judgments, and general insurance practices and regulations vary from state to state. However, the overall trend is for large awards, when judgments are made against agencies, and for higher insurance premiums. As a result, some agencies have instituted such practices as setting aside money for possible claims rather than buying insurance (self-insuring) or cooperating with other agencies in buying insurance.[35]

Who Can Be Sued?   The answer to this question is that almost anyone can be sued.

> In the United States almost anybody can be sued for anything at any time— and the area of physical education, athletics, parks and recreation is no exception.[36]

Guadagnolo observed that suits may involve all persons related to any agency's service delivery system.

> With fewer and fewer exceptions everyone on the agency's organization chart, together with volunteers, parents, or college interns, may be vulnerable to claims of negligence.[37]

At one time, governmental agencies were immune to suits, due to the doctrine of "sovereign"—or governmental—immunity.[38] The basic premise for this immunity was that since governments serve the general welfare of the public and establish the laws that are enforced, a suit against the government would be inappropriate.

In practice, immunity has been based on whether an agency's function has been determined to be *governmental* or *proprietary*.[39] The distinction between these two categories is difficult to make. An approximate difference is that a governmental function serves the general public welfare; a proprietary function is more of a private service for a segment of the general public, even though the general public may benefit indirectly. Part of the distinction is based on whether the service is mandated by state law (and therefore is a governmental function) or is offered at the discretion of the agency providing the service. Governmental functions have been less subject to liability claims than have proprietary functions.

This distinction is not of great significance to recreation and park agencies. There is no general rule that can be applied in determining whether leisure services are governmental or proprietary.[40] Further, the concept of immunity applies only to governmental agencies, when it is determined to be applicable; and the concept is being applied by the courts with less frequency. In many states, laws have been enacted that repeal governmental immunity provisions.[41] The safest assumption for recreation and park personnel to make is that their agencies can be sued, and that they also can be sued as individuals.

Under What Conditions Can You Be Found Negligent?   Establishing liability is an extremely complex matter. Principles vary from state to state, and decisions are made in courts of law.[42] There are no hard and fast rules. However, some generalizations can be made about negligence and liability.

Nickolaus suggested that recreation and park agencies and their employees can be liable in three broad categories of cases: injuries resulting from the physical condition of land and water areas, either natural or improved; injuries related to equipment and facilities; and injuries caused by the negligent acts of personnel.[43] The suggestions for creating and maintaining safe conditions, which were described earlier, will help to reduce liability risks in all three of these categories. However, the possibility of employee negligence raises some additional questions.

What is negligence? Like other legal terms, negligence cannot be easily defined. In essence, it means doing something—or failing to do something—that causes damages to or for someone else, where the probability of the damages could have been reasonably foreseen.[44] Rankin provided this interpretation.

> Liability is likely to occur when someone has been hurt as the result of a wrongful act or omission of another who owed a duty of protection to the injured party.[45]

According to Prosser, four conditions must be present for negligence to be established.[46]

1. *Legal Responsibility.* The staff member involved must have a legal duty to protect others from unreasonable risk or harm. Guadagnolo and van der Smissen both used examples of a drowning swimmer to distinguish legal duty from moral duty.[47] If you were at the beach as a private citizen, and if you were a competent swimmer and had been trained in lifesaving methods, you might have a moral but not legal obligation to attempt a rescue. However, if you were one of the lifeguards employed to protect swimmers, you would have a legal duty to do so. The authors caution that you can be held liable for your actions if you decide to attempt a rescue even though you had no legal duty prior to your attempt.

2. *Failure to Take Reasonable Care.* It must be shown that the staff member failed to provide an acceptable standard of care. A key factor here is the determination of actions that would be taken by a "reasonably prudent person" in the same situation.

> The courts have held that the standard of care owed to the park and recreation participant is that of a reasonably prudent person under the circumstances.[48]

Guadagnolo pointed out that the basis for comparison in cases involving park and recreation employees is accepted professional competence.

> Under standard of care, it is extremely important to recognize that the care given will not be compared to that of a reasonable person but rather that of a prudent professional.[49]

In such cases, it will be expected that performance will be higher or more effective.

In determining standard of care, some consideration may be given to the conditions under which a participant uses a recreation and park facility. Three broad categories of users have been defined—trespassers, licensees, and invitees.[50] *Trespassers* are those who use recreation and park facilities without permission, and where no benefit from the use results for the owner or agency. *Licensees* have permission to enter, which may be implied or stated, but again the agency or owner receives no benefit. Knudson provided these illustrations.

> Examples of licensees are cross-country skiers who receive permission (no fee paid) to use company land or a farm, a person who asks permission to hunt pheasants in a cornfield, or a fisherman who is allowed to cross private land to reach a stream.[51]

Invitees are those who benefit from their use of areas and facilities, and from whose visit the agency or owner also receives a benefit. In most cases, the users of recreation and park services are considered to be invitees.

Standards of care generally require that invitees will be given the greatest protection from harm and trespassers the least.[52] The agency has no obligation to the trespasser until such use is discovered. Some courts have ruled that trespassers must be warned about hazardous conditions if their presence is known to the agency or owner.

The no-obligation provision changes somewhat in the case of trespassers who are children. If a trespasser is a child who is judged to be too young to know better (usually twelve years old or younger, but in some cases up to sixteen), if the agency or owner of the land upon which the child trespasses is aware that the area is attractive to children, and if a dangerous condition exists that is not a natural hazard, the existence of an "attractive nuisance" can be established.[53] Owners and agencies can be held liable for creating attractive nuisances. Van der Smissen noted, however, that applying this concept to some public recreation and park facilities is inappropriate.[54] In most cases involving playgrounds, it cannot be established that children are trespassers; usually they are considered invitees.

There has been a tendency not to emphasize these different use classifications. Instead, courts have tended to consider each case on its merits against the standard of prudent performance.[55] In some states, the different classes of users have been dropped from the law.[56]

3. *Cause.* For negligence to be established a casual relationship must be present between the actions of the staff member and the injury or damage received by the participant. It must be proven that the staff member did something that should not have been done, or did not do something that should have been done—and that the behavior resulted in the injury or damage. The issue of "proximate cause" becomes involved at this point.[57] The staff member's behavior must be related directly enough to the injury to be judged a primary cause of it.

> Generally, the test employed in determining whether an individual can be held liable for his negligent conduct is whether such conduct was a *substantial factor* in bringing about the injury. A substantial factor has usually been interpreted to mean any such factor which in and by itself would have caused the injury.[58]

Several categories of staff behaviors might be involved in judgments of proximate causes.[59] An *act of commission* is an instance where an individual did something that should not have been done. If the individual failed to do something that should have been done, it is referred to as an *act of omission*. These terms are similar to another set of descriptions of behavior that might be ruled as negligent: "nonfeasance," "misfeasance," and "malfeasance." *Nonfeasance* describes those situations where duty is neglected totally; the staff member does nothing. *Misfeasance* is where the staff member either does not perform a required lawful act (omission) or performs the act improperly (commission), and injury results. *Malfeasance* is the performance of an illegal act that causes injury.

Two categories of behavior on the part of participants may reduce the degree of liability to which a staff member may be held.[60] One of these is *assumption of risk,* where it can be established that the injured person knew about the normal hazards of engaging in the activity in which the injury occurred. This provision usually is applicable only to cases involving teenagers and adults, where it is assumed that normal risks can be recognized and understood. The other category is *contributory negligence,* or *contributory fault,* where the actions of the participant caused the injury, either wholly or in part. Where this condition is applied, judgments against the agency may be reduced in proportion to the degree of contributory fault found to be present.

4. *Proof of Injury or Damage.* The fourth condition requires proof of injuries or damages. Typically, claims are based on physical injury or property damage. However, judgments may be made because of psychological factors.

> Many cases are receiving substantial settlements on claims of psychological trauma, fright, humiliation, and other forms of pain and suffering.[61]

The various conditions discussed in this section can be illustrated, in a summary fashion, by the earlier illustration of the boating accident. As a senior citizen leader, you had taken a group to a resort area. Once there, you rented a power boat and took several of the older adults for a ride on the lake. In doing this you collided with a rock sticking up in the lake, and two persons in your boat received injuries. If these individuals sued, you would be named as a defendant. Probably your immediate supervisor and the agency administrator also would be named as defendants, on the premise that they may have failed to provide proper training that would enable you to provide for participant safety. Perhaps the agency that owns the lake or manages the resort also would be named. You probably would be held negligent if it were judged (1) that you had a legal duty to protect the well-being of the passengers in your boat, (2) that you failed to perform as a reasonably prudent professional would under the circumstances, (3) that this failure was the proximate cause of the injuries, and (4) that the injuries could be proved to exist. The extent of your liability might be reduced if it could be shown that the passengers knew that the boat might hit a rock and they went anyway, or that they contributed to the accident (for example, that one of them was operating the boat at the time of the accident). An additional defense against liability would be if the courts ruled the accident to be due to natural causes—for example, that an unexpected and unusually strong gust of wind blew the boat into the rock.[62]

How Can You Protect Yourself? As indicated earlier, liability law is very complex. Clear-cut answers to questions of negligence cannot be given without considering the specific circumstances, nor except by someone with legal training. Usually, court decisions are involved. But again, there are some things that recreation and park personnel can do to reduce the probabilities that they will be sued successfully.

Van der Smissen provided a general summary.

> The best defense, of course, is that one or more of the four elements . . . have not been proven—that a duty was not owed the injured, that reasonable care was exercised in the performance of the act, that the act was not the proximate cause of the injury, or that there was not in fact injury to the plaintiff.[63]

Know the law. The possession of relevant knowledge appears to be a significant factor in avoiding liability. Farina made this observation.

> Municipal governments, officers, agents, and employees consistently perform negligent acts. Many of these acts result from ignorance of the laws, poor administration, and lack of preparatory training.[64]

Staff members should know what their responsibilities are; they should carry these out as diligently as possible; and they should have a basic knowledge of factors that are considered in establishing negligence and liability. This does not mean that we must become lawyers. Rankin, who like van der Smissen is a lawyer as well as a recreation professional, made this point in discussing legal risks in innovative programming.

> It is neither necessary nor desirable for the recreation professional to learn and practice law prior to initiating innovative risk programming. What is necessary is for the programmer to utilize the special skills of recreation education and experience to make informed judgments which will account for not only the participant's physical safety and the agency's need to be free of litigation, but also the requirements of balanced program activities and the participant's needs for risk-incurring experiences.[65]

She also identified the element of common sense.

> In all of these matters, common sense augmented by professional education and experience remains the critical common denominator.[66]

One thing seems apparent: While recreation and park personnel need to be knowledgeable about general liability law and conscientious in discharging their duties, we cannot prevent all lawsuits. We can do our best to provide citizens with opportunities for enriching leisure experiences, and we can attempt to reduce the risk of legal action against ourselves and our agencies even if such action cannot be prevented.

We cannot close our parks and recreation facilities in fear of a suit. Proper planning, the retention of quality personnel, effective supervision, and in-service education should and will effectively lessen opportunities for adverse judgments to be rendered.[67]

Have insurance. We also can make certain that we have adequate insurance protection to cover possible judgments against us. This involves knowing whether our agency carries liability insurance. If so, are individual employees included in the coverage? Does the coverage extend to volunteers? If the agency self-insures, what provisions are made for protecting staff members? Guadagnolo suggested that the agency's financial protection against liability should be reviewed periodically.[68] He observed that coverage frequently is nonexistent, or inadequate in terms of the amounts of money awarded in judgments against the agency. He also pointed out that only certain job classifications may be covered. Regardless of the protection provided by the agency, individual staff members may want to consider buying personal liability coverage for themselves.

Special cases. Two special considerations should be noted in minimizing one's exposure to liability. One of these has to do with the transportation of participants in a staff member's own (private) vehicle. Transporting people in agency vehicles requires particular caution.[69] This need for caution is not lessened if private vehicles are used; it may be increased. This is true whether the automobile is owned and operated by a staff member or a volunteer. Before transporting participants in your own car, you should check with the insurance carrier who insures the vehicle to be certain that you are covered adequately for such use. It is advisable for volunteers to obtain this information also, from their individual carriers, if they will be transporting participants.

A second consideration is the use of permission slips. As a prerequisite for participating in a recreation activity, such as a trip or an athletic contest, children often are asked to submit parental permission slips to the agency. On these slips, parents frequently are asked to waive any right to sue for injuries that might occur to a child. In a sense, the agency is attempting to protect itself from liability; it is asking the parent to assume the risk involved in the activity. Van der Smissen cautioned that this is false security. She indicated that parents cannot waive the right of a child to bring suit against the agency at the time the child reaches the legal age for doing so.[70] Rankin noted that signed statements, in all cases, are invalid if the risks of the activity are not understood.

> Having a signed disclaimer clause will not provide an adequate defense if the participant was not really aware of or able to comprehend the dangers involved.[71]

While parental permission slips do not relieve an agency of legal responsibilities for a child's safety, they are useful in informing parents about the child's participation and assuring that they approve of it.

CRIME, VIOLENCE, AND OTHER DISRUPTIVE BEHAVIORS

The older couple had parked their travel trailer in a spot near the lake at the state recreation area. All of the other camp sites were occupied. It was late evening; the couple had gone to bed, after attending a campfire talk given by a ranger. Around midnight, the man was awakened by a noise outside. In looking out the window, he saw what appeared to be someone breaking into his car. He had been fishing earlier and had left his equipment and a camera inside the vehicle. He had thought that he should bring the camera, at least, inside the trailer. But instead, he left the things in the car and locked it. Now it appeared that someone was trying to steal them. He quickly put on a pair of pants and slippers and went outside. He confronted the person, who by that time had a wing-window pried open, and was partially in the car. The apparent thief backed out of the car with the camera, then struck the older man in the face and ran from the area. The man fell to the ground, bleeding from a cut on his mouth.

Recreation and park settings are not immune from violent or criminal acts, vandalism, and other disruptive behaviors; and the people who use leisure services may become victims. Another dimension of managing resources for safe use is to minimize the potential for this happening.

Some types of disruptive behaviors are neither crimes nor violent. Sixth-grade boys who are noisy and boisterous during a community drama production are disruptive. Teen-agers who play loud music in a campground are disruptive. Eighth-grade girls who splash water on other swimmers are disruptive. None of these behaviors poses a direct threat to the safety of other participants. Such behaviors fall into the general category of discipline problems, which were discussed in Chapter 7. The focus in this chapter will be on disruptive behaviors that threaten people's safety or property.

Types and Rates of Crime. Two types of criminal behavior to which users of recreation and park areas are exposed are offenses against persons and offenses against property. In the camera theft illustration, both types were involved—the car was broken into, the camera was stolen, and the owner was struck in the face. Connors, reporting on the findings of two nationwide studies, noted that crimes against property are more prevalent than crimes against persons.

> Property offenses (larceny, breaking and entering) and vandalism are the most extensive serious crimes and account for the greatest dollar loss. . . . Personal offenses (murder, rape, assault) are minor but evident.[72]

Some violence results from conflicts among users.[73] These arise because of variations in lifestyles, different perceptions of appropriate uses of parks, or because different groups feel possessive of certain park areas.

> Issues such as nude sunbathing, snowmobilers versus cross-country skiers, and park use by motorcycle clubs, for example, can generate considerable

controversy. In other cases, certain user groups may feel they have a proprietary right to certain facilities and may object to sharing or changing them.[74]

Sometimes conflicts arise between age groups, especially where use by young adult visitors might involve drug or alcohol consumption, the use of high volume sound equipment, and other behavior seen as inappropriate by older park users.[75]

Overall rates of crime are somewhat difficult to assess.[76] The available statistics suggest that nonurban recreation and park areas may be safer than urban environments. For example, Westover, Flickinger, and Chubb, commenting on felonies (homicide, rape, assault, robbery, burglary and larceny) reported by the National Park Service, indicated a crime rate of 2.9 per 100,000 user days in 1978. Expansion of this figure by approximately 40 percent to account for the probability of unreported crimes, yielded a rate of 4.9 per 100,000 use days. The authors observed that this was very much below the national crime rate, as reported in 1978.[77] Based on this, an individual's chances for becoming a victim in a national park would be fairly small.

There is some suggestion that users of state parks feel that their exposures to crime are not great. Westover, Flickinger, and Chubb also reported on a study of Ohio state park visitors conducted by Flickinger, in which over 90 percent of the respondents said they felt safe and protected in the parks.[78] However, these same respondents indicated that they felt less safe in urban parks. Eighty-seven percent reported this feeling; 27 percent indicated that they avoided local, neighborhood parks because of fears about crime.

A survey of over 4000 individuals in California also indicated that fear of crime is a barrier to urban recreation participation.

> Fear for personal safety is a major deterrent to recreation for many Californians living in urban areas. Many respondents indicated a personal experience with crime in a recreation setting, or knew someone who had such an experience. The need for safe, secure recreation areas is explicit throughout the study.[79]

The studies reported by Connors verify that crime does occur more often in urban recreation and park areas.

> In terms of the occurrence of crime, the studies revealed that criminal activity in park and recreation areas is most likely to occur: in a developed area as opposed to an undeveloped area; near an urban atmosphere, or an urban-simulated environment; at a well-attended facility. . . .[80]

Most of the offenses (95 percent) were committed by males; 44 percent of the offenders were juveniles.[81] The most likely time for crimes was reported to be weekends (especially Saturdays) in the period from 8 P.M. to midnight during summer months.

Actual exposure to crime and violence in recreation and park areas probably is greater than the statistics indicate, for two reasons. First, many crimes are not reported.[82] Second, people spend considerably less time in parks than in other settings. While the reported crime rates are relatively low, the limited amount of time people actually spend in parks gives them added significance.[83]

Connors contended that criminal activity in recreation and park areas is increasing.[84] Kraus also observed increases in antisocial behavior, and in damages to facilities and equipment. Based on studies conducted in 1971 and 1979, he reported a growth in the indications from municipal recreation and park departments (from 69 percent to 76 percent) that these problems were "severe" or "moderate."[85]

Included among the findings were two of particular interest. The number of departments reporting that drug addicts, alcoholics, gangs, and other potentially disruptive groups dominated playgrounds or small parks increased from 29 percent to 41 percent. The number reporting attacks on department personnel increased from 4 percent to 7 percent.[86]

A precise description of overall risk to users is impossible. However, it is clear that users of recreation and park areas may become victims of criminal or violent behavior.

Minimizing User Exposure to Risks.[87]   In working with people, we have an obligation to do what we can to protect them from criminal activity. It has been noted earlier that people tend to not use recreation and park areas that they consider unsafe. This is common sense and it is congruent with Maslow's theory of needs.[88] As much as possible, we want to create conditions that will encourage people to use our facilities and services, and we want to minimize their exposures to risk while they are there.

Providing for participant security and minimizing the potential for offenses against property are complicated responsibilities. In this sense, they are similar to maintaining accident-free environments and avoiding liability. However, dealing with criminal and violent activity has an added dimension, in that a third party (the offender) is involved in most cases. In avoiding accidents, the primary relationships are between participants and staff members. Occasionally, interactions between participants contribute to or are the cause of accidents. However, rarely is there a premeditated intent to harm. In crime and violence, the primary relationship is between the participant and another participant or nonparticipant (although crimes and acts of violence sometimes are committed against staff members, also). And the intent to harm usually is present.

Know how far to go.   Each agency must decide how far it wants its personnel to go in handling violent or disruptive persons. One part of the question is deciding whether staff members will function as law enforcement personnel or if the agency will rely primarily on outside police assistance. In some recreation and park situations, personnel are empowered as law enforcement officers. This is most true in public resource managing agencies at the federal, state, and county or regional levels. These individuals will have received specialized training. In application though, it is not an either-or decision. All agencies benefit from options to call officers from other jurisdictions; often as backup help for their own law enforcement personnel, if these exist. Also, agencies cannot create a police force without appropriate authorization. In some cases, security officers are used. These individuals may have no greater legal authority to make arrests than the average citizen. However, they usually have the advantages of training and symbols of authority (such as badges and uniforms).

Several other decisions emerge when an agency decides, and is authorized, to have staff assume police duties. A significant one is whether authorization will be sought for security or police personnel to be armed.

For the average worker these matters will have been decided prior to his or her joining the agency. Most of us work in situations in which we do not have police power; we will not be armed and we will not be expected to make arrests. However, most of us will be in situations that have the potential for criminal acts, and we will be expected to take appropriate measures to minimize participant risk. There are things we can do.

Try to prevent crime. Obviously, it is much better to prevent crimes than to deal with them after they have occurred. Assume that you are a ranger at a state desert park and that you have law enforcement authority. A group of off-road vehicles (four-wheel drive jeeps and pickups) has pulled into a group campground area, and the drivers and riders have set up their tents and camps. Several of the pickups are carrying trail bikes (motorcycles designed for off-road use). Most of the area in the park is closed to motorized use. Except in a few areas, vehicles are restricted to established roads. Signs are posted informing the public of the restrictions.

You probably would assume, correctly, that in this situation a problem could occur. If so, you have two alternatives: You could wait until someone drives into a restricted area and then issue a citation. Or you could visit the group before a violation occurs. You might approach the group, welcome them to the area, remind them of the restrictions, and point out the area where off-road vehicle use is permitted. You would be making certain that they are aware of the park's regulations, and you would be seeking their cooperation. You would be making contact in a positive, nonthreatening way.

This approach would not guarantee that the group will follow park regulations. They might drive their vehicles into restricted areas, and you might have to take corrective action. But it will be much easier, less hazardous, and probably less costly in terms of personnel time to prevent violations and disruptive behavior if you can do so. Making contact also lets the group know of your presence. Frequently, that is sufficient encouragement to follow regulations. If you are equipped with a radio, your presence also informs users, by inference and nonverbally, that you are able to request assistance if needed. Sometimes, users of park and recreation areas can be encouraged to police themselves. This might be especially possible if you can contact the leader or spokesperson of a group. Explaining your position and asking for support might lead to positive action.

These kinds of actions are designed to defuse problems before they occur. They are facilitated if you can develop the attitude that most users come to parks to have a good time. Relatively few come looking for trouble. Often, problems that occur do so because people lack knowledge or because their activities are in conflict with the activities of other people. If you can learn as much as possible about what users want and expect, you have a better opportunity to work with them on a positive basis.

Assume the same desert park situation. Suppose a group of young adults had set up camp in the campground and were playing loud music on a portable stereo set. Is this a legitimate activity? By whose standards can it be judged? It may or may not be appropriate in a park setting. But it probably is bothering other, older campers in the area; and you have a potential conflict situation with which to contend. By prohibiting the music, you may be failing to meet the needs of the younger group. Maybe you can get them to move to an unoccupied area in another part of the park, where their activities will not disrupt other campers. If so, you have defused a problem and still allowed users to have enjoyable experiences.

It would be unrealistic to think that you can prevent all problems or to assume that all users will respond positively to you. However, it is better to try the positive approach initially and to follow up with corrective measures as needed. If you initially assume that an individual or group is certain to cause problems, your own behavior may increase chances that the problem will occur. This is the self-fulfilling prophecy mentioned in Chapter 4. You do not need to ignore cues. You can be alert and sensitive to the possibility of a problem without assuming automatically that one will occur.

In the illustration of the desert park, the ranger had law enforcement authority. Most personnel will not. The point of the example still is valid. If you can make contact with users, increase your visibility, and approach them positively, you may be able to prevent some problems that would otherwise occur.

Keep records.   You should keep records on criminal and disruptive acts that occur in the areas for which you are responsible. If possible, this should be done with police assistance. This may help to identify those locations and times when risks to participants are higher. If patterns of criminal behavior or conflicts can be established, security measures can be strengthened in those locations at the appropriate times. If, for example, other recent robberies had occurred in the trailer camping area where the visitor lost a camera, extra security measures could have been taken. These could be focused more specifically, if the thefts tended to occur on certain days or certain times.

Participants or visitors should be encouraged to report offenses. As indicated earlier, many crimes in park and recreation settings go unreported. Connors suggested some reasons for this: People often don't know to whom they should report incidents; the means for reporting (telephones or direct contact) often are not available; and lack of coordination among law enforcement agencies sometimes results in information about crimes in parks not being transmitted to park personnel.[89] Sometimes visitors do not report problems, especially thefts, because they attribute them to their own negligence.[90] While we want to encourage visitors to report problems, we must take care in doing so. We do want visitors to be sufficiently aware of possible crimes, to take reasonable precautions, and to report any problems they have. But we do not want to so emphasize these possibilities that visitors become overconcerned. Their preoccupation with personal safety or property loss can discourage park use completely, or so inhibit it that their enjoyment is minimized. To make people aware but not overconcerned is a task that requires sensitivity, but it is one that recreation and park personnel should attempt.

Consult with local authorities. Probably the most important step that you can take to increase security, in those agencies that do not employ regular law enforcement personnel, is to consult with the local police or sheriff's department. This brings expert judgment to bear upon the agency's security problems. It also benefits law enforcement personnel, since they probably will be called to handle problems that continue to arise. Their work is made easier if problems can be minimized or prevented.

Police should be notified, for example, if events are being held at which problems might occur. Examples would be events that attract large crowds or that bring groups together where hostilities might be sparked. These characteristics sometimes are present at such events as dances that are attended by adolescents from different high schools or towns, athletic events where rivalries have been running high, or mass entertainment of various kinds.

Sometimes, additional staff are required in an area. They serve at least two purposes in terms of security. First, they are available to observe and report disruptive behavior or to cope with it if it is within the range of their capacities. Second, as suggested earlier, their visible presence may deter some criminal acts.

Know traffic patterns. Another element in security is related to traffic patterns (foot or vehicular) in a park or recreation facility. We should know how visitors get access to and leave our areas. By observing these points, we can obtain useful information about how many visitors are in the area and see any unusual entry or exit behaviors. At times, it may be advisable to lock certain areas (with due regard for exit needs). Limiting vehicular access to park areas can reduce vandalism and other disruptive acts. The ability to visually supervise other locations in an area contributes to security. Sometimes, shrubbery can be trimmed or lights can be placed to facilitate observation.

Know how to call police. Procedures for requesting assistance from local law enforcement personnel should be understood clearly by agency staff members. While it is difficult to define, there may be a stigma against calling the police. Staff members might see it as a sign of weakness, as an admission that they cannot handle the problem. Certainly, an agency does not want staff members calling for assistance unnecessarily. Nor do police want to be responding to unwarranted calls. However, if you are going to make an error, it will be better to err by requesting help when it is not needed. This is far better than waiting until it is too late or until a situation is out of control or someone has been harmed.

As suggested in Chapter 8, in the discussion on referrals, communication with other agencies (in this case, the police department or sheriff's office) is facilitated by prior positive contacts. It is useful for agency staff members who might be requesting assistance to get to know some of the officers in the law enforcement agency before they find themselves making an emergency call. These informal contacts help both agency staff and police to function more effectively under stress conditions.

In some recreation and park situations, radios can be useful for contacting law enforcement agencies directly or for calling some other central base station and requesting that information be relayed to proper authorities.

Protect yourself.   In any situation where criminal or violent behavior is a possibility, you need to think of your own safety as a staff member. This is especially important if you have not been trained in law enforcement techniques. You do need to protect the participants for whom you are responsible, but good judgment is needed. If you exceed your capabilities and become a victim yourself, your usefulness to others probably will be over. Use common sense.

The specific security measures taken by any leisure service agency depend upon the specific circumstances. A variety of different methods was reported by Kraus in the studies mentioned earlier.

> Respondents described a wide variety of efforts designed to improve safety or control vandalism, ranging from new designs and building techniques and fixed, vandal-proof equipment to the use of security alarm systems and the establishment of park ranger patrols. In some cases, departments were closing parks earlier or closing certain park areas. In others they had eliminated the use of difficult-to-control restrooms. One department was producing a "vandalism awareness" film for use in public schools, and another was considering the use of "rent-a-dog" guards in key facilities.[91]

Kraus noted that departments generally reported "little success in this area."[92]

Disruptive Behavior and Staff Responses.   A criminal or violent act is a type of behavior. It is goal directed: The criminal has a purpose (or purposes) in mind, defines a "plan" for achieving his purpose, and engages in the overt behavior that he believes will lead to the goal. The elements of behavior and the generalizations described in Chapter 3 apply also to disruptive or antisocial behavior.

A staff member's response also is behavior. In the camera theft incident described earlier, assume that a park ranger was notified immediately following the crime. Several different but related goals would then motivate his behavior. He would want to see that the injured victim of the crime was cared for; he would want to initiate actions to apprehend the thief; and he would want to strengthen or modify existing procedures for protecting visitors. For each of these goals, he would choose different plans and select appropriate responses, as described in Chapter 3.

A general concept of the interactions between a disruptive act and staff actions taken in response to it can be defined. A criminal or violent act exists over time. That is, the act itself is usually preceded by other behaviors. To an experienced observer, these antecedent behaviors can provide cues to the later acts of crime or violence. For example, assume that a small group of adolescents is grouped around two cars parked in front of a recreation center. A fight erupts between two of the teen-agers. Before the first blow is struck, there probably will be several cues that a fight is likely. These include the words exchanged between the two individuals, changes in the body positions of the two, and changes in the general behaviors of the other teens who are in the immediate area.

Another example might be drawn from the camera theft illustration. Prior to breaking into the car, the person who committed the act may have been in the area observing the car and the actions of the older adult. An experienced observer might have noted something unusual about the individual's behavior. This possibility, of course, can be overstated. Often suspicious behavior is not that at all. And there is need to guard against the myth that you can tell a criminal by his or her appearance. However, cues may be evident that would alert an observer to possible problems.

The roots of problem behaviors for any individual may go back to such things as relationships with parents or peers, environmental influences, or other past experiences. The discussion here is concerned only with those antecedent behaviors that are observable.

At some point, the problem itself occurs; the fight starts, the camera is stolen. If the antecedent cues are strong enough that the observer is convinced a problem will occur, preventive action can be taken. If you act before you are convinced clearly that a problem is developing you may be wasting your time, and if your actions are inappropriate you create negative feelings on the part of those toward whom the action is directed. If you wait too long, prevention may not be possible and corrective action will have to be taken. As suggested earlier, it is preferable to prevent problems; and it is much better to err in the direction of caution. Usually, the earlier that action is taken, the easier it is to prevent or solve problems. However, it is possible to respond too rapidly on the basis of less-than-adequate evidence. Once the problem erupts, it then becomes necessary to take corrective action. This assumes that the problem is severe enough that something must be done about it. Both preventive and corrective actions will require some time to take effect; a reduction in the negative behavior may be nearly instantaneous or it may not be apparent for an extended period of time.

Following preventive or corrective action, there may be a period of adjustments or residual effects. In the teen disturbance illustration, the fight might have been prevented by the intervention of the center director. Or, if it had already started, the director might have stopped it. In either case, there would be a period immediately following the action during which time other supportive actions might be required. The teens might be taken to the director's office, individually or together, for a discussion of the events leading to the problem. Parents might be called and informed of the situation. The crowd that assembled might have to be dispersed. The specific actions depend upon the situation, as assessed by the director.

SUMMARY

Recreation and park personnel provide leisure opportunities for people. To do so, they interact with those whom they are attempting to serve using a variety of different resources. These include money, physical facilities and supplies, and legal authority. They function also within the framework of legal restraints.

Financial resources are required if an agency is to provide leisure services. These resources come from a variety of sources, depending on the agency: tax revenues, membership fees, voluntary contributions, and expenditures for services made by participants. Systematic and effective use of these revenues depends on using budgets and following appropriate expenditure procedures. Staff members should become familiar with budgets and procedures used in their respective agencies. They should know what funds are available to them, how these funds can be expended, and how they can participate in developing future budgets.

Physical resources such as parks and recreation centers also are used by personnel. One primary responsibility they have is providing for safe use. Accidents can be caused by natural hazards in the environment, the kinds of facilities developed by agencies, the condition of these facilities, the types of activities participants engage in, and the quality and extent of supervision provided. Staff members can minimize the possibility of accidents by identifying and correcting potential hazards, following proper maintenance procedures, and considering the safety of users in the design of new facilities. Safe use can also be promoted through educational efforts and through appropriate regulation of participant behavior. Procedures should be established for what to do if accidents occur.

And even with conscientious attention, accidents will occur. When they do, leisure service agencies and personnel may be held liable. Any staff member can be sued. Whether a judgment of negligence will be made against a staff member or an agency will depend upon whether the staff member behaved as a reasonably prudent, professionally trained person would, under the circumstances. The best protection against being held liable for injuries or damages to another person is to know clearly what your responsibilities are and to carry these out as faithfully as possible. You should behave so that your actions, or failures to act, do not cause accidents. You should also consider having personal liability insurance coverage in addition to any insurance carried by the agency.

Another threat to the safe use of recreation facilities is the possibility of criminal and violent acts. Both participants and staff members may become victims of such acts. The most common are property offenses, such as burglary and vandalism; however, offenses against persons also occur. Some agencies employ individuals who are trained and have authority as police officers. Most agencies, however, rely on support from police departments and sheriffs' offices. Agencies should establish relationships with these agencies and consult with them about security measures to reduce risks to participants and staff. They should also keep records of criminal or violent acts that occur at agency facilities. Patterns might be established from these records that would enable more effective security measures to be taken. These measures include assigning additional staff to potential trouble spots, knowing traffic patterns at recreation facilities, observing exit and entry points, knowing how to request police assistance, and informing law enforcement agencies when events are held at which disruptive behavior is likely to occur. Along with a concern for participants, recreation and park personnel should be alert to possible risks to themselves. They should not attempt to handle situations that are beyond their capabilities.

Disruptive behavior, and staff responses to it, can be thought of as a sequence of behaviors, beginning with the first evidence of the problem and ending with the solution. In the initial stages, preventive action can be taken. After a point, prevention is no longer possible and corrective action must be initiated. In some problems, the time period between the first evidences and the need for corrective action is very short; in others, the problem develops more slowly.

REVIEW QUESTIONS

9-1 What basic kinds of budgets are evident in our field? What different components do these usually include?

9-2 In what way is a budget like a plan?

9-3 What factors or conditions are potential contributors to accidents in recreation and park settings?

9-4 In general, how can accident potentials be minimized? That is, what can leisure service personnel do to reduce risk to participants or users?

9-5 What is liability? What is negligence? What conditions are necessary for negligence to be charged against staff members?

9-6 In general, what can staff members do to reduce the possibilities that participants will become victims of crime?

TO DO

9-A Select some group (a real one in your community or a hypothetical one). It could be a group of senior citizens, adults working at an industrial plant, residents at a facility for the developmentally disabled, students in an environmental education program, or any other group. For this group, plan a recreation event that lasts no more than one day. Develop a budget for the event. Consider needed staff time, equipment and supplies, transportation (if any), publicity and promotion, and any other probable expenses. Assume that you had to cover all of these expenses by charging a fee for the event. How large would the fee have to be? Is this a realistic amount considering the group involved?

9-B Visit a playground, park, recreation center, or other leisure service facility. As you look around, make a list of the things you would want to check, for safety purposes, if you were responsible for the facility. Why would you want to check each (that is, what potential hazard is involved)? How often would you want to check each? What would you be looking for, specifically?

If you are taking a class related to this topic, visit the facility with one or two other students. Make your observations independently. Then, compare notes to see where you overlap in your observations or where one of you might have missed something.

9-C   Interview a representative from an insurance company in your community. Find out what you can about liability insurance. What kinds are available for individuals? What coverages are provided? What do they cost?

9-D   Read a local newspaper for several days, giving particular attention to the reporting of crimes. Notice the nature of the crime, where it happened, characteristics of the victim, and other related information. Did any of these occur in leisure settings? Could they have occurred at a recreation and park facility? If so, can you think of anything that could have been done to prevent the crimes or to avoid similar crimes in the future?

END NOTES

1. Suggestions in this section are adapted from "Competency Assessment Processes in Recreation Curricula," 1973–74. Report filed at the Office of the Chancellor, California State University, Long Beach, California, pp. 136–39.

2. Richard G. Kraus and Joseph E. Curtis, *Creative Administration in Recreation and Parks* 2nd ed. (St. Louis: The C. V. Mosby Company, 1977), p. 201.

3. Kraus and Curtis, *Creative Administration in Recreation and Parks*, p. 201.

4. Christopher R. Edginton and John G. Williams, *Productive Management of Leisure Service Organizations: A Behavioral Approach* (New York: John Wiley & Sons, Inc., 1978), pp. 299–310.

5. For discussions of criteria for defining capital outlay items (or properties) see Kraus and Curtis, *Creative Administration in Recreation and Parks*, pp. 205–6; Edginton and Williams, *Productive Management of Leisure Service Organizations*, p. 303; and Dennis R. Howard and John L. Crompton, *Financing, Managing and Marketing Recreation & Park Resources* (Dubuque, Iowa: William C. Brown Company Publishers, 1980), p. 280.

6. National Committee on Governmental Accounting, *Governmental Accounting, Auditing, and Financial Reporting* (Chicago: Municipal Finance Officers Association of the United States and Canada, 1968), p. 191.

7. See Kraus and Curtis, *Creative Administration in Recreation and Parks*, pp. 204–5; Edginton and Williams, *Productive Management of Leisure Service Organizations*, pp. 305–10; and John Gundersdorf, "Management and Financial Controls," in Wayne F. Anderson, Bernard J. Frieden, and Michael J. Murphy, *Managing Human Services* (Washington, D.C.: The International City Management Association, 1977), pp. 274–75.

8. Gundersdorf, "Management and Financial Controls," p. 275.

9. For examples, see Howard and Crompton, *Financing, Managing and Marketing Recreation & Park Resources*, pp. 290–93; and Thomas I. Hines, *Budgeting for Public Parks and Recreation* rev. ed. (Arlington, Va.: The National Recreation and Park Association, 1974), pp. 12–13.

10. Edginton and Williams, *Productive Management of Leisure Service Organizations*, p. 317.

11. Hines, *Budgeting for Public Parks and Recreation*, p. 17.

12. National Committee on Governmental Accounting, *Governmental Accounting, Auditing, and Financial Reporting*, p. 166.

13. This illustration is based on a general purchasing procedure commonly used in recreation and park agencies, outlined by J. D. Schwarz, instructor of recreation and park finance classes at California State University, Chico; June, 1981.

14. Hines, *Budgeting for Public Parks and Recreation*, p. 25.

15. Ibid., p. 26.

16. Richard Kraus, "Urban Recreation: A Greatly Exaggerated Demise," *Parks & Recreation* 16, no. 7 (July 1981): 28.

17. Thomas I. Hines, *Fees and Charges* rev. ed. (Arlington, Va.: National Recreation and Park Association, 1974), p. 28.

18. Howard and Crompton, *Financing, Managing and Marketing Recreation & Park Resources*, pp. 414–18.

19. Ibid., p. 416.

20. Kraus, "Urban Recreation: A Greatly Exaggerated Demise," p. 28.

21. Howard and Crompton, *Financing, Managing and Marketing Recreation & Park Resources*, pp. 417–18.

22. Ibid., pp. 407–10.

23. Ibid., pp. 428–46.

24. Hines, *Fees and Charges*, pp. 30–31.

25. James P. Negley, "Are You Liable?," *California Parks & Recreation* 35, no. 2 (June/July, 1979):14.

26. Reported by George F. Nickolaus, "Liability in Parks and Recreation," *Parks & Recreation* 16, no. 2 (February 1980): 56.

27. Diana R. Dunn and John M. Gulbis, "The Risk Revolution," *Parks & Recreation* 11, no. 8 (August 1976): 14.

28. Alan Jubenville, *Outdoor Recreation Management* (Philadelphia: W. B. Saunders Company, 1978), pp. 156–59.

29. Jubenville, *Outdoor Recreation Management*, p. 150.

30. Janna Rankin, "Legal Risks and Bold Programming," *Parks & Recreation* 12, no. 7 (July 1977): 48.

31. Jubenville, *Outdoor Recreation Management*, pp. 221–23.

32. Betty van der Smissen, *Legal Liability of Cities and Schools for Injuries in Recreation and Parks* (Cincinnati: The W. H. Anderson Company, 1968), pp. 208–9.

33. Van der Smissen, *Legal Liability of Cities and Schools for Injuries in Recreation and Parks*, pp. 50–51.

34. Negley, "Are You Liable?," p. 14.

35. Frank Guadagnolo, "Legal Aspects of Managing Recreation and Park Agencies," in Howard and Crompton, *Financing, Managing and Marketing Recreation & Park Resources*, p. 178.

36. Van der Smissen, *Legal Liability of Cities and Schools for Injuries in Recreation and Parks*, p. 71.

37. Guadagnolo, "Legal Aspects of Managing Recreation and Park Agencies," in Howard and Crompton, *Financing, Managing and Marketing Recreation & Park Resources*, p. 171.

38. Van der Smissen, pp. 1–6.

39. Ibid., pp. 6–8.

40. Ibid., p. 34.

41. Guadagnolo, "Legal Aspects of Managing Recreation and Park Agencies," in Howard and Crompton, *Financing, Managing and Marketing Recreation & Park Resources,* p. 171.

42. Van der Smissen, *Legal Liability of Cities and Schools for Injuries in Recreation and Parks,* p. iv.

43. Nickolaus, "Liability in Parks and Recreation," p. 54.

44. Van der Smissen, *Legal Liability of Cities and Schools for Injuries in Recreation and Parks,* p. 51.

45. Rankin, "Legal Risks and Bold Programming," p. 48.

46. William L. Prosser, *Handbook of the Law of Torts* (St. Paul, Minn.: West Publishing Company, 1941), p. 8, cited in van der Smissen, *Legal Liability of Cities and Schools for Injuries in Recreation and Parks,* pp. 51–52; also see: Guadagnolo, "Legal Aspects of Managing Recreation and Park Agencies," in Howard and Crompton, *Financing, Managing and Marketing Recreation & Park Resources,* pp. 172–74; and Rankin, "Legal Risks and Bold Programming," p. 48.

47. Guadagnolo, "Legal Aspects of Managing Recreation and Park Agencies," in Howard and Crompton, *Financing, Managing and Marketing Recreation & Park Resources,* p. 172; van der Smissen, *Legal Liability of Cities and Schools for Injuries in Recreation and Parks,* p. 80.

48. Rankin, "Legal Risks and Bold Programming," p. 48.

49. Guadagnolo, "Legal Aspects of Managing Recreation and Park Agencies," in Howard and Crompton, *Financing, Managing and Marketing Recreation & Park Resources,* p. 173.

50. Douglas M. Knudson, *Outdoor Recreation* (New York: Macmillan Publishing Co., Inc., 1980), p. 583.

51. Knudson, *Outdoor Recreation,* p. 583.

52. Guadagnolo, "Legal Aspects of Managing Recreation and Park Agencies," in Howard and Crompton, *Financing, Managing and Marketing Recreation & Park Resources,* pp. 172–73.

53. Ibid., pp. 172–173; Knudson, *Outdoor Recreation,* pp. 583–84.

54. Van der Smissen, *Legal Liability of Cities and Schools for Injuries in Recreation and Parks,* pp. 92–93.

55. Rankin, "Legal Risks and Bold Programming," p. 67.

56. Guadagnolo, "Legal Aspects of Managing Recreation and Park Agencies," in Howard and Crompton, *Financing, Managing and Marketing Recreation & Park Resources,* p. 173.

57. Van der Smissen, *Legal Liability of Cities and Schools for Injuries in Recreation and Parks,* pp. 86–92.

58. Ibid., p. 88.

59. Ibid., pp. 78–81.

60. Ibid., pp. 94–100.

61. Guadagnolo, "Legal Aspects of Managing Recreation and Park Agencies," in Howard and Crompton, *Financing, Managing and Marketing Recreation & Park Resources,* p. 174.

62. Van der Smissen, *Legal Liability of Cities and Schools for Injuries in Recreation and Parks,* p. 92.

63. Ibid., p. 94.

64. Albert M. Farina, "Accident Liability: What Is Your Legal Responsibility?," *Parks & Recreation* 14, no. 3 (March 1979): 31.

65. Rankin, "Legal Risks and Bold Programming," p. 69.

66. Ibid., p. 68.

67. Nicholaus, "Liability in Parks and Recreation," p. 56.

68. Guadagnolo, "Legal Aspects of Managing Recreation and Park Agencies," in Howard and Crompton, *Financing, Managing and Marketing Recreation & Park Resources,* p. 178.

69. Ibid., p. 177.

70. Van der Smissen, *Legal Liability of Cities and Schools for Injuries in Recreation and Parks,* p. 96.

71. Rankin, "Legal Risks and Bold Programming," p. 68.

72. Edward F. Connors III, "Public Safety in Park and Recreation Settings," *Parks & Recreation* 11, no. 1 (January 1976): 20.

73. Theresa N. Westover, Theodore B. Flickinger, and Michael Chubb, "Crime and Law Enforcement," *Parks & Recreation* 15, no. 8 (August 1980): 32.

74. Westover, Flickinger, and Chubb, "Crime and Law Enforcement," p. 32.

75. Ibid., p. 32.

76. Connors, "Public Safety in Park and Recreation Settings," pp. 20–21.

77. Westover, Flickinger, and Chubb, "Crime and Law Enforcement," p. 29.

78. Ibid., p. 30.

79. *Recreation Needs in California: Report to the Legislature on the Statewide Recreation Needs Analysis* (Sacramento, California: State of California Department of Parks and Recreation, 1982) p. 25.

80. Connors, "Public Safety in Park and Recreation Settings," p. 21.

81. Ibid., p. 21.

82. Westover, Flickinger, and Chubb, "Crime and Law Enforcement," p. 30.

83. Connors, "Public Safety in Park and Recreation Settings," p. 21.

84. Ibid., p. 21.

85. Kraus, "Urban Recreation: A Greatly Exaggerated Demise," p. 29.

86. Ibid., p. 28.

87. This section is based, in part, on suggestions made by U. F. (John) Bullerjahn, Chief of Police, City of Chico (California), and Clifford Wade, Manager II, Peace Officer Standards and Training Coordinator, Department of Parks and Recreation, State of California; July, 1981.

88. Abraham H. Maslow, "A Theory of Human Motivation," *Psychological Review* 50, no. 4 (July 1943): 370–96.

89. Connors, "Public Safety in Park and Recreation Settings," pp. 20–21.

90. Westover, Flickinger, and Chubb, "Crime and Law Enforcement," p. 30.

91. Kraus, "Urban Recreation: A Greatly Exaggerated Demise," p. 29.

92. Ibid., p. 30.

chapter 10

Working with Human Resources

PREVIEW

The resources with which recreation and park personnel work include other staff members. These are the human resources through which agency objectives are met and through which leisure services are provided.

The basic process in working with staff resources is supervision. Chapter 10 will begin by examining a concept of supervision, as a process. Then, we will review those activities that personnel use in supervising other staff members. These will be followed by a discussion of the factors that contribute to effective supervision.

The human resources involved in recreation and park agencies include paid staff members and volunteers. This chapter will consider the types of recreation and park agencies that utilize volunteers, the kinds of responsibilities they carry out, and the characteristics of volunteers. Motivations for volunteering will be examined. The benefits of volunteering, to the agency and the individual, will be discussed; and potential problem areas will be identified. Finally, several suggestions for working with volunteers will be presented.

The head recreation therapist (supervisor) in a large psychiatric hospital was meeting with a member of his staff. The staff member had been employed in the hospital's recreation therapy unit for three years. The head therapist and the staff member were reviewing the member's performance evaluation for the previous year. The supervisor had just completed the evaluation, and was explaining his comments. The staff member was reacting to the evaluation and to the supervisor's explanation. It was a positive interchange—on all but a few aspects, the staff member's performance had improved over the previous evaluation. The supervisor and the therapist then moved into a discussion of how he could improve these aspects of his performance in the coming months.

Following the conference with the staff member, the head therapist drove across town to the local community college. He was scheduled to speak to one of the recreation classes about the general topic of recreation in a psychiatric institution. He also wanted to discuss the role of volunteers in recreation therapy, and he hoped to interest some of the students in volunteering to work at the hospital.

As indicated in the last chapter, paid and volunteer staff members are resources with which recreation and park personnel work. These are the human resources that enable leisure opportunities to be made available. The recreation therapy program at the psychiatric hospital could not be provided for patients without staff members to do the necessary planning and to provide the necessary leadership. The quality of the program depends upon how well the therapists function. Therefore, the head therapist, like all recreation and park personnel who are responsible for the work of others, is concerned about effective use of staff members.

Effective use of staff members (the human resources with whom we work) involves the process of supervision. This process is used by anyone in an organization who is responsible for the work of other people.

A CONCEPT OF SUPERVISION

There is a temptation to think of supervision solely in terms of seeing that employees do not make mistakes and that they carry out their work at acceptable levels. However, this is an extremely limited concept of supervision. Williamson presented a concept of the process that is much broader.

> Supervision is a dynamic enabling process by which individual workers who have a direct responsibility for carrying out some part of the agency's program plans are helped by a designated staff member to make the best use of their knowledge and skill, and to improve their abilities so that they do their jobs more effectively and with increasing satisfaction to themselves and to the agency.[1]

This concept emphasizes the primary objective of supervision, which is to make the agency's services more effective by helping staff members become more effective. Supervision is seen as an *enabling* process—a process that enables workers to become more effective. It recognizes that supervision is best when it leads to employee satisfaction as well as agency satisfaction.

Williamson's concept is very appropriate for the field of recreation and parks. It is consistent with a philosophy that values the integrity of persons and their personal growth. If we expect members of our staffs to work with people in humanistic ways, then our supervision of those staff members should be humanistic. The supervisor should model the behavior expected of staff members who work directly with users of the agency's services. Williamson's concept recognizes that agency objectives are met largely through staff members. Therefore, whatever helps them to be more effective will contribute to the effectiveness of services. For that reason, supervision is largely an educational process. It enables workers to learn how to be more effective.

Williamson's concept is also appropriate because of the nature of those who provide direct services in recreation and parks, and because of the settings in which they work. Our field uses relatively large numbers of part-time, or seasonal, workers and volunteers. Hoff noted the prevalence of part-time recreation personnel and reasons for their use, as revealed in a 1976 survey.

> With part-time employees promising budget savings in light of their lower wages, fewer benefits, and flexible scheduling opportunities, only 15 percent of the surveyed cities employed full-time activity specialists and only 13 percent employed recreation program leaders on a full-time basis.[2]

He commented on the special problem this situation raises for supervisors.

> Thus at the face-to-face level of programs and services, where our philosophies and goals are actualized, we are often counting on people who may be only partially educated and experienced in recreation.[3]

Hoff's comments relate particularly to recreation activity leadership. However, the prevalence of part-time personnel is evident also in other aspects of the field. For example, park agencies employ relatively high numbers of seasonal workers. And volunteers are used widely throughout the field of recreation and parks. For such persons, supervision that helps them to learn appropriate skills, knowledges, and attitudes will contribute most to their effectiveness.

There is less opportunity for direct, on-site supervision in recreation and parks than in some fields. There is some, of course. For example, a swimming pool manager directly supervises the instructors or guards who are on duty at the time the manager also is on duty. The head therapist might be on some wards together with volunteers when they are working with patients; if so, he would provide direct supervision at those times. However, recreation and park personnel often work in situations where direct observation by the supervisor is impractical or impossible. Sometimes, the supervisor and a staff member are separated geographically; for example, a supervisor of centers and playgrounds may have an office in a central location, and the various center and playground directors all may be at different specific sites. Or there may be separations in time. The manager of the pool might leave work at five P.M., but the guards for the evening recreational swim period may be on duty until the pool closes at 9 P.M. In such situations, it is advisable to designate someone to be in charge when the supervisor is not present. Even so, when staff members are expected to work with relatively little direct supervision, it is necessary that they know what to do, and that they have appropriate confidence in their abilities to do it. An educational approach to supervision helps to develop competency and confidence.

WHAT DO SUPERVISORS DO?

In Chapter 1 it was noted that typically there are three levels of responsibility in most recreation and park agencies: administrative, supervisory, and functional. The process of supervision is used at all three of these levels. It is used by any staff member who has responsibility for the effectiveness of other staff members. The park supervisor supervises the work of maintenance workers, the preschool director supervises the teen-age aides, the head therapist supervises the work of other therapists and volunteers. The swimming pool manager supervises the work of guards and instructors. They all use supervision as a process. In this section on using staff resources, the term *supervisor* will be used to designate any staff member who uses supervisory processes.

Teaching and Leading. Teaching is a big part of supervision. At times, the instruction is on a one-to-one basis; at other times, the supervisor teaches in a group. Supervisors also use leadership processes. In general, leadership is the act of influencing others to engage in certain behaviors or to achieve certain goals. When a supervisor works with staff members in the planning and implementing of leisure services, different staff members must carry out different responsibilities and must work together to achieve the overall goal. The supervisor influences these behaviors through leadership.

Supervision involves several other major responsibilities. All of these fit within the concept of supervision as an enabling process.

Selection of Staff. Assume the situation with the park supervisor and the maintenance workers described in the last chapter. At some point, the groundskeepers had to be recruited, screened, selected, and employed. This process sometimes is the direct responsibility of the supervisor; in most cases, the supervisor is involved in the process one way or another. An important element in this process is the *written job description*.[4] The job description usually gives the title of the position, the requirements (in terms of education and experience, or knowledges and abilities), and the duties. The job description may be used to announce the position and recruit applicants. Perhaps its most important function is to inform the person who is to carry out the responsibilities of the position what those duties are. It serves as a framework for providing needed training, and it becomes the basis for making later evaluations. Workers need to know what is expected of them, and on what factors their performances will be judged. A well-written job description enables the worker to meet agency expectations more effectively.

In-service Training. Once the groundskeepers had been recruited, it was necessary to provide appropriate in-service training. Van Dersal described four types of training undertaken by supervisors: (1) orientation to the job, (2) training related specifically to the position for which the employee was selected, (3) training to keep the worker up to date, and (4) general career development.[5] These are broad types found in both business and governmental settings, and they are applicable to recreation and park agencies. The groundskeepers needed to be given an orientation to their jobs, to the structure and policies of the park department, to the other staff with whom they will be working, and to the ways in which their work fits into the overall organization. This orientation would be given individually if each person joined the department at a different time; or a group orientation would be conducted if several were employed at one time.

Career development would be concerned with enabling the worker to develop abilities that could lead to greater responsibilities. This might involve opportunities to attend special classes or workshops, or the encouragement to complete recommended readings. The other two types—job training and training to maintain or refresh proficiencies—are directly related to the worker's position. The supervisor might provide this instruction individually or in groups, probably in both. The instruction would be ongoing. Some of it would occur in scheduled meetings or classes; while some teaching would be woven into the day-by-day interactions between the supervisor and staff members.

Scheduling Staff. Another supervisory responsibility is the scheduling of work assignments for staff members. In some situations, staff members are provided with a general framework within which they have considerable freedom to plan their own schedules. For example, a supervisor of playgrounds and centers may outline, for staff, the hours when the various individual facilities will be open, the general program responsibilities at each site, dates when overall staff meetings will be held, when certain reports are due, and the budgets that are available to each playground or center director. Within this framework, the staff at each site may develop its own working schedule, subject to the approval of the supervisor. In other situations, the supervisor might define work schedules directly.

Generally, involving staff members in decisions about their work leads to better morale. The park supervisor meets with the groundskeepers at the beginning of each week to review any areas needing special attention because of heavier use than expected or unusual weather conditions. Based on this information, plus his general knowledge of the turfed and landscaped areas in the city and the work capacities of his staff, he makes assignments for the week. Staff members have the opportunity to comment or raise questions if they wish to do so. To make realistic work assignments, the supervisor has to know how much time is required, on the average, to complete certain tasks—for example, the amount of time required to mow an acre of grass using the department's gang mower.[6]

Evaluation. Most of the teaching efforts of the supervisor are intended to enhance staff members' effectiveness in carrying out their responsibilities in the agency. To plan the kinds of learning experiences that are needed, the supervisor must evaluate staff performance. The head therapist evaluates his staff members in various ways. He completes a hospital rating form for each therapist at set time periods, after six months for new employees and annually after that. He goes over these with each individual, pointing out strengths, as he perceives them, and areas where improvement is needed. Each staff member is asked to sign the rating, along with the supervisor. It then becomes part of the employee's personnel file. The supervisor also engages in on-going, informal evaluations of each staff member.[7] As he has opportunities to do so, he observes each therapist at work. Usually he holds an individual conference with the person afterward to discuss his impressions and to listen to the staff member's reactions and perceptions. This was the conference described at the beginning of the chapter. Conferences such as this are valuable opportunities for open communication.

The supervisor periodically reviews the work produced by staff members. In the case of the groundskeepers, the park supervisor checks the appearance of turf areas in the city parks and other city-owned landscaped areas. As he hears comments about the parks, from citizens, he notes them. As the head therapist visits with patients, he picks up their reactions to the activity program in the hospital. These sources of information help supervisors complete rating forms. These forms are reviewed when employees are being considered for promotion; and supervisors use them to help individual workers improve performance. They become the basis for planning future in-service training.

Providing Resources.   One aspect of enabling staff members to function efficiently is the provision of appropriate resources. The groundskeepers need dependable equipment, such as power edgers and mowers, if they are to carry out their duties with satisfaction to both themselves and the park department. They also need such things as fertilizers and pesticides. They need transportation for themselves and their equipment to the different park sites. The playground and center directors need part-time clerical help to type letters and reports and maintain files. The work of the therapists is expanded by volunteer assistants. In most situations, it is the responsibility of the supervisor to see that these resources are available.

Linking Administrative and Functional Levels.   Supervisors are the communication links between administrators and those workers who interact with the users of agency services, or who are the first line of the agency's service. In the example at the beginning of this chapter, the head therapist is the link between the therapists and the person to whom the supervisor reports, which in this case is the director of the hospital. This is not to say that all communication within the agency follows the lines of the formal organization. However, the supervisor has both responsibilities and opportunities for interpreting agency policies and other relevant information from the administrative level to workers at the service level.

The communication channel flows the opposite direction, also. The supervisor passes along to management personnel information from the service providers that will help in the ongoing process of making administrative decisions. The head therapist picks up much information from his staff about patients and the reactions of their relatives who visit the hospital. He also knows how his staff members are responding to any changes in hospital policies. These data are important to efficient agency operation.

Not all information needs to be passed up and down the line; to do so would take unnecessary energy and time. One of the tasks of the supervisor is to judge what information to pass along. The flow of relevant data keeps communication lines open and functioning, minimizes the possibility of conflict, and makes it easier to deal with conflict when it does develop.

Directing, Controlling, and Taking Corrective Action. The concept of supervision as an enabling process assumes that workers want to be effective and productive. This assumption is in contrast to the notion that they will get by as easily as possible. These two assumptions are related directly to McGregor's "theory X and theory Y."[8] McGregor contended that there are two opposing sets of attitudes held by management personnel toward workers: One set sees staff members as disliking work and avoiding it when possible (theory X); the other set sees workers as desiring responsibility and as being willing to work with commitment and creativity under the right conditions (theory Y). Supervisors who assume that staff members dislike work give considerable attention to controlling and directing. Van Dersal summarized this view.

> In order to get people to work as well and hard as possible, management has to take a strong hand. It must direct people's activities, persuade them, reward them, punish them, control them.[9]

He noted that while this approach (theory X) is prevalent in business and government, there are significant advantages in basing management practices on the assumptions of theory Y.

> Where this is taking place, remarkable results are coming in. The people in the organization are being encouraged to develop and use their knowledge, skills, abilities, and imagination to help reach the objectives of the organization. They do this because the company's objectives are theirs also. And in working toward these objectives the people find deep satisfaction in their achievement.[10]

As indicated, theory Y, which assumes that staff members are interested and responsible, is most consistent with an enabling approach to supervision. It is consistent also with a humanistic philosophy. This does not mean, however, that supervisors should avoid giving directions and controlling the work of staff members.

Just as there are times when autocratic leadership is more effective than a democratic approach, there are times when the supervisor will need to give directions. When the requirements of the task are clear, and when they must be completed as defined, it is appropriate for the supervisor to provide clear directions. Under these conditions, staff members expect directions; if they are not given, the staff may become unnecessarily confused and frustrated.

Also, at times the performance of an individual staff member may call for discipline and corrective action. Suppose, for example, that one of the therapists had begun coming to work late. Assume that the head therapist had talked with her, had sought her perceptions about what was going on, and had explained the importance of getting to work on time. If the tardiness continued, the supervisor would have to take some kind of corrective action. The supervisor has options that range from giving the worker a reprimand, verbally or perhaps in writing, to discharging her from her position. In some work settings it is possible to use losses of certain privileges, fines, temporary layoffs or suspensions, or demotions.[11] It is likely that the supervisor's initial corrective action, after talking to the employee, would be a verbal reprimand. If this did not lead to the desired changes, more severe disciplinary measures might be taken.

Flippo provided a description of appropriate practices in taking disciplinary action.[12] When correction is required it should be handled in private, to avoid embarrassment and the creation of unnecessary hostility. The action should be taken as soon as possible after the need for it has been established. At the same time, the decision to take such action must be considered carefully. The worker should be told clearly why the action is being taken, and what he or she can do to correct the situation. And, of course, discipline should be fair and consistent. Individual workers may respond differently to different corrective measures, and the supervisor will be more effective if these differences are known and considered. However, taking different actions with different individuals for the same behavior may lead to employees feeling that the supervisor is biased or favors some workers over others.

Other Activities.   Both the head therapist and the park supervisor will carry out many other activities that enable their staff members to work with greater satisfaction to the agency and themselves. It is appropriate to mention two of these.

Planning, in the broad sense, is a major activity for most supervisors. The park supervisor had to plan the power edger workshop. He has to plan for seasonal changes in the deployment of the maintenance crew. He has to project (plan) budget needs for the coming year. The head therapist needed to plan a program of patient activities for the year, with detailed plans for each month. All of these activities facilitate staff work and contribute to staff effectiveness and efficiency.

To plan and carry out most departmental operations, appropriate records must be kept; and they must be filed or stored so as to be available when needed. The park supervisor needs to know such things as the performance ratings of staff members, the work schedules for prior months, the types and amounts of fertilizers and pesticides used and where and when they were applied, and the dates and other details of accidents that happened on park property. The head therapist needs information about the involvement of individual patients in past program activities. The need for ready access to relevant information calls for an effective record keeping and filing system.[13] Good judgment is needed in making decisions about the kinds of information to keep and the length of time for which it should be available in current files.

Remember that all of the activities engaged in by supervisors are justified primarily by their contributions to staff effectiveness in the delivery of quality leisure services.

EFFECTIVE SUPERVISION

Some people are more effective supervisors than others. They are able to enable their staff members to function more effectively; they can do the things supervisors do in such ways that agency goals and individual employee satisfactions are achieved more fully. Why is this? What are the differences between effective supervisors and ones who are less effective?

Since leadership and teaching are key elements in supervision, the factors that make leaders and teachers effective also will contribute to supervisory effectiveness. The ability to work with groups is another factor.

Basic to all supervision seems to be the ability to relate effectively to people.

> Human relations difficulties head most lists of supervisory failures. The supervisor has difficulty in getting along with his subordinates, fellow managers or his boss. This failure in human relationships is usually due to a lack of understanding of human behavior and needs and an inability to relate successfully with others.[14]

In Chapter 4, different aspects of interpersonal relationships were discussed. These are applicable to supervisory relationships. The things we know about evidencing empathy, giving nonthreatening feedback, disclosing our own feelings appropriately, and resolving conflicts can be useful in the interactions we have, as supervisors, with our staff members.

One particular dimension of the supervisor-staff member relationship is important to note. This is the ambivalence felt by the workers we supervise.

> One of the strange things about being a supervisor is that we have to learn that it is possible for our people to love us and hate us at the same time. Perhaps these words are too strong, but they identify the problems brought about by the phenomenon of "ambivalence."[15]

This phenomenon occurs because supervisors represent authority, and therefore might be seen as potential sources of restriction or punishment. They also represent sources of reward and security: They can give praise, recommend raises, and help to make work easier. Supervisors who are aware of the likely presence of staff member ambivalence, at some point in their relationships, will be in a better position to deal with it.

Staff morale is a major factor in staff effectiveness. The supervisor who can contribute to good morale will be more effective. Morale is the result of many work and nonwork-related conditions. Sessoms and Stevenson suggested that a very important element is the sense of accomplishment staff members feel; they observed that this is particularly true in fields such as recreation and parks.

> People like to feel they are needed and are making some contribution to the agency's goals. Financial rewards in many park and recreation agencies are not as great as they are in some other services; consequently a sense of accomplishment in what one is doing becomes more critical.[16]

The authors also identified such factors as rules and regulations that are appropriately related to policies and are evaluated regularly, the involvement of staff members in decision making, and personnel practices that are enforced fairly and equally as contributors to morale.

A study by Herzberg, Mausner, and Snyderman also indicated that a sense of achievement and recognition are important contributors to employee satisfaction.[17] They identified five factors that lead to people being satisfied with their work. Achievement was the factor most frequently mentioned by the respondents to the study. The other factors were recognition for work well done, the challenging and interesting nature of the work itself, the opportunity to accept and carry out responsibility, and chances for advancement. The authors identified five different "job-dissatisfying factors." These were ineffective management and policies, incompetent supervision, salary inequities, poor interpersonal relationships with supervisors, and inadequate work conditions. Again, supervisors who create conditions that lead to work satisfaction will add to their effectiveness.

Frost used a "critical incident" technique to study the effectiveness of first-line supervisors (those who supervise functional level personnel) in municipal recreation departments.[18] She collected reports of effective and ineffective supervisory incidents from 466 observers (recreation leaders, first-line supervisors, and second-line supervisors). From these, she distilled 1213 behaviors, which she grouped into categories and classes.

> At the class level of generalization, the greatest numbers of effective behaviors were reported in the following classes: "effective in training subordinates"; "effective in maintaining good interpersonal relations"; "effective in exerting dynamic leadership"; and "effective in allowing subordinates to participate in decisions and choices which concern them." The classes of ineffective behaviors containing the greatest number of behaviors were "ineffective in transmitting information"; "ineffective in disciplining, reprimanding and controlling subordinates and patrons"; "ineffective in exerting dynamic leadership"; and "ineffective in carrying out commitments."[19]

Frost's study underscores the importance of interpersonal relationships in effective supervisory behavior, and the contributions of leading and teaching to such behavior.

Perhaps the most influential contributors to supervisory effectiveness are the attitudes of the individual supervisor. If you place value in the staff members you supervise, if you recognize the potential contributions they can make, and if you see your role as one of enabling them to make those contributions, you will optimize your chances to be effective. Broadwell provided this useful summary.

> What have we said about our attitudes toward our subordinates? We have said that we must realize that they have a storehouse of brain power and experience for which the successful supervisor will find keys. . . . These are the same people that will determine to a large degree just how well we do when we are appraised, because our job is really one of getting the work done through them.[20]

EMPLOYMENT PRACTICES

There are some special considerations related to the employment and supervision of paid staff. These can be categorized together under the general term *employment practices*.[21] Included are such things as affirmative action guidelines, which relate to the employment of women and minority persons; employee rights in such areas as minimum pay, paid time off, and access to personnel files; types of personal work clothing and equipment supplied by the agency; and agency and staff participation in such programs as Workman's Compensation and Social Security insurance. Some of these programs and practices are mandated by law. Others are beneficial in developing and maintaining staff effectiveness and morale. It is the supervisor's responsibility to become familiar with those practices that are followed in the agency in which he or she is employed. Personnel regulations and employment practices defined by the federal and state governments change frequently. Supervisors should be certain that their understanding of related laws is current.

VOLUNTEERS IN LEISURE SERVICE AGENCIES

One special category of human resources includes the hundreds of thousands of volunteers who carry out various duties in all different types of recreation and park agencies. Volunteering—working in an unpaid capacity—is not unique to our field; it is a widespread phenomenon in the United States. For example, in 1974 approximately 37 million Americans volunteered their time to a broad diversity of organizations, carrying out a wide variety of responsibilities.[22] This figure was up from an estimated 21 million volunteers in 1965.[23] The range of volunteer responsibilities has expanded considerably in the past several years. Weinberg cited some examples.

> More and more volunteers are working in the most intimate areas of people's lives—birth control, abortion, drugs, counseling, therapy, rape, suicide prevention, child abuse. They are taking on the problems of a technological society—air, water and soil pollution; nutrition; the quality of education; the cultural environment.[24]

Swanson defined the types of assignments that are carried out by volunteers.[25] She identified 399 different jobs, in twelve different categories based broadly on the type of agency involved.

While volunteers work in many types of agencies, the leisure services field has utilized volunteers widely and for many years. Nonpaid staff workers have provided services from the beginning of the recreation movement, and through the years the numbers have increased. They work in such diverse settings as youth agencies, employee recreation programs, and hospitals and treatment centers. In 1975, 5,800 individuals volunteered an estimated 177,306 hours with the National Park Service. They did such things as providing assistance for disabled visitors, teaching outdoor skills, interpreting environmental features, and conducting historical research.[26] Millions of hours are also volunteered in municipal recreation and park departments. For example, Crawford indicated that in the Philadelphia Department of Recreation in 1975 approximately 20,000 individual volunteers gave service.[27] Howard and Crompton observed that 62,421 volunteers gave well over 850,000 hours in 1976–77 in Baltimore County, Maryland, and that in the first six months of 1978, 428,000 hours were donated to the Los Angeles Recreation and Parks Department by approximately 6,000 volunteers.[28]

Types of Volunteer Service.   The categories of volunteer roles defined by Graham and Klar are representative: administration and consultation, program activity leadership, and operational services.[29] The administrative category includes such roles as serving on a recreation and park commission, on a board of directors, or as a fundraiser. Activity leadership is working directly with participants in the various areas of the recreation program. Operational services is a broad category that involves activities such as clerical assistance, public information, and park maintenance. While not every volunteer position can be classified neatly into one of these categories, they do represent the general duties carried out by volunteers in leisure service agencies.

Who Volunteers?   In the past, the majority of volunteers tended to be white, middle-income females. Poor people, minority persons, and males were underrepresented in those volunteer jobs for which records were kept. That situation has changed.

> For many years the image of the volunteer . . . has been that of a middle-aged, middle-class woman with time on her hands. Today the public image is changing, slowly catching up with reality. According to the Census Bureau, 59 percent of all volunteers are women. Volunteers may be very young sixth graders tutoring first graders in reading and math. They may be old, eighty-year-old men and women working with retarded children. They are all ages between, all races, and come from every economic and social background.[30]

This diversity is reflected in recreation and parks. Senior citizens are serving in a variety of leisure settings, as are teen-agers, and even elementary-school children. An auto worker and an orthopedic surgeon help to coach a youth soccer team. A black social worker spends part of his free time developing a community theater group. A university student majoring in economics spends a summer leading nature hikes in a state park. Her major professor and academic advisor works weekends in the activity program at a nearby children's hospital.

Myths About Volunteers. Despite the widespread use of volunteers in leisure services and in many other fields, there are some inaccurate beliefs and attitudes about them that are counterproductive. Naylor identified several of these "myths."[31]

One of the myths is that volunteers are a source of "free help"—that since volunteers work without pay, no agency funds need be expended. The fallacy of this attitude is that volunteers, like other staff members, require supervision; they need training, supplies, and most of the other considerations required by paid staff. True, they do not receive salaries; but they are not free. A second myth is that volunteers do not need to be trained. It is easy to assume that because they often come to the agency with special skills further training is unnecessary. In fact, we sometimes think volunteers will be offended if we suggest training. In describing his own early experiences in twenty years of volunteer service, Barnes made this statement.

> Because of this myth, assumptions were made about my abilities and competence, and I was not offered any orientation or training. This lack of training deterred my effectiveness as a volunteer and inhibited my development as a viable community resource.[32]

Another myth is that volunteers can carry out any function that is carried out by professional staff. This leads to the belief that volunteers depress the labor market by filling positions that would otherwise be filled by employees. Volunteers often *are* highly skilled, and they may increase their general competencies beyond their specialized skills through in-service training. However, they usually do not have the same capabilities as professionally educated staff. Agencies tend to find that it is most effective if volunteers and employed staff complement each other, rather than occupying the same types of positions.

A contrasting myth is that volunteer effort is worth less to the agency than regular staff time. Volunteers enrich agencies in ways that cannot be duplicated readily by employed personnel. Their contributions are different, but no less valuable. One perception that may contribute to a depreciation of the worth of volunteers is the feeling that they are interested only in their area of specialization, that they are not concerned with overall agency objectives and policies. This may be true in some cases, but there is no support for the belief generally.

Obviously, not all volunteers will be effective, even with appropriate screening and supervision. This reality is the basis for another myth—the belief that it is very difficult if not impossible to evaluate volunteers or to discharge them if it is needed. It is not easy to release a person who is giving time and energy freely. However, it can be done. And, in the best interests of providing effective service, it must be done if an individual is a detriment to such service. Volunteers need supervision. They need to be evaluated honestly. They need to know if they are not performing adequately, and they need opportunities to make corrections and to grow.

On occasion, paid staff members are threatened by the presence of volunteers. They may feel that volunteers aspire to their jobs. Or they may believe that volunteers will criticize the way they operate, that they will cause embarrassment. Agencies have found, instead, that volunteers usually become supporters of the program and advocates for the agency in the community.

A final myth is that the volunteer program in an agency is a separate, isolated element. There are special considerations in the implementation, development, and maintenance of such a program. But it will be most effective if volunteers are seen as an integral part of the overall agency operation.

Realities: How the Agency Benefits From Volunteers.   While there are many myths that are counterproductive to effective and full utilization of volunteers, the clear reality is that agencies do benefit from using volunteers. Volunteers expand and enrich the delivery of leisure services. Frequently they bring to the agency specialized skills and knowledges that would not be available otherwise. For example, a retired bank executive who is a skilled woodcarver can teach this art as a program offering in a municipal recreation and park department. It may be impossible to employ someone with this skill, and the retired individual has no interest in paid work. Further, the department could not afford to offer the class for the limited enrollment it attracts if a paid instructor were found.

Volunteers usually bring to their assignments enthusiasm and a freshness that benefits regular staff as well as participants. Kraus and Bates referred to this as an "emotional ingredient."[33]

If the experiences volunteers have in a leisure services agency are satisfying, they usually become interpreters and supporters of the agency in the community. Because they are not employees, their favorable perceptions about the agency often are accepted much more readily. They also can serve as "pulses" of the community, informing agency personnel about prevalent citizen feelings that exist and needs that are unmet.

In some situations, volunteers will be able to work more effectively with those whom the agency is attempting to serve.

> Particularly in metropolitan areas, today's *volunteers are often recruited from the same area as the clients* of the human service organizations. Consequently, they have a much closer association with the clients, more sensitivity to their situation, and greater ease in getting accepted than the professionals.[34]

Providing volunteer opportunities allows the recreation and park agency to extend its services in another way. Volunteering itself is a leisure activity; the agency which makes the experience possible contributes to the leisure satisfactions of those individuals who become involved.

> For many individuals rendering volunteer service represents a type of participation in the program—it is "program" for them—so they gain satisfaction and value that is comparable to that resulting from their participation in other types of recreation activity.[35]

While the potential benefits to an agency are real, there also are some real disadvantages.

While it is a myth that volunteers typically are not interested in overall agency objectives and policies, it is true that their commitment to an agency usually is a secondary one. The volunteer service usually is not the most important part of their lives. There are many exceptions to this generalization, but it is a logical one. Regular jobs and family responsibilities often are given higher priorities. Therefore, there is some possibility that volunteers will be less accountable and less responsible. Again, there are many exceptions; some volunteers will be extremely conscientious once they have accepted an assignment.

It does require tact and sensitivity to supervise volunteers. Since they are giving their time, supervisory methods that threaten or coerce them are inappropriate. These methods also are inappropriate in most cases with employed staff members; but while they sometimes may be necessary with employees, they have limited use with volunteers. Volunteers cannot be "fired." They can be reprimanded, and they can be released. These actions are appropriate if a volunteer proves to be incapable or engages in inappropriate behavior. These methods should be used only after the nature of the problem has been discussed with the individual, and opportunities for change have been provided. While this is true also for regular staff, their use with volunteers must be carried out carefully to avoid creating a public relations problem. Even so, action must be taken when a volunteer is not doing the job adequately. The welfare of the users of agency services, the reputation of the agency in the community, and the morale of other staff members require that it be done.

Volunteers may come to an agency with ulterior motives. Graham and Klar identified three: the desire to gain political advantage by being visible in the community in a prestigious way, the wish to exercise power over other people, and an interest in obtaining paid employment with the agency.[36]

> In and of themselves, these motives may not prove detrimental to the agency. But, too often volunteers once having achieved their ulterior motive (or having failed to do so) terminate their relationship with the leisure service program. Such action can lead to a disruption of the normal program operations. . . .[37]

Also, inappropriate motives such as the desire to exercise power over others can have detrimental effects on participants.

These possible disadvantages reinforce the need for sound supervisory practices in working with volunteers. Effective recruitment and screening, adequate orientation and training, and appropriate evaluation procedures all enhance the values of using volunteers and minimize the disadvantages.

What Motivates Volunteers?   Volunteering is behavior. All of the generalizations about behavior in Chapter 3 are applicable to volunteer behavior. People volunteer to achieve certain goals or meet certain needs;

they are motivated to volunteer. The nature of the behavior is influenced by the volunteer's perceptions—awarenesses of the available opportunities and assessments of which behaviors will be most likely to contribute to goal achievement or need satisfaction. Personal and environmental conditions, such as age and place of residence, also are influencing factors. Volunteer behavior may be motivated by multiple goals, both immediate and long range. The influences of conflict and levels of aspiration may be felt. Some needs may be more potent than others, as suggested by Maslow.[38]

Several social motives were discussed in Chapter 3, motives such as the desire for affiliation and for recognition. These social motives, along with physiological needs such as food and shelter, seem to influence the behaviors of most people at different times and to different degrees. Henderson has suggested that wishes for affiliation, for achievement, and for power are basic motivations for volunteering.[39] Power, as Henderson described it, is a positive motive; it is the desire to engage in leadership, to exercise authority and to encourage achievement in other people. It is not the type of power that is used to the detriment of others. One dimension of the power motive might be the satisfaction that results from causing things to happen. Schindler-Rainman and Lippitt concluded from their analysis of motives that

> a major motivating factor for volunteers is the opportunity to participate in problem-solving and significant decision-making.[40]

Henderson indicated that these different social motives suggest different types of volunteer experiences.

> Volunteers who have evident affiliation needs should be given opportunities to work with others. Persons with power needs might best serve on committees and boards and in leadership positions. Achievement-oriented people need specific goals that they can reach and feedback on how they are doing.[41]

An additional social motive, suggested in Chapter 3, is the wish to express altruism.[42] This also would seem to be a strong motive for volunteer behavior.

Swanson reported on a study in which more than 500 individuals were asked why they did volunteer work. The following reasons were ranked highest:[43]

Ranking	Reason	% of Respondents Rating Reason Important
1	"I like to be helpful."	96.4
2	"It is very important [that] the work be done."	94.3
3	"My relationship with those I serve is very rewarding."	92.4
4	"I enjoy being with people."	89.1
5	"The work is extremely interesting."	85.1
6	"I feel it is my duty to do volunteer work."	72.3
7	"I like to feel needed."	71.9

The motives of affiliation, altruism, and perhaps achievement can be seen in these reasons. Several reasons were ranked as relatively *unimportant:* "Volunteer work gives me prestige" (88.5 percent of the respondents rated this as unimportant); "It is important to my family that I do volunteer work" (85.4 percent); "My close friends do volunteer work" (84.9 percent); and "I like to get out of the house" (76.2 percent).

Schindler-Rainman and Lippitt observed that motives for volunteering are changing. They contended that altruism and a sense of duty are less prevalent as motivating factors today than in prior years.

> Today the motivations to volunteer may include: preparation for and/or exploration of paid employment; causing change to happen; people with similar problems counseling each other (e.g. breast cancer patients, drug users, etc.); wanting to be where the action is; deep concern about causes such as ecology, the women's movement, minority rights, etc.; self-development and growth; wish to be with like-minded people; staying in the mainstream (this is particularly true for the older volunteer).[44]

Hayes and McDaniels implied that people sometimes volunteer as a way of meeting needs that are not met through regular jobs.

> The donation of time and effort on one's own volition for another's benefit, volunteerism during leisure time can provide the personal contact and the opportunity for individual accomplishment and identification so often lacking in today's work experience.[45]

The authors suggested a variety of other potential motives and benefits related to volunteering. They developed the concept that different benefits result at different stages of life. For adults, a search for satisfactions not found in employment might motivate volunteer behavior. Older adults, with much free time, might gain a sense of meaning and self-fulfillment by helping others. Young adults and adolescents might use volunteer opportunities to explore possible career choices. And for children in the elementary years, volunteering can contribute to a sense of accomplishment and the development of self-esteem.[46]

The central theme developed by Hayes and McDaniels is that volunteering is a leisure activity. For this reason, volunteers expect to get something from the experience. Schindler-Rainman and Lippitt noted this idea and related it to motivation.

> To increase motivation, most volunteer opportunities should provide for both self-actualizing personal development and meaningful service to the needs of others.[47]

Henderson identified the dual responsibility that volunteers' expectations cause for agency personnel.

> The supervisor of volunteers in a leisure service agency is challenged with a double programming duty: to provide services that may only be possible with

volunteer help, and to enable the volunteer to have a recreative experience through volunteering. . . . Gone are the days when the volunteer's role was solely to provide service altruistically for the good of the organization or the community. Volunteers still have this goal, but they also want to feel some kind of personal growth and fulfillment.[48]

Henderson noted, as did Hayes and McDaniels, that with time the reasons why people volunteer may change. The same person will be motivated at different times for different reasons. And, as suggested earlier, different individuals may have different motivations for giving their time and effort without pay. The supervisor's challenge is to match the agency's needs and the task the volunteer is asked to carry out with the individual volunteer's motives.

Finding People With the Needed Talents. A prerequisite to looking for volunteers is an identifiable need for them. Obviously you should not recruit people unless you have opportunities for them to provide meaningful service. Your appeal for volunteers might be general, but it should be based on the existence of specific jobs that need to be done. For example, a park and recreation department might make a general announcement on a local television channel that volunteers are needed for various jobs in the department, without defining the responsibilities. However, when people respond it should be possible to tell them the details of the specific jobs. People are more willing to volunteer if they know what is expected of them.

An exception to this generalization is when an agency conducts a general survey to identify potential volunteers. For example, a church might ask members of the congregation to fill out forms, indicating their particular talents and interests, and requesting information about their possible availability for volunteer work in the future. Graham and Klar talked about the development of a "volunteer resource file."[49] They suggested that data about potential volunteers be obtained by personal contact, by phoning or sending mailed requests, or through the use of mass media. This information then is recorded on 3×5 cards or in some other form in which it is readily accessible as needs arise. They advised that the file be updated periodically.

The usual methods used for recruiting volunteers for specific and current or anticipated needs include the types of contact mentioned in the last paragraph. Announcements can be made using media sources: television, radio and newspapers. Information can be posted in public places, such as supermarket bulletin boards, in buses, and at libraries. Personal contacts can be made directly or by phoning or writing; this probably is one of the most productive methods. The contacts can be with personal friends and acquaintances or with people to whom you are referred by someone else.

Current volunteers in an agency are good sources for referring you to other potential volunteers. For example, the teen-agers who are helping with the preschool program described in the last chapter probably know other teens who might be interested in helping. If two or three of the community college students decide to volunteer in the psychiatric hospital, they might persuade a few out-of-class friends to help also. Participants in program activities may be willing to help others in ways related to their special interests; for example, a ceramicist might help teach a children's class, or a member of a softball team might volunteer to officiate in another league.

Another method which is usually productive is to appear before community groups to request help. Service clubs, chambers of commerce, and churches are examples. As suggested, colleges and universities also are sources of volunteers. The possible contacts here are with the student governments and with the various clubs and organizations that exist on most campuses, as well as appropriate classes. At some colleges and universities, there will be a person or group especially concerned with the coordination of volunteer activities.

Some academic programs (such as recreation and parks, social welfare, and community services) require their student majors to complete fieldwork experiences. While the motivation of fieldworkers may be different, they are sources of assistance very similar to volunteers.

In some communities, there will be volunteer bureaus; organizations with responsibilities for recruiting and placing volunteers. Volunteer bureaus usually are supported by funding programs such as the United Crusade. If a community has a "welcome wagon," or a similar program for newcomers, this avenue might be used. Volunteering is an excellent way to meet people and get more established in a new neighborhood.

Corporations frequently encourage their employees, including management personnel, to become involved in community efforts and projects. They have interests in the well-being of the communities in which they are located. They also see the potential public relations benefit of employees becoming more visible in the community in positive ways.

As indicated earlier, today's volunteers come from varied backgrounds. People of all ages, both sexes, different income levels, and different racial and ethnic identities can be found in volunteer ranks today. Even so, some groups are more prevalent than others. Schindler-Rainman and Lippitt contended that opportunities for volunteering still are not equally available.[50] They identified groups of volunteers who are "underutilized" and "more highly utilized."[51] More highly utilized volunteers included such groups as middle-aged, white, married, middle-to-upper-income women (and to a lesser degree men); high-status minority persons; business and professional people; those who are identified with organized religion; and those who are members of certain community organizations and social groups.

The underutilized category included blue collar workers and labor union members, older adults, the young, large numbers of minority persons, disabled individuals, people who live in rural areas, single men, those who lack formal education, and men and women who are "nonjoiners" or unaffiliated with the typical community organizations. The authors recognized that many volunteers come from some of these different categories, and that the tendency for them to do so is increasing. However, because of our recruitment practices and various social conditions, these groups are not yet as evident as they might be.

Schindler-Rainman and Lippitt suggested that we need to extend our recruiting efforts to locations and sources where they will be most likely to contact people who are potential but unidentified volunteers—to places like labor union halls, neighborhood improvement associations, adult education classes, and informal neighborhood social groups. They believed that "informants" can be used—people such as beauticians, social workers, bartenders, ministers, and gas station attendants, who might be able to refer you to someone who is a potential volunteer.[52] Of course, you would have to know the contact person. In some cases, it might be better in terms of respecting people's privacy to ask the informant to suggest that the potential volunteer contact you.

Naylor emphasized the need to develop ways to reach out to individuals whose lifestyles have not included volunteering but for whom the experience would be important.

> We cannot simply wait for them to come to us to offer to volunteer. We must develop a network of people in the community who believe in what we are doing and who will help private citizens see what they can do within our program.[53]

By whatever method we use, if a broader range of backgrounds can be represented in our volunteer groups, our programs will be both expanded and enriched.

> The challenge to all agencies, organizations, and movements is to find the important underutilized volunteer resources in areas that have not previously been tapped.[54]

Working With Volunteers. The suggestions for using supervisory processes, discussed earlier, apply to volunteers as well as to employees. Volunteers are staff members. No less than paid staff members, they benefit from effective supervision—supervision that enables them to function more effectively in achieving agency goals and personal satisfaction. Training is a supervisory method that is especially important in working with volunteers.

There are, however, some special considerations related to volunteer involvement. Some of these also apply to working with paid staff.

1. *Planning for Volunteer Involvement.* Schindler-Rainman and Lippitt suggested several devices for initiating community-wide volunteer programs.[55] One of these is to convene a community conference on volunteering, to which key leaders from government and industry are invited. The general purposes are to heighten awareness of the values of volunteering, to assess community needs, and to initiate overall planning. Another strategy is to solicit the help of a local college or university in conducting a community-wide survey of volunteerism. The resulting information can be used to make decisions about implementing a program. All agencies in a community that presently use volunteers might participate in a "training-of-trainers" institute. In such an institute, those who presently work with volunteers get together (often with outside consultants) to share ideas, improve competencies, and discuss ways of expanding volunteer opportunities in the community.

At the agency level, several steps are involved in initiating volunteer programs. In describing a specific example of the development of a program, Holmwood provided a useful outline of the six major steps.[56] A first step is to inventory the current use, if any, of volunteers in the agency. Second, staff members are surveyed to get ideas about the use of (or additional uses for) volunteers and about the kinds of things the agency would have to do if a program were initiated or expanded. The third step is a recruitment effort. This involves use of media, personal contacts, and other methods to inform the public about opportunities for serving. Fourth is a selection process, in which individuals who respond are placed according to their talents and interests and the agency's needs. Fifth is to establish training, scheduling, evaluating and other on-going supervisory practices. Finally, a system is initiated for recognizing and expressing appreciation to the volunteers.

In planning for the use of volunteers, consideration should be given to budget implications.[57] Added staff means additional supervision; this may create needs for additional hours for paid staff. Also, it is desirable for employed staff members to receive training in working with volunteers. This may influence the agency budget. It is possible that an agency might wish to provide funds for mileage or conference expenses incurred by volunteers. Will volunteers be covered by any accident or liability insurance the agency carries? If not, consider providing this coverage.

In some situations, relations with labor unions will influence planning. On occasion, unions object to volunteer use on the basis that it takes jobs away from employees.[58] These objections can be minimized if the agency adopts a written policy stating that volunteers will not be used to replace paid staff, except in the event of documented budget cuts that result in layoffs. If you anticipate objections, you might involve local unions in the planning. Also, as suggested earlier, unions are possible sources where volunteers might be recruited.

2. *Conditions That Maximize Volunteer Effectiveness.*[59] As with any staff members, volunteers need to be informed about the agency in which they are working—its overall purposes, its basic organizational scheme, and its relationships to other community agencies. This information, however, often is overlooked in orienting volunteers. It should not be. They can be effective in carrying out their specific assignments and in serving as interpreters of the agency in the community if they have relevant, overall information about the agency. These purposes are served also if they know how their specific jobs fit into the overall scheme. It helps, too, to encourage them to view their assignments as part of the broader agency operation.

Volunteers will function best if they feel they are integral parts of the agency. The relationships they have with other staff members on a day-by-day basis will influence these feelings. Obviously, they wish to be treated with equal respect as partners in the service delivery system. They may want to be involved in planning and decision making. If so, and if they are involved at appropriate times and in appropriate ways, this will contribute to their identification with the agency. Identity also can be enhanced by such things as sending agency newsletters to volunteers, and providing them with identifying symbols (such as name tags and jackets) when appropriate, especially if these are worn by other staff members. Providing for parking spaces and individual work areas, if the nature of the work calls for it, also contribute. Volunteers should be informed about relevant in-service training opportunities and conferences. All of these things help them feel that they are part of the agency.

One special kind of information that will be useful to volunteers is information about income tax deductions they may be able to take for attending training and conferences, as well as for other activities related to their volunteer work.

Probably the most important determiner of whether or not volunteers are satisfied is the nature of the work they are asked to do. If it is well matched with their talents, and if it is important that it be done, they probably will be happy with their assignments. To provide the best match of individual abilities and jobs, get to know volunteers with whom you will work. Doing so shows your respect for their individuality. Volunteer assignments are best when they are challenging but not threatening—within the individual's abilities but not so easily achieved as to be boring. We probably err most often by not providing sufficient challenge.

> Often we don't expect enough of volunteers, do not give them enough responsibility, don't delegate authority when we delegate responsibility. Then they feel demeaned and underestimated by being given a stupid task. So why bother?[60]

At the same time, it is important not to exploit volunteers, not to overuse them.

Naylor noted the effect of self-fulfilling prophecies.[61] If volunteers are expected to perform effectively, they tend to do so. If we expect them to be irresponsible, we tend to experience that kind of behavior.

Like other staff members, volunteers appreciate opportunities for promotion within the agency. They enjoy variety and the chance to accept new responsibilities of which they are capable. This suggests that we review volunteer assignments periodically.

> We don't review volunteer jobs often enough, we don't check out feelings, we don't give people an opportunity to move about and have a variety of experiences. If one is doing a good job, we tend to give our attention to someone else.[62]

Another key factor in working effectively with volunteers is appropriate and timely recognition for work well done. This can take many forms. Praise from other staff members may be one of the most potent types of recognition. Agencies often use various kinds of awards, such as certificates and service pins. Recognition luncheons and banquets also are used. News releases announcing the contributions of specific volunteers are also effective. Promoting a volunteer to a more responsible position also is a form of recognition.

3. *Helping Other Staff Work with Volunteers.* The effectiveness of volunteer workers will be enhanced considerably if the paid staff members are good at working with them.

The attitudes of paid staff toward volunteers are important. Regular employees sometimes resist the addition of volunteers to an agency. As indicated in the earlier discussion of myths, regular staff may feel threatened. They also may feel a possessiveness about the agency, its programs, and the people it serves. Employed staff usually receive considerable satisfactions from providing services to people, and they may be unwilling to share these with volunteers. They may feel that volunteers cannot perform effectively, and they may resent their involvement for this reason.

Involving paid staff in the decision to use volunteers, and in the planning and implementation of a program, can help to develop positive attitudes. Encouraging paid staff to talk about their anxieties and concerns can help to get feelings out in the open. Often, this makes it easier to correct inaccurate perceptions and to begin to build acceptance for volunteers. If the policy-making body for the agency (such as the board of directors or council) values volunteers and communicates this to staff, it will encourage acceptance. This will be particularly true if the board or council provides additional staff time for working with volunteers.

Training sessions can be provided that help employed staff to know more about using volunteers—how it helps the agency, how it benefits the volunteers, and how they can help volunteers to be most productive.

Involving paid staff and volunteers in joint projects or in joint training can also help to build a team feeling in the agency. However, it probably would be better to do this after some initial and separate orientation has occurred.

As indicated earlier, a key factor in the effective use of volunteers is giving recognition for work well done. This is a two-way street. When volunteers express appreciation to the staff for support given, staff members tend to be strengthened in their commitment to the program.

A Concluding Word About Volunteers.   The use of volunteers is prevalent, overall and in recreation and park settings. This use seems to be expanding.

We often speak of volunteer programs. The term has been used in this section. However, remember that the volunteers should not be seen as isolated from the other aspects of agency operation. Their effectiveness is maximized if they are seen as integral parts of the agency.

Volunteers provide significant services to agencies and their publics. In doing so, they benefit personally in various ways. Volunteering can be a very satisfying leisure experience.

Principles of effective supervision apply to volunteers as well as to employed staff members. In addition, there are some special considerations agencies should keep in mind.

In some ways, it is inappropriate to talk of "using" volunteers. Naylor suggested that the term might indicate an attitude that is counterproductive to both agency and volunteer welfare. In a lecture series on volunteering, she made the following statement:

> I hope, as we think together how to keep volunteers, we can consider that they are free, autonomous individuals who have a right not to be used, but to be given an opportunity to do something important and to put in their own point of view about what we are doing in such a way that we enrich and extend the programs that we believe in.[63]

While her concern may seem to be a problem of semantics, the basic point is a useful one for recreation and park personnel. The use of volunteers essentially is the provision of opportunities for people to help others. It is consistent with a humanistic philosophy, and it is another way of working with people.

SUMMARY

Recreation and park agencies carry out their responsibilities through staff members. Administrators, supervisors, and functional level workers are the human resources that enable an agency to provide leisure opportunities for people. If people are to be served well, staff members must be enabled to work effectively. The process that facilitates this is supervision. This process is used by any staff member who is responsible for the work of other staff members, not just by those who have a job title of "supervisor."

Supervision is an enabling process. It helps workers to perform more effectively, with the result that they and the agency receive greater satisfaction. In addition to teaching and leading, it involves such responsibilities as selection and scheduling of staff, evaluation of performance, provision of resources, and serving as a communication link between different personnel levels in an agency.

Some supervisors will be more effective than others. Those that are tend to operate more democratically, are more skillful in the uses of leadership and instructional processes, and are able to develop appropriate interpersonal relationships more easily. They give staff members opportunities for accepting responsibilities and for advancement, and they provide recognition for work well done.

Two basic categories of human resources are paid staff members and volunteers. Paid staff includes full-time, part-time, and seasonal workers. Volunteers are those staff members who receive no pay for their services.

Volunteers are involved extensively in recreation and park agencies. They serve in a variety of ways: on boards and commissions, as activity leaders and teachers, and in such activities as clerical assistance, providing transportation, fund raising, and park maintenance.

Volunteers include people of all ages, males and females, and differing income levels, educational levels, and racial and ethnic identities. They are motivated by a variety of reasons. Needs for achievement, for affiliation with others, and for causing things to happen are strong motivations. The wish to express altruism is another primary reason. Volunteering is a leisure activity, and it provides for satisfactions in that sense. It also may provide benefits for volunteers such as personal growth and opportunities to explore new career possibilities.

The benefits that agencies receive also vary. Volunteers permit the extension and enrichment of leisure services. More or different opportunities can be provided for the people served by the agency. Volunteers usually contribute to favorable public relations. They help to interpret the agency in the community.

Possible disadvantages to the use of volunteers include the reality that it is more difficult to hold them accountable than paid staff, and they may come to the agency with inappropriate motives. Proper supervision, including training, can minimize these disadvantages.

Volunteers can be recruited through the use of mass media, contact with schools, corporations and community organizations, and personal contacts with individuals.

Before involving volunteers, an agency should clearly identify the need for them. Job descriptions should be developed. Budget implications should be considered. When recruited, volunteers should be treated as integral parts of the agency, and their talents and agency needs should be matched as closely as possible to maximize chances for accomplishment and satisfaction. Good work should be recognized. These conditions, and others that contribute to effective involvement of volunteers, can be achieved most readily if staff members grow in their abilities to work with volunteers. In-service training helps to bring this growth about.

REVIEW QUESTIONS

10-1   What are the basic purposes of supervision?

10-2   In what ways are the processes of leading, teaching and supervision related?

10-3   What are the characteristics of effective supervision? In what ways do effective supervisors differ from ones who are ineffective?

10-4   How can volunteers be used in the delivery of leisure services?

10-5   What are the advantages of using volunteers? What are the potential problems?

10-6   What agency conditions or staff activities are associated with the effective use of volunteers?

TO DO

10-A   Volunteer for work in a recreation and park agency, or some other human service agency. If this is not possible, recall some prior volunteer experience which you have had. After a period of time (a month or so), or based on the memory of your prior experience, answer these questions:

1. How did you learn about the volunteer opportunity? What did the agency do, if anything, to recruit you?
2. Why did you volunteer? What did you hope to get out of it (other than complying with this "to-do" item)?
3. Did the agency give you an orientation? If so, what was involved?
4. What supervisory techniques seem (or seemed) to be especially effective, which are (or were) used by your supervisor? Which ones would you change if you were your supervisor?
5. Does the agency evaluate its volunteers? If so, what techniques are used?

10-B Review some announcements of full-time leisure services positions. These usually are available for examination on the bulletin boards of college and university leisure service departments, or at college and university placement offices, or from state and national professional societies. What information is included on the announcement? Is there a description of duties or responsibilities required in the position? Is something said about such things as vacation time, sick leave, and unemployment insurance? What other information would you like to have included that would be appropriate on a job announcement? Write a job announcement for the position you described in item 1-A (Chapter 1).

10-C Look back at the job you described in item 1-A (Chapter 1). For that job, answer the following questions:

1. Which will be the most important factor you will consider, in selecting it over some other job? The salary, other fringe benefits, the geographic location, the people with whom you will be working, or the nature of the responsibilities and duties of the job itself? Why is this factor the most important one?
2. Will you prefer the job to be one in which there is considerable routine or frequent change (in terms of your duties and responsibilities)? Why?
3. Will you want it to be highly structured, highly flexible, or something in between these two extremes? What are the reasons for your choice?
4. Will you prefer your supervisor to be more autocratic or more democratic? Will you want this person to use more of a task-oriented approach or a relationship-oriented approach? Why?

END NOTES

1. Margaret Williamson, *Supervision: New Patterns and Processes* (New York: Association Press, 1961), p. 19.

2. Michael K. Hoff, "Part-time Workers Take Full-Time Management," *Recreation & Parks* 16, no. 1 (January 1981): 77.

3. Hoff, "Part-Time Workers Take Full-Time Management," p. 77.

4. Several examples of job descriptions are provided in Richard G. Kraus, Gay Carpenter and Barbara J. Bates, *Recreation Leadership and Supervision: Guidelines for Professional Development* 2nd ed. (Philadelphia: Saunders College Publishing, 1981), pp. 36–41.

5. William R. Van Dersal, *The Successful Supervisor in Government and Business*, rev. ed. (New York: Harper & Row, Publishers, Inc., 1968), pp. 99–108.

6. For a discussion of procedures for analyzing work loads and developing work schedules, see Van Dersal, *The Successful Supervisor*, pp. 158–69.

7. The methods described here are discussed in Kraus, Carpenter and Bates, *Recreation Leadership and Supervision*, pp. 297–98.

8. Douglas McGregor, *The Human Side of Enterprise* (New York: McGraw-Hill Book Company, Inc., 1960), pp. 33–57.

9. Van Dersal, *The Successful Supervisor*, pp. 89–90.

10. Ibid., p. 91.

11. Edwin B. Flippo, *Principles of Management*, 3rd ed. (New York: McGraw-Hill Book Company, 1971), p. 414.

12. Flippo, *Principles of Management*, pp. 415–17.

13. For suggestions on setting up and using filing systems in recreation and park agencies, see J. R. Needy, *Filing Systems*, rev. ed. (Arlington, Va.: National Recreation and Park Association, 1974).

14. W. Richard Plunkett, *Supervision: The Direction of People at Work* (Dubuque, Iowa: William C. Brown Company Publishers, 1975), p. 43.

15. Martin B. Broadwell, *The New Supervisor* (Reading, Mass.: Addison-Wesley Publishing Company, Inc., 1970), p. 9.

16. H. Douglas Sessoms and Jack L. Stevenson, *Leadership and Group Dynamics in Recreation Services* (Boston: Allyn & Bacon, Inc., 1981), p. 181.

17. Frederick Herzberg, Bernard Mausner, and B. B. Snyderman, *The Motivation to Work* (New York: John Wiley & Sons, Inc., 1959) cited in Van Dersal, *The Successful Supervisor*, pp. 68–76.

18. Ardith B. Frost, "Crucial Behavioral Dimensions of First Line Supervisors in Municipal Recreation" (Ph.D. dissertation, University of Southern California, 1963), reported in *Dissertation Abstracts* 24, no. 1 (July 1963): 175.

19. Frost, "Crucial Behavioral Dimensions of First Line Supervisors in Municipal Recreation," reported in *Dissertation Abstracts*, p. 175.

20. Broadwell, *The New Supervisor*, p. 12.

21. For a discussion of various considerations related to employment practices, see Frank Guadagnolo, "Legal Aspects of Managing Recreation and Park Agencies," in Dennis R. Howard and John L. Crompton, *Financing, Managing and Marketing Recreation & Park Resources* (Dubuque, Iowa: William C. Brown Company, Publishers, 1980), pp. 163–70.

22. Isolde Chapin Weinberg, "Volunteering Comes of Age," *Parks & Recreation* 10, no. 12 (December 1975): 13.

23. Harriet H. Naylor, *Leadership for Volunteering* (Dryden, N.Y.: Dryden Associates, 1976), p. 203.

24. Weinberg, "Volunteering Comes of Age," p. 46.

25. Mary T. Swanson, *Your Volunteer Program: Organization and Administration of Volunteer Programs* (Ankeny, Iowa: Des Moines Area Community College, 1970), pp. 11–26.

26. "Washington Scene," *Parks & Recreation* 10, no. 12 (December 1975): 8.

27. Robert W. Crawford, "How to Get and Keep Volunteers," *Parks & Recreation* 10, no. 12 (December 1975): 16.

28. Howard and Crompton, *Financing, Managing and Marketing Recreation & Park Resources*, p. 99, citing information from the Heritage, Conservation and Recreation Service, *Volunteer Handbook*, H.C.R.S. Pacific Southwest Regional Office, September 1978, p. 1.

29. Peter J. Graham and Lawrence R. Klar, *Planning and Delivering Leisure Services* (Dubuque, Iowa: William C. Brown Company, Publishers, 1970), pp. 164–65.

30. Weinberg, "Volunteering Comes of Age," pp. 14, 46.

31. Naylor, *Leadership for Volunteering*, pp. 205–11

32. Robert E. Barnes, "Maximizing Human Resources," *Parks & Recreation* 10, no. 12 (December 1975): 27.

33. Kraus, Carpenter, and Bates, *Recreation Leadership and Supervision*, p. 308.

34. Eva Schindler-Rainman and Ronald Lippitt, *The Volunteer Community: Creative Use of Human Resources* 2nd ed. (Fairfax, Va.: NTL Learning Resources Corporation, 1975), p. 43.

35. George D. Butler, *Introduction to Community Recreation* 4th ed., (New York: McGraw-Hill Book Company, Inc., 1967), p. 160.

36. Graham and Klar, *Planning and Delivering Leisure Services*, p. 168.

37. Ibid., p. 168.

38. Abraham H. Maslow, "A Theory of Human Motivation," *Psychological Review* 50, no. 4 (July 1943): 370–96.

39. Karla A. Henderson, "Programming Volunteerism for Happier Volunteers," *Parks & Recreation* 15, no. 9 (September 1980): 62.

40. Schindler-Rainman and Lippitt, *The Volunteer Community*, p. 61.

41. Henderson, "Programming Volunteerism for Happier Volunteers," p. 63.

42. David Krech, Richard S. Crutchfield, and Egerton L. Ballachey, *Individual in Society* (New York: McGraw-Hill Book Company, Inc., 1962), pp. 97, 99.

43. Swanson, *Your Volunteer Program*, p. 7.

44. Schindler-Rainman and Lippitt, *The Volunteer Community*, p. 41.

45. Gene Hayes and Carl McDaniels, "The Leisure Pursuit of Volunteering," *Parks & Recreation* 15, no. 9 (September 1980): 54.

46. Hayes and McDaniels, "The Leisure Pursuit of Volunteering," pp. 55–57.

47. Schindler-Rainman and Lippitt, *The Volunteer Community*, p. 61.

48. Henderson, "Programming Volunteerism for Happier Volunteers," p. 62.

49. Graham and Klar, *Planning and Delivering Leisure Services*, p. 172.

50. Schindler-Rainman and Lippitt, *The Volunteer Community*, p. 36.

51. Ibid., pp. 100–101.

52. Ibid., p. 66.

53. Naylor, *Leadership for Volunteering*, p. 157.

54. Schindler-Rainman and Lippitt, *The Volunteer Community*, p. 66.

55. Ibid., pp. 130–33.

56. Joseph H. Holmwood, "Kettering, Ohio—Where Volunteers Make the Difference," *Parks & Recreation* 15, no. 9 (September 1980): 59.

57. Schindler-Rainman and Lippitt, *The Volunteer Community*, p. 39.

58. Schindler-Rainman and Lippitt, *The Volunteer Community*, p. 104; and Howard and Crompton, *Financing, Managing and Marketing Recreation & Park Resources*, p. 104.

59. This section is based on suggestions in Butler, *Introduction to Community Recreation*, p. 162; Henderson, "Programming Volunteerism for Happier Volunteers," pp. 63–64; Naylor, *Leadership for Volunteering*, pp. 13–16; Schindler-Rainman and Lippitt, *The Volunteer Community*, pp. 61–63; and Anne K. Stenzel and Helen M. Feeney, *Volunteer Training and Development: A Manual* rev. ed. (New York: The Seabury Press, 1976), p. 18.

60. Naylor, *Leadership for Volunteering*, p. 13.

61. Ibid., pp. 13–14.

62. Ibid., p. 14.

63. Reported in Naylor, *Leadership for Volunteering*, p. 153.

chapter 11

Support Processes

PREVIEW

As recreation and park personnel engage in processes such as leading, teaching, working with groups, using advocacy and referral, and supervising, they rely also on several other processes. These, too, are competencies that enable staff to work with people more effectively.

Communication is basic to every interaction between staff members and participants, or the general public, or other staff members. The success of these interactions depends upon communication. Chapter 11 will present a general model of communication and give attention to such considerations as barriers to communicating effectively, the skill of listening, making oral presentations, and writing clearly for understanding.

Staff members of leisure services agencies engage frequently in planning. In a sense, any activity is based on some type of planning. The intensity, amounts of time involved, and consequences of planning vary greatly. A therapist may sit at his desk and plan how he will interact with a client who has an appointment in thirty minutes; a recreation center staff may meet all day to plan the fall schedule of activities; and a park planner may spend several months designing a five-acre neighborhood park. This chapter will provide an overview of basic planning processes.

Planning and problem solving are similar activities. Recreation and park personnel often encounter problem situations. The kinds of problems are very diverse—such things as inadequate financial resources, conflicting uses of areas and facilities, events that create undesirable public relations, and disputes among staff members. Chapter 11 will present a basic problem-solving process.

Both planning and problem solving require the gathering of relevant data. This process also will be examined as part of the discussion on planning. Attention will be given to different types of data and methods of collecting and using it.

Any expenditure of effort by a staff member involves organization. We organize our own time, we organize programs of activities or services for participants, and we may organize programs of work for staff members. The chapter discusses some principles of organizing and gives some suggestions for time management.

A human service organization develops linkages with other people-serving organizations. Recreation and park agency staff members interact with personnel in other leisure service agencies, health and welfare departments, law enforcement offices, environmental organizations, and other diverse groups. Considerations related to working with community groups will be briefly reviewed.

The recreation director of the apartment complex sat the hot cup of coffee down on her desk. It was 8:30 A.M., and she had just arrived at the office. The manager of the complex was not in yet. The office secretary had been there since 8:00 A.M., and was typing the rough draft of the weekly bulletin. Preparing the bulletin copy, which was distributed to all residents, was the responsibility of the director.

The director sat down and looked at her appointment calendar, and the "to-do" list for the day. It was going to be a busy one. She started to sort out the high priority items, and to organize her day's activities. The phone interrupted. It was a call from one of the residents with some questions about a new policy on the use of the tennis courts and swimming pool by nonresident guests. She welcomed the opportunity to talk to him, because he seemed to have some misconceptions about the policy. After hanging up, she decided to write a general clarification of the policy for the bulletin.

She returned to the task of organizing her day, and shortly had listed the things she wanted to accomplish. She wanted to spend some time planning the summer activity schedule. The initial step in this process would be to look over the evaluations of last summer's program. She asked the secretary to pull the file on last summer. Then she spent until about 10:00 A.M. reviewing the comments she had written last September and the evaluation sheets participants had turned in during the summer.

At 10 o'clock, she had an appointment to talk with the president of the residents' association. He arrived a few minutes after the hour. By 10:30 A.M., he had explained the details of his concern. He had received reports from parents that there was increasing evidence of drinking among teenagers living in the complex. Problems of this sort were not entirely new, but there seemed to be considerable increases in recent months. He asked her to "do something about it, if possible." She agreed to think about possible courses of action, and to meet with the president and a small group of concerned residents next week.

After he left, she sat for a few moments reflecting on what they had talked about. There had been minor occurrences before, but not recently. Yet the president was not an alarmist; he had said that more than a few parents were worried. Several questions ran through her mind. How prevalent was teen drinking in the complex? Was drinking the real problem, or was it a symptom of something more basic? She decided that the first step was to get more precise information. She asked the secretary to make several appointments for her later in the week—one with the principal of the nearby high school, one with the juvenile officer of the local police department, and one with the teen coordinator in the city recreation and park department. She also asked the secretary to phone the officers of the complex teen club, and ask them to meet with her the next day after school.

In the course of a typical day, recreation and park personnel engage in a variety of activities that might be called *support processes*. They are supportive in that they help people to use the basic processes described in earlier chapters. Leadership and instruction rely on communication, as do all interpersonal processes. Any teaching must be based on planning to be effective. The processes of advocacy and referral assume that personnel have relevant data about the group targeted for the advocacy attempt and possible referral sources. Resource management problems frequently occur, and problem-solving processes are used to find acceptable solutions. Also, the manipulation of resources requires organization as well as planning. Personnel must use evaluation in all of the processes if they are to do valid planning in the future. And in many referral cases, the worker must establish some kind of ongoing contact with the referral agency. Other illustrations could be given.

The distinction used here between basic processes and support processes is arbitrary. All of the processes are found commonly in the work of recreation and park personnel, and all might be equally important under varying circumstances.

The intent of this chapter is not to discuss the various support processes fully. Instead, it will identify the key aspects of each process and present some generalizations about each.

COMMUNICATION

The apartment complex recreation director just described was engaging in the process of communication at several points: when she wrote the draft of the bulletin, when she instructed the secretary about typing it, when she telephoned one of the residents, when she asked the secretary to pull the evaluation file and make appointments for her, and when she discussed the teen problem with the association president.

Communication is involved in all of our interpersonal contacts. In fact, communication might be seen as a part of all behavior where two or more people are involved. Smith and Williamson suggested that we attribute meanings to other people's behavior and they attribute meaning to our behavior. In this sense, the behavior becomes a message and as we behave, we communicate.[1] As the recreation director talked with the association president, she might have paused and looked out the office windows. This behavior (the pause or silence), or her gestures, might have communicated as much as what she actually said. The way she walked into the office in the morning might have communicated something about her mood to the secretary. While all of our behaviors do communicate, this section will focus more directly on those directly intended to communicate.

Because communication is so much a part of our lives, we tend to assume that we communicate effectively. This seems to be true, even though there is much interest in communication and much awareness about communication problems. Brooks and Emmert suggested that we take communication for granted because we start to communicate very early in life and rather automatically. They observed that this does not assure that we will be effective communicators.

> The truth is, however, that *interacting with others* "effectively" *is not automatic.* Bad habits as well as good habits become ingrained in our communication behavior. . . . Mere interaction with others, without knowledge and without insight, will not of itself guarantee the development of good interpersonal communication skills or the correction of counterproductive communication behaviors.[2]

There are no easy or concise rules for improving the effectiveness of our communications, that apply to all situations. However, there are some basic understandings and some generalizations that we can examine.

The Nature of Communication.   Many different models of the communication process have been developed.[3] Most of these models include the following elements: an individual who wishes to communicate (a *sender*); the *message* the individual wants to send, which may include both verbal and nonverbal cues; the means chosen to send it (such as by talking, writing, using the telephone, or other *vehicle* or *channel*); and an individual who is the intended *receiver* of the message. The receiver may become the sender, and send a return message. That is, the *direction* of the communication will be reversed; it will become a circular process. As it does, it will exist over *time*. Different factors may prevent communication or interfere with it. These are called *barriers* or "*noise*." The sender *encodes* the message and the receiver *decodes* it. The interference may occur at these times.

These elements can be represented as shown in Figure 11-1. The recreation director's discussion with the association president can be used as an example. Suppose that she mentions to him that she has not noticed teens drinking at any events sponsored by the complex. She is the *sender,*

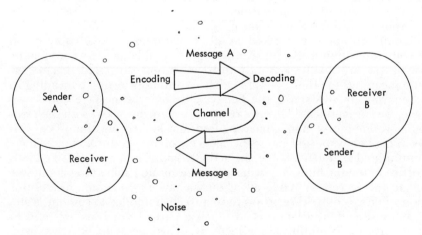

Figure 11-1   Elements of the communication process.

and the *message* she *encodes* is, "I haven't seen any evidence of drinking." The *channel* is the spoken word. The president is the intended *receiver*. But suppose he interprets her comment (*decodes* the message) as disagreement with his belief that drinking is occurring. He might hear this message: "I don't believe that the teens are drinking." His assumption or perception of what she meant becomes a source of *noise* or interference. He then becomes the sender; his message to her is, "You don't get around enough to know what's going on." The interference has caused the beginning of what could become an interpersonal problem.

Barriers to Effective Communication.   The communication that is evolving in this illustration probably will not be effective. This is because the message that the receiver heard carried a different meaning than the sender intended. In this case, the barrier was an incorrect assumption by the association president. There are several different types of barriers.[4]

Differences in perception, from one person to another, can be the sources of interference. As noted in Chapter 3, perceptions influence behavior generally and they frequently cause problems in communicative behavior. Our perceptions are influenced by such things as past experience, attitudes, and biological limitations. Sometimes we make assumptions or expect conditions to exist. These assumptions and expectations affect our perceptions. For example, the association president may have expected the recreation director to doubt his word. Maybe this expectation grew out of past experiences. Since he expected doubt, he perceived it even though the director did not feel that way. This kind of a situation sometimes is referred to as a self-fulfilling prophecy.

The kind of responses receivers give may lead to interference. Several different response styles were identified in Chapter 4. Some of these tend to discourage effective communication. One that might is a judgmental response, such as the association president made. In effect, he was saying that the director should be more aware of what is going on. This probably would elicit some kind of a defensive statement from the director or a counterattack.

These kinds of interference, or *noise,* are associated with the sender and the receiver. As such, they might be thought of as types of psychological interference. Other interferences of this type would be fear, anxiety, distrust and anger. For example, if the recreation director were preoccupied with a problem at the complex swimming pool, her worry might prevent her from listening carefully to what the president is saying.

Other interference types are associated with either the form of the message or the vehicle or channel used to send it. Tubbs and Moss used the terms "technical interference," and "semantic interference."[5] *Technical interference* is channel related. Examples would be such things as a poor phone connection, a loud stereo that makes it hard to hear the telephone, or a carbon copy of a letter that is so indistinct that it cannot be read easily. Tubbs and Moss noted that the sender may create technical noise if he mumbles, speaks too softly, or fails to project his message clearly.[6] *Semantic interference* is related to the symbols chosen for the message. This is sometimes called *code noise.* Suppose the recreation director were to use technical terms, related to a problem with the swimming pool water treatment system, in a discussion with the apartment complex manager. If the manager were unfamiliar with these terms, semantic interference would occur.

Borman and others discussed several types of barriers to communication.[7] Included are two sender orientations that lead to misunderstandings. In *source-orientation,* the sender is overly interested in his own objectives, and he assumes that other people will assign the same meaning to his message that he does. This orientation is likely to lead to code noise, or to psychological interference if the sender is insensitive to the feelings and reactions of the receiver. In *message-orientation,* the sender is preoccupied with what is being said—with the message. Again, he is apt to be insensitive to the receiver, and semantic or psychological interference could result. The authors contended that the most productive orientation is a focus on the receiver. This encourages the sender to encode the message so that the receiver's interests and understanding are considered.

Another barrier to understanding is that of *status differentials.*[8] Sometimes wide differences in the perceived positions of two individuals can cause misunderstanding. The person of lower status may be unwilling to give accurate or honest feedback to the higher status person. If the association president had considerable authority and if the status of the recreation director in the apartment complex were low, she might say what she thinks he wants to hear. She might agree that something should be done about teen drinking, even if she feels that no problems exist.

The Nature of Messages.   As indicated earlier, effective communication depends upon the sender's message being understood by the receiver as the sender intended.

Various kinds of messages are sent as we communicate. Smith and Williamson, after reviewing the work of other authors, identified four "primary message systems"—language, gesture, space and sexuality.[9]

> *Language* is self-explanatory. It consists of the verbalizations of human speech as well as the linguistic structures and rules for using these verbalizations. *Gesture* is defined as any act that can be assigned significance by one or both parties in a transaction. *Space* includes the use of territoriality, distances, and angles of interaction and inclination to create meaning. *Sexuality* is a general classification that designates the use of the body to integrate interpersonal transactions. Critical elements of this message system are touch and touching, body image, and body rhythms.[10]

The authors noted that these categories are tentative and that the sexuality message system is somewhat controversial. They suggested, however, that the four systems provide a framework for understanding different kinds of messages.

Other authors have used a two-category conceptualization—verbal and nonverbal communication. Ronald Smith noted that verbal communication involves the use of words to represent objects and ideas; all other forms of messages are nonverbal.[11] He divided nonverbal communication into five subcategories: sign language, action language, object language, space, and time. *Sign language* and *action language* include such things as the use of gestures to communicate an idea, facial expressions, and body movements and postures. *Object language* results from what we wear, the kinds of cars we drive, and other tangible things that communicate roles and status. *Space* involves the messages that result from how close or how far we stand from the receiver. *Time* involves such things as punctuality and tardiness—how quickly we respond or if we do not respond are acts that send messages, whether we intend them or not.[12]

Tubbs and Moss also described these five types of nonverbal communication.[13] In addition, they included "vocal cues."[14] Essentially, these are messages about other people's feelings (emotions) that we infer from such things as tone of voice, how loudly or softly people speak, or how rapidly or slowly.

Tubbs and Moss noted that 65 percent of all social meaning in interpersonal communication is attributable to nonverbal stimuli, while about 35 percent is verbal.[15] They indicated that nonverbal messages influence verbal messages in one of three ways—they replace, reinforce, or contradict them. Assume that when the recreation director asked the secretary to type the draft of the weekly bulletin, the secretary said, "There's nothing I'd like to do better." If her tone of voice and facial expression when she said this communicated that she was tired or had other things which needed to be done, the verbal message would be contradicted or replaced. On the other hand, her nonverbal cues might have reinforced the message by communicating an eagerness to get the bulletin typed and mailed. If the secretary's verbal cues and nonverbal cues were not congruent, the director would tend to rely on the nonverbal message. "In general, if as receivers we are caught between two discrepant messages, we are more inclined to believe the nonverbal message."[16]

The essential characteristic of messages is that they communicate meanings. In Chapter 7, the relationship of meaning to learning was discussed. The ideas presented there are applicable to communication. What we hear or see in a message will be influenced by the needs we have at the time. If the resident who inquired about the policy on use of the complex's facilities reads in the bulletin that adult guests may be invited, this message will have more meaning for him than for the resident who is not interested in inviting guests. Also, our existing meanings influence our interpretations of messages. If we want juvenile guests to be able to use the facilities, and if we expect from past experience that they will be able to do so, we may read this into the bulletin statement, even if the policy applies only to adults.

Smith and Williamson contended that there are three levels of meanings in most communication transactions: "the denotative level, the interpretive level, and the relational level."[17] The *denotative* level is the literal meaning of the words or symbols in the message. The *interpretive* level consists of cues that tell the receiver how the message should be interpreted. The *relational* level also consists of cues that indicate the relationship between the sender and receiver. Consider the earlier interaction between the recreation director and the secretary. The denotative level of the secretary's response included the words, "There's nothing I'd like to do better." These words have a literal meaning. However, the secretary's tone of voice and facial expression provided cues to the director about how to interpret this message; these cues constituted the interpretive level. There also may have been cues that reinforced or modified the relationship between the two people. Perhaps the secretary's nonverbal communication indicated her awareness that the director was the supervisor and she was a subordinate; perhaps it reinforced a personal friendship between them. The relational level could be evident in verbal cues. The secretary might have said, "There's nothing I'd like to do better, but you're the boss." Or, "There's nothing I'd like to do better, but I'll do it for a friend."

Communicating Effectively.   At the most basic level, effective communication results from eliminating noise or interference and assuring that there is congruence between verbal and nonverbal cues. Several more specific considerations are involved in achieving these objectives.

Johnson suggested some sender activities that increase the chances that the message will be understood as intended.[18] One way is to increase the "redundancy" of the message. This can be done by repeating it or reinforcing it with such things as examples, pictures, and greater volume. The recreation director might explain the guest policy by posting copies of it in the recreation center, at the tennis courts, and at the pool; she might write a clarification for the bulletin, and she might give a verbal explanation at the monthly general meeting of residents. These would be ways of increasing redundancy. Another way is to make the message as complete and as specific as possible and to inform the receiver appropriately about your assumptions and frame of reference. Identifying your own feelings and opinions helps. Organize your thoughts before expressing them. While the message should be complete, do not communicate too many unrelated ideas at one time.

Tubbs and Moss described several speaker responsibilities that contribute to effective communication.[19] Speakers should speak loudly enough to be heard easily. They should be as clear as possible, and they should be aware that listeners might misunderstand their messages. Checking listeners' understanding of your messages and being willing to restate and clarify them also helps.

The authors also described several listener responsibilities.[20] It helps if you let the speaker know how you are reacting. Is the message audible? Is it clear and understandable? Be attentive, and let the speaker know that you are by appropriate verbal and nonverbal responses. Paraphrase or restate the speaker's message to check that your understanding of it matches the speaker's intent.

Johnson provided additional suggestions for listening and responding.[21] Listen to the speaker's entire message before responding. Often, we start thinking about our own responses before the sender has finished speaking. Listen for meaning in the message, rather than focusing too much on details. Try to avoid giving evaluative responses.

The suggestions in Chapter 4 about response styles that contribute to good interpersonal relations, and about appropriate feedback, are useful in communicating effectively. Especially, be aware of your own feelings and attitudes and, as suggested earlier, let the sender know what these are, as appropriate.

Paraphrasing and giving feedback involve two-way communication—communication in which messages are exchanged, and the persons involved in the exchange participate both as senders and receivers. Two-way communication assures greater accuracy in messages. It permits the sender to know how the receiver is decoding the message.

Giving appropriate feedback helps to reduce discrepancies between verbal and nonverbal cues. If we let the sender know when we get mixed messages, we create an opportunity for clarifying the intended message. Also, if we can become more aware of the nonverbal cues we are giving, we can do a better job of making them congruent with our verbal messages; or we can make the verbal cues congruent if the nonverbal cues are expressing the real message we wish to convey.

One of the most important factors in effective communication is the credibility of the sender as perceived by the receiver. Tubbs and Moss provided this definition, and observation.

> In its broadest sense, **credibility** refers to *our willingness to trust what a person says and does.* It is undoubtedly the single most important influence on our judgment of a speaker.[22]

The authors identified several different dimensions of credibility. *Source credibility* is a function of the expertise or prestige of the speaker, and the speaker's character. *Character* includes such things as objectivity and reliability. There are two aspects to credibility: the reputation or image the speaker has before the communication effort, and the impression he or she makes during the communication. Tubbs and Moss spoke of these as *extrinsic* and *intrinsic* credibility.[23]

Johnson indicated that the perceived intentions of the sender influence credibility.[24] He suggested that we should be open about the effect we want our message to have; this makes our intentions clearer to the receiver. He also noted that such things as dynamism, warmth and friendliness, and favorable opinions other people have of the sender, contribute to credibility.

Both Johnson and Tubbs and Moss emphasized that the perceptions of the receiver are the key factors in creating sender credibility. If we believe that a speaker is trustworthy and competent, we will see her as credible whether she is or is not.

Effective Communications in "Transracial" Settings.[25]   Some considerations in effective "transracial communication" were presented by Arthur Smith. These are applicable in any situation where different past experiences or the identities of those involved might increase the probability of barriers or interference.

Smith defined transracial communication as verbal interaction between persons from different ethnic or racial backgrounds. He noted that in such interactions, communication barriers often are intensified. This is more probable if one person in the transaction has formed opinions of the other person on the basis of race or ethnicity. In such situations, several things contribute to effective communication. Sensitivity to the other person's point of view and open-mindedness are important contributors. Smith observed that, while the responses of people involved in transracial interactions cannot be predicted with any assurance, it can be assumed safely that closed-minded or dogmatic individuals will be less effective than those who remain open.

> Open-minded persons will receive and evaluate messages on their merit. This means that it is possible for two open-minded persons to disagree about the merit of an idea. In fact, transracial communication is only truly accomplished when verbal interaction is normalized to the extent that people of different races can disagree, evaluate each other, and express deep feelings without the matter of their racial difference entering into the conversation.[26]

Smith contended that the end result of effective transracial communication is *normalization,* which is characterized by openness, honesty, and maturity.

Another condition that contributes to effective interactions is the sharing of a "common coding system"—verbal and nonverbal cues that have common meanings for both the sender and receiver.

> Much conflict, interracial and otherwise, could be resolved and indeed prevented if people had some knowledge of each other's verbal code. When source and receiver share a codification system, their chances of achieving understanding are considerably improved.[27]

Smith pointed out that differences in meanings of verbal and nonverbal cues, or codes, may produce incongruity between what a speaker says and the nonverbal cues perceived by the receiver. This can occur in any communication. A person may intentionally send a verbal message that does not represent his real feelings, which may be communicated clearly through nonverbal cues. In transracial communication, the sender's messages may be congruent, but they may seem incongruent to the receiver because of a misinterpretation of either the verbal code or the nonverbal code. The two do not match according to the receiver's understanding, based on his experience. However, they may be quite congruent on the basis of the sender's experience and intent.

Transracial communication is facilitated by reducing the distances between people. Smith spoke of participants becoming available to each other. This idea includes more than geographic proximity, though this is necessary.

> Some of the mistakes of perception can be corrected if the communicators sincerely want to transcend boundaries. Nothing can happen if genuine willingness to become available to the other person is lacking. You can become available through research into the cultural background, the issues of interest, and the historical contributions of the persons you seek to understand. But more importantly, you must become geographically available.[28]

In Chapter 4, we examined the relationship of self-awareness to the development of good interpersonal relationships. Smith suggested that self-awareness also is an important factor in transracial communication. We need to be aware of our own perceptions, values, and biases before we can effectively interact with someone who may have different perceptions, values and biases.

These suggestions apply also to other communication efforts where there is diversity between the sender and receiver, for example between senior citizens and young adult leaders, between disabled participants and nondisabled staff members, between male patients and female therapists, and between low-income residents and middle-income board members. Referring to the works of several other authors, Smith made an observation that supports this generalization.

> Interpersonal communication is liable to be more difficult to achieve, and is less likely to occur, the greater the contextual differences between source and receiver. This is to say, when communicators share a similar verbal code, are mutually available, and have similar values, their chances for understanding each other are immensely increased.[29]

Speaking to Groups.   Recreation and park personnel frequently have opportunities to speak to groups. The apartment complex recreation director might address the monthly meeting of the resident's association on the topic of future leisure programs, or she might speak at a meeting of the professional organization.

There are four different types of presentations to groups: impromptu speeches, extemporaneous speeches, speeches that are memorized, and ones that are read from prepared manuscripts.[30] *Impromptu* speaking usually is spontaneous and informal, with little or no prior preparation. You may be called upon to do this, on occasion. However, it is much better to do some preparation if you have the opportunity. *Extemporaneous* speeches are planned. The main characteristic is that the speaker uses notes in the delivery. Often, the notes are in the form of an outline that is made up of phrases or key words. A *memorized* speech is just that; you write the speech, memorize it, and give it. The disadvantages of this approach are that the delivery tends to sound mechanical, and you might forget some of it. You may have experienced that dry-mouthed, panicky feeling that comes with the realization that you are not sure what to say next. *Reading a speech* is appropriate if you want to be precise and make certain that you cover every point. The problem with this approach is that you have to concentrate so much on your manuscript that you often miss cues from the audience that tell you how they are reacting. Also, it can be difficult to hold people's attention unless they are quite interested in the topic. Probably, most of the speeches that you will give will be extemporaneous ones.

Many of the generalizations that apply to person-to-person communication apply also to speaking to groups. In a sense, speaking to groups is one person communicating with several other individuals who happen to be together. The differences are that the speaker alone is responsible for giving the message, there is less opportunity for feedback from the listeners, and the speaker may be less comfortable in front of a group. However, the considerations related to listener perceptions, noise, congruency between verbal and nonverbal cues, and speaker credibility generally are applicable.

Define the purpose.   There are two basic dimensions in speaking to groups: The speech must be prepared (except in the case of impromptu deliveries) and it must be given. Tubbs and Moss provided a useful framework for preparing a speech.[31] First, you must decide your purpose. The two main purposes of most speeches are to inform or to persuade. What do you want to accomplish? This question, and other aspects of the preparation and delivery, might be influenced by your audience. If possible, you should know your audience. What are their interests? How receptive are they apt to be to your message? Is it probable that they know anything about your topic? If so, how much? Are there any biases or dominant values that may be prevalent among members of the audience?

Select the topic.   Next, you need to decide upon your topic and upon the central idea. The recreation director, in her speech at the annual conference of the professional organization, might wish to persuade members that more attention should be given to apartment complex recreation. Her topic might be the importance of this aspect of the field, and her central idea might be that too little emphasis has been given to this subject in past conferences and in the organization's monthly journal.

Prepare an outline and notes.   Having defined your purpose, topic, and central idea you should develop an outline of the points you want to cover. Then gather materials to support your main and secondary points: examples, quotations, statistics, or other types of evidence. Finally, you should develop an introduction to your speech and a conclusion. These, with the body, constitute the main parts of the presentation. Transitions are needed to connect the various main points, and to lead from the introduction into the body, and from the body to the conclusion. These are sentences that help the listener move smoothly from one concept to the next.

The notes you will use in the actual presentation can be written from your outline of main points and supporting information, perhaps in the form of an abbreviated outline. Key words or phrases should be identified. Some speakers prefer to type their notes on 4×6 cards, and use a colored flow pen to highlight main points. Probably by the time you have developed your outline and written your notes, you will know the material well enough that you will not have to rely heavily on the notes. Tubbs and Moss offered the opinion that the mistakes most often made by inexperienced speakers are to rely too heavily on notes or to try to memorize material, with the end result that the presentation lacks interest.[32]

Practice speaking.   The authors also noted that fluency, the use of supportive and congruent nonverbal cues, naturalness, and poise are elements of an effective delivery.[33] Fluency is related to the rate at which we speak and the continuity or flow of the ideas. We want to aim for a delivery that is neither so fast that listeners have difficulty following it nor so slow that people become bored or distracted. Long or frequent pauses should be avoided. Also, many speakers have distracting habits such as the needless repetition of such words as "you know" or vocalizing pauses with "ahs" and "uhs." Tubbs and Moss spoke of these as *nonfluencies*.[34] As much as possible these should be eliminated, since they detract from the content of the presentation. Naturalness and poise seem to result from experience.

Probably the best advice is to practice a speech before you give it. Ask someone to listen to you and give you reactions. Or tape-record your presentation, and play it back. These suggestions also permit you to time the speech to be sure it is the proper length. Being well prepared and knowing your audience add to poise. Also, it helps build naturalness and confidence if you can get as much experience speaking as possible. Take advantage of opportunities to make presentations to groups, even though you might be afraid to do so at first. Your confidence will build and you will have developed a valuable skill.

Written Communication.   The recreation director in the illustration at the beginning of the chapter probably wrote several things during the course of the day: the bulletin copy, mentioned in the example, perhaps a memo to the manager, and maybe a letter to a colleague in another community. Like oral communication, writing is an important responsibility for most recreation and park workers.

Define the purpose.   Defining the purpose of communication is as important in writing as in speaking. It also is important to know something about the person or persons who will read what you have written. As much as possible, you should write for a particular audience, keeping in mind the probable interests and understandings of its members. Code noise can cause disruptions in writing as well as speaking. For example, the use of technical terms in a report written for a general audience may lead to lack of understanding. Other types of noise also are potential causes of ineffective written communication. Psychological factors such as the perceptions, attitudes, and feelings of readers may cause problems. Channel noise might occur if handwritten notes are illegible, if carbon copies of letters are not distinct, or if the quality of printed materials is not good. All of these factors suggest that many of the things you can do to improve the quality of verbal messages apply also to written communication.

Decide on form and routing.   The types of writing that you might use in a recreation and park agency include memos, letters, reports, publicity releases, narratives to accompany budget requests and grant applications, staff and volunteer newsletters, and information bulletins such as the one used at the apartment complex. Effective written communication involves using the right type for the purposes you want to achieve and for the setting within which you are writing. You should know standard forms for each of the types or the accepted form used in your agency.

Another consideration is to whom should your communication be sent. Obviously, you will have in mind a primary recipient or recipients: the person to whom you are writing the letter, or the individuals who will receive copies of the newsletter. But are there others who should receive copies? Should carbon copies of your letter be sent to anyone other than the addressee? Should you give a copy of the newsletter to your supervisor? Should a memo you are sending to your staff be routed through the agency administrator for approval? Some of these questions can be answered by checking agency policies or by asking other staff members; others will require your own judgment. One particular question concerns reports, news releases, and other written materials that are distributed outside of the agency. Usually, policies will have been established that indicate if approvals are needed and, if so, how they are to be obtained.

Write clearly.   In writing, clarity is an important factor. You will want to write clearly so that your memo or report can be understood easily. Generally, it is better to be as brief as possible, as long as you write what needs to be written and give the details needed to accomplish your purpose. If what you are writing must be lengthy, a summary of the main points will be helpful to your readers. For example, you may have written a long and detailed report to your supervisor. A brief summary of the main points presented at the beginning will give her an overview and save her time. If she wants the details, she can read as much of the rest of the report as is necessary. Also, it usually is preferable to write as simply and as directly as is consistent with your topic.[35]

Write carefully.   In addition to clarity, the quality of written communication is influenced by such things as accuracy, logic, unity, and emphasis. If you are describing something, you and your readers want it to be accurate. If you are arguing for or against something, logic is expected. You want the writing to be a unified whole rather than a collection of unrelated parts. And you want to emphasize the important points.

Use proper English.   Quality also depends upon proper use of paragraphs, correct spelling, sentence structure, punctuation, and grammar. Of course, communication can occur in spite of misspelled words and improper punctuation, but errors detract from the message. Often they create an unfavorable impression that decreases the writer's credibility. Using a dictionary to check words you are unsure of can be very helpful. Also, a handbook on style and usage can be very useful for such things as punctuation and grammar.[36]

Proofreading what you have written and rewriting where necessary contributes greatly to effective writing. Sometimes, it is useful to ask someone else to proofread your work. You may be too close to it to catch errors in form or in overall meaning.

Meet deadlines.   Finally, in writing it is important to be aware of deadlines. If your administrator wants a report on a certain date, give yourself plenty of time to complete and submit it by that time. If you send a memo to staff members informing them of a meeting, it should arrive far enough in advance of the date so they can plan for it in their schedules. If you want to write to a volunteer to thank him for helping with a special program, your letter will lose some of its value if he doesn't receive it until a month after the program.

Clear and accurate writing and effective oral communication enable recreation and park workers to accomplish their purposes. These activities are used in all of the processes discussed earlier in this book. They are also used in the other support processes we will examine in the remainder of this chapter.

PLANNING

Staff members in recreation and park agencies do various kinds of planning. The apartment complex recreation director was beginning to plan the summer activity schedule. Program planning is one major type of planning. The planning of areas and facilities is another major type. Budgeting also is a planning process, and the development and utilization of staff requires planning.

1. *What is planning?* At the most basic level, planning is a means of deciding what you want to accomplish and determining the steps that have to be taken to achieve the objective. Bannon provided this definition.

> In simple terms, planning is the recognition of an existing or anticipated need and the devising of specific steps for fulfilling that need.[37]

Murphy and others offered a similar definition.

> *Planning is basically the setting of organizational, divisional, district, center or park goals and establishing a procedure to accomplish them.*[38]

Gold's concept identified characteristics of the process.

> Despite semantic difficulties, the literature and practice generally agree that planning: (1) deals with the future and (2) develops alternatives for more rational decisions. Most authors and professional planners feel that planning should be representative of what people want, imaginative in projecting what might be, and realistic in recognizing what is possible.[39]

Planning permits us to make considered decisions about what we want and it allows us to determine the best ways to go about meeting our objectives. In a sense, everything we do involves planning. The model of behavior discussed in Chapter 3 includes the stages of thinking out alternative responses that might achieve goals, and selecting (or engaging in) those that seem most promising. This is planning; the phrase used at that point in the model is "the participant's plan for achieving the goal(s)." When the apartment complex recreation director arrived at work at 8:30 A.M., she had a tentative plan in mind for the day's activities. Her arrival at 8:30 rather than at 7:30 or at 9:30 probably was based on a plan. When she organized her day, she was planning. When she thought about how she would respond to the association president's concern about teen drinking, she engaged in planning. This kind of planning is inescapable. However, when we talk about planning in recreation and parks, we generally are referring to a more systematic, identifiable process related to one of the four major elements mentioned earlier: program services, areas and facilities, financial resources, and staff development.

2. *Program planning.* In program planning we are attempting to provide leisure opportunities for people. Their wishes, the purposes and philosophy of the agency, and the resources with which we have to work are primary considerations. When the recreation director plans programs for residents, she must be aware of what they want. She also must consider the philosophy of the complex. What does management see as its responsibilities to residents? The answer to this question will influence the resources she has, or can obtain, for implementing any plans she makes.

Select an appropriate method.   The director might select one or a combination of several methods for planning programs. She might review past programs, including evaluations of them that are on file, and base her planning on these. She might find out what kinds of services and activities have been successful in other apartment complexes. She could visit or phone colleagues in other communities; or she might have information on file from meetings or from printed materials (such as professional journals and activity reports). These could become the basis for planning. She could ask residents what they want by taking a survey, calling a meeting, or inviting suggestions. Or she might rely entirely on her own professional judgment. Danford identified these four general methods as the *traditional* approach, the *current-practice* approach, the *expressed-desires* approach, and the *authoritarian* approach.[40] Each has advantages and disadvantages.

While successful past programs probably have good potential for future success, the needs and interests of participants can change. Services that meet needs effectively in other communities and agencies can give some good hints about what will be successful in your agency. However, the people you serve may have different interests from those who are served by the other agencies.

Asking people what they want is very appropriate, and, as suggested at various places in this book, the users of services should be involved in planning. More input may be needed, though. People may not know what is possible; their perceptions may be limited to their own past experiences. An additional problem with this approach is the difficulty of knowing who really represents the public. It would be relatively easy for the recreation director to talk to every resident in the apartment complex. It would be almost impossible for a city recreation supervisor to talk to everyone in the community. Also, people's expressed desires often are not compatible. Older residents and teens in the complex may have very different ideas about how the recreation center should be used.

The authoritarian approach has the advantage of utilizing expert judgment. It has a serious disadvantage in its assumption that the professional knows what is best for people, and it fails to provide for the personal growth of participants that can happen when they are involved in planning.

Edginton and Hanson also described a variety of approaches to program planning.[41] Several are similar, in essence, to the ones identified by Danford. Two give particular emphasis to the value of involving participants. The *indigenous development* and the *interactive discovery* theories are based on the ideas that people should be involved in planning and that

citizens and leisure service professionals can work effectively—and bene-
ficially—together. These approaches are consistent with a humanistic philosophy that values personal growth and self-determination.

The apartment complex recreation director probably would use all of
the sources of information available to her. She certainly would review past
programs; and she would want to be aware of successful programs in other
settings similar to hers. She would plan cooperatively with residents to
discover their needs and interests, and she would bring her professional
training and experience to her decisions.

Consider time, content, and resources. The types of programs that result
from such planning can be varied both in terms of time periods and content. Program plans can be developed annually, by season or by month,
and for each day or specific session. Most agencies develop an overall,
yearly program that indicates, at least tentatively, the types of services
which will be offered. Based on this, quarterly plans (fall, winter, spring,
summer) or monthly plans might be defined. Detailed plans for each specific program will be worked out. These will include answers to the following questions: What activity will be offered? For whom is it intended?
When and where will it be offered? What staff will be needed? What other
financial considerations are involved? For example, will fees be charged?
What supplies and equipment are needed? Finally, how will the program
be publicized?

The content of specific programs tends to be drawn from the major
categories of games and sports, aquatics, the arts (art, crafts, music, drama,
dance, literature) social activities, hobbies, nature activities and outdoor
recreation, travel and sightseeing, and various kinds of special events. Different agencies include or emphasize different aspects. As indicated earlier, the specific activities that are included in any one program are influenced by the agency's objectives, the needs and wishes of the users, and the
available resources. Additional considerations are the offerings of other
leisure service agencies in the community. For the most effective use of
resources, agencies should attempt to avoid overlapping programs that are
intended to serve the same participants' needs and interests.[42]

Kraus provided a comprehensive list of guides to program planning.[43] Some of these apply to overall leisure services available in the
community; others apply to the programs of specific agencies. Recreation
programs should meet community needs and should provide opportunities
for all citizens to enjoy enriching leisure experiences. This includes disabled persons, as well as different age groups, both sexes, all income levels,
and people with different ethnic and minority identities. Planning should
take into consideration the services offered by other community agencies;
cooperative rather than competitive relationships should be developed
with these agencies. The overall community program should provide for
diverse interests, without undue emphasis on one type of activity or one
user group. Opportunities should enable people to continue to participate
in activities already learned, and to advance in terms of the level of their
skills. For any particular group, activities should be adjusted to interests
and abilities so that the chances for successful experiences are maximized.

Opportunities should be offered at appropriate times for the intended participants. Programs should be planned to make the most efficient use possible of available resources. This includes effective deployment of well-qualified, professional staff who can work with participants and supervise part-time staff and volunteers. It also includes adequate funding to implement program plans. The program should be interpreted to the public. They should have been involved in the development of it, and they should know clearly what is available. Finally, services should be evaluated regularly and systematically.

3. *Planning areas and facilities.* A second major type of planning is related to areas and facilities. These range from small neighborhood parks to large natural areas, which might include several thousand acres. Buildings and other physical developments might be involved, such as recreation centers, swim pools, and golf courses. Usually, this type of planning is carried out by someone with specialized training. Agencies, particularly larger ones, might employ planners as regular staff members. Others might use the services of a private planning consultant on a contract basis.[44]

Determine the scope of the plan. Two basic types of plans for areas and facilities can be identified: comprehensive plans and specific site plans.[45] *Comprehensive plans* are concerned with overall park and recreation developments for a particular agency, governmental jurisdiction, or geographic area. For example, all states have comprehensive outdoor recreation plans. Most local governments have recreation and park sections in their general plans that are intended to guide overall development in the particular geographic area. Commercial recreation enterprises, such as ski areas and resorts, usually have a plan for continuing or future development that considers the entire facility. *Site plans* are concerned with specific locations, such as a specific neighborhood park or a particular recreation building. Typically, a master plan will be developed for each site. The master plan details the various elements on the site: locations, number, sizes, and relationships to each other.

Ideally, a relationship will exist between plans for different developments. For example, the location of a neighborhood park will be influenced by the location of other recreation and park facilities in the community as well as by such factors as population densities, transportation routes and natural terrain features. Each specific facility will be shown on the city general plan, which also includes land use designations (zoning), the location of other public service facilities, and major traffic circulation patterns.

Follow a planning sequence. Most agencies use a similar approach to planning recreation and park facilities. A series of steps can be identified. Lankford developed a "composite planning process" that describes steps typically taken.[46] The composite was based on a review of planning literature in the field and on an analysis of planning methods used by five representative resource-managing agencies: three federal, one state, and one commercial operation.

The composite process includes these steps: (1) Identify the problem or issue that leads to the need for planning. (2) Organize the planning effort (develop procedures and assign staff). (3) Establish goals and objectives. (4) Gather and analyze data about user needs, the resources involved, and planning restraints. (5) Develop possible alternative plans. (6) Determine the environmental, social and economic consequences of each alternative. (7) Evaluate alternatives and select the best plan. Additional steps, related to implementation, include presentation of the plan to the policy-making group for approval, allocation of resources, actual implementation, and evaluation of the process and results. Lankford noted that citizen involvement is sought at various points in the process.

The agencies studied in the development of Lankford's composite process were resource-managing agencies. Four of the five operated at state or federal levels. Bannon developed a detailed planning model directed more toward urban settings.[47] It is comprehensive in that it considers all aspects of the delivery of leisure services at the local level. The model itself includes the basic steps of formulating administrative policy related to the plan; gathering necessary background data and information about the community; determining citizen attitudes and interests by survey methods; analyzing current resources, programs, and administrative and organizational patterns; and developing and presenting conclusions and recommendations. The model, and these steps, can be thought of as parts of an ongoing planning process that includes the establishment of goals, strategies and programs for achieving these goals, and evaluations of the effectiveness of plans as implemented.[48]

Bannon's concept and the composite process defined by Lankford contain similar elements. In fact, Lankford included Bannon's model in the review of literature that was the partial basis for the composite method.

Specific site planning involves similar considerations. Population characteristics and the needs to be served by the facility have to be determined, the site upon which the facility is to be developed must be analyzed, and the best alternative for meeting identified needs has to be defined. Usually, this process results in a *preliminary plan*, or a *schematic plan*, that shows the elements to be included and the relationships they will have to each other. This preliminary plan leads to the development of the final plan after appropriate citizen input. The final plan then is presented to the policy-making body for approval. Specific facilities should be planned so that they are as conveniently located as possible to those who will use them. They should be designed so as to be functional, aesthetically pleasing, and easily maintained.

The other major types of planning, in addition to program services and facilities, are financial and staff development. Considerations related to these areas were presented in Chapters 9 and 10.

4. *Needs assessment.* All planning involves the assessment of needs. The term *needs* can be thought of in various ways. Moroney and others have identified four different categories of needs: normative needs, perceived needs, expressed needs, and relative needs.[49] *Normative* needs are those that result from the differences between what people presently have and some standard. Professional judgment is involved in establishing standards and assessing needs based on these standards. Various standards have been developed for the field. For example, a standard for neighborhood parks might be 2.5 acres of park land for every 4,000 people in the community, or one tennis court for every 2,000 residents.[50] There are disadvantages in using standards, and they are not absolutes.[51] Instead, they are guidelines to be considered in planning, and adjusted on the basis of local situations. In this example, if a community of 32,000 people had a total of 10 acres in neighborhood parks, and if the adjusted standard were 2.5 acres per 4,000 residents, then the normative need would be for an additional ten acres. If the community had sixteen tennis courts and the adjusted standard were one per 2,000 residents, no need would exist. Frequently, normative needs are based solely on professional opinion without reliance on a previously established standard.

Perceived needs are those that people feel they have. They are what people say they want. Often, they are referred to as *felt* needs.

Expressed needs are related to demand, that is, to the number of people who seek particular recreation services but who cannot be accommodated. If 200 family or friendship groups appear at a campground on a holiday weekend, wishing to occupy sites that can accommodate only 150 groups, there is an expressed need for 50 additional sites.

Relative need is influenced by the particular conditions that exist in different areas. Godbey used the term *comparative need.*

> One framework for making allocation decisions in leisure service agencies is the use of comparative need—resource models, which establish priorities for service within the population. This framework is based on the assumption that people vary in their "need" for the leisure services of a given agency and that this variation can be systematically related to social or economic statuses or conditions.[52]

He suggested that areas in which high numbers of poor people, older adults, youth, or racial or ethnic minority persons live often will have higher relative needs for leisure services. Areas with greater incidences of juvenile delinquency and with higher population densities also will have higher relative needs. Bannon presented several methods for estimating demand for leisure services, which include consideration of relative need.[53]

Godbey identified a fifth category—*created needs.*[54] These are needs that people did not have previously but that are created when an agency stimulates awareness of and interest in an activity.

Another distinction in types of needs can be made. The term *needs* can be thought of as the needs society has for certain developments to happen on the part of individuals, and the needs of the individuals as they perceive them. For example, the growing child needs to develop skills for effective citizenship. However, this essentially is a need that society has for young people. The second meaning is similar to personal wishes, desires, or aspirations. These are perceived or felt needs.

Obtain information by asking and observing.   As indicated earlier, we cannot see people's motives. We either must ask them about their goals and aspirations, or we must observe them and make as valid inferences as possible. One way of being more assured that recreation and park services will meet people's needs as effectively as possible is to involve people in planning processes. This is a way of asking people what they want. In a larger sense, it is an approach that helps people grow in their own capacities to be self-determining, and this is consistent with a humanistic philosophy discussed in Chapter 1.

Obviously, there are constraints in this approach. Leisure service agencies rarely have sufficient resources to meet all of the wishes of the citizens they serve. And, sometimes these expectations are in conflict. For example, the wishes of the cross-country skier and the snowmobiler will not be met at the same time in the same setting. However, our agencies do exist to provide for people's leisure needs or to enable people to meet their own needs. We will be effective to the degree that we know what the needs are. The most direct way of accomplishing this is to plan with people rather than for them, that is, to involve them in the planning.

There are times when this is not possible. While planning is a continuous process, and while feedback of information during the course of service delivery often results in modifications, much planning must be done before the initiation of programs and services. Sometimes this means that we must estimate people's needs before we are in direct contact with them. In these cases, we usually base assumptions about need on typical or average individuals. For example, if we were doing initial planning for a senior citizen function, we would consider the needs of a typical older adult. This approach is valid, if we recognize the necessity of checking our assumptions with the people who are to receive the services when we have the opportunity to do so. In reality, there probably is no "average" older adult, teenage, or preschooler. The average is a construct comprised of characteristics commonly found, but that may not be found in entirety in any one person.

We can make some assessments of needs by observing people. Combs talks about "reading behavior backward." By this he means inferring the causes and influences on the behavior, based on observations of it.

> If a person's behavior is a function of perceptions, it follows that if we observe behavior carefully, it should be possible to reconstruct the feelings, attitudes, purposes, in the perceptual field of the behaver that produced the acts we observe.[55]

In attempting to infer the needs of others from observations of their behavior, or from estimates about the needs of "average" individuals, we must guard against assuming that the needs we feel are felt by all people. That is, we should be aware of our own needs and recognize that the needs of another person might not be the same as our own. The development of self-awareness, discussed in Chapter 2, helps us to recognize and account for our own needs as well as our own values and biases.

Use surveys. Surveys of various kinds can be used to gather data about needs.[56] They are most frequently used to assess perceived needs. Information also can be obtained concerning the awarenesses people have about available leisure services, the extent to which they use these services, their reactions to them, and feelings they have about proposed developments. To obtain information, we can conduct telephone interviews, mail questionnaires to citizens requesting that they be returned, or contact people directly in groups that meet regularly or through door-to-door surveys.

Usually, it is not feasible to contact every citizen, so sampling methods are used. The purpose is to survey a smaller segment of the service area that is representative of the entire population. Systematic biases should be avoided. For example, if you used a telephone interview, you would not have contact with those citizens who do not have telephones. Frequently, random samples are used in which, theoretically, every individual has an equal chance of being selected for inclusion in the survey. Care must be taken also in developing the survey form. Questions should be stated as clearly and unambiguously as possible. Otherwise, it will be difficult to interpret responses. The objective is to obtain information that is accurate and in direct response to the questions asked. It is desirable to pretest the survey form and method using a small group of respondents similar to those who will participate in the actual survey. This helps to assure that you will obtain more useable data.

One additional consideration is dealing with nonresponses. You may mail out 1,500 questionnaires, and receive 1,000 responses. Can you assume that the returns represent the entire 1,500? Probably not, but you rarely will achieve a 100 percent return. You will want to obtain as high a return as possible through careful attention to methods, including follow-ups (such as sending a second request to nonrespondents). And, you will need to consider whether or not the "no responses" are significant enough to make the results questionable. Finally, of course, when all the information from the survey has been collected, it must be analyzed and interpreted.

Other methods for assessing needs include the use of relevant information that already exists, such as census data, surveys taken by other agencies or organizations, and pertinent statistics that have been collected. Also, public hearings can be used to determine needs.[57]

The planning process usually results in a report; frequently maps and other illustrative data are included. These reports, if they are done well, provide guidelines for serving people more effectively. They facilitate our efforts at working with people. However, they must be implemented. While this seems obvious, it does not happen automatically. Bannon provided a caution and a suggestion that serve as an appropriate concluding statement on planning.

> We are too easily won by the seemingly completed task of a spiral-bound plan report. My advice is to throw away the binder and dig into the implications and prescriptions of the report itself. Don't be misled by a fancy report in an attractive binder and lose sight of the unmet needs which have been articulated on paper only—another impressive report to grace our bureaucratic bookshelves with only a printer's or consultant's bill demanding our real attention. Plans abound in every aspect of human services; unless they are used as guidelines for development, they are worthless.[58]

PROBLEM SOLVING

We have a problem when a condition exists that we do not want, or when there is a condition we want but there are blocks to achieving it. The association president wants something to be done about teen drinking in the apartment complex. Something is preventing this from happening, at least at the time of his meeting with the recreation director. Therefore, he has a problem. The recreation director also may want teen drinking to stop. Or it is possible that she may feel that the president's concern is unnecessary, that drinking on the part of teen-age residents is not a problem. In that case, the condition she wants to achieve is to convince him that nothing needs to be done. Her problem becomes one of dealing with the feelings of the president and his request for action.

Problem solving is closely related to planning. At the most basic level, it involves determining goals (usually involving changes in the conditions that constitute the problem), generating alternative solutions, and selecting the most promising one. These steps are similar to the basic steps used in planning. They also are similar to the last phase of the helping process, presented in Chapter 4.

Components of Problems. Ackoff suggested that problems have five different components: the person (or persons) with the problem, the aspects of the problem that the person can control, those that he cannot control, the restraints within which the person must operate, and the possible outcomes.[59] Take the example of the apartment complex recreation director. The president of the association called her attention to a problem—teen-age drinking in the complex. In this case, several people could "have" the problem. If drinking exists, it will be a problem for the director, since at least the president expects her to do something about it. Probably the drinking is a problem to parents of the teens who are involved, and it may be a problem for some of the teens themselves. All of these persons are possible decision-makers, in terms of doing something about the problem.

From the viewpoint of the director there are several controllable aspects. For example, she can refuse to let teens who are known to have been drinking use the recreation facilities at the complex. Other factors will be beyond her direct control, such as the availability of alcohol and variations in the responses of parents to the problem. The restraints under which the director will work include possible management policies that govern resident use generally, and the amount of time she can give to finding a solution. Possible outcomes are a function of what the decision-maker does and the uncontrolled variables. Perhaps some action that the director takes in cooperation with parents will solve or minimize the problem. Maybe the availability of alcohol and the fact that adult supervision is not available at all times, means that teen drinking will continue.

Problem-solving Steps. Bannon developed a problem-solving model that has broad applicability in recreation and park settings.[60] The first step is to identify and analyze the problem. Next is to define the objectives.

Following this, you must determine the factors that are blocking change or preventing a solution to the problem. Keep in mind possible resistance to change and conflicts in points of view and expectations. This information becomes the basis for developing alternative solutions. Bannon suggested a "brainstorming" technique for doing this. Alternatives are evaluated and the most promising is selected. Finally, you must develop strategies for implementing the decision that has been made. The author provided a large number of case studies, based on actual experiences, that give opportunities to apply this model.[61] These are indexed by subject matter and references related specifically to each case are listed.

Bannon cautioned that problem solving is a complex process, and that the model is not intended as a "cookbook" method to be followed rigidly. Often, the facts surrounding a problem are vague and difficult to determine. The problem itself may be hard to isolate. Some problems, for various reasons, may not be solvable. The method does encourage a more systematic approach to problem solving and less reliance on intuition.

> Be assured of one thing: if you carefully pursue each step of this model, you will improve your pattern of thinking, which should enhance your daily efficiency and decision making and problem-solving ability. It is hoped that continued use of this model will develop a more analytical and creative approach to problem-solving.[62]

The first step in any problem solving is to define the nature of the problem. Part of this will be a determination of who is responsible for solving it and which elements can be controlled. The main problem will have to be differentiated from symptoms and subproblems. The main problem or "key" problem can be thought of as one that, when solved, will result in the solution of (or reduction of) the symptoms and subproblems.[63] In the teen drinking example, there probably will be various symptoms and subproblems. The association president is concerned and wants something to be done. Some parents probably are worried. Some teen participants may be behaving disruptively at the recreation center. Perhaps the high school principal has observed that students who live in the complex have more unexcused absences than other students. Maybe merchants in the shopping area near the complex have complained about the behavior of adolescents. All of these may be related to the drinking problem. Perhaps the drinking itself is a symptom of a deeper problem. All of the people just mentioned (the association president, parents, teens, the high school principal, and merchants) as well as the recreation director will have viewpoints about the problem. Some of these may conflict. There probably will be differences in their perceptions of what should be done.

If changes in the behavior of teen residents are to be accomplished, the problem-solver or solvers will have to deal with the key problem rather than with the symptoms. Symptoms merely provide the evidence that a problem exists. We can assign priorities to these symptoms, starting with the ones about which we are most concerned. This can help us to define the main problem and the subproblems.

Van Gundy also presented a problem-solving model similar to Bannon's.[64] Three basic elements are included: a problem-definition phase, a phase devoted to generating possible solutions, and a phase for evaluating these and selecting one. The process begins when stimuli are perceived that indicate a problem and ends with the implementation of the solution.

The author provided a useful flow chart for determining if a problem actually exists and if problem solving should be undertaken.[65] The sequence consists of a series of questions. The initial condition is an awareness that a problem might exist. The initial question is, Does a problem gap exist? A problem gap is a discrepancy between actual conditions and desired conditions. If the answer is *no*, then no problem exists and the problem-solving process can be terminated. If the answer is *yes,* the next question is asked. Is the gap measurable? Essentially, this means, Can the problem be described precisely enough to be solved? Again, if the answer is *no*, the process ends. The remaining questions are, Do you need to solve the problem? Are the required resources available? Is the problem within your sphere of influence? If the answer to all of these questions is *yes*, then a problem exists and problem-solving is appropriate.

Van Gundy provided other guidelines for analyzing and defining problems, generating ideas for solutions, and evaluating and selecting alternatives.[66]

Recreation and park personnel routinely encounter problems. Just as planning, in a sense, is part of behavior, so is problem solving. We have goals we wish to achieve; frequently there are barriers that stand in the way. When we encounter these, we consider alternatives and select the one that seems most likely to lead to the goal. When the goals we have are related to working with people, effective problem solving can enable us to provide more effective service.

ORGANIZING

Organizing is a process that enables recreation and park personnel to use resources efficiently. Resources include staff members' own time and energies. They should be able to organize themselves to accomplish what they need to do effectively and without feeling pressured. In the illustration at the beginning of the chapter, the recreation director was organizing her day, looking at her calendar and developing a "to-do" list. These activities are related to personal organization. She also would have engaged in the process of organizing many times as she set up programs and worked with the ongoing delivery of services to residents.

1. *Program and service organization.* The agencies within which we work are organizations. They are composed of staff members who are related to each other, in both formal and informal structures, and who interact to accomplish agency objectives.[67] We also create suborganizations within our agencies. Many of these are fairly short-lived. For instance, the recreation director might appoint a committee of residents to help plan a picnic for the entire complex. The committee is a temporary organization.

Its members interact with others for the purpose of planning the picnic. Probably, a chairperson will be appointed or elected and different responsibilities will be assigned. As this happens, a structure will develop. In reality, the committee is a group, and the elements just described are elements of a group. But it also can be thought of as a temporary organization.

Break the task into units. The process of organizing for delivering leisure services is a matter of creating organizations. It involves determining the objective to be accomplished, breaking this into logical components, assigning responsibilities (and authority for carrying them out) to staff members, providing appropriate resources, and then structuring the relationships between staff members so they can operate efficiently. The basic process is division and reconstruction. The task to be accomplished is divided into units. Generally, the basis for doing so is used consistently throughout the organization and the units that are defined are mutually exclusive.[68] In the picnic example, the total task is to plan and conduct the event. The various subtasks that must be done include such things as arranging for a location, arranging for food service, selecting and scheduling entertainment, publicizing the picnic, and signing up those who plan to attend. Individuals may be assigned to subcommittees responsible for each of these elements.

The basis for division of the task in this illustration is *purpose.* Lining up a facility is a purpose. Letting people know about the event is a purpose. In a large department, providing aquatic programs may be a purpose. Maintaining park areas may be a purpose. If so, these might be represented in the organization as separate units, that is, as the aquatic division and park maintenance division.

Sherwood and Best identified four other bases: process, clientele, area, and time.[69] A *process* classification is based on the skills used by staff members. Processes and purposes often are closely related. *Clientele* refers to the individuals and groups who are served by the agency. An *area* classification is based on geographic distribution of services. *Time* refers to the periods when the agency operates. This last basis for subdividing into units rarely is used in recreation and park agencies. The two that are used most frequently are purpose and area. Sometimes, in larger agencies, both will be used. For example, a city recreation and park department may be broken into several geographic districts, with a general supervisor responsible for each. Within each of these, there may be functional units, headed by other supervisory personnel: supervisors of sports; art, music and drama; playgrounds; and others.

Assemble the Units. The reconstruction phase of organizing occurs when different subunits are assembled and related to each other in some systematic way. Usually, this can be represented by an organization chart. An example of a typical organization chart was given in Chapter 1. In developing a chart, and in relating staff members to each other so they can work together effectively, three fundamentals of organization should be considered.[70] First, each staff member should know to whom and for whom he or she is responsible. Part of this concept is that each person should be supervised directly by only one other person. The ambiguity of receiving conflicting instructions from two different sources should be avoided. Second, the number of staff members for whom a supervisor is responsible should be reasonable. The number should not be so great that the supervisor is pressured and staff members feel neglected, nor so few that oversupervision occurs. (The appropriate number will be influenced by various factors.) Third, staff members who have responsibilities should be given the necessary authority to fulfill or complete them.

An organization chart shows the formal structure of an agency, but there usually is an informal structure also. This is comprised of established lines of communication and groupings of staff based on such factors as friendship, respect, and mutual support. Normally, we do not set up an informal structure. It evolves as people interact in the agency.

2. *Personal organization.* This book has emphasized the importance of interpersonal relationships and the use of self. Your own talents, and your time and energies, are your resources to use in working with people. To do this most effectively, you need to be organized personally. The key to personal organization is time management. Recreation and park staff members often feel pressured and overworked. Usually the responsibilities we accept in agencies are demanding. The feelings we experience of being too busy and of not accomplishing all that we want to do are sometimes the result of unrealistic work loads or of inefficient work methods. Effective time management can be useful in either case. A comment by Lakein provides an appropriate overall framework. We need to "work smarter, not harder."[71] He contended that time is the most important thing in our lives. Everything we do takes time. We all have twenty-four hours a day. While the demands upon those twenty-four hours will vary from person to person, we can enrich our lives by learning to use time more wisely. And we can become more effective in our jobs.

Know how you use time.   An initial step in time management is to become aware of how you are using time presently. There are two major aspects to this consideration. One is your overall *style.* Are you always late for appointments? Do you usually put off doing things until the last minute? Scott described several types of compulsive time use—ways of using time and responding to demands that we do almost without thinking about them.[72] Compulsive time use is the opposite of using time consciously. Compulsive uses often become our overall style. They include the following: Some people are always in a rush. Scott labels this a *hurry-up* style. Others waste time trying to do everything perfectly when it is neither needed nor expected. Another style is a consistent tendency to overcommit one's self and an inability to say *no.* In a *try-hard* approach, people concentrate on "getting an A for effort" rather than on results. Finally, some people adopt a stance of being strong, of not relying on anyone else, and of never appearing weak. Scott observed that people typically spend from 50 to 90 percent of their time in compulsive roles.[73] These are not necessarily bad, but they are less efficient. She suggested that we often engage in time-inefficient behaviors because they meet certain psychological needs. For example, some people may unconsciously mismanage time as a way of getting attention, as a way of exercising power, or as a way of avoiding responsibility. If we are aware of our styles or consistent patterns and the possible motivations, we can substitute more efficient behaviors.

A second dimension of time management is the determination of specifics. What activities are you engaging in, and how much time are you devoting to them? Simpson advocated keeping a log of activities for a two- or three-week period.[74] This log should be detailed enough to identify specific categories of activities, the purposes, and the time spent. Scott also commented on the usefulness of knowing where your time goes. She noted that interruptions and demands cause the greatest time problems for most people, and suggested particularly that these be identified.[75] Both Scott and Simpson indicated that this kind of record keeping can be done quickly, and that it is worth the investment.

Adopt useful attitudes.   Another aspect of time management is to adopt useful attitudes toward time and modify unrealistic ones.[76] One reality is the twenty-four-hour day. If you want to improve your uses of time, you cannot wait until you have more time. You cannot extend the twenty-four hours you have each day; those are all anyone has to work with. Another realization is that interruptions are inevitable. You cannot eliminate them, but you might be able to manage them more effectively. Keep in mind that you have some choices; if you feel overloaded, at least part of the fault probably is your own. As suggested earlier, some of the excessive demands people face are the result of their not being able to say *no*. Recognize that, in most cases, you do not have to be responsible for everything. That is not to suggest that actual responsibilities be neglected, but rather that we sometimes overestimate our own importance. Another useful attitude is that your personal worth does not depend upon how hard you work. It is true that your value to your agency is related directly to how effective you are. But if you can avoid becoming overcommitted for the sake of proving yourself, you will be able to make better decisions about the best use of your time.

Set priorities.   Most time management literature emphasizes the need to set priorities. If you are to use time effectively, you have to know what things you want to accomplish and which of these are most important. Lakein suggested the use of an A,B,C system.[77] A tasks are the most important; Cs are the least. The As are those things you want most to accomplish; the ones which will have the greatest payoff. The Cs are tasks that you might decide are not worth doing, in terms of the time required. Some As are decided for us by other people—our supervisors or family members or others to whom we are responsible. For the most part, however, we can set our own priorities. Lakein suggested identifying the tasks that are most important by developing a list of long-term goals. These become the framework for determining shorter-range goals and activities. Priorities among A goals can be developed; some will be more important than others. These become A-1, A-2, and so on. These priorities may change with time. As may become Bs or vice-versa. Your list should be reviewed periodically.

Plan.   The priority list is the basis for your weekly and daily planning. Planning is the key to controlling your time. This is true even if you feel you have no time left to plan; those are the times when planning is most needed.[78] The use of a daily calendar or a "to-do" list is necessary for most people. This allows you to plan what you want to accomplish. It encourages you to organize your time. And it gives you the satisfaction that comes as you check off completed items.

Lakein cautioned that your A items might be big enough that it will take some time to complete any one of them, perhaps a long time. He uses the term *overwhelming As* to identify high-priority tasks that are so large we might be discouraged by them.[79] These need to be broken into smaller subtasks that can be accomplished more readily. Otherwise, it is easy to put off starting on the total job. This is one form of procrastination. A defense against this is the use of *instant tasks*—things you can do in a short amount of time that accomplish part of the overwhelming A. The completion of an instant task provides satisfaction and usually motivation to continue with the larger responsibility.

Another caution is that it often is tempting to do C tasks instead of A tasks because they are easier. They provide temporary satisfaction, while working at an important but difficult A task might be frustrating.[80] C items may become high-priority tasks, but usually not without some warning. Most Cs can be put off for a while and some, you will decide, do not have to be done at all.

Adopt appropriate techniques.   In attempting to improve your use of time, it is important to *adopt techniques that work for you.* Time management cannot be a rigid, mechanical process. Time, and the uses of it, are personal matters. Your own uniquenesses and the relationships you have with other people must be considered. Different people consistently work best at different times. If you can discover your best times, you can take advantage of them. Changing moods may influence your productivity. Take advantage of the times you really feel like working and either look for ways to motivate yourself when you cannot get going or take a break. Recognize when you need to relax and when you need to give yourself a pep talk. Again, your own style is important. If that style is inefficient or built on inappropriate attitudes toward time, you should work for changes. But what you end up with still will be your unique style.

There are some techniques, in addition to those already mentioned, that seem to work for most people. The importance of *planning* and the use of a calendar or "to-do" list have been mentioned already. In developing your overall schedule, try to *anticipate recurring tasks*—things that you have to do every week or month or annual responsibilities such as budget preparation or summer staff recruitment. For more specific planning, it is helpful to *set aside blocks of time* to accomplish the major tasks you have to complete. Usually it takes some time to get going on a task; if you can keep with it once you are involved you will be more efficient. If you can *group tasks* so that you do similar things in the same time period, it also is helpful. For example, you might set a time aside to write all the letters you have to write or to make several phone calls. *Do not plan your schedule too tightly.*

Interruptions will happen, and you need to leave some time for these, and for unexpected and unavoidable demands. You might also be able to *delegate some tasks to others,* depending upon your situation in the agency where you are working. Learning to delegate appropriately is an important skill. It helps you, and it recognizes the talents of other staff members and their needs to accept responsibility and grow.

Learning to *make decisions* is another time-saver. In a sense, decision making is problem solving. It involves knowing what you want to achieve, and evaluating the alternative courses of action. Scott suggested the use of a "timeline" or a personal deadline schedule to make sure decisions are made without wasting time.[81] Determine the date by which a decision must be made. Then back up from that date and set deadlines for clarifying your objective, collecting needed information, and developing decision alternatives. The decision date is the date when you must pick the best alternative and implement it.

To be most effective in terms of future time use, major decisions and the processes that led to them should be evaluated afterwards. Let the other people with whom you are working know that you are trying to improve your use of time. They may be able to help you directly or to give you encouragement and support. If other staff members are disorganized it probably will make your job more difficult. But this does not have to stop you from improving; your example may help them.[82]

Correct time-wasting habits.   Procrastination is a problem for many people. *Putting things off* is a way of avoiding unpleasant tasks, or difficult tasks. It also may be a subconscious way of getting attention, "getting even" with someone else, or creating excitement by starting projects at the last possible moment. But putting things off can lead to some unpleasant consequences.[83] If you wait to the last minute and things do not go as you planned, you may be in trouble. An unexpected illness might keep you from finishing the job. Something else may come up that also has to be completed quickly. Or the original task may take longer than you expected. While working under pressure may be exciting for some people, it usually does not encourage high-quality performance. Scott suggested that you recognize when you are procrastinating and be sensitive to why you are doing it. Often, if you recognize your own motivations and the probable consequences, you can direct your energies and substitute the satisfactions of accomplishment.[84]

Being *late for appointments* is another pattern. Part of the solution, as with procrastination, is to be aware that it is happening consistently, if it is, and to see what the satisfactions and the consequences are. A conscious decision to be early, and finding satisfaction in arriving before the appointment often help. Planning is involved. Obviously, if you are due at a meeting at 11 A.M., and it takes thirty minutes to go from your office to the place of the meeting, you must leave by 10:30. Better yet, leave at 10:15 and give yourself time for unexpected traffic problems or to relax for a few minutes before the meeting.

Handling paperwork inefficiently may create time problems for some people. Lakein's A, B, C system can be used to identify top priorities.

Incoming mail can be sorted according to the kind of attention you need to give to it. The less you have to handle each item, the better. If you can answer a letter when you first receive it, or pass information on to someone else who should have it, you will save time. Messy desks suggest the possibility of inefficient paperwork management. The problem is not the untidiness itself; it is the loss of time trying to find papers you need. Scott observed that there is no direct correlation between neatness and productivity; what *does* influence productivity is knowing where things are. It is important that you put papers that are necessary to your work in special places where you can find them when you need them.[85] In most offices, this means developing and consistently using an appropriate filing system.

Efficient time management is not a cure-all for the problems faced by recreation and park personnel. However, all of what we do requires time. We will be more effective if we are aware of how we use time to accomplish our purposes; and if we learn to use that time more wisely. Lakein contended that every person has enough time to do the things he or she feels are the most important. The problem is knowing what we want to do or have to do and then doing those things as best we can. Lakein suggested that whenever you have any doubts about how you are using your time, you ask Lakein's Question: "What is the best use of my time right now?"[86] The answer will help you decide whether or not you are managing your time wisely.

WORKING WITH OTHER AGENCIES

As indicated in Chapter 1, human service organizations are characterized by linkages between agencies. These are based on a wholistic philosophy. People are not collections of independent, isolated needs, feelings, and capabilities. Each person is an interacting, interdependent totality. What affects one aspect of the person can affect all parts. This reality influences leisure services. People come to our recreation programs and to our areas and facilities with different needs. Their aspirations and expectations are conditioned by such things as health, family relationships, work environments, and the availability of transportation. Some of these conditions prevent people from using our services. We can serve users better and extend opportunities to nonusers more fully by developing liaisons with agencies that address other human needs. As we do so, we will help to minimize the fragmentation of services that citizens often perceive when they seek help.

Different aspects of working with other agencies were discussed in Chapter 8. These include learning about community resources and developing lines of communication with staff members in other agencies. Some of the behaviors that contribute to good interpersonal relationships contribute also to interagency contacts. Staff members who understand another agency and are sensitive to the viewpoints of the personnel who work in it will facilitate good relationships between the agencies. Being willing to cooperate, consistently keeping commitments, and following agreements will help to build trust.

Agencies can help each other in various ways. The apartment complex recreation director was seeking the advice and assistance of the high school principal, a juvenile officer from the police department, and the city recreation department teen coordinator as she began to work on the teen drinking problem. Other illustrations could be developed. Often, cooperative arrangements between leisure service agencies can enhance the effectiveness of both. As an example, agencies sometimes jointly plan and conduct training sessions for volunteers. A community-wide survey of recreation interests might be most effective if it were conducted cooperatively by all of the agencies that provide leisure services. This could lead to an ongoing structure for assessing community needs, determining areas of overlap and gap in service, and developing procedures for addressing needs that are discovered. Agencies can engage in joint programming. The apartment complex recreation director might work closely with a local travel agent, setting up tours for residents. Or she might make arrangements with a bowling alley or a golf course to sponsor lessons or tournaments.

Working with other agencies yields benefits for the people we serve. To do so effectively, we need to be aware of the limits of our authority to commit resources. Some of these are legal in nature, others are based on policies and regulations, and still others are the result of community expectations. We also need to overcome any barriers related to interagency competition and vested interests. Sometimes traditional ways of thinking need to be examined carefully and perhaps challenged.

EVALUATING

An earlier section identified the importance of planning in the delivery of leisure services. Planning and evaluation are related closely. Like planning, evaluation is a necessary part of delivering leisure services.

> The manager of the lakeside inn stood on the dock with the member of her staff who is responsible for operating the beach area and the stable. They were discussing the use of the two facilities by guests. The inn offers horseback riding, fishing, swimming, and sailing. The inn also has an arrangement with a nearby golf course that allows guests at the inn to play for reduced green fees. The manager's discussion with the staff member is part of her overall evaluation of the inn's operation for the season. She has spent time with the food service staff and the employees who are responsible for cleaning and maintenance. This afternoon, she will sit down with the accountant and review the financial status of the inn. She also will read again the written reactions that are requested from guests before they check out. The invitations to comment on services and the facilities are available at breakfast on the last morning of each guest's stay.

The manager of the guest inn is evaluating the services she is responsible for providing. She will talk to staff members, observe services being delivered, analyze the condition of the physical properties (dining room, lodge, beach, stable, and other facilities), review guest reactions and analyze the financial health of the operation. From these evaluations, she will write an end-of-season report. She also will have conducted periodic and ongoing evaluations of the different aspects of operation throughout the entire season.

We evaluate past events or events that are in progress to make better decisions about the future. Information about the effectiveness of past actions or current efforts makes planning possible. The manager of the inn will be deciding on staff hiring and guest fees for next season, based on the experiences of the current season. The apartment complex recreation director discussed at the beginning of the chapter was reviewing evaluations of the previous summer program before making up this year's schedule. In this case, evaluation facilitated program planning.

1. *Purposes of evaluation.* While many different concepts of evaluation can be identified in the literature, the essential features of the process are (1) establishing criteria on which judgments or measurements will be based, (2) assessing the degree to which the criteria have been met, and (3) using the resulting information.[87] In the strict sense, use is not part of the process. However, how evaluative information will be used influences the kinds of information that will be gathered and sometimes how it will be gathered. Therefore, evaluation techniques must be designed and carried out with use in mind. There is no purpose in evaluating, unless you use the information you have obtained.

Evaluation can serve several purposes. The overall objective is to obtain information that facilitates decision making and planning.

The specific purposes to be achieved by evaluation influence when it will be done. Assessments of services can be made during the times programs are operating or at their conclusions. In-progress evaluations enable us to monitor services and to take any corrective actions that might be needed. These have been called *process or formative evaluations.*[88] They provide feedback that is of immediate use. They are done periodically—how often depends upon the type of information needed in the specific situation. Where new services are involved, or where problems exist, evaluations might be frequent. Frequent feedback will permit agencies to adjust services to be more effective or to find solutions before problems intensify. In any case, formative evaluations should be done frequently enough to produce needed data but not so often that staff time is used needlessly. Of course, informal evaluation goes on daily as we assess our own efforts and the efforts of those with whom we work.

Outcome or summative evaluations[89] are completed at the end of a program. They enable us to decide whether the service should be offered again in the future and, if so, what features to retain and what changes to make. Rossi suggested that two different aspects should be considered in a summative evaluation—the *impact* of the service on individual users, and the *extent* of the service (the coverage, or number of users served).[90] Some programs produce important benefits for participants but serve relatively few people. Other services are very broad in coverage but are only moderately beneficial. Both dimensions should be considered.

Formative and summative evaluations serve somewhat different purposes. Both yield useful data, and both are necessary in the provision of leisure services.

Information from evaluation can be directed toward different "audiences."[91] Evaluation information can be used by *direct-service providers*, such as the guest inn manager and apartment complex recreation director, to monitor and modify programs. It can be used by *administrators* to make decisions about organizational changes and resource allocation. Because some of these decisions require the approval or support of *policy-making groups*, evaluations can assist these groups in the development of policies, and information can aid administrators in convincing policy-makers of the need for continued support. The *users of agency services* and communities in general want information about the degree to which services are meeting needs and are accomplishing what they are intended to accomplish. They want to know if they are "getting their money's worth." This desire is consistent with the general emphasis on accountability mentioned in Chapter 1. Each of these different groups, or audiences, may have different specific needs for evaluative information, even though the overall purposes of assisting with planning and decision making may be the same.

Also, different agencies will have different specific purposes for evaluation. For example, a commercial recreation enterprise such as the guest inn will be interested in information about profits and losses; a hospital might want to know the effects the recreation therapy program is having on patients. Both agencies may be interested in budget efficiency and influences on users. However, the specifics will differ in emphasis and in type of information desired.

2. *Different approaches.* Several different approaches to evaluation can be identified.[92] These vary in terms of the types of data collected, the criteria used for determining effectiveness, the times when evaluation occurs, and the methods employed.

One commonly used method is the *comparison of conditions in the agency with previously established standards.* Examples of standards for areas and facilities were given in the planning section earlier in this chapter. There are also standards for other aspects of the leisure service delivery system, such as programming and administration. Illustrations can be drawn from van der Smissen's standards and evaluative criteria for public recreation and park agencies. For example, *Standard 21* is part of eleven standards defined for personnel. It reads as follows:

> There should be a written job analysis for each position (full-time, part-time, volunteer, professional, non-professional) which is made available to the employee.[93]

Criteria for this standard are expressed in terms of the job analysis. The job analysis should:

    a. Include a job description—title, line of authority, scope and range of authority; duties, functions, responsibilities, amount and kind of supervision exercised and received.

   b. Include job specifications—education, certification, and registration, experience, special skills, etc.

   c. Be reviewed and updated annually in conjunction with the employee.
Provision should be made for review at both staff and board levels.[94]

Degrees of compliance can be checked for each criterion according to this
scale: Yes, Almost, To some degree; No; Does not apply.[95] A scoring
system is provided, with procedures for weighting different standards and
developing profiles that represent comparative degrees of compliance.
Overall, thirty-five standards are defined in the six general categories of
philosophy and goals, administration, programming, personnel, areas and
facilities, and evaluation.

The major use of a standards approach is as a self-study—an evaluation of an agency carried out by agency personnel. It serves this purpose
well. However, there are some disadvantages to keep in mind if you choose
this approach. Both Bannon and Theobald observed that the relationships
of standards to program effectiveness are based on assumptions rather
than empirical evidence. Also, standards must be adapted to differing situations, and they may change over time. Agencies may focus so much
attention on the standards that they become goals in themselves, obscuring
the needs of people in the actual situations.[96]

Another approach to evaluation measures effectiveness as the *degree
to which goals are achieved*. The goals may be set by the agency, or an outside
source might establish them for general use by various agencies. Hatry and
Dunn developed a method of this latter type. The goals are reflected in a
statement of the general objectives of recreation services.

> Recreation services should provide for all citizens, to the extent practicable, a
> variety of adequate, year-round leisure opportunities which are accessible,
> safe, physically attractive, and provide enjoyable experiences. They should, to
> the maximum extent, contribute to the mental and physical health of the
> community, to its economic and social well-being and permit outlets that will
> help decrease incidents of anti-social behavior such as crime and
> delinquency.[97]

Hatry and Dunn developed eleven different measures they thought were
linked to these objectives.[98] These include participation rates, percentages
of people living within, or beyond, certain distances from agency facilities,
numbers of accidents and criminal attacks occurring at recreation sites, and
others. Collectively, the eleven measures cover all the general objectives.
The evaluation method involves collecting and analyzing data on each of
these different measures. These data may be compared with similar data
for prior years or with different geographic areas served by the agency.

Hatry and Dunn suggested ways to collect data for the eleven measures. They also recommended when to collect different types of data. The
authors noted that some types of information are not easily obtained and
that it is difficult to correlate some measures with recreation participation.[99] Bannon also observed this problem and said that it detracts from
the value of the method.[100]

An interesting modification of goal-achievement approaches is the *goal-free method*. This type of evaluation is based on the idea that when goals are used as criteria, the goals themselves may bias the evaluator.

> According to this view, the central question in evaluation should be, Is the program any good?, rather than, Has the program attained its goals? To answer this first question, goal-free evaluation employs an outside evaluator, who is screened from contaminating program influences while conducting a performance analysis.[101]

The goals of participants rather than the goals of the agency might be the basis for evaluation. Iso-Ahola stated that we should assess leisure services in terms of the characteristic outcomes of recreation behavior. We should ask participants about the degrees to which they perceived freedom and competence, the extent to which they were aroused optimally, and whether their expectations for social interaction (if any) were met.[102]

Cost-benefit evaluations, another group of methods, measure the benefits of recreation and park services in relation to the costs. Higher ratios of benefits to costs indicate efficiency. As an example, Meserow, Pompel and Reich outlined a method for evaluating leisure services using "participant-hours" as measures of benefit.[103] Participant-hours can be compared to leadership costs, maintenance costs, costs for equipment and supplies or to either gross or net overall costs for leisure services.

Wilder assigned dollar values to participant-hours using his "economic equivalency index (EEI)."[104] The EEI is based on the assumption that time has monetary value, that if participants chose to invest a given amount of time in work rather than recreation, they would earn a certain amount of money. Wilder used the minimum wage as the amount which could be earned. Multiplying participant-hours by the minimum wage yields a dollar value that represents benefits; that is, participants presumably would be willing to pay this amount since theoretically they are giving it up by not working. This dollar value then can be used to compute cost-benefit ratios. Wilder provided a method for calculating the influences of age on the minimum wage, and for making adjustments based on the special needs of elderly and disabled persons.

The method has the advantage of quantifying benefits in the dollar values that are used in assigning costs. Theobald noted a significant problem, however.[105] The cost-benefit method assumes that all leisure experiences are of the same intensity, and that there are no differences in benefits for different participants or different activities.

Another approach to evaluation is to rely on *professional judgments*. Of course, whenever recreation and park personnel review their own programs, professional judgment is involved. The recreation director at the apartment complex was using her judgment when she reviewed program evaluations from prior years; in fact, some of the evaluations were her own made at the conclusion of the programs. Similarly, the guest inn manager relied on her knowledge of hospitality services in judging how well the inn was doing. The approach also may involve the use of outside experts, either individually or as a panel: The manager intended to consult with the accountant about financial matters. The recreation director might ask two or three administrators from complexes in other communities to visit her facilities, observe services provided, perhaps talk to residents, and provide her with their reactions. This approach is implemented easily, but it tends to be subjective. Two different directors might observe the same program and have quite different opinions about it. If the director uses her own professional judgment to evaluate the programs that she planned and provided, she might be biased.

Some evaluation methods properly can be called *evaluative research*. Sapora noted the differences between evaluative research and evaluation.[106] He suggested that evaluation essentially is a status review. It describes what is going on in a program or what went on and measures these events against some kind of criteria. In evaluative research, a typical approach is to manipulate some conditions while holding others constant. The objective is to evaluate the effect of various recreation methods or services—to show correlations between methods used and outcomes, and where possible, to establish casual relationships. This kind of research, which manipulates some variables and controls others, is based on an experimental design. Kiresuk and Lund discussed this approach; they also identified a second type of design based on an *observational approach*.[107] In this type, there is no direct manipulation of variables. Instead, such methods as field studies, case studies, and survey research are used. These methods qualify as research efforts if they are conducted systematically and carefully. Ellis and Witt contended that all evaluations should use *systematic methods* to collect valid evidence. They described several methods for doing this.[108]

Nolan pointed to the value of a scientific approach.

> The closer the evaluation is to the scientific method, the more it can answer the question why and the more findings can be generalized to other programs. The less scientific, the more the evaluation should answer specific questions as to what went on in a particular program.[109]

She observed that evaluation methods can be viewed as existing along a continuum, with simple checklists for assessing compliance with criteria at one end and complex scientific experiments at the other end.

Nolan also pointed out that all recreation programs consist of three different aspects, each of which should be given attention in a complete evaluation.[110] The three aspects are the planning phase, the period during which the program is in operation, and the time when the program is concluded. Nolan identified these as the "input," "process," and "outcome" phases. Different kinds of data can be collected for each phase. *Input* data include such information as the amounts of money spent for the program, the numbers of personnel assigned, the allocation of other resources, and the efforts used to promote the program. *Process* data focus on techniques used during the program. *Outcome* data measure the success of the program against previously established goals. Nolan observed that outcomes may be influenced by other factors, such as conditions within the agency and services offered by other community organizations. These also should be considered in the evaluation.

Kiresuk and Lund identified outcome assessments as one of four major types of evaluation. These categories are effort evaluation, outcome evaluation, efficiency evaluation, and impact evaluation. The authors subdivided these into specific subcategories, and provided a detailed breakdown for each one.[111] The *effort evaluation* category includes specific methods for assessing programs or services. These generate data similar to the information collected for Nolan's process phase. *Outcome evaluation* data are similar to Nolan's outcome phase. Kiresuk and Lund defined two subtypes—evaluations of *program-level outcomes,* which focus on the benefits of services, and *client-level outcomes,* which examine the effects of services on specific individuals. Program-level evaluations include the goal-achievement and goal-free types mentioned earlier. Client-level evaluations would be most useful in therapeutic settings. *Efficiency evaluations* compare costs to outcomes, using cost-benefit methods. *Impact evaluations,* like effectiveness evaluations, assess the results of services. However, they examine the impacts of programs on a larger scale. They look at effects on communities, including such areas as economic contributions and helping to solve or minimize social problems.

A question related to all the approaches is, who should conduct evaluations? The two possibilities are to do them "in house," using regular staff members, or to use an outside consultant or other qualified evaluator. Theobald provided a useful summary of the advantages and disadvantages of each approach.[112] The basic advantages of an outsider are objectivity, the ability to concentrate on the evaluation effort, and often more technical expertise in evaluation processes. However, such a person may pose a threat to staff and, of course, cannot know the program as well as agency personnel do. The advantages of using regular staff are that they do know the intricacies of the program and therefore should be able to evaluate it more thoroughly. Also, they are in a much better position to carry out ongoing evaluations. However, they are more subject to pressures within the agency and the public might have less confidence in their findings because of their possible lack of objectivity.

Theobald suggested that both types of evaluators be used, as appropriate. He also suggested involving participants and the general public in evaluation, particularly in determining general goals and objectives to be achieved.[113]

3. *Selecting a method.* It should be apparent from the previous discussion that there is no single most effective approach to evaluation. Nolan contended that "the all-purpose evaluation is a myth."[114] Theobald took a similar position.

There is no standardized or uniform formula for administrators or evaluators to select the "best" design or method of pursuing an evaluation study.[115]

Theobald and others have suggested questions that should be asked in selecting any specific approach.[116] What information is needed? Why is it needed? How will it be used? The approach that is selected should be capable of producing information that is objective, accurate, and relevant. The data that is generated should identify positive and negative factors. It should be constructive, enabling needed changes to be made. Is the approach feasible? Is it possible in terms of available funds and staff time and expertise? Is it a method which is acceptable to those who are involved?

Howe's work indicated that a "multimethod" or "triangulated" approach might be selected in some situations.[117] This approach combines elements from different methods to strengthen the evaluation process and to generate data in which more confidence can be placed. Howe used a multimethod approach in several separate evaluations of university curricula and continuing education programs in the field of recreation and parks. She pointed out the general advantages and disadvantages.

> The main benefit of this approach is that it is descriptive, orderly, easily replicable, and collects information from a number of sources and perspectives. The drawback is that the evaluator who uses the model must be capable of analyzing and interpreting a variety of data, or have access to people who can do so.[118]

Bullock also suggested the advantages of using multiple methods. He spoke of this as an *interactionist approach*.[119] He noted that since leisure involves varied and changing perceptions and behaviors, different methods of evaluating produce more useful information. These methods interact with each other. They reinforce each other by verifying information, or by covering different dimensions of that which is being evaluated.

4. *The overall evaluation process.* As indicated earlier, it is possible to identify three basic steps in the evaluation process: determine criteria to be used, gather data related to the criteria, and implement the findings. This third step is included because the intended uses of evaluative data may influence the selection of criteria and methods of collecting data.

This three-step process can be expanded. A review of several general evaluation models and descriptions of processes[120] leads to the identification of the following major steps:

Set the framework for the evaluation. This step involves a determination of when an evaluation is needed, the audience to whom it will be directed, and the purposes to be achieved. Background information, such as agency philosophy and relevant policies, might have to be clarified at this point if there is any ambiguity or if these are not known by the evaluator.

Clearly identify goals and objectives of the service being evaluated. As mentioned earlier, the goal-free approach suggests that evaluations might be biased by focusing on established goals rather than assessing overall effectiveness. However, in most evaluation models, identifying goals and objectives is a critical step. Theobald contended that effective evaluation is possible only if the purposes of the service are clear.[121] To the extent possible, they should be specific and measurable. It is most appropriate if members of the public served by the agency participate in setting program goals and objectives.

Establish criteria that will be used to assess services.   What will be considered as evidence that the services are effective, that they are accomplishing their goals and objectives? Bannon noted that the public should participate in this step, as well as in the identification of goals and objectives.[122] He suggested that criteria statements will be most useful if representatives of the public and agency staff develop their expectations separately and then meet to agree on a combined statement.

Consider resources and constraints.   Whatever method is chosen to produce the appropriate data must also be feasible in terms of agency resources and other constraints. These factors may require a compromise between what is desirable and what is possible.

> The function of evaluation is to provide information that can be used to make decisions. The quality of such information, the degree of confidence that can be placed in it, is in turn dependent upon the technical integrity of the procedures by which it was derived. . . . At base, the nature and quality of an evaluation is a compromise between the level of exactitude required by a decision-maker and the constraints that may be imposed by the immediate situation.[123]

Select an appropriate evaluation method.   Consider the kinds of data that are needed, how they will be used, and the constraints. The method should produce information that enables decisions to be made about services. Ways of gathering data need to be identified. Instruments may need to be selected or developed.

Conduct the evaluation.   It is helpful at this stage to have a timeline in mind, with target dates for completing the effort. Also, it is appropriate to monitor the progress of the actual evaluation as it proceeds. Modifications may be needed.

Analyze the data collected.   The types of analyses will be influenced by the data and the purposes of the evaluation. It is inappropriate to submit superficial data to detailed analysis; and it is inefficient to fail to get as much out of detailed data as is needed for the purposes of the evaluation. In some cases, computer processing of data may be useful. Strobell suggested that recreation and park personnel take advantage of computer technology and abandon what she saw as biases toward the use of quantitative methods.[124] However, computer processing will not make poor data better. Its use should be determined by the data and the uses to which the analyses will be put. Another consideration is the nature of the audience. The analyses of data should be useful in terms of those who will be using them—including the decision-makers.

Draw conclusions from the analyses and *make recommendations* to the appropriate persons.   Unless the results of the evaluation reach the appropriate persons, it is of little use.

5. *Some general suggestions.* You will be engaged in the process of evaluating frequently as you work with people in recreation and park settings. The evaluations may range from informal, day-by-day assessments to efforts that are highly organized and systematic. You probably will be involved with both kinds. The information presented here is intended to give you an overview of factors to consider and processes to use. In both your informal, day by day evaluations and the ones that you plan and organize more thoroughly, it is important that you know what you are doing and why. Even informal evaluations should not be haphazard.

Often you might be evaluating your own work. Frequently, however, you will be evaluating the work of others. Evaluation can be threatening to them. This threat can be minimized by letting people know what is happening and why it is being done. Be thorough and careful, even in informal assessments. Nolan provided this advice.

> Be aware that you are evaluating aspects that are of personal and professional importance to the people working in a program. Don't dismiss a person's work without giving it careful attention.[125]

She also noted the importance of establishing ground rules about how the results of evaluations will be handled. People, including those being evaluated, need to know who will have access to the results, and how they will be released.[126]

Evaluations are conducted to assure that our services meet people's needs. This is the most basic reason. If we approach them constructively with a view toward positive results, many of the potential threats are minimized and the probabilities of making needed changes are enhanced. However, the evaluation process can be misused. Suchman and Weiss both identified this possibility. They described several inappropriate uses.[127] Evaluation can be undertaken as a way of putting off difficult changes that have already been identified. It can be used as a delaying tactic. It also can be misused to justify a failing program or to destroy an unpopular program—by manipulating or misrepresenting data or giving undue emphasis to selected aspects of it. If we know why we are evaluating and we communicate these purposes to others who are involved with or affected by the process, these misuses should not occur.

Evaluation is essential in delivering effective leisure services. It is necessary if we are to plan realistically for the future. Decisions about continuing, modifying, or terminating specific aspects of our operations must be based on a knowledge of how well these operations functioned in the past, and of the degrees to which they achieved organizational objectives. Evaluation includes assessments about the adequacy and condition of areas and facilities, the efficient and proper use of financial resources, and the quality of staff performance. (Suggestions related to these dimensions were included in Chapters 9 and 10.) It also includes analyses of program effectiveness and overall management efficiency. This chapter has discussed these dimensions and the overall process of evaluation.

The dimensions to be evaluated are interrelated. You cannot assess facility maintenance or program effectiveness without considering the availability of financial resources. Staff performance is affected by the facilities within which individuals operate and the supplies that are available. Therefore, evaluation of any specific dimension should take other influences into account.

Evaluation helps us make decisions. It also can contribute to confidence. It lets us know how we are doing. If we are doing well, that knowledge enables us to move ahead with assurance. If we need to change, we will know more about how to do so if our evaluations are appropriate. These benefits apply to all staff members.

SUMMARY

This chapter has provided information about several processes that support the activities of recreation and park personnel as they work with people. These are processes that enable staff members to be more effective in leading, working with groups, teaching, making referrals, engaging in appropriate advocacy, and using resources.

Communication is the most basic support process. It is part of all interpersonal relationships, involving both staff and participants. The primary concern in communicating is that messages are understood by the receiver or receivers in the ways that the sender intended. The messages include both verbal and nonverbal cues. For accurate meanings to be transmitted, these should be congruent. If not, there is a tendency for the nonverbal aspects of the message to be the parts which are believed or understood. "Noise," or interference, can distort meaning. The use of words that do not have common meaning is a source of noise. Other sources of noise include psychological factors such as fear, anger, and differences in perceptions. "Two-way" communication, in which the receiver responds to the sender's message, enables the participants to check each other's meanings. This contributes to effective communication.

Planning is a way of determining where we want to go and the best way to get there. It includes the establishment of specific goals and the development and evaluation of possible alternative courses of action. Most of our activities involve planning. In the professional sense, we plan such things as budgets, areas and facilities, and programs and services. Planning permits the most effective use of the resources with which we have to work, including our own time and energies.

Problem solving is similar to planning. We frequently encounter problems in providing services for people. These are blocks that stop us from doing what we feel should be done, or they are existing conditions that we feel should not exist. Like planning, problem solving involves knowing what you want to accomplish, identifying possible ways of reaching this goal, and selecting the one that seems most promising.

Planning and problem solving should lead to action. Plans should be implemented, and solutions to problems should be carried out. This is where organization is important. Organization is a process in which a task to be completed is divided into logical subtasks. Responsibility and authority for these subtasks are assigned and necessary resources are provided. Time lines for completion of the tasks are determined, if appropriate. The subtasks are then coordinated; that is, the relationships between the people who are responsible for each element are clarified. This usually involves the development of an organization chart that shows lines of responsibility and accountability.

In some cases, you will be the only one involved in carrying out the overall task. You will be responsible for all the subparts. There will be no need, obviously, to relate these different parts to each other according to staff members assigned to them. However, it is useful to define the different aspects of the task and to know how you will do each of these—to know what resources are needed and when the different subparts will have to be completed.

An important element in personal organization is time management. Most recreation and park personnel feel pressured on occasion and feel that there is not enough time to do what they want to do. Managing time wisely permits you to be more effective and to enjoy your work more thoroughly. The skill most useful for good time management is the ability to set appropriate priorities for things you want to accomplish and to concentrate on high-priority tasks.

In working with people, we often become involved with other agencies. These contacts may be for the purpose of helping those who use our services but who have needs we cannot meet directly. In such cases, referral and advocacy processes may be used. In other cases, our interactions with other agencies may be of direct benefit to us. We may seek the help of other agency personnel in solving a common problem; or we might share resources in some ways that are of mutual benefit. In developing good interagency relationships, it is useful to get to know individual staff members in other related agencies. It also is important to develop trust, to evidence a willingness to cooperate and to follow through faithfully with commitments when they are made.

Evaluating enables us to know how we are doing. Are we being effective? Are the services we are providing appropriate? Evaluating is tied directly to planning and to decision making. The primary purpose of any evaluation is to provide a logical base for taking action. The action may be to recognize the good work of a staff member. Or it may be to make major modifications in agency services to the public. Evaluations range from informal assessments that are parts of our everyday responsibilities to highly planned and systematic efforts that involve other staff members, the public, and possibly outside consultants. Many different approaches to the process can be taken. Most of them include the basic steps of clarifying goals and objectives, identifying criteria to be used in the evaluation, collecting and analyzing the necessary data, drawing conclusions, and making recommendations to the appropriate persons.

This chapter has not tried to say all that could be said about the various processes. Instead, the intent was an overview and a discussion of how the activities relate to working with people. If you are interested, much additional information can be obtained by reading any of the references cited in the chapter.

REVIEW QUESTIONS

11-1 When is communication effective? That is, what are the characteristics of effective communication? What barriers detract from effective communication?

11-2 What different basic elements can be identified in a model of communication?

11-3 What are the purposes of organization, in terms of agency operation and in terms of the efficiency and effectiveness of individual staff members?

11-4 In what ways are the processes of planning, problem solving, and evaluation related? What are the basic purposes of each of these in the delivery of leisure services?

11-5 What is meant by *needs assessment*? What different categories of need have been identified? What methods can be used to assess needs?

11-6 What different approaches to evaluation can be taken? In what ways are these similar? In what ways are they different?

TO DO

11-A In item 9-A (Chapter 9) you planned a recreation event for a group of people, and then developed a budget for the event. Look back at that plan. What factors did you consider in developing it? If you were planning an actual event, would you go about planning it differently (that is, would your planning method be different)? If so, in what way? If you wanted to assess the needs of the group for whom the event was planned, how would you do this? List the steps you would follow in planning an actual event for this group.

11-B Identify some specific problem you presently are facing. It might have something to do with school, if you are taking classes. Or it could be something related to money matters, or your job, or your relationships with another person. The main thing is that it should be a real problem that you are experiencing now. Using the information on problem solving in this chapter, develop a solution to the problem. After trying the solution you developed, evaluate whether or not the process helped in this situation. That is, evaluate the process you used.

11-C Look back again at the organization chart you drew in item 1-B (Chapter 1). Answer these questions about it:

1. What was the basis for the organization you developed? That is, why did you select the particular type of organization that you did?
2. Is the chart consistent with the fundamentals of organizations described in this chapter?

11-D Keep a log of how you use your time for the next two weeks. In a small noteboook, that you can carry with you, or on 3×5 cards, make brief notes on what you have done, and the approximate time it took to do it. At the end of each day, take a few minutes to review these notes and make necessary additions or corrections. After two weeks, look back over your log and answer these questions:

1. Does your use of time seem effective? Are you getting done what you want to get done?
2. What activities seem to take most of your time? Are these the activities that are most important to you?
3. Do you seem to have many interruptions in the activities you plan? That is, do most days go about the way you planned them or the way you thought they would?
4. What could you do to make more effective use of your time?

11-E Consider the job you defined in item 1-A (Chapter 1). Keeping in mind the duties and responsibilities of the position, develop a checklist or a rating scale that you would like to have used in an evaluation of your performance on the job.

11-F Consider some task that you have to accomplish in the near future. For that task, develop a method for evaluating how effectively you perform it. Then, after you have completed what you wanted to do, evaluate your performance using the method you developed. Or, if it is possible to do so, ask someone else to evaluate you, using the method.

11-G Engage in the following communication experiences:

1. In a group of three (you and two other people), discuss your career goals. Use this format. One person will be the speaker (1), another person will be the listener (2) and the third person will be the observer (3). The speaker will have two minutes to talk about his or her career goals and plans. The listener can ask questions for clarification or expansion, but cannot otherwise add information to the story. The observer keeps time for the speaker, observes the communication process, and later shares his or her perceptions about what went on. Was the speaker understandable and easy to follow? Did person 2 listen actively? After the first person has been the speaker, the roles switch. Person 2 becomes the speaker, 3 the listener, and 1 the observer. Then, switch roles again so that every person has the experience of being the speaker, the listener, and the observer.
2. Again, form a small group with two other people. Select some controversial topic—one for which two distinct and different points of view can be identified. You should take one side, with the other person taking the other. (It does not matter whether you or the other person really agrees with the position taken.) Now, start a discussion of the issue. However, after the initial statement by one person, before either person can make a point he or she must give a brief accurate summary of what the other person just said. That is, you must paraphrase the other person's position before arguing against it or stating your own position. Discussion of issues should continue on in this manner for ten or fifteen minutes, or until the topic seems to be exhausted. The third person serves as an observer to make sure that paraphrasing takes place and to give feedback after the discussion.

3. Write a short speech to be given to a group of people. It should be related to recreation and parks. Identify the group to whom it would be given and, of course, determine the topic. Plan the speech according to the suggestions in this chapter. Then practice giving the speech. Stand in front of a mirror, and if one is available use an audio recorder to tape it. Keep track of the time it takes to give it. Play it back and think how you can improve it. Later, give the speech to an actual audience (the group for whom it was planned, or some friends) if that is possible.

4. Write one of the following: a letter of application for the job you described in item 1-A (Chapter 1); a memorandum to your immediate supervisor in that position, requesting funds for travel to a meeting of the professional organization; an article for the local newspaper that publicizes the recreation event you planned in item 9-A (Chapter 9), or a letter to a friend explaining why you decided to work in the field of recreation and parks. Then go back and read what you have written, keeping in mind the suggestions on writing discussed in this chapter. Make any corrections you feel are needed. If possible, ask a friend to check it for clarity and correctness. Also, go back yourself and check the letter you wrote in item 8-C (Chapter 8).

END NOTES

1. Dennis R. Smith and L. Keith Williamson, *Interpersonal Communication: Roles, Rules, Strategies and Games* (Dubuque, Iowa: William C. Brown Company, Publishers, 1977), pp. 61–62.

2. William D. Brooks and Philip Emmert, *Interpersonal Communication* (Dubuque, Iowa: William C. Brown Company, Publishers, 1976), p. 4.

3. For examples of communication models see Larry L. Barker and Robert J. Kibler, eds., *Speech Communication Behavior: Perspectives and Principles* (Englewood Cliffs: N.J.: Prentice-Hall, 1971) pp. 25–42; Sarah A. Barnhart, *Introduction to Interpersonal Communication* (New York: Thomas Y. Crowell Company, 1976), pp. 4–21; George A. Borden and John D. Stone, *Human Communication: The Process of Relating* (Menlo Park, Calif.: Cummings Publishing Company, 1976), pp. 56–91; David W. Johnson, *Reaching Out: Interpersonal Effectiveness and Self-Actualization*, 2nd ed. (Englewood Cliffs, N.J.: Prentice-Hall, Inc., 1981), pp. 74–76; Thomas C. Neil, *Interpersonal Communications for Criminal Justice Personnel* (Boston: Allyn & Bacon, Inc., 1980), pp. 15–19; Herman and Zelda Roodman, *Management By Communication* (Toronto: Methnen Publications, 1973), pp. 38–40; Smith and Williamson, *Interpersonal Communication*, pp. 27–32; and Stewart L. Tubbs and Sylvia Moss, *Human Communication: An Interpersonal Perspective* (New York: Random House, Inc., 1974), pp. 21–37.

4. In addition to other sources cited in this section, see William V. Haney, *Communication: Patterns and Incidents* (Homewood, Ill.: Richard D. Irwin, Inc., 1960) for a useful presentation of barriers, with many illustrations and exercises.

5. Tubbs and Moss, *Human Communication*, pp. 31–32.

6. Ibid., p. 32.

7. Ernest G. Borman and others, *Interpersonal Communication in the Modern Organization* (Englewood Cliffs, N.J.: Prentice-Hall, Inc., 1969), pp. 145–66.

8. Borman and others, *Interpersonal Communication in the Modern Organization*, pp. 149–50.

9. Smith and Williamson, *Interpersonal Communication*, pp. 80–81.

10. Ibid., p. 81.

11. Ronald L. Smith, "Theories and Models of Communication Processes," in Barker and Kibler, eds., *Speech Communication Behavior*, p. 21.

12. Ibid., *Speech Communication Behavior*, p. 21.

13. Tubbs and Moss, *Human Communications*, pp. 143–55.

14. Ibid., pp. 155–61.

15. Ibid., p. 163.

16. Ibid., p. 163.

17. Smith and Williamson, *Interpersonal Communication*, pp. 84–91.

18. Johnson, *Reaching Out*, pp. 79–80.

19. Tubbs and Moss, *Human Communication*, pp. 13–14.

20. Ibid., pp. 14–15.

21. Johnson, *Reaching Out*, pp. 89–91.

22. Tubbs and Moss, *Human Communication*, p. 262.

23. Ibid., pp. 262–66.

24. Johnson, *Reaching Out*, p. 81.

25. This section is based on an article by Arthur L. Smith, "Interpersonal Communication within Transracial Contexts," in Barker and Kibler, eds., *Speech Communication Behavior*, pp. 305–18.

26. Smith, "Interpersonal Communication Within Transracial Contexts," p. 307.

27. Ibid., p. 311.

28. Ibid., p. 315.

29. Ibid., pp. 308–9.

30. Tubbs and Moss, *Human Communication*, p. 267.

31. Ibid., pp. 268–72.

32. Ibid., p. 267.

33. Ibid., p. 266.

34. Ibid., p. 266.

35. For suggestions on writing concisely, see William R. Van Dersal, *The Successful Supervisor in Government and Business* rev. ed. (New York: Harper & Row, Publishers, Inc., 1968), pp. 128–34; Peter Swiggart, *Anatomy of Writing* (Englewood Cliffs, N.J.: Prentice-Hall, Inc., 1966), pp. 1–19; and Richard A. Lanham, *Revising Prose* (New York: Charles Scribner's Sons, 1979).

36. For example, see James K. Bell and Adrian A. Cohn, *Handbook of Grammar, Style and Usage* 2nd ed. (Beverly Hills, Calif.: Glencoe Press, a Division of Benziger Bruce & Glencoe, Inc., 1976).

37. Joseph J. Bannon, *Leisure Resources: Its Comprehensive Planning* (Englewood Cliffs, N.J.: Prentice-Hall, Inc., 1976), p. 1.

38. James F. Murphy and others, *Leisure Service Delivery System: A Modern Perspective* (Philadelphia: Lea & Febiger, 1973), p. 126.

39. Seymour M. Gold, *Urban Recreation Planning* (Philadelphia: Lea & Febiger, 1973), p. 119.

40. Howard G. Danford, *Creative Leadership in Recreation* (Boston: Allyn & Bacon, 1964), pp. 107–8.

41. Christopher R. Edginton and Carole J. Hanson, "Appraising Leisure Service Delivery," *Parks & Recreation* 11, no. 3 (March 1976): 44–46.

42. Richard G. Kraus, *Recreation Today: Program Planning and Leadership*, 2nd ed., (Santa Monica, Calif.: Goodyear Publishing Company, Inc., a Division of Prentice-Hall, Inc., 1977), pp. 91–93.

43. Kraus, *Recreation Today*, pp. 85–91.

44. A useful discussion of procedures for selecting and working with a consultant is presented in Bannon, *Leisure Resources*, pp. 38–62.

45. Planning terminologies vary somewhat. The terms used here were suggested by Fred Brooks, instructor of recreation and park planning classes at California State University, Chico, May, 1981.

46. Samuel Vinson Lankford, "A Study of Planning Processes Used by Selected Recreation Resource Management Agencies" (Master's thesis, California State University, Chico, 1981).

47. Bannon, *Leisure Resources*, pp. viii–xv.

48. Ibid., p. 3.

49. Robert M. Moroney, "Needs Assessments for Human Service," in Wayne F. Anderson, Bernard J. Frieden, and Michael J. Murphy, eds., *Managing Human Services* (Washington, D.C.: The International City Management Association, 1977), pp. 136–37. See also Leo H. McAvoy, "Needs of the Elderly: An Overview of the Research," *Parks & Recreation* 12, no. 3 (March 1977): 32–34; and David Mercer, "The Concept of Recreational Need," *Journal of Leisure Research* 5, no. 1 (Winter 1973): 38–47.

50. For other examples, see Bannon, *Leisure Resources*, pp. 208–25; and Betty van der Smissen, *Evaluation and Self-Study of Public Recreation and Park Agencies: A Guide with Standards and Evaluative Criteria* rev. ed. (Arlington, Va.: National Recreation and Park Association, 1972), pp. 10–53.

51. For a discussion of the disadvantages of standards, see Geoffrey Godbey, *Recreation, Park and Leisure Services: Foundations, Organization, Administration* (Philadelphia: W. B. Saunders Company, 1978), pp. 263–68.

52. Godbey, *Recreation, Park and Leisure Services*, p. 273.

53. Bannon, *Leisure Resources*, pp. 225–39.

54. Godbey, *Recreation, Park and Leisure Services*, p. 347.

55. Arthur W. Combs, Donald L. Avila, and William W. Purkey, *Helping Relationships: Basic Concepts for the Helping Professions* 2nd ed. (Boston: Allyn & Bacon, Inc., 1978), p. 132.

56. For suggestions related to use of surveys in recreation and park settings, see Bannon, *Leisure Resources*, pp. 128–65; and Godbey, *Recreation, Park and Leisure Services*, pp. 241–57.

57. Moroney, "Needs Assessment for Human Services," in Anderson, Frieden, and Murphy, eds., *Managing Human Services*, pp. 142–48.

58. Bannon, *Leisure Resources*, p. 2.

59. Russell L. Ackoff, *The Art of Problem Solving: Accompanied by Ackoff's Fables* (New York: John Wiley & Sons, Inc., 1978), pp. 11–12.

60. Joseph J. Bannon, *Problem-Solving in Recreation and Parks* (Englewood Cliffs, N.J.: Prentice-Hall, Inc., 1972), pp. 46–47.

61. Bannon provided 100 case studies in the 1972 edition of *Problem Solving in Recreation and Parks* (pp. 155–340). In a second edition of the book published by Prentice-Hall, Inc., in 1981, Bannon presented an additional 100 case studies (pp. 125–387). These include problem areas that became more apparent after the first edition was published.

62. Bannon, *Problem-Solving in Recreation and Parks*, p. 48.

63. Ibid., pp. 52, 56–59.

64. Arthur B. Van Gundy, Jr., *Techniques of Structured Problem Solving* (New York: Van Nostrand Reinhold Company, 1981), pp. 5–8.

65. Van Gundy, *Techniques of Structured Problem Solving*, pp. 18–21.

66. Ibid., pp. 21–42.

67. A discussion of the basic elements of organizations is presented in Herbert G. Hicks, *The Management of Organizations: A Systems and Human Resources Approach* 2nd ed. (New York: McGraw-Hill Book Company, 1972), pp. 22–35.

68. Frank P. Sherwood and Wallace H. Best, *Supervisory Methods in Municipal Administration*. (Chicago, Ill.: The International City Managers' Association, 1958) pp. 115–16.

69. Sherwood and Best, *Supervisory Methods in Municipal Administration*, pp. 116–19.

70. Ibid., pp. 121–27.

71. Alan Lakein, *How to Get Control of Your Time and Your Life* (New York: The New American Library, Inc., 1973), p. 17.

72. Dru Scott, *How to Put More Time in Your Life* (New York: The New American Library, Inc., 1980), pp. 51–63.

73. Scott, *How to Put More Time in Your Life*, p. 62.

74. B. G. Simpson, "Effective Time Management," *Parks & Recreation* 13, no. 9 (September 1978): 61.

75. Scott, *How to Put More Time in Your Life*, p. 67.

76. Ibid., pp. 11–17, 34–41, 73.

77. Lakein, *How to Get Control of Your Time and Your Life*, pp. 25–29.

78. Ibid., pp. 25, 45.

79. Ibid., pp. 102–5.

80. Ibid., pp. 69–77.

81. Scott, *How to Put More Time in Your Life*, pp. 95–96.

82. Ibid., p. 14.

83. For a discussion of the disadvantages of procrastination, see Lakein, *How to Get Control of Your Time and Your Life*, pp. 134–39.

84. Scott, *How to Put More Time in Your Life*, pp. 117–24.

85. Ibid., p. 172–73.

86. Lakein, *How to Get Control of Your Time and Your Life*, p. 96.

87. Thomas J. Kiresuk and Sander H. Lund, "Program Evaluation and the Management of Organizations," in Anderson, Frieden, and Murphy, eds. *Managing Human Services*, (Washington, D.C.: The International City Management Association, 1977), p. 284.

88. William F. Theobald, *Evaluation of Recreation and Park Programs* (New York: John Wiley & Sons, 1979), p. 58; Kiresuk and Lund, "Program Evaluation and the Management of Organizations," in Anderson, Frieden, and Murphy, eds., *Managing Human Services*, pp. 285–86.

89. Theobald, *Evaluation of Recreational Park Programs*, pp. 58–59; Kiresuk and Lund, "Program Evaluation and the Management of Organizations," in Anderson, Frieden, and Murphy, eds., *Managing Human Services*, p. 285.

90. Peter H. Rossi, "Boobytraps and Pitfalls in the Evaluation of Social Action Programs," in Carol H. Weiss, ed. *Evaluating Action Programs: Readings in Social Action and Education*, (Boston: Allyn & Bacon, Inc., 1972), pp. 230–31.

91. Kiresuk and Lund, "Program Evaluation and the Management of Organizations," in Anderson, Frieden and Murphy, eds., *Managing Human Services,* pp. 286–87.

92. For discussions of different approaches see Bannon, *Leisure Resources,* pp. 268–75; Kiresuk and Lund, "Program Evaluation and the Management of Organizations," in Anderson, Frieden and Murphy, eds., *Managing Human Services,* pp. 287–97, 299–303, and William F. Theobald, *Evaluation of Recreation and Park Programs* (New York: John Wiley & Sons, Inc., 1979), pp. 76–102.

93. Van der Smissen, *Evaluation and Self-Study of Public Recreation and Park Agencies,* p. 38.

94. Ibid., p. 39.

95. Ibid., p. 39.

96. Bannon, *Leisure Resources,* p. 269; Theobald, *Evaluation of Recreation and Park Programs,* p. 77.

97. Harry P. Hatry and Diana R. Dunn, *Measuring the Effectiveness of Local Government Services: Recreation* (Washington, D.C.: The Urban Institute, 1971), p. 13.

98. Hatry and Dunn, *Measuring the Effectiveness of Local Government Services,* p. 17.

99. Ibid., pp. 32, 35–36.

100. Bannon, *Leisure Resources,* p. 274.

101. Kiresuk and Lund, "Program Evaluation and the Management of Organizations," in Anderson, Frieden, and Murphy, eds., *Managing Human Services,* p. 291.

102. Seppo E. Iso-Ahola, "Intrinsic Motivation: An Overlooked Basis for Evaluation," *Parks & Recreation* 17, no. 2 (February, 1982) 32–33, 58.

103. L. Hale Meserow, David T. Pompel, Jr., and Charles M. Reich, "Benefit-Cost Evaluation," *Parks & Recreation* 10, no. 2 (February 1975): 29–30, 40.

104. Robert L. Wilder, "EEI: A Survival Tool," *Parks & Recreation* 12, no. 8 (August 1977): 22–24, 50–51.

105. Theobald, *Evaluation of Recreation and Park Programs,* pp. 90–91.

106. Allen V. Sapora, "Evaluation of Park and Recreation Operations: Who Should Do It?," *Parks & Recreation* 4, no. 12 (December 1969): 35–36.

107. Kiresuk and Lund, "Program Evaluation and the Management of Organizations," pp. 299–303.

108. Gary Ellis and Peter A. Witt, "Evaluation by Design," *Parks & Recreation* 17, no. 2 (February, 1982) 40–43.

109. Monica M. Nolan, "Evaluating Recreation Programs," *Parks & Recreation* 13, no. 12 (December 1978): 41.

110. Nolan, "Evaluating Recreation Programs," pp. 40–41.

111. Kiresuk and Lund, "Program Evaluation and the Management of Organizations," in Anderson, Frieden, and Murphy, eds., *Managing Human Services,* pp. 287–97. The four types of evaluation are based on categories developed by Edward A. Suchman, *Evaluative Research Principles and Practice in Public Service & Social Action Programs* (New York: Russell Sage Foundation, 1967), pp. 60–71.

112. Theobald, *Evaluation of Recreation and Park Programs,* pp. 66–68.

113. Ibid., pp. 67–68, 154.

114. Nolan, "Evaluating Recreation Programs," p. 41.

115. Theobald, *Evaluation of Recreation and Park Programs,* p. 152.

116. Ibid., p. 152; Nolan, "Evaluating Recreation Programs," p. 41. Criteria for selecting an evaluation approach are suggested by Harold Koontz in *Appraising*

Managers as Managers (New York: McGraw-Hill Book Company, 1971), pp. 12–15, cited in Bannon, *Leisure Resources,* p. 276.

117. Christine Z. Howe, "Current Strategies for Evaluating Leisure Programs," *California Parks & Recreation* 37, no. 2 (April/May 1981): 24. Also, Christine Z. Howe, "The Use of Ethnographic Research Techniques: A Case Study of a Continuing Education Program" (Paper presented at the National Recreation and Park Association Symposium on Leisure Research, Phoenix, Arizona, October, 1980).

118. Howe, "Current Strategies for Evaluating Leisure Programs," p. 21.

119. Charles C. Bullock, "Interactionist Evaluators Look for '*What Is*' Not '*What Should Be*'," *Parks & Recreation* 17, no. 2 (February, 1982) 37–39.

120. Bannon, *Leisure Resources,* p. 281; Howe, "Current Strategies for Evaluating Leisure Programs," p. 24; Kiresuk and Lund, "Program Evaluation and the Management of Organizations," in Anderson, Frieden and Murphy, eds., *Managing Human Services,* pp. 303–4; and Theobald, *Evaluation of Recreation and Park Programs,* pp. 154–55.

121. Theobald, *Evaluation of Recreation and Park Programs,* p. 152.

122. Bannon, *Leisure Resources,* pp. 290–91.

123. Kiresuk and Lund, "Program Evaluation and the Management of Organizations," p. 297.

124. Adah Parker Strobell, "Modernizing Evaluation Techniques," *Parks & Recreation* 12, no. 6 (June 1977): 31.

125. Nolan, "Evaluating Recreation Programs," p. 48.

126. Ibid., p. 48.

127. Edward A. Suchman, "Action for What? A Critique of Evaluative Research," in Weiss, ed., *Evaluating Action Programs,* p. 81; Carol H. Weiss, *Evaluation Research: Methods for Assessing Program Effectiveness* (Englewood Cliffs, N.J.: Prentice-Hall, Inc., 1972), pp. 11–12.

Conclusion

The main theme in this book has been that recreation and park personnel work with people in various ways. These ways are designed to help people live more enriched lives—to grow personally and to become more self-determining in meeting their leisure needs. Our ways of working with people should recognize that these needs are influenced by all of the other needs, aspirations, and conditions that comprise each person's life situation. The field of recreation and parks cannot be all things to all people, but it can be a strong part of that collection of agencies that exist to serve the citizens of our communities and nation. It can develop linkages with these other agencies for the mutual benefit of all who are involved. To the extent that it does so, it becomes a human service field.

The recreation and park field is comprised of many separate and diverse agencies, departments, organizations, and enterprises. Each relies on the efforts of those staff members, paid and volunteer, who carry out its purposes and programs. While the responsibilities and duties of these individuals vary, some processes are common to most. Several of these are directly related to working with people. All are related indirectly since the primary justification for any position is its eventual contribution to the service function of the agency. Competency in these common processes can be thought of as the ability to use processes effectively in recognition of both personal characteristics and situational demands.

When we work with people, we are working with behavior. When people engage in recreation, they are behaving. When we interact with other staff members, they and we are behaving. For these reasons, it is appropriate to have some general understandings of behavior. We need to know why people engage in recreation and some of the factors that influence their participation. It also is useful to know why people might not participate.

The primary processes we use include leading, working with groups, and teaching. In all of these, interpersonal relationships are involved. In all of them, we use ourselves as instruments. We accomplish much of what we do by the use of our own personalities, by the ways we uniquely relate to each person with whom we work. We can do this best if we become aware of our own needs, biases, and perceptions.

Leading, working with groups, and teaching are supported by certain resources: recreation areas and facilities, other staff members, and the finances necessary to provide for them. To be most effective we need to know how to get the most use from what is available. We need to be able to create or maintain environments that promote and enable leisure behavior. This involves planning, problem solving, organizing, and other support processes. In some cases, either we will not be able to provide direct services to people or it will be inappropriate to do so. In these cases referral or advocacy processes might be advisable. All of these various processes are made possible through communication.

Volumes have been written about these processes. This book has presented some information about them. It has attempted to give an overview of basic considerations and to show how the processes together constitute a way of working with people, a way of providing leisure leadership. There is no "cookbook" answer to providing such leadership. The people with whom we work represent a vast array of personalities, lifestyles, and personal circumstances. The agencies through which we operate are extremely diverse. And, perhaps most important, each of us is unique. Even so, basic knowledge about the methods upon which we can draw should help us to be more effective. In a sense, our field is both art and science. Science is reflected in the developing knowledge base from which we can work. This results from growing research in recreation and parks, from the findings of investigations in other related fields, and in the accumulation and documentation of successful experience. The art is in using this knowledge skillfully and creatively.

At the beginning of this book, an illustration was given in which a student wanted to enroll in a university recreation and park curriculum. He told the advisor that he wanted "to work with people." He might not have known all that was entailed in that vague wish. No doubt it represented some of his major aspirations. It was his career choice—what he wanted to do with his life, professionally. Many people have made that choice. There is great satisfaction in working with people in recreation and park settings. At times, certainly, there are frustrations and disappointments. But the feelings that come from knowing you are helping others lead more enriched lives are more than worth the occasional problems. The opportunities afforded by our profession are unique in that people who use our services do so voluntarily, seeking enjoyment. The services we provide have potential for benefiting participants in many ways, some immediate and some far-reaching. These conditions make our work important. We have reason to feel both proud and humble—proud because we are parts of a significant profession and humble because of the responsibilities we accept.

Index

AUTHORS

*See *End Note* sections.

SUBJECT

Accidents:
  contributing factors, 263–64
  prevalence of, 262–63
  prevention of, 264–67
  procedures, 266
    giving first aid, 266
    reporting accidents, 266
Advocacy:
  concepts of, 233–34
    political-social and individual dimensions, 233
  conditions for, 231–32
  conflicting interests, 241
  differing views, 238, 241
  justifications for, 234–35
  methods, 234, 235–41
    community organization, 232, 236–37, 239
    confrontation, 237, 239
    different levels, 238
    informational, 236
    letter writing, 243–44
    negotiation, 236, 239
    organizational alliances, 240
    petitions, 244
    public hearings, 244
    selection of, 237–39
    uses of pressure, 236, 239
    working with legislators, 244–45
  in recreation and park settings, 231–35
  resistance to change, 239–40
  risks in uses of, 237, 241
Age, as an influence on behavior, 78
American Red Cross, 201, 265, 266
Antecedents to recreation behavior, 62, 64–65, 75
Aspiration, level of, 70, 75
Assertive discipline, 211–15
Assessment:
  of needs, 335–38 (*see also* Needs Assessment)
  in the referral process, 230
  in teaching, 199 (*see also* Evaluation, in teaching)
Attitudes, 76–77, 107, 191–92, 206–8
Autocratic leadership, 138–40
Awareness:
  as a factor in recreation behavior, 85–87
  of self (*see* Self-awareness)
  of sociophysical settings, 67–68

Budgets (*see also* Financial procedures):
  calendar, 258
  considerations in using volunteers, 308
  preparation, 258–59
  types, 255–58
    functional, 257
    line-item, 256–58

object-classification, 256–57
program, 257–59

California Park and Recreation Society, 17
Cohesion, in groups, 159
Communication:
  barriers, 321–22
  between diverse groups, 327
  as a core process, 35
  effectiveness, 324–27
    listener responsibilities, 324–25
    speaker credibility, 325
    speaker responsibilities, 324
    in *transracial* settings, 325–27
  elements, 320–21
  influences of perception, 321, 325
  levels of meaning, 323–24
  non-verbal, 322–23, 326
  speaking to groups, 327–29
    fluency, 328–29
    how to prepare, 328–29
    types of speeches, 327
  types of interference:
    psychological, 321, 329
    semantic, 321–23, 329
    technical, 321–29
  types of messages, 322–23
  types of responses in helping, 105–6, 113 (*see also* Helping)
Communication, written, 329–31
  types, 329
  writing effectively, 329–31
Competency:
  concept, 27
  core processes, 32–42
    communicating, 35
    developing public relations, 42
    evaluating, 37
    helping, 42
    implementing services, 38
    leading, 35
    managing resources, 37–38
    obtaining relevant community information, 39
    organizing, 36–37
    performing technical skills, 41
    planning, 35–36
    problem-solving, 38–39
    supervising, 42
    teaching, 36
    using a special language, 41
    verbalizing a professional philosophy, 40–41
    working with community and professional groups, 39–40
    working with groups, 38
    working within legal frameworks, 40
  in the leisure services, 27–34
    commercial recreation, 28–29